In Search of the Origin of Pyramids
and the Lost Gods of Giza

In Search of the Origin of Pyramids and the Lost Gods of Giza

OR
Centering Creation

165 illustrations

Dr Charles R. Kos

Plus Ultra Books

A Plus Ultra Book.

http://www.plusultrabooks.com.au

Melbourne, Australia.

First published by Plus Ultra Books, Melbourne, 2015.
1 3 5 7 9 CS 10 8 6 4 2

National Library of Australia Cataloguing-in-Publication entry

Creator:	Kos, Charles, author.
Title:	In search of the origin of pyramids and the lost gods of / Dr Charles R. Kos.
ISBN:	9780987420824 (paperback)
Notes:	Includes bibliographical references and index.
Subjects:	Pyramids—Miscellanea. Mounds—History. Cairns—History. Religion.
Dewey Number:	726

Certain figures used in this book have additional authorship attributions as listed
in the Picture Credits.

Cover design: 'Listoghil' in the foreground at Carrowmore Megalithic Cemetery,
Ireland. Queen Medb's tomb on Knocknarea looms in the background. The Great
pyramid of Giza with Milky Way are in the overlay.

Typeset in Computer Modern Roman using the LaTeX typesetting system.

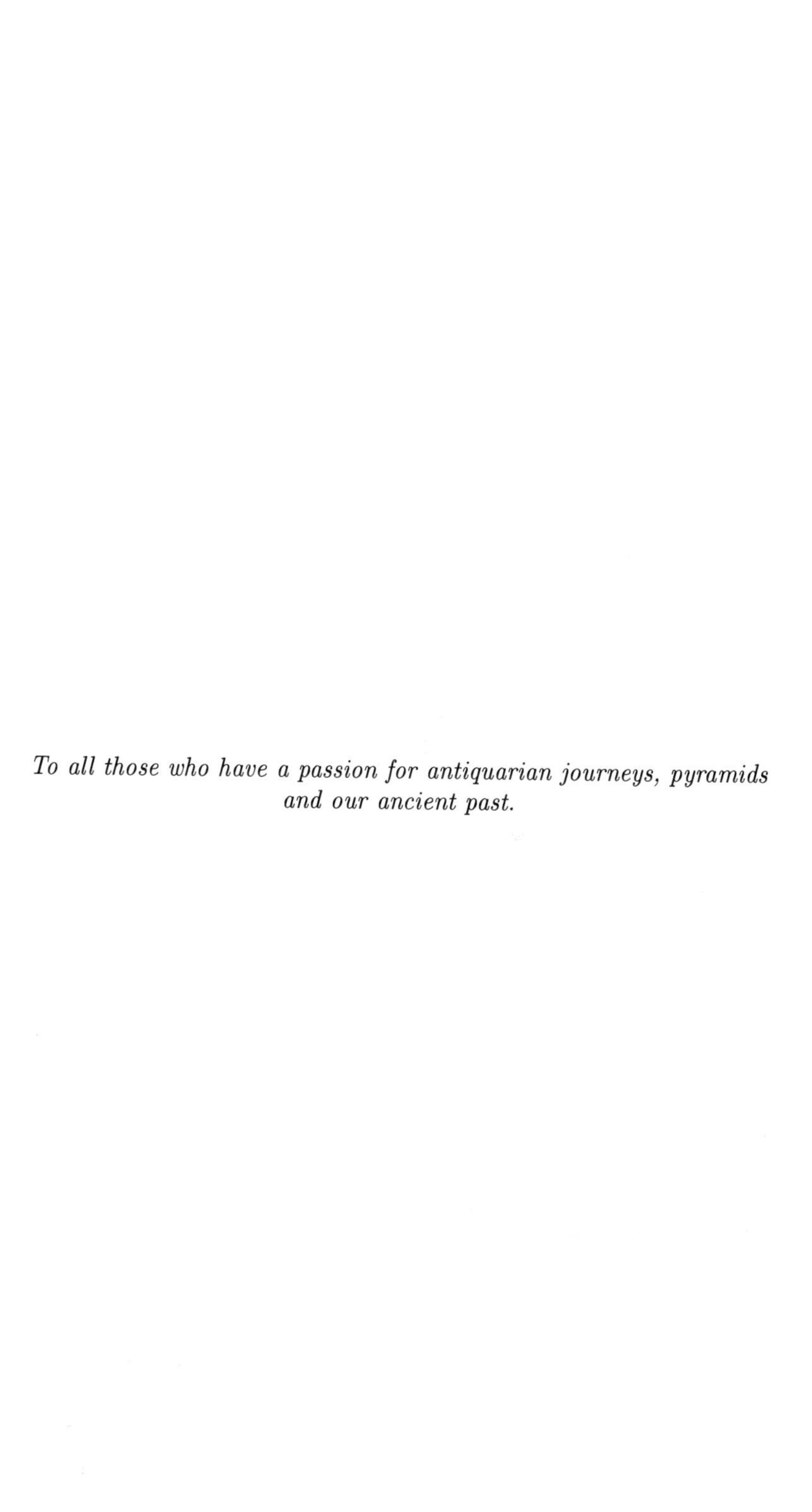

To all those who have a passion for antiquarian journeys, pyramids and our ancient past.

Contents

Acknowledgements

A great many seemingly unrelated events, people and chance encounters, at home and abroad, interact like a cog-wheel, with existing knowledge, and things yet to be learned. If the process goes on long enough, these elements conspire to make a book. I would like to thank wonderful friends. There is my mother and brother, Daniel who deserves a massive thank you for his computer and typesetting skills. I acknowledge my antiquarian friends (mentors and teachers), academic friends and mentors whom I will never be able to repay, firstly for their magnificent past assistance, and secondly for training me up to think as well as write, in a hopefully reasonable and detective-like manner. I thank the originators and maintainers, essentially the people, for the great system in my mother country of Australia. This has essentially blessed me with an almost free-of-charge postgraduate education in the humanities, an opportunity denied to millions of hopeful aspirants across the world. I would also like to thank my father, for escaping from both the Germans and Soviets, in order to come here. I would like to thank all my other friends, and everyone who is now about to read this book. It has been a utterly tremendous pleasure to research as well as write, as well as to watch the process unfold.

I wish to acknowledge future assistance. Science is never complete but always evolving. As such, nothing is ever utterly right, but hopefully moving in an appropriate direction. This is especially the case in any book, more-so than a journal article which has rather exacting standards and therefore limitations upon what one may theorise. In this work I have tried to be as honest as possible with the reader, pointing out similarities as well as differences, as well as making allowance for various points of view, pointing out where deficiencies lie in the arguments presented. Above all I try to base everything upon hard evidence. Naturally in the world of mythology research, dealing with civilisations and peoples without extant written record, it is hardly possible to be definitive, or present something which is falsifiable. Various lengthy time periods seem to intervene. This is possibly one of the reasons few have attempted to apply mythological ideas to pyramids in explaining their representation and function. If anybody, however, can spot any glaring or minor errors I will be extremely grateful to take them on board in a possible future, expanded edition, as well as subsequent publications.

I would like to thank authors Dr Robert Schoch and his co-author Robert Aquinas McNally, as well as Robert Temple for their excellent recent books, which I feel bring scholarship, credibility and honour, as well as public awareness to what is essentially a difficult as well as emerging interdisciplinary field. It is essentially the field of seeking out the identity and beliefs of a widespread Stone-Age culture, about which we know almost nothing, and whose perishable products are mostly gone.

This is the story of the pyramid religion, of tribes, migrations, and the murky mythical ideas of a nomadic people who upon settling, began to build ancient wonders. The insights of the mentioned authors, and many others, have turned this, what essentially was going to be a travel book, highlighting for a wider audience the existence of pyramid-equivalents in Europe, into a work which seeks to tie the strings together, tentatively.

It is now a work which, after rationalising some of the mythologies of European mound-building, makes remarks regarding Giza and the Sphinx, the very purpose of pyramids, interpreted through a stone- and bronze-age mythological perspective. I feel this work has never really been done before on such a broad scale. I take heart from the older works of Dr Leon Stover, as well as Professor Gerald Hawkins (*Beyond Stonehenge*), who acknowledged that we need to de-specialise just a little, to look beyond one's borders (a 'country' as we know it is a modern phenomenon anyway. Before that we have kingdoms. Before that, polities, and then 'cultures' which would often overlap), to explain what is going on in the Stone Age, regarding particular monuments. Hopefully my brush is not too broad.

Other authors I would like to thank are to be found in the Bibliography. Among them, some exceptional favourites are Rodney Castleden and Paul Devereux. They have each written a consistent series of fascinating works. These are often interdisciplinary and deal with widespread themes, even if not directly related to uncovering the basis for what would become a rather widespread pyramid religion.

It is often fascinating to watch as different authors come to similar conclusions, even with parallel pieces of evidence at their fingertips. Over time, newer stronger pieces of evidence, in particular newer genetic models of evidence, are found by others, which show that certain ideas and mentioned coincidences often had a stronger foundation behind them than hitherto realised.

I apologise in advance to any authors I may not have been able to get around to, who may have presented arguments relevant to those presented in this book. I am attempting to assist in sculpting a new field (interactions of various pyramid-building cultures, in Egypt) out of hundreds of sources. There are just too many good books out there.

I have had a great deal of trouble with the title, trying to make it incorporate aspects of Egypt, or Britain, or Ireland, or 'Myths', or 'Giza' or 'Egypt'. I even wanted to use: 'using mythology to locate lost pyramids', which is something I do in this book, but also keep it short. Titles are all important, in terms of providing a suitable metaphor which explains a central argument, as well as including searchable terms. Thanks to all those I have endlessly rebounded them against, especially my fantastic brother Daniel.

Thank you to the antiquary Sylvia Joiko, Barbara McNeill, as well as others, for the excellent, lengthy and insightful discussions and co-discoveries made in terms of relating Indo-European mythology to an older, rather widespread tradition. I would also like to thank all those who have a passion for pyramids and the ancient past, wherever they are.

Introduction

The Old Testament as we know it, contains rather fascinating and strange tales. Many of them seem to defy explanation or understanding. People seeking to interpret the Bible as ancient history also run into a wall. Relating anything in ancient history or archaeology, to most stories or characters in the Bible, does not work very well, as many archaeologists have and continue to discover.

That is probably because this relation compares two very different examples of evidence: religious texts, and rocky remains. There are stories in the Bible which cannot be readily explained, such as a primordial idea about the origins of humanity, which seems to include a look at a former religion, a fleeting glimpse, before rarely again being mentioned.

Such a tale, among many, can inspire us to carry out an historical and archaeological investigation, however perilous, into the matter:

> And the whole earth was of one language, and of one speech. And it came to pass, as they journeyed from the east, that they found a plain in the land of Shinar; and they dwelt there. And they said one to another, Go to, let us make brick, and burn them thoroughly. And they had brick for stone, and slime had they for mortar. And they said, Go to, let us build us a city and a tower, whose top may reach unto heaven; and let us make us a name, lest we be scattered abroad upon the face of the whole Earth.

> And the Lord came down to see the city and the tower, which the children of men builded. And the Lord said, Behold, the people is one, and they have all one language; and this they begin to do: and now nothing will be restrained from them, which they have imagined to do.

> Go to, let us go down, and there confound their language,

> that they may not understand one another's speech. So the
> Lord scattered them abroad from thence upon the face of
> all the earth: and they left off to build the city. Therefore
> is the name of it called Babel; because the Lord did there
> confound the language of all the earth: and from thence did
> the Lord scatter them abroad upon the face of all the earth.

— Genesis, 11: 1-9.

The tale appears to tell of a nomadic people who wished to establish a civilisation. To accomplish this, they reach 'Shinar', thought to be Sumer, from the East. To prevent further scattering they need both a city and a 'tower'.

The tower is not a defensive fortification but a religious building, of vast size, needed to talk to God. Without this they would be scattered again. That is presumably return to nomadic life, or suffer invasion, and so lose their civic identity. The Bible does not necessarily approve of this early religion, for the people were scattered nonetheless. Even so, despite the fact the Jews of the Bible-Era in the first millennium BC did not build these great towers, they were still built for worship of their same 'Lord', written with a capital. What is going on here?

This book seeks to answer that question! History began at about the end of the fourth millennium BC. Several centuries afterwards pyramids started to be built in various places around the world at about the same time, by about 2800 BC. These pyramids are strange and are a source of controversy to this day as to their purpose. Are they tombs or something more?

In high school I had been taught that the Egyptian pyramid evolved from a succession of increasingly smaller mastabas or tetrahedral-looking square tombs, placed on top of one another. 'Right', I thought. This explanation implied to me at the time that six kings would have been buried on top of each other. The final shape would have been a pyramid, thus giving them the inspiration to simply build a pyramid in future.

The classic example is that in the third dynasty, King Djoser decided to turn a mastaba into a pyramid in this way. He allegedly placed six mastabas on top of one another. It is an explanation which places the pyramid, and its understanding, within the realm of the Egypt specialist, for clearly it implies that the pyramid was invented there.

In looking at a cross section, I was surprised to discover that it actually reveals that the pyramid started from one real mastaba, a genuine burial, subsequently enlarged directly into a four-tiered step pyramid.

This was thence enlarged into a six-tiered pyramid, by enlarging lower mastabas, and then stacked further. But these were pseudo-mastabas, lacking internal chambers. One also cannot stack a mastaba and have it remain as one, since burials are placed in the ground underneath. These are therefore not stacked mastabas.

It seems that stacked sloping-mastaba architecture was a convenient way to carry out a royal order to make a large stone mound, which is a rather different religious device. Researching the matter further, I found that the mastaba itself often actually contained an internal mound, since first dynasty times, the beginning of Egyptian history. Furthermore, in 1912, Egyptologist James Henry Breasted suggested that the pyramid actually evolved from the primordial World Mound, a old idea of what lay at the centre of creation. Archaeologists ever since have tended to agree. Mark Lehner, representing an orthodox Ancient-Egypt opinion, writes in *The Complete Pyramids*, that the pyramids *are* temples as well as tombs. He says that the pyramid complex was a sacred place built to what he calls the Horus-Osiris divinity, which is merged with the Sun god, in terms of the pyramid as central icon. In other words, the pyramid was a solar representation, as well as of the regeneration god Osiris (he is a figure who comes back to life after being killed, to possibly bring back the springtime) and Horus, an overriding sky god.

This world mound, however, is not unique to Egyptian mythology, but part of world mythology. It is part of the older primordial stone-age mythology of the mound builder. We are no longer just in the realm of Egyptology, but 'world prehistory' and mythology, that is to be found from Eurasia to the Americas. Lehner's idea of worship at a pyramid complex is I think a correct one, but the gods he describes are later ideas formulated to be superimposed upon far earlier stories and earlier god names which did not originate in Egypt. Osiris is just another name for the Neolithic bleeding god, and Horus is a sky figure with aspects of Thor and Zeus. These gods are found everywhere, but under different names, and the pyramid is also potentially to be found everywhere, and it venerates similar ideals of regeneration to what Lehner discussed. World mythology is perhaps a field which one can study, in order to begin to enter the mind of the pyramid builder. Mound builders seem to have entered Egypt before the first dynasty, and also in the second or third or fourth dynasties in repeated invasions, and possibly from different directions.

There is another point of view. There is an excellent book, reflecting current opinions, *Pyramids: The Real Story behind Egypt's Most Ancient Monuments*, 2004, by Joyce Tyldesley. Early Egyptologist Flinders Petrie wrote that an invasion of new people was responsible, in part, for a certain change in very early Egyptian culture, and civilisation.

Tyldesley writes that his views are not necessarily correct, and that they were based upon 19th-century ideas of colonisation and empire. I disagree. Her conception, shared by many others, is largely one of Egypt's original, organic development, expounding the idea of a clearly visible evolution from burial mound to pyramid, in Egypt. It would imply early Egypt's pyramid development is isolated from elsewhere. This book, and many before it, show that not to be the case, *because there were other pyramid or mound-building cultures developing elsewhere*, at the same time, to the north, east, west, and possibly even to the south of the Delta.

Due to rapid changes in archaeology as of the late 1990s and 2000s, we now know that pyramids were even being developed right across the world in the Americas, at about the same time as the Egyptian pyramids were going up. A neighbouring culture may have invaded Egypt, mixing their pyramid culture with Egypt's pyramid culture, to create a new flavour of pyramid design. The resulting architectural fusion would not necessarily be seen by archaeologists as an invasion.

Naturally the counter to the rationalisation that Petrie's thinking is merely based upon colonisation ideas, is to suggest that the no-colonisation theory is a modern trend, a product of 1960s decolonisation-era thinking! To follow the thinking of 'no invasion,' is to have a situation where early Egypt (a murky time of lost history) is immune to invasion. Later Egypt for almost its entire extant history, from the New Kingdom onwards, by contrast, (over three thousand years) has seemingly been ruled by one set of foreigners after another. Some of these eventually became the new Egyptians, as they mixed with the natives.

Nonetheless, Tyldesley says that the northern Delta Egyptians mixed their blood and culture with people from the Near East, whereas those of Upper Egypt, in a harsher climate, were more inward looking. She also says that the Delta was at a greater risk of foreign invasion. I think the pyramids, aspects of Lower Egypt and the Delta, are a product of some of these mixings. Egypt cannot be treated in isolation. It lies along an invasion corridor which has persisted since early man left Africa. Although its large Nile-fed population gave it some protection from invasion and cultural annihilation, this was by no means a guarantee.

When people investigate the early pyramids of Egypt, there are potentially two lines of inquiry that have perhaps not been given sufficient attention, and deserve to be followed up. These are an investigation into the Stone-Age mythology of nomads who migrated into Egypt at various times. The other line of inquiry is pyramid-building practice, around the world, taking note of when it occurred.

Widespread, similar pyramid construction at an early stage, in the third millennium BC would indicate that one requires knowledge of gods and religion as they were *before* 3000 BC, in order to interpret that culture, before it began to spread. Since we have very little information about times before 3000 BC, people have always tended to interpret pyramids from the perspective of later eras, including our own. 'The pyramids are larger than they need to be, and also contain a sarcophagus. Therefore they are tombs built by tyrannical individuals as a folly.' Since we know that people can be tyrannical, and build follies, the explanation 'works.' It is not, however an explanation which encourages interest in the representation of Giza itself, and other pyramid complexes. When we examine that, we must, I would suggest, begin to re-assess the former working assumption.

In this book, I am suggesting that the pyramid practice is not only more widespread than we appreciate, but also takes many more forms, while utilising the same function, than we appreciate. It is almost not so much a question of asking 'where' are the pyramids, but where *aren't* they! I would suggest that by analysing Stone-Age mythology of nomad or migratory tribes, who may have entered Egypt at the beginning of Egyptian history, one can start, in my humble opinion, to grasp what it was all about, including some of what might have been memorialised on the Giza plateau. This book tries to supply some of the details.

Tyldesley re-iterates a popular and traditional view, in saying that the rise and fall of the Nile gave rise to notions of a world mound of creation emerging from waters of creation: an Egyptian idea. Not so. The world mound is found around the world in early mythology, and represented in third-millennium BC mounds in Europe which preceded or paralleled the building of many Egyptian pyramids.

I think the pyramid, found everywhere, is merely an expression of the idea of the world mound, also found everywhere. The Egyptian mound religion is merely another version of the *Axis Mundi* (world axis) legend. This is primordial, certainly at least ten thousand, if not more years old (as shown in the Göbekli Tepe section, and also by older Clovis peoples migrations, also discussed later). It is found in stories about *Shambhala*, to Atlantis' central mountain, to the Bible Isaiah 19:19, which writes of an 'altar' in the midst of Egypt. In these legends, there is a mountain at the centre, and is found across the world, in almost every culture, and is therefore an incredibly old legend.

In this legend, there is a tree on a mountain. It points to the north. Underneath is the underworld. It is a symbolic axis and centre of creation. In this book I visit several ancient *Axis Mundi*, in different countries, even if they are not yet recognised as such. The alternate title, *Centering Creation* might suggest this is an *Axis Mundi* book. In a way it is, but it is really also a pyramids book. In the final chapter, Synthesis, I suggest that the primordial *Axis Mundi* mythology is represented on the Giza plateau. It *is* the pyramid religion.

There is an unfortunate neglect of what I would call the 'pyramids' of Europe, as well as in Asia. Everyone knows that China has pyramids, but in Europe it is a little different. 'Europe has pyramids?' That is a fair question. Before I define what I mean by 'pyramid', I would like to continue to start this book off with a 'bang'. I would like to put it to the reader that Europe not only has pyramids, but effective pyramid 'complexes' which vaguely parallel the pattern found at Giza, both in time period as well as design. These 'pyramid' structures found in Europe, are really too big to be considered mere cairns or tombs, even if they are described as such. Like the Giza pyramids, they have never been found to contain any burials, and yet tradition invariably seems to ascribe some kind of burial to them.

There is one more conception I would like to introduce. The pyramid religion is based upon the mound religion, widespread across the world. This is far older than the Egyptian religion, and covers a wider area. Egyptian mythology as we know it, is largely a city-state mythology, perhaps more-so than a Stone-Age one. I envisage that a nomad culture swept into Egypt at a very early time (as they did in later times, *c.f.* the Mameluks or Hyksos tribes). Think of Germans inheriting the culture of Rome in the Dark and Middle Ages.

Possessing gods which were perhaps rather different to those of the indigenous inhabitants, they found themselves in possession of a large labour force. These people were able to give vent to their ideas and create a landscape reflecting their own underworld, but also of the imagination, according to their own principles. The puzzle of what is going on at Giza is thus explained well by employing a fusion of ideas from Stone-Age mythology from pre-state nomads, as well as the later more civic Egyptian mythology, which has been an established empire for a very long time indeed.

Let us rewind. Europe and Asia contain a number of what I would term 'lost pyramids'. Now the reader has another question on his or her lips. Why *lost* pyramids? One answer is that most of what I would like to refer to as 'pyramids' found in Europe do not even look like the conventional idea of the paved Egyptian pyramids, of which we know a lot more. Silbury Hill in Southern England is unquestionably pyramid-like, built out of packed chalk and clay, which has been covered up by topsoil. Its interior shape seems to be polygonal, or a cone.

Some of what perhaps should possibly be called pyramids are referred to as *cairns* yet are clearly pyramid in both size and appearance, and even have altars next to them. Some are step pyramids which are not even called by that word (the Marlborough Mount for instance, dating to 2400 BC). Some, in particular the hemispheres, are known as *tumuli*, or a *tumulus* in the singular. Some structures are perhaps even eroded or smoothed out deliberately and look like hills. The Olmec *La Venta* pyramid, in Mexico is conical and composed of heaped earth, looking like a European mound, yet the indications are that it was once rectangular, damaged by erosion. In this way pyramids may be a product of their environment and building materials available.

If it is difficult to make a square or rectangular pyramid out of packed chalk, clay and heaped earth, one makes a cone. In the desert however one does not have these substances, so one uses stone or mud-brick. Since these are shaped like cubes and rectangular prisms, the pyramid becomes square or rectangular. In fertile lands the old Germans put up a huge totem pole called an Irminsul, possibly around their sacred burial complexes. This may have had an astronomical use. In the Middle East one does not have suitable trees so one perhaps aligns the pyramid itself to the compass points, and with astronomy.

Some of what could even be referred to as pyramids, within the definition I am proposing, are completely natural hills yet still were seemingly treated as sacred, by ancient peoples, perhaps according to similar principles. What would be important is a Stone-Age conception, rather than our conception. For Stone-Agers, lacking the Internet, or a library, for comparison between world pyramids, any huge mound or mountain may well have been built by the gods. I do not think it is building material which is what makes the pyramid, but what the mound actually represents.

The mound religion seems to be from where the pyramid religion was derived. An early pyramid was a burial, or placed on top of a burial, as it was in pre-dynastic Egypt. It was raised so it could be seen, possibly by a god in heaven.

A tree was sometimes planted on top as a nice gesture. Its roots reached into the underworld. Its branches reached into the sky, to perhaps help the buried body commune with the sky god. Over time the memory of *who* was buried became forgotten. Perhaps it was now that the pyramid itself became important. What followed was an indiscernible mixture of cultural diffusion and isolation, over a long time period.

The 'pyramid builders' as author Dr Robert Schoch calls them, slowly carried their culture around most of the world, but did so in a haphazard manner. Initially, he says, they spread to many regions. With this as a foundation, trade networks and the migration of culture may have fostered similarities in the mounds/pyramids of various places, even oceans apart. The motive would have been expansion of trade and religion.

There may not have been an entirely common source, though the pyramids themselves do seem to emerge from the Old World, spreading subsequently to the Americas, with later cross-cultural influences and modifications occurring between both sets of cultures, creating a strange kind of 'co-evolution'. In Europe, one can just build a mound from topsoil. That does not quite work in Egypt, so one needs by necessity, to use stone or mudbrick to make an enduring structure. I envisaged a scenario in which proto-Indo-Europeans and Asians (who seem to be an early adopters of the mound-building idea, but not necessarily the original founders) spread out over a huge area, Europe to Asia, and began to spread this culture from different points, thousands of miles apart. The spreadings may have converged and overlapped, cancelling out or reinforcing existing ideas, but always changing them.

This idea would create an interplay between Egypt, and the fact that Europe seems to contain several hundred to several thousand lost 'pyramids'. Most of these look like small suspicious hills, often lacking a burial. There are also stone pyramids, haphazardly arranged, built more for gods than for men. There are lost religions in Europe, no longer known to us, perhaps associated with these structures. Given the general lack of awareness of these structures, I thought it might be necessary to make a book about them.

'Pyramid' is a bizarre word. As it is known, a pyramid is generally found in Egypt and is an ancient-Greek word based on an ancient-Egyptian word. In the last century, the term has been applied to similar structures from Mexico to Japan. A pyramid is therefore not just something found in Egypt. The original and rather lost religion of the pyramid or hill, of which we have a very shaky understanding, remains something of a mystery. It would seem that another, earlier, set of cultures managed to spread its ideas far further than the great Iron-Age cultural spreaders, the Celts, ever dreamed of.

We should clarify what the word pyramid actually perhaps means and why it seems fitting to apply it. The term being used in this book does not apply to a geometrical pyramid, with straight sides. The Greek term *pyramis*, plural: *pyramides* would at first glance seem to inspire a geometrical explanation due to our association between Ancient Greeks and Platonic solids. On the contrary, it does not apparently refer to this because its etymology seems to be the phrase *fire in the middle*. It should also be said that the etymology is uncertain. 'Pyramis' in Greek means 'wheaten cake,' and it was assumed that the pyramids could have looked like cakes. Alternately, the pyramids seem also to have been called *mer* in ancient Egyptian. The word *per-em-us* is also an Egyptian word found in the Rhind mathematical papyrus, which is used to denote the height of a pyramid.

The suggestion being made in this book is that geometry is not required to imply a particular religion or god is being worshipped. Nor is the pyramid one of the classic Platonic solids. The idea of a mound itself may be more important. 'Pyramid' as we know it is an ancient word, but appears, maybe due to our association with the 'perfection' of the Great Pyramid, to be almost a modern mathematical term, probably based upon drawings and photographs made in Egypt. Furthermore, if we hold to this definition then only very few structures will pass and the pyramid-like structures in countries outside Egypt, including even inside Egypt, such as the Bent Pyramid, cannot pass as pyramids. In addition the step pyramids of Mesopotamia, which may have even influenced the beginning of some trends of pyramid-building in Egypt, would not be called pyramids either.

The research of Dr. Robert Schoch has been a game-changer in terms of the idea of investigating a pyramid culture, which spread in an unknown complex manner, from one area to another. In his groundbreaking *Voyages of the Pyramid Builders* he presents the 'there are too many similarities, so let us explore it' argument in the best way it has ever been done. By cautiously interpreting various ideas, rejecting many, he comes up with ideas to compare and explain the bizarre similarities of appearance of pyramids in different parts of the world, presumably based upon similar ideas.

Schoch is hesitant to ascribe the phenomenon of pyramids found in various countries across the Earth as the spread of a culture. Rather he states that a mythology spread its wings after some catastrophic event which triggered a migration. This mythology then inspired the building of slightly different pyramids in each country, probably based upon a disaster which originated from the sky.

This was a good step forward because it begins to define, for modern humanity, what can only really be termed as the spread of an almost world-wide pyramid-building proto-culture. This would have a common origin, reinforced by further migrations, over many thousands of years, even if later instances of it were not in contact.

As repeatedly mentioned, I would go a step further and will argue that this is all an expression of the earlier widespread mound-building culture. In that instance, pyramids would have been built to venerate the primordial past actions of many different gods in a syncretic unity, fostering further creation and good luck for the future.

Unfortunately there seem to be no mythological references to the veneration of a mathematical object with square corners, a crystal-like geometrical structure, in any mythology, which could account for the spread of the pyramids. Rather there is lots of mythology venerating the cosmic mound or mountain, or the underworld, where creator gods live, as a centre point of creation. True, there is the possible religious aspect of there being four equal corners (on an Egyptian pyramid) which often centre the pyramid in terms of geographical coordinates, but there are other mechanisms for highlighting north, where easier building materials than cut stone were available.

Possibly one of the best pyramid books ever written is *The Complete Pyramids*, by Mark Lehner. With a title like that, one would expect it would contain information about all sorts pyramids, anywhere. On the contrary, the book treats pyramids according to *shape* (the Egyptian style), and country, namely Egypt, with a final chapter on where pyramids of the Egyptian geometry are built elsewhere, by those inspired by Egypt.

It is such a good book that the reader is not disappointed to find it mainly contains information about Egypt, as well as more modern buildings inspired by the Egyptian-pyramid shape in a final chapter. Naturally this is fine, for pyramids are known as an Egyptian phenomenon. However the overall picture it creates is that pyramids began in Egypt, in the pre-dynastic, as mounds over graves (Egypt is still seen as one of the first civilisations, so why not?), and subsequently diffused, in much more recent times. A Roman for instance, built himself a Egypt-style pyramid, and the current Louvre is inspired by Egypt. The book is excellent, though it tracks pyramids, not from their beginnings, from their global point of origin, but from their apparent point of origin in Egypt, where they reached their world zenith.

This book, *Origin of Pyramids*, is designed to take whatever is the reader's assumption, and challenge him or her to come up with their own definition of what a pyramid intrinsically is! Is a pyramid categorically a tomb for a king, built in Egypt (or America or China)? Alternately, are the pyramids in Egypt and elsewhere in fact based upon a type of earlier widespread religious ritual designed perhaps to assist the communion of Mother Earth (Or even a god imprisoned in the underworld) with Father Sky, as well as an assortment of other underworld gods, to ensure a good harvest?

This religion and pyramid practice alternately developed on its own in Egypt, but was also perhaps carried *into* Egypt by invaders during various inter-dynastic periods. This book argues that it certainly did *not* develop there exclusively, as is a prevailing opinion relating to the evident evolutionary development of the pyramid from step pyramid, and mastaba (a tomb-like platform) before that (or world mound). (A similar evolutionary idea is commonly presented for American pyramids, as evolving from a small raised platform. In my studies of Asian stupas at university, as a student I gave a similar presentation espousing the orthodox view that stupas or hemispherical mounds in Asia also evolved, in Asia, from simple mounds of earth with a stick in the top) This is presented, among the other arguments of this book.

One old book is called *The Ancient Burial-mounds of England*, by L. V, Grinsell. The title seems to carry the assumption that all mounds in England are for burials. Lots of mounds cannot fit into this category, hence the need for this book. Europe contains cenotaphs (shrines with no burial) like Silbury Hill which appear to contain no burial, no matter how many times they are dug up. Its mysterious purpose is unknown.

A problem which may develop for the hypothesis expounded in this book is that eventually superior archaeological methods will detect cremations inside some of these mounds. Whether that constitutes a burial or not is up for debate. Until then, the hypothesis developed here is that the pyramids of Europe, as elsewhere, being among the largest ancient structures built by man, far superior to regular burials, are perhaps to be considered burials of gods.

So what *is* a pyramid? Let us define the term more closely. A pyramid seems to be a huge structure, designed to awe the masses, with which some kind of sacrificial ritual is often associated, often for agricultural fertility. They are bigger on the bottom than on the top, and often, like certain Egyptian pyramids, contain *no* burial. Despite this they are surrounded by burials in much smaller mounds or smaller pyramids. This is something to be noticed over and over in Europe, a large mound or tumulus with a cemetery or small burials around it. The hypothesis advanced supports certain existing ideas, from a more mythological perspective, that they are built largely to create a God in a mountain. This often seems to be a female god-in-the-mountain, which communes with a male god of the sky, but it does not always have to be that way. In the old days, in pagan times, male gods had their female consorts and they often came in pairs. One could not always separate them.

As well as creating gods in mountains, other, often lesser pyramids were also built as a tomb for men. Some of the latter, may have later been associated with tombs of actual gods in later times. Some were built *specifically* as tombs for men and gods, or simply gods, or *specifically* for ancestor gods, those long dead, as seems to be the case for Navan Fort in Ireland. The whole thing is very complicated. There are even tenuous hints regarding a very primitive kind of what I would like to call 'proto-Buddhism', which once extended beyond Asia, and even into Europe and Egypt, giving rise to such ideas as Gnosticism and perhaps Stoicism, as well as perhaps Hermeticism and even Christianity in later times, but which existed well before the days of Gautama Buddha, as Buddhists acknowledge, who lived in the sixth century before the common era. Perhaps his teachings became associated with earlier prophets who had a similar system of teachings, and were later known as earlier incarnations. As the Buddhists point out, their religion is truly ancient.

I wish to highlight some of these ideas also and how they seem to relate to the worldwide pyramid religion. What I choose to call the pyramids of Europe, seem to be the religious equivalent of the pyramids of the Middle East, as well as the hemispherical *stupas* of Asia, built to worship Buddha or for good luck. It would seem that the religion being practised at the pyramids, in Europe anyway, but also perhaps to some extent in Egypt and even in the Americas was based upon a precursor mythology, reflected in the ideas now known as the Indo-European, or Indo-Germanic mythologies.

'Indo-Germanic' is an older term for current 'Indo-European,' which I will bring up sometimes in order to highlight the fact that extant Germanic mythology seems fairly close to the much older, and extinct Indo-European religion, than certain other mythologies which had a more local reach. (This is perhaps because it survived on the Scandinavian island-like outpost, safe and well-defended from invasion via the Baltic, but being spread elsewhere whenever the population increased.) Yes, we can even seemingly relate early Germanic mythology to certain Egyptian gods and ideas, as will be shown later on. This book does not really aim to fully elucidate various instances of what may have been a pyramid religion, with regard to ritual. Rather it is all about providing a general idea on the subject, and what the pyramid represents according to now-extinct mythologies.

We have mounds and then we have cairns. Mounts or mounds are often built on a high position, close to heaven, as are cairns. *Encyclopaedia Britannica* states that a 'Cairn' is a 'pile of stones'. It goes on to state that cairns are used as boundary and track marks, and for burials. (That makes sense if a cairn was vandalised and its stones were used to subsequently build a farmer's wall.)

Ireland seems to have cairns as other countries have mounds, but, I would argue for a very similar purpose, especially when they are very large. In my travels I would note that despite all such structures being called cairns or mounts, some are tiny, yet others are of monstrous proportion! Are they all really used for the same purpose? (The answer, we know today, seems to be 'no', but that is a rather recent opinion, and few hazard to make it or draw implications from it.) The article in the *Encyclopaedia* goes on to state that cairns exhibit 'a great variety in shape and size, from the conical form covering a single grave to a more elaborate structure comprising several chambers.' It states further that in Britain the burial chamber is seldom found under the cairn but rather within the structure itself, unlike elsewhere. This deviation reminds one of the Egyptian pyramids, where some burial chambers are to be found within the structure. Others are to be found underneath.

This brings us to another point. What is new in this book, is that some strings are brought closer and tied together, which have not hitherto been considered to have had much, if any connection. As connections arise, ancient structures can begin to make sense, even in terms of traditions which were still alive as of the 20th century, descending from earlier ideas. These are ideas an archaeologist will seldom touch, due to the presence of the associated mythological aspects needed to rationalise and understand why a structure was built, assuming it was built for mythological value.

The consideration of the importance of myth seems to be part of a 'new wave' of recent academic thinking which acknowledges that the appropriate scholarly approach is not always exclusivist or black and white, accepting everything from one source and rejecting utterly everything from another. That method certainly leads to respectability, apparently steering away from making drastic errors. It is a good thing because we are taught only things we absolutely know for sure, or think we do, supported by overwhelming evidence. It is also a bad thing as it is like closing the box, ending the enquiry, and not allowing anything inside which might harm the hermetically-sealed environment, so diligently established, which may or may not reflect reality.

One is encouraged by the fact that there seems to be a growing realisation that histories and traditions can contribute to archaeology, and have their part to play in giving the general public an understanding of what structures once related to, providing we acknowledge that those sources are obviously contaminated by the tides of time, space and migration, and so cannot be taken too literally.

The especially scholarly reader may wonder what on Earth I think I am doing in comparing different cultures in the way this book does, ultimately tying the strings together in making a case for a stone-age pyramid-building society which was similar in various countries. It is certainly not the speciality-academic thing to do. Men are meant to specialise, to find everything they need to know about the monuments in a country within a study of that country's culture. For instance, if one investigates Egypt, one should really be an Egyptologist, which means that one stays in Egypt. I would retort that in this case, this restriction would not cover what needs to be done, because we are dealing more with cultural ideas, a Stone Age religion, which precedes the existence of Egypt as a polity. The existence of the pyramid religion forces us to reinterpret both ideas, and methods of thought.

Here is where I answer any criticism of this interdisciplinary process, and show that my arguments lie on rather firm ground. Firstly, the notion of country and even culture as limited to certain 'nations' ('kingdoms' before that) are rather modern ones. It is known for instance that the Celtic culture spread over a wide area in Europe including many different kingdoms. DNA studies of haplogroups also suggest that for a large part of the last ten thousand years there was one large, intermixing culture stretching from Europe to central Asia. It is also known that the Sami, the earliest aboriginal Europeans of the northern regions of Scandinavia, still herding reindeer in some cases, share 'U51b' with the Berbers of North Africa, and thence the old (and modern) Egyptians. The link is estimated at 9000 years old. Geneticist Alessandro Achilli and his colleagues have argued for a radiation of this haplogroup from what they call a Franco-Cantabrian refuge area in southwest Europe. Some of the proto-Sami clearly did not like reindeer meat. (Incidentally the Clovis peoples of the Americas may have in part originated from Spain, also about 9000 years ago).

I think that some of these peoples went to set up early civic bodies in North Africa, mixing with African gods, to create the proto-Egyptian religion. Egypt was then repeatedly invaded by people from the North and West (and from the south) bringing newer ideas, variations on older ones. For instance the religion of priests with masks seems to be of fourth-millennium BC origin, in Vinca areas of SE Europe, as well as on walls of Egyptian tombs later on. This book hopes to establish that the pyramid religion in Egypt did not evolve altogether out of the mastaba and step pyramid. Rather it is more the mound-builder religion of Eurasia, with an Egyptian flavour.

Populations in those days were lower. There were tribes rather, which migrated. The men went off to hunt and the women looked after the food around the house, doing a little farming, brewing, baking and general housekeeping as well. This was the time of the Neolithic farmers, who built the megaliths of Europe. The wandering nature of tribes, especially in times of crisis meant they did not see themselves as necessarily tied to a particular region. Kingdoms did not really exist. A druid might have been able to travel a very long way indeed and still be seen as a druid, and afforded respect.

The more I researched, the more I found to indicate that the lost religion of the pyramids may have common origin or overlap with the lost religion of mountain worship. It is also linked to mound worship and worship at the primordial wishing, World Tree, Tree of Life or 'Yggdrasil' as it is known in Germanic mythology. This realisation meant, for me anyway, that the mounds in Europe were in fact pyramids. Where I looked, I noticed similar ideas. The pyramid is associated (not always) with the tree of knowledge on top, the mountain, the snake, and a body of water.

In the supposed centre of the world the Earth swells up in a huge mountain to meet the heavens. This is the location of *Shambhala*, a legendary kingdom surrounded by inaccessible peaks. It is a sanctuary of heaven on Earth, and a place of knowledge. There are lakes shaped like the moon, and filled with jewels, to either side. The kingdom is surrounded by eight other kingdoms in the shape of a lotus flower. One can only find it when one is not looking for it. One must also be worthy.

This folk-tale, purportedly about the lost kingdom of *Shambhala*, (a mythical kingdom north of Tibet), or subsequently associated with it, seems to be a major basis for many of the ancient pyramid religions. It is also related to the idea of the mandala, or even ideas of the impenetrable grail castle. In the 20th century it was found generally only in Asia, yet reflects other ideas seemingly based upon the pyramid or large mound and its landscape, as found in Europe or elsewhere. This among other ideas, was a clue that looking towards mythology, from east and west, might help to explain some of the mysteries of the mounds, and even myths relating to the foundations of the worship of various past gods of Eurasia, and beyond.

Centuries ago antiquarian illustrators ventured into the countryside with their sketchbooks and made idealised Enlightenment- and Romantic-era drawings of what they considered to be the strange geometrical relics of a lost civilisation. They could have no fathoming how truly old these structures were. They simply knew them as medieval or ancient, possibly Roman or Post-Roman (or even Celtic Druid if they truly wished to venture into the distant past). They associated them with figures of recorded mythological antiquity, like Arthur or Merlin. I hoped to retrace a few of their footsteps with some sense of wonder, and see what it was like to chance upon these structures and see what they looked like. I also wanted to try and find out about what the extinct religion surrounding them might have been.

Despite this being a decent-size book I was only able to scratch the surface, in four countries, of uncovering facts about this lost pyramid religion that the mounds and pyramids represent. I encourage others to follow the path and visit the locations and ask locals questions about the ancient lost religion that the mounds may represent. There is still a good deal of surviving strange and bizarre folklore out there, which is fun to collect, and which one cannot find in books. This brings us to the final reason that some pyramids are 'lost'. We tourists do not really know about them. Even if we know *of* them, and go to explore, hoping to uncover a lost world, we are still puzzled. There is no history about them, for they were built largely in the 3rd millennium BC, regardless of their international location. We know nothing *about* them. There is nothing much out there in the way of information. I was once asked by someone: 'Stonehenge... I'd love to go... what's the deal with that?'

I tried to answer as best I could. 'Well, it's the home of a summer ritual, it was built about four thousand years ago, and... we don't know much more than that! The rest is speculation.' It is a pity!

In all, much of the book discusses and describes observations regarding burial complexes in Europe, drawing certain conclusions. Since this is a book about travels as well as pyramids, I concentrate on the locations which I was fortunate to have personally visited and investigated in my humble capacity.

As the book progresses, the travel-book component drops out and we can start to piece together the puzzle of what was going on or represented *mythologically* at the Giza complex in Egypt, in a final chapter entitled *Synthesis*. Giza is a place of great mystery.

The hypothesis here is that it is a place mainly reflecting a fertility cult of the primordial triple goddess and her hound. The pyramids may also may have been used as tombs for the kings of Egypt, but it need not have been that way. In my research, I was quite surprised to notice common themes at Giza, which are to be found elsewhere, but are rarely or never spoken of in any publication. The book ends with this and other rather startling conclusions regarding the pyramids and Sphinx of the Giza plateau. In all it ties the pyramids of Egypt to what I call the 'pyramids' of Europe. The ideas are radical, yet quite plausible if we change our understanding of what a pyramid actually is, shifting the definition from geometrical object, to religious mound. I would rather reveal some of these ideas in greater depth at the end, rather than here. The reader must be prepared, and there is a good deal to be argued before we can get to that eventuality!

The photographs were taken personally unless otherwise stated in the *Photo Credits*, or in which case they are public domain. It is with all this that I humbly invite you to accompany me on a journey to discover some fascinating old ruins left by the Celts and proto-Celts of Europe, and indulge in a bit of a detective journey as well. I had great enjoyment in going off the traditional tourist trail to seek out some of these structures and climb them. (One cannot climb an Irish *cairn*, it might collapse!) I wish to share some of this enjoyment with the reader. Although I try to keep it scholarly and accurate, this is not intended to be a dry academic tome, rather a read for everybody. This author is humbly hopeful that it will prove an enjoyable read as well.

'Pyramid,' a tentative definition

This is a peculiar term. The encompassing definition being suggested in this book is that a *pyramid*, wherever it may be found, and generally in earlier periods, is often really a huge fertility hill and place of worship, defined by Rodney Castleden as a 'harvest hill'. This may be natural or partly shaped, or entirely built by man.

It is built not necessarily as a tomb for a king, as is often thought, (such a tomb could be too-easily plundered) but rather as a tomb for Stone- or Bronze-age gods. These may have included a shining god or fertility deity which returns annually, as well as other underworld deities such as a serpent and trickster god. There may also have been an associated 'world tree' or yggdrasil, or totem pole, marking the site as a centre of creation.

In a place lacking trees, the pyramid may be built of stone rather than turf (this book does not really discuss the pyramids of America). Such a pyramid would then be square-shaped, as that is the shape of stone blocks, and incorporating north-south astronomy in its alignment, or in relation to other pyramids. There may also have been an associated triple deity, often female. The three components are seen as the weavers of mans' fate. These are all responsible, together with an interaction with sky deities, for the promotion of the fertility of the land.

A pyramid may or may not be astronomically aligned. The mound was seen as a centre of creation, a point from which Earth, its geological patterns, water, and all creatures, were originally born. As such the pyramid may also contain various soil or plant samples from across the landscape, presumably an act of sympathetic magic to raise fertility in various locations.

A pyramid is also a mountain representation. Nutrients are washed down a mountain to a fertile valley below, where crops may be grown. In an area lacking a mountain, was a pyramid built instead?

A pyramid or pyramid complex is like a replica of the underworld, probably built for political purposes, in order to actually practice a Stone-Age religion whose ideas are encapsulated in part by very old mythology. It was all done for the resurrection of the bleeding god, sometimes synonymous with the Sun god, and as a tomb for him during the winter months.

A pyramid may have been used as a tomb for a king, perhaps due to its resemblance to a regular tomb, or it may not have. Much larger pyramid or tomb-like structures lacking a burial are often surrounded by smaller mounds which almost invariably are the burials of once-important figures. The king may have been buried rather close, if not in the actual pyramid, in order to take advantage of the proximity of these gods and their representation, for his own afterlife. Above all a pyramid is a mound for the promotion of fertility, for rebirthing the agricultural god near suitable farmland, and perhaps also for associated good luck.

This, I would suggest, is what a pyramid perhaps really is.

Chapter 1

Into Ireland
(*The cairns of Medb*)

While agricultural fields above Europe are regular, industrial and come in varying organic shades of yellow, we see something quite different when we fly above Ireland. We see irregular, misshapen small fields, which are covered in thick juicy green grass all the year round. There are few if any crops but plenty of sheep and cows. From the windows of the descending plane one can see a patchwork of dry stone walls, assembled hundreds to thousands of years ago, now frozen in time, but whose building had once been accompanied by bloodshed and warfare. This was the product.

We enter a land never graced by the Industrial revolution. Because of this I would in time be told that 'every river in Ireland is safe to drink from'.

On the *Emirates* flight in there are stars on the ceiling when it is 'night time'. Before meals they hand out a wet facewasher with chemicals on it, on a peg. They also do this after the meals, and just before and after a snack, before we landed in Ireland. Two Irish larrikins were sitting next to me, coming home from ten weeks bouncing all over South East Asia. 'We only planned the first week, then we just winged it... Laos, Cambodia, China, Indonesia, Malaysia.' As I was to slowly realise, it appeared that the Irish are among the greatest natural born-travellers in the world, even if they share the very human characteristic of not travelling much in their home country. It is in their blood. There is also the consideration that anybody dwelling on any island must have had ambitious travelling ancestors.

They were ordering three beverages at a time, and then going up to pester different stewardesses for more. Previously ordering only one drink at a time, I thought it would be a good idea to emulate this, and rehydrate. The stewardesses are just pretty young things and too overworked to argue.

'A drink? I'll have a Heineken, and in addition I'd like a vodka on ice, with a whiskey, and and also another couple vodkas with tomato juice and tabasco sauce, thanks!'

We had all assembled quite a little collection of those little bottles and beers. It was eventually too much for me and I simply couldn't take it anymore.

'That's what is known as a ladies' drink', I was told. In spite of the plausible veracity of that statement, I still could not keep up, so I gave them the left-overs, which they sloshed down in a few seconds. Later they were warned to keep the noise down.

Before we touched down, I had tears in my eyes, looking over the remarkable timeless green fields which I had never seen before, separated by those stone walls, not seen in the rest of Europe, which might have dated to the Neolithic. I imagined what ancient people visiting Ireland by boat, this land of eternal springtime and rain, would have thought. Having heard of its repute, they would have considered the magical qualities of the place, as perhaps we would today consider visiting something mystical like Atlantis.

In Ireland, snow does not settle in winter for more than three consecutive days. Ireland has a very curious weather pattern where a mere 33 degrees Celsius (91.4 Fahrenheit), is the standing summer heat record. Alternately it does not really frost up like the rest of Europe either. Ireland behaves like an island in the middle of the Atlantic, rather than something alternately attached to the Siberian refrigerator, or the Sahara, as the rest of the European peninsula is.

'This is going to be epic,' I was thinking. I now had eight weeks to explore as many ancient mysteries as I could pack in, and Ireland is full of them.

I woke in the hostel the following morning. 'What's the time brohther?' said a man on an adjacent bed. They certainly talk differently in Ireland. Later, on the street a homeless person was saying 'can ye spare some change brother?' I instantly had thoughts of the *Clockwork Orange* movie. That is how they talk, in Dublin anyway!

If you are a historian, you go to Ireland for the ruins. The oldest visible archaeology in Europe seems to be found on the peripheries. This is the archaeology we do not really need shovels and geophysical detectors to notice, like in more densely populated Britain.

The places, Malta, Ireland, the Balaerics, the Azores, are islands of ruins and vanished trading civilisations. These islands were exposed to the religious ravages of invading peoples far less often than those in more central regions. England has a far greater medieval and dark-ages history than Europe. Their history, which has been mostly corrupted by mythology, but which nonetheless exists, actually goes back to the time of a leader called 'Brutus', who supposedly led some migration, in about 1100 BC, the time of the Sea-Peoples attacks on Egypt, from a place near Greece in the Mediterranean. These men swept across Europe, ending the days of Achilles and the *Iliad*, and Odysseus.

'Why does England have abundant archival records of the Middle Ages, yet the continent does not?' my research supervisor once asked me. 'Because they have rarely suffered invasion,' he said, answering his own question.

If Britain has suffered little invasion, what about Ireland? First, take a Central-European country like Poland. It lies on a flat, natural invasion corridor between Europe and Asia. Polish history only goes back one thousand years as a result. Every empire which occupies the place first burns everything and often kills the intellectuals. Some of the most ancient Polish history and geography in fact comes from Ptolemy, the Arabs and Byzantines. I shudder to think of all the continental druids who passed down their culture for generations, meticulously memorised, only to have it obliterated in one fell swoop.

Due to their protected (in relative terms) geographical location, their academic nature, natural curiosity and European Dark Ages-period Golden Age, it may amaze the reader to learn that the Irish can boast of a history extending backwards over two thousand years before the common era, in various Irish chronicles.

The chronicles are not merely idle tales. Certain very early dates, around a thousand years before Christ, amazingly, provided in the chronicles as containing disastrous years, have been verified with tree ring studies as being bad years. The implication is that all the past invasions of Ireland were never enough to fully kill off the Irish intellectual spirit, and never took over the whole country. The fabled invasions merely took over or integrated with one of the four historic quadrant-kingdoms into which Ireland was perpetually divided.

After several generations of contact, invaders invariably saw themselves as Irish (as the English colonists to Ireland often have, for the past eight centuries) and identified with the traditions of their countrymen. If only Minoan history went back as far, we would know the identities of fabled 'Minos' and his descendants and begin to comprehend the mystery of the Bull dance, depicted so elegantly on Minoan reliefs.

Crete however, tragically formed a natural stopping-off point for any ancient fleet of war-like ships, crossing anywhere in the Eastern Mediterranean, to re-supply. The Sea Peoples of 1100 BC and other invaders had flocked to that island like bees to honey. Its proximity to the Near East meant that huge armies on the move had periodically destroyed it. He who controls Crete controls the entire Eastern Mediterranean and its commerce. This includes access and partial control to set prices for the economies of Egypt, Greece, and the Hittites. Meanwhile, he who controls Ireland controls... Ireland, and the trade between Dublin and... some obscure place in Wales or Western England. 'It's er... just not the same.'

In rough general terms, Ireland can be thought of a mixture of two races, ancient Spanish, and Viking. The Mediterranean element seems to be the strongest in Dublin, where the men are approaching Leprechaun height in some respects, and with a darker complexion. Other towns by contrast look very Viking, especially in the north. Cork people really look very English, like a bunch of Errol Flynns, bandying about, arrogantly. At least that is one Dublin perception.

Armagh

I had experienced six days of exceptional weather in Belfast, as it was a week with only one day which was truly rainy. Apparently that is unheard of. I had been informed it is not unusual in Belfast for it to rain every day of the year! I was therefore very pleased with the 'goddess' for providing six days minimal rain. It was also pleasant to 'escape' the impending Belfast rains in the morning, with a coach trip to the interior. The whole following week was forecast to have been an absolute shocker.

In between rain showers it is quite warm. A t-shirt is fine in late spring. I took a coach inland towards Armagh, the ancient, and modern spiritual capital of Ireland. It is only a few miles from the now-vanishing border with free-state Ireland. It is a nice town of ten thousand. Inland, it certainly rains less. I wrote in my diary that from my hostel window,

I could see a huge rain cloud in the Belfast direction, which was not approaching, merely hovering over that city making everyone miserable.

This hostel was actually purpose built a couple of years ago. It looks like it would be good for school groups and is indeed quite ambitious in build. Yet the place was deathly quiet, with no noise at all. In the late afternoon I conjectured that there might be only one other guest, or that I was the sole guest in the entire hostel. Nevertheless, it was one of the best hostels I have ever been in. It felt like a hotel since it had no other guests, and it certainly reminded me of the ski hotel in *The Shining*, with the gloomy atmosphere outside.

Being in the UK, Belfast was bombed heavily in World War II. (The Free State was neutral). They have never experienced a disaster on the scale of Eastern Europe in the wars. Therefore the main frame of reference, the main event they look back to is not 20th-century genocide, but 19th-century famine/genocide. Apart from the famine, by which their frame of reference is different to other European countries, they did not have massive industrial protests and communism or socialism on the scale of other nations.

The main relic of old Ireland is feudalism. Rather than having an internal revolution to break out of feudalism, they concentrated their attentions upon the lack of home parliament, the English landlords, and upon a movement for independence and reform, in addition to emigration, which was the personal form of rebellion. Due to feudalism until the twentieth century, there was never much opportunity for anyone to rise above their station in Ireland. Due to these, and other factors, Ireland has a low population of several million. The ratio of Britain to Ireland in population used to be 2:1 in the eighteenth and nineteenth centuries. Now it is 10:1.

Emigration, I was told, was the mainstay of Irish culture until the 20th century. Another one of the great Irish disasters was the Titanic. It was built in Belfast. The last part of call was in Cobh ('Cove'), a delightful town whose two attractions are the Titanic and another old naval disaster.

The Irish were really nice to me on my first day in Armagh. I have the feeling that they do not realise how welcoming they are compared to other people on Earth. It is the old Viking spirit. I was walking up and down medieval Abbey Street looking for the hostel. I asked directions from two men outside an exhibition. One went inside, onto the computer to check where it was. The other told me to come and see the exhibition later.

The hostel was one of those small ones which kick everyone out in the morning and open again at 5pm. I was stranded, but then the cleaning woman opened the door so that I could leave the bags in the luggage area. Thank goodness!

The exhibition in the Methodist Church, was about the Armagh rail disaster. I learnt lots from the guide who told me all about it. Armagh really has a small-town feel. They were discussing the new visitor amongst themselves.

'He says he's looking for the 'ah-stel, we give him directions, I tell him to come back later, and here he is!'

'Hey, stick around after the exhibition, I'll give yer a treat!'

I will now relate the events which took place a century ago, in this ancient capital-city of Ireland. One hundred years ago, the population of Ireland was greater than today. There was to be a great church outing to the beach by train. All train companies in those days, as in Australia, were privately run. 'To save costs', they did not bother putting the latest braking system on the train. Everyone wanted to go to the beach, so over one thousand people showed up. To cover that, they had to hitch on a few extra carriages to a small engine. Going up a long incline, the engine stalled so they decided to leave a few carriages behind and chock them up with stones, and come back for the left carriage later.

The problem happened as soon as they left and the carriages were disconnected. The train accidentally nudged them. The stones moved and got crushed. The carriages which had been left on the hillside began to move. They built up momentum and went careening a few miles back down the hill. The people could not just jump out because in those early days, doors were locked from the outside. The windows were only small enough for children to escape so they threw babies and children out. The last thing they would have heard was the whistle of the train coming from behind which smashed into them. There were even old people at the exhibition saying they remember that the windows on old trains were too small.

The whole exhibition was told in photographs, in the cute little church. It was all volunteers and very kind people at this exhibition. I went back to the man who introduced me to it.

'Arrgh! let's go!'

We went into the cafe room. It was composed of middle-aged to elderly people but a few young couples as well. He took out five quid and gave it to the cashier. 'Ca-ching!' They gave me such a huge amount of food, as was really befitting a huge celebration, rather than lunch. The Irish do believe in eating far beyond the recommended calorie limits, as the travel book stated. With all the rain I don't blame 'em.

First it was an excellent home-made veggie soup, similar to how everyone's mother makes it, with tea. Every time the food woman went past the tea got filled up, which was very nice. Then my soup got filled up as well so I drank that down.

The women kept bringing me more and more. Now it was trays full of sandwiches.

'Just keep eating, you may as well fill yerself op, there is plenty more!'

She placed several trays of sandwiches, cupcakes and other cakes before me and refilled the tea.

'Is that enough, would you like some more?'

'Are all these for me?' I was incredulous.

'Oh of course!'

'That's awesome!'

Since I had to fill myself up, I made sure I did. I had lots of scones with jam and then whipped cream on top.

A woman approached me. 'Are you English?'

'No.'

'Are you French?' someone else asked, approaching the table.

'No, actually I'm Australian.'

'Do you have Irish ancestry then, since you're over here?'

'No, none.'

They were excited to hear about Australia. One man was a German language teacher and he was incredibly excited to hear about my travels to Germany in 2012. It seems we had both visited the same region. He said the skytrain in Wuppertal was over a century old (built in the 1930s). He said he really enjoyed hitchhiking in Germany but you cannot do that in France because drivers do not always stop!

'That was in Normandy. And if you try it in southern France, well they'll just kill yer.'

I remarked about the ever-present rains in Ireland. The Irish do not always notice this as it is 'normal'. He had his own spin on it.

'Ireland is the sponge of the Atlantic. It soaks everything up, and that's why it floats.'

It sounded to me a lot like Atlantis! Change the costume and he may as well have been a curious Irish medieval monk, quoting Aristotelian theory, with Pythagorean variations, though the comment was of course told as a joke. I love the way the Irish can come up with theories based on their own experiences. There is something different about their character, not to be encountered elsewhere in Europe. I was prepared to accept the thought for the time being, considering how old everything seemed to be in this country, at least compared to every other European nation I had been to, including England. The only other places with such old things are the Mediterranean islands. There is also a golden treasure from Bulgaria, from a civilisation which came after the Vinca. That even predates Schleiman's jewellery at Troy by millennia. The tombs near Sligo, Ireland, however were dated to 5000 BC and no other country in Europe has such golden ornaments in their museums, from say 2000 BC, as the Irish do. Ireland seems to have been in suspended animation for thousands of years, ever since the crops failed from too much rain. Sheep took over from that early instance of farming.

They kept feeding me food so I kept eating it and chatting. After all that, I said thanks to all of them and it was already three o'clock. I said my goodbyes and popped into the tourist information. The lady inside was incredibly friendly, reflecting the overall mood of the town, which seemed to be an intense friendliness to anybody. She was saddened I had only one further day to enjoy the place. She began to suggest some places, then stopped.

'OK, would you like me to just go through it all?'

'Yes, give me the works.'

Eventually I asked her to kindly ring up the planetarium to book me in. The planetarium is I suppose a modern mound in a 'city' of huge ancient hills which look like man-made mounds, at least in shape. I wonder about the hills of Armagh. Did the ancients think they were made by a strange race of giants? The Armagh planetarium is simply awesome for such a tiny town and reflects the input of U.K. money. The U.K. needs to allocate certain monies to building certain museums in tiny Northern Ireland, so where to put it all? There are not a lot of places to choose from, about which we really know anything.

How cyclical and convoluted everything is! Here I was going to this 'modern' mound. Then... an astronomy lesson! First a presentation of the northern sky, followed up by a zoom into some galaxies in Virgo and Leo. Then Saturn.

Later, a really funny dark-humour cartoon movie about how fragile astronauts are in space. Basically space travel is impossible for the human body. In space one immediately starts to get osteoporosis and the blood concentrates in the heart instead of legs, causing the heart to swell. There were also some heartswelling ladies running the place. There was also an exhibition here. It was about different probes and stuff, amazing replicas of satellites.

Armagh is Ireland's answer to Polish Gniezno, or possibly Avebury or Windsor in England. It is a seat of kings, kingly burials and an ancient capital, now reduced to a small town. Brian Boru, who defeated the Viking invasion a thousand years ago, despite the fact he was likely mainly a Viking himself was buried here, or was he?

There are other ancient ruins nearby. Oddly, this small town is the capital of the Roman and Protestant churches in Ireland. I went to the Catholic cathedral twice. The first time, they were doing confirmations. Later on it was empty. Wow! I suppose this is Ireland's 'Aachen' since this is where kings were crowned, along with Tara. The *Lonely Planet* guidebook claims the Catholic cathedral looks 'Byzantine.' Instead it is, architecturally a huge gothic affair, yet with what one might call very (very) late (modern in fact!) Romano-Celtic mosaics, everywhere inside. This is Ireland's unique spin on Hagia Sophia and the Eastern Empire.

Armagh itself was the capital of Ulster, or ancient Northern Ireland. This was one of the four kingdoms into which Ireland was always divided. St Patrick came here and allegedly started his church, converting the pagans. It appears there were two main pagan temples here.

Patrick's church is on top of a hill which would have been of holy use in older times, and is the Archbishopric of the Anglican Church of Ireland, on Sally hill, near the centre of town. It seems the Anglicans have access to this 'original' site of St Patrick. The other Catholic cathedral looks like it occupies a rival hill, Sandy Hill, just a little further out, which looks a lot like it has been placed on top of some stepped pyramid, though seems to be modern terracing, built in the late 19th century at the time of the church, as it is observed to wrap tightly to the shape of the cathedral. I would be happy to hear from anyone who knows if this has been done in continuation of an older tradition.

What is supposed to have happened is that St Patrick arrived at Sally hill, in the centre or Armagh, around the year 445, coming from Britain. On the hill, he spotted a deer and its fawn. His followers wanted to kill these animals. Patrick however took the fawn on his shoulders, (the deer followed) and took it to Sandy Hill, fig. 1.2. The incident has been interpreted by some as his prophetic notion that this

Figure 1.1: When I first saw this I imagined that early Christians had, as they did, placed a church on top of an earlier pyramid-mound in order to convert the natives. What looks like the terracing of a possibly ancient structure is in fact rather modern. The mound itself upon which the cathedral sits may not be, for this was an ancient shrine, where St Patrick possibly paid his respects. The mound sits on top of Sandy hill, Armagh, which is ancient in terms of ceremonial significance. Mounds on top of hills seem to be part of a deeply ancient religion.

modern cathedral would be built in his honor, 1400 years later.

On the contrary, I would suggest he was merely bearing away the pagan artefacts to a nearby hill, whilst claiming the more central Sally hill, for his own use. He bore the 'fawn', possibly some pagan idol, on his head, to show it honor (and so perhaps he would not be slaughtered by the natives), whilst the mother only followed, perhaps because it was a religious procession. It was the old Christian idea, popular in the first millennium, of showing that the old religion is not destroyed by violence, rather simply superseded by similar, yet different, monotheistic ideas.

I walked around St Patrick's Anglican cathedral back in town. As mentioned, around on one side it, it was written that Brian Boru was buried 'about here'. He was the national-hero king in the time

Figure 1.2: The Catholic church of Armagh on top of a modern pleasant terraced hill, which is itself on top of a hill. It was to here that St Patrick possibly banished a set of what seem to have been pagan idols, when he took up preaching residence on the nearby Sally Hill, in the fifth century.

of Mieszko of Poland, the early 1000s. He successfully defended the Dublin area against the Vikings, even if he and his people seem to have been descended from an earlier invasion of Vikings themselves. I would personally have my doubts. It is easy for the idea of an unknown great king being buried in some mound, natural or artificial, to have become mixed up with ideas of what we know today as Ireland's greatest king.

Boru's era was one in which we see a pattern around Europe, of petty princedoms and chiefdoms coalescing into mini-empires which became the early nation states we recognise today on the map. It was only in this era, somehow, that history around Europe, was able to begin again, after centuries of darkness, in which the old Indo-Germanic religion of the tree and the mound, was slowly replaced by the religion of the 'One God.'

Navan Fort

On the glorious following sunny morning, I walked three kilometres out
of town to the 'Navan Fort', getting directions along the way from the
very helpful Irish.

This town of Armagh was a very important place, deeply ancient,
but it may have grown out of a nearby greater city. It may have been
a place where the peasants lived, just as the town of Amesbury several miles away from Stonehenge is the remnant of possibly a Stone-Age
farming community, near the political/ceremonial capital-city at Stonehenge. Another analogy would be the fact that people live in London,
whereas the Queen lives a little further out in Windsor. Here, Navan
fort was the ceremonial capital of the Armagh region, with Armagh
being the possibly newer, associated former population centre.

My shoes simply got so wet, but that is part of the magic of Ireland!
On approaching, one sees that something is wrong with 'Navan Fort'!
It is not really a fort but a sort of henged hill. Walking around it one
can surmise that yes, it *could* well have been used as a fortress, but
only in a drastic emergency, for it is literally nothing at all compared
with a proper hill fort, with enormous battlements, that one fights ones
battles on, and which can be seen around Europe. It is more like one of
the famous Irish 'Fairy Rings' (either Bronze-Age henges or Iron-Age
ring forts, which is a fortress on flat land with a ditch around it, rather
than necessarily on a proper defensive hill).

It is all rather insufficient to be used for defensive purposes. It
would have been good of course as a ceremonial hill fort, the way some
charming but indefensible country houses have a 'moat' or decorative
crenulations. Later on, I wandered into next door, which was the museum and told the man behind the desk there, about my observations,
to which he repeated to me, basically the same ideas.

On the hill, I imagined that it was indeed a royal hill. It has a
sweeping and beautiful dramatic view and would be excellent for a
royal palace, a nice large wooden roundhouse or two. I imagined some
nice royal red banners and flags fluttering in the breeze and saw where
I could imagine people would come from across the rolling hills and up
the path, guarded by men in royal uniform, who would enter. Being
caught in torrential rains and hiding in a thicket for half an hour or
so did not dampen my enthusiasm. We were really in the realm of
Irish mythology. This is truly Northern Ireland's (The old kingdom of
Ulster's) answer to the Hill of Tara.

Now, what is going on in the middle of this huge ring fort? Inside

Figure 1.3: The first and obvious mound at Navan Fort.

there appeared to be two circular shallow hills. This reminded me of the two hills inside Tara or the two circles inside Avebury in England. (The man inside the museum had told me that, yes indeed it is quite similar to Avebury in the respect of a circle containing two smaller circles.)

Examining what these two hills actually were, was something of a challenge! Both were clearly artificial. The first, a steeper more prominent though smaller mound in area (both are about the same height) had some ancient oaks around it. I fancied they were left overs from the druids, and their rituals, but there is no evidence. I sheltered under one during the rains, and sat on a large root, the only 'chair' around, to make my notes. All I needed was a harp, to crown the bucolic setting.

This smaller hill was the kind of ringed barrow, or a sort of henged mound. One climbs to the top and then ambles back down again, and that is that. It is not as large even as the Wanda Mound near Cracow, fig. 2.7, which we shall get to later, so it is rather disappointing. See fig. 1.3.

I walked around for a while, not even noticing the next mound which is much larger in area and very shallow, and therefore hard to see. One does not actually 'see' it. Rather, one has more of a dawning realisation that one is on a kind of strange incline, which continues in various directions. I forgot its existence until I started looking for it, imagining that which was under my nose and in front of me, to be a mere hill or very large slope. See fig. 1.4.

'Perhaps if I get to the top of the hill, the mound would be revealed,' is what I was thinking. But no, this was simply a strange innocuous slope, in various directions, which turns out to have been a huge mystery for everybody involved. I would later realise that understanding this unknown hill in Armagh, a town of no tourists, would perhaps be one of the keys to unlocking the pyramid religion, worldwide, and its origins.

While investigating, the heavy rain caught me and I pressed myself into a thorny thicket under a tree next to the fortress' ring. I was very pleased with the effectiveness of the shelter. The rain just went on and on for an hour or so, whilst the thicket became less and less effective at keeping the rain out. I pressed deeper into the thicket, wishing I had something to hack into it, like a machete, to make a small room. A drenched man in a t-shirt ran past with a dog, oblivious to my existence. I was grateful for the experience to spend a little more time in such a sacred location.

In his book *Britain BC*, Francis Pryor says he feels a sense of *déjà vu* at Navan, as it feels oddly like Stonehenge or the tombs of *Bru na Boinne*. I would argue that in fact we are dealing with very similar themes and a very similar religion, though by no means precisely the same religion. Too much time, and space, has elapsed between each site for that eventuality.

Before meticulous excavation by archaeologist Dudley Waterman at Navan fort in the 1960s, it was assumed that the two mounds in the fort were simply Bronze-Age barrows. A question arises which must have puzzled everybody. What are Bronze-Age barrows doing in the middle of an Iron-age ring fort, and taking up such an inconsiderate amount of room, in an area which otherwise seems to have been an excellent location for some sort of a palace? The Navan fort complex is really not that big and the larger mound really might have made life inside a bit tiresome.

It turns out the mounds *were* the palace, before they were mounds that is. That is where we fall into difficulty about what a barrow, normally thought of as a burial, actually is. The larger mound at Navan fort seems to have originally been a series of large round houses,

Figure 1.4: Next to the first mound is this less obvious mound. The museum curator believes this was built to symbolically house the imprisoned Loki. Imagine how many of these might lie around Europe, disguised to the untrained, and trained eye, as natural hills? Both mounds are in the middle of what appears to be a largely ceremonial ring fort. It is this less obvious mound, which resembles a hill, that the neighbouring museum is mainly dedicated to. For decades, archaeologists struggled to uncover the mystery of what this manmade hill was supposed to accomplish. Cairn? Mound? What is it? The *Concise Oxford* says that a cairn is a 'pyramid of rough stones as a memorial, sepulchre, landmark, etc.' This mound contains round stones, a lot of burnt wood and various layers of soil.

or royal palaces, renewed down the centuries. These rotted and were rebuilt again and again in different locations, about eight times.

The larger less-obvious mound, Site B, is about 40 metres in diameter, a respectable size. It began as a ring ditch in the eighth century BC before it became a series of large roundhouses, possibly royal palaces erected in the same place, time and again, as they rotted away, for several centuries.

In 95 BC, things got very strange indeed as the thing was burned and filled in with soil, as well as stones, and covered up in strange ceremonial fashion. Why? Perhaps the palace had become 'haunted'. Maybe the superstitions were finally taking over.

Chris Lynn, archaeologist, believes that Site B was a 'bruidne' or a magic hostelry, comparable to an Iron-Age Valhalla. In Irish epics, the kings feasted inside, and at the end the thing burnt down around them, immolating them. That immolation business does sound rather like an Aryan tradition from India, or even, I would hazard, a pyramid-builder tradition. The king dies, so everyone dies. They are after all, needed to serve him in the afterlife. Fair enough. Yet if this is so, it is a symbolic immolation, for no bodies were found.

After I was fully satisfied that I had worked out as much as I could, I went to the Visitor Centre. They have a huge exhibition. There is actually a lot more to see in this museum than outside on the hill. After I bought the ticket, a woman dressed in Iron-Age costume appeared, standing next to me, and with a huge smile on her face. It is a really good museum, cursed with being in the middle of nowhere, a small town, and in Northern Ireland with a low population. I believe that I was the only customer all day long.

'This is Jenny, and she will take you to her dwelling,' the man behind the desk said.

Jenny, a middle-aged blonde woman with obvious Viking ancestry was standing there with the mentioned big smile, dressed in rags and furs, holding a crook. I could not wait to see what sort of place this would be. But that is when everything started to become weird. After preliminaries, she asked where I was from.

'Melbourne.'

'Oh my daughter lives there, but I'm not supposed to know where that is.'

'Uh, OK.'

'Tell me, have you brought any salt?'

'Um... not particularly.'

'Hmmm! You have come across the seas, and you have not bought any salt? It would have helped us.'

'OK.'

It deteriorated from there as the confusion level increased. At first I thought we were simply having a communication problem, but then I saw it was simply part of the 'show', except I was to become part of the show for them.

After a bit of walking we passed some little vegetable gardens and saw a dwelling which Bilbo Baggins would have been pleased to call home. It was a reconstructed Iron-Age roundhouse.

'You are most welcome to come into our dwelling.'

'Thank you so much, it's a great honour!'

There was a girl in there of about twenty. Like the older woman, she too was also dressed in Iron-age clothing. We all began chatting. For most of the time she simply sat, playing with threads and wool in a sort of hand loom. She sat in front of a fire which was in the middle of the round house. It had a pot boiling over it.

One question I forgot to ask was whether they know that boiling water makes it safe to drink. If they did know, how would an Iron-Age person have been able to explain it? Would they say that the fires of the joker God Loki, or perhaps Hephaestus, assist mankind with their love and curiosity?

Perhaps they might have remarked that by some secret action, the fire works at the water, 'tempering' it, into something which is now holy enough to drink, purged of the curse of the unclean?

'As you can see, we need no chimney, the smoke just goes through the roof, and yet there is no smell.'

'We can hang things over the fire, from the ceiling, in order to smoke them,' the woman continued.

It was most cozy. There were furs everywhere on the floor. The walls were thick, caulked up in places with mud and grasses, and the living area was large. It was a fine house! Many would like to live that way today! I certainly would love to give it a try. The floor was thick with furs everywhere, in particular in about one fifth of the hut, which was the communal sleeping area. How cozy it must have been in any season!

There are two doors on opposite sides of the hut. I had come in through the big door, which I was told is reserved for people from other tribes, or for druids. Normally they just use the small door.

'If we don't like who is crawling through the door, we can simply chop off his head,' the girl said.

'Really?'

'I think that I might clean that door... it looks like there is still some blood on it,' she continued.

'But then again I might leave it as it is, as a warning... just in case some shoddy person wants to get inside.'

'Um... yeah that's a good idea actually!'

'How much longer are you staying?'

'Two weeks.'

The woman began to think. 'Ah... two passes of the moon!'

She turned to the girl. 'I am picking up his language,' she explained.

It was becoming really frustrating to talk to these people in my own language so I basically adopted their stone-talk. Although I started speaking in their lingo, or attempted to, it was a maddening experience. Despite being extremely curious they kept resorting to variations upon:

'I don't know what he's talking about... strange stories... he must be a bard.'

'Yes, a storyteller... we could use a bard around here!'

They wanted me to tell of my travels. I told them about the Krakus Mound in Poland, which I was going to go to.

'I have never been across the sea. The furthest I have been is the sea itself, a four day walk.'

They said that they grow barley and that their wealth is held in cows.

'I know someone with thirteen cows,' the girl said.

'Do people own land?'

'I... I do not know what he speaks of.'

'He is a bard, his ways are uncertain to us,' the girl replied.

'Do you own this house? Is there a title?' I asked.

'Who... who owns the land!? Did you hear what he asked? How can anyone own the land?'

'I suppose the king might own it, but everyone uses it really,' chimed in the woman.

'Please tell me about the king!'

'We call him a king, but he is really an elected ruler.'

The women said that they said they live thirty to thirty-five summers. That seems about right. I sometimes think this is down to teeth, which seem to go a little bad in many people by around age thirty. Even if people had fewer cavities back then, there were no fillings either! It must have been a dream-like pastoral existence of harps and hardship. To have had such a short existence, and to know it, must have enriched their leisure days with feelings of sentimentality and love for nature, the likes of which we today do not understand.

'You have come so far... such a big bag... and yet no salt. We could have used it.'

Again I felt like I had committed a serious indiscretion. Salt must have been important back then.

'Sorry, I'll err... bring some next time?' I offered this as a gesture of goodwill, eager to regain lost fidelity.

They took me outside their amazing house and showed me the herb garden. They grow parsnip and purple onion flowers. One thing I did not know is that in Europe they have honeybees which are really a small type of bumblebee. Neither exist in Australia.

They picked spring onion with flowers to take with me on my journeys (I was still digging out some rotting remnants from the bottom of the bag, on the way to the airport). They also had a trough outside, and said that one can cook a cow in the trough for a feast. As for bread, they make it themselves in a bread oven in the ground with a stone in front of it for a door.

'Do you have a baker?'

'What's that?'

They made bread themselves and as for alcohol, the answer is 'yes'. They make beer themselves as well! I was informed that beer is safer than water for drinking. As for the lack of specialisation of industry. This would have meant there was really no time for anything. Men were always hunting or training. The priests did not have any economic basis for the supply of paper or writing materials. They had to manage with whatever they could scratch into stone.

As for relations, they had a trial marriage when they were fourteen years old, which lasted for a year and a day. I was reminded that medieval loans would also take place for a year and a day, a relic of Stone-Age ritual, and also a marriage of sorts.

If the trial marriage does not work out, they stand back to back and walk apart, like in a duel. I wondered which shaman culture they pulled that one out of. Grounds for divorce? If the man is lazy, the woman can divorce him. If one speaks badly of the other, that is also grounds for divorce.

I told them about ancient Celtic mounds and told them of the mounds I had seen on tops of natural hills, overlooking cities of the west coast, like over Galway and Sligo (more on that presently). Then,

I asked who the pyramid god was. Unfortunately they did not really know what I was talking about, and it was an uncomfortable situation, because they really wanted to give a convincing answer.

I guess back then the Stone-Age mothers would have told their children, 'Look if you don't behave, I'll have you taken up there to the mound, and the priests will slice you open as a gesture to the fertility god, so everything turns green next year!' 'Furthermore... the man with the horse mask will scream at you the curses of death!' It must have been terror to the kids, looking up at that big temple on the hill and imagining screams coming down at midnight, along with the howling of the wolves in the nearby primordial forest.

As they listened to the noises of the night, they would have huddled by the fire in their incredibly cozy furs, close to their parents. They would have learned fear at a young age, and learned to respect the authority of the priest-kings. However my stone-age couple did not speak of this.

'Our god is Taranis.'

'Tyranus?'

'Taranis.'

'I've never heard of him.'

'You've—' They could not accept this revelation.

'Please tell me about Taranis! Who is he?'

'He is... he is the sky god. He is everywhere.'

Later on I looked him up. Taranis is almost another way of saying 'Thor,' god of thunder (Thunor in Anglo-Saxon England). Thor is a weather god. Mythologically, he is the child of the union of Earth Mother and Sky Father. These are represented by Jord and Odin.

They asked me about work. I said I had just finished university.

'It must be that school you start when you are eight... to become a warrior.'

'Well... not quite.'

The Irish are wonderful people in their hospitality and I really did feel quite at home and would have stayed for weeks in their little stone-age hut, if I had been invited.

'Do you have any more questions? You have come such a long way to see us!'

'Ummmm, OK... what is your main crop, wheat?'

'We can't grow wheat due to the rains.'

'I noticed that flying over.'

'Flying? So he *is* a druid, or some sort of magician?'

'We have another plant. We grind it up and put it in a drink.'
'Oh, like coffee?'
'Yes,' said the girl.
'You're not supposed to know what coffee is, because it was brought from America by Columbus,' I said.
'Oh. Columbus?'
'If you weren't dressed in that garb, I would almost think you were modern people,' I added.
'He speaks so strangely, but he is from another land', said the woman.
'Strange names and far-away places,' added the girl.
'But I am becoming convinced that he *is* a bard', said the girl.
'Well, I hope we can learn more from him. It's not often we have the honour of a bard in our house. We'd love to live with you, but yes he does seem suspicious. But then he would be, being so far from home.'
'And yet, if only he had brought some salt for all his troubles.'
Finally, it was time to go. It was time for the 'handshake.'
'No, like this!' It was really an *arm*shake to prevent stabbings.
'But then I can stab you like this with my free hand!'
'No, no! I'd manoeuvre you like this!' (the Amazon woman then demonstrated some stone-age martial arts on me).

A bizarre theory

I said my farewells to the wonderful Iron Age people. The adjoining museum was simply awesome. Enlightened and unpretentious, it has evidently been designed recently by a genius curator. I would say it is one of the finest museums in the world. One wears headphones the whole time, but not for the robotic-like guided tour where one dials in a number based on a place marked on a map in one's hand, as is usual. Instead, the headset relays one's position to the program, as well as the direction in which one's head is pointed. As such it supplied funny creepy music at appropriate moments, so I felt like I was watching a wonderful ancient mysteries program.

The shallow mound that I thought was just a slope really puzzled archaeologists. They found out that this less obvious (from the ground) mound was originally a huge forty-metre roundhouse temple built for ritual. The museum makes the claim that it is the largest tribal Iron-Age building of which we know. I am really not sure about that claim.

Figure 1.5: While standing on the Navan ring fort and looking over the landscape, I imagined the ancient houses, banners and turrets. This is Ireland's ancient heritage. People would have watched foreign delegations, traders approaching, coming over the hill, from a distant land. They would have told their partner and children about it at night.

After having built their almost-round temple, there seems to have been a odd non-circular perambulatory between the interior wooden posts. There was a huge oak, possibly a totem pole in the middle which the people may have walked around. After this it gets a little bizarre. The people then brought stones from everywhere which had been weathered and rounded. In other words Thor had presumably blessed these stones and given them great wisdom. They had seen much. The stones were possibly from other monuments. (Stonehenge was also supposedly brought from elsewhere) Then they filled the house with these rocks, making a kind of conical cairn or 'pyramid', a word I like to use for unusual very large cairns.

That, however, was not enough to even begin to satisfy the Iron-Agers, so they set the whole thing on fire and then covered it all up with specially-selected layers of soil brought some distance from different parts of the kingdom. The brought soils were carefully layered. They were making a kind of wedding cake. This created the mound we see today. All that work to make a natural-looking hill? Unbelievable! The Celts were amazing.

Information provided in the museum makes the suggestion that they were trying to create a god or genius in the mountain like Germanic Loki. Firstly, let us have some background. In Germanic/Viking mythology, Loki is a trickster god, similar to Lucifer, which has the same root. He is a bit evil, but nothing approaching the Christian conception of 'Satan'.

There is another god called Baldr, who is similar to Percival or Early Christ or Apollo, as he is a god of light and purity. Baldr, evidently similar to the Greek Apollo, is essentially Christ before Christ. He is the son of the Sun or sky god. I would suggest, as have many others, such as Brian Branston in *The Lost Gods of England*, that it was easy to convert most of Europe to Christianity because Christ was seen as an updated version of this 'bleeding god', who is also a shining solar god. Hercules also is a kind of Baldr, but instead of twelve stations of the cross like Christ, he had twelve arduous labours to deal with.

In mythology, like Christ, Baldr makes prophesies about his own death. This leads his mother to making everything in existence promise not to hurt her poor son. Everything promises except for the mistletoe, sacred plant of the druids. Presumably mistletoe grows differently to other plants so it does not have to follow regular rules, or anybody's orders. The gods meanwhile, found a new pastime. This was hurling objects at Baldr, which would simply bounce off of him without harming him. We will continue the story in the present tense. The trickster Loki hurries over with a spear he just made from a branch of mistletoe and encourages Hoor, a blind god and brother of Baldr, to throw it at at him. Baldr is slain. This ends the good relations between Loki and the gods.

Thor arrives and threatens Loki variously with knocking the head off of his shoulders, or throwing him up on the roads to the east (possibly a reference to mounds in the east). Loki mocks him for these threats. Eventually Thor declares that he is sending Loki to 'Hel', which seems to be an underground place or deity, but probably aspects of both.

Loki is bound inside Hel with a snake suspended above him. The snake drips poison from its fangs. For a while Loki's wife (old gods often have consorts of the opposite sex) holds a basin over Loki to prevent the poison touching his skin, but she cannot be there all the time. When the poison touches Loki, it causes him to write in agony, causing earthquakes. It sounds like a fiery dragon might fit into that story as well, instead of a snake.

Why venerate Loki? As a fire god and an underworld god, presumably fire is his special gift to humanity!

While at the museum, the wheels started to turn and I began to consider other mounds. Pyra-mid is a Greek word which means 'fire within'. I got the feeling that the pyramid builders in Egypt had similar ideas about venerating some god, when they built their pyramids. Lacking inscriptions, the Old Kingdom pyramids do not seem to be truly dedicated to the power of pharaoh, like they might have been. They seem a lot like the summer 'harvest mounds' of Europe, which are huge and largely anonymous.

The Egyptian pyramids also *do* seem to have been intended as tombs for kings but this was not really a successful enterprise, for they do not contain burials. Making a tomb out of a pyramid/mound, or being buried near one might have occurred for reasons of prestige (a king possibly wanting to be buried near his great project) but also for religious reasons akin to being close to the gods, and so 'hitching a ride' into the afterlife.

It was such a good museum! It also reflected what seems to be a current and developing trend. This is that there is more of an acknowledgement that ancient hearsay, in the form of chronicled stories or myths, has a part to play in understanding not only history, but also archaeological structures. That is, we might use such sources to explain archaeological remains, if we wish to examine them from a more humanist perspective, rather than simply an architectural one. Archaeology can explain what *they* did, but not always why they did it!

The museum explanation: 'A home for their god to reside forever, like the genius Loki.' I came up with my own little explanation as to why the Iron Agers layered soils from perhaps six different (or more) territories of the kingdom, in this unique hill-cake.

The answer is 'sympathetic magic'. What is that? Voodoo is a type of sympathetic magic. Take a sample of something associated with someone and use it to manipulate them. As above, so below. Can't catch a fish? Encourage a *pattern*. One primitive 'spell' mentioned by Frazer in his *The Golden Bough*, is this. Throw your fishing partner in the water and then pull him out. Fish will come and then you will pull them out, because the pattern has been established. With knowledge of sympathetic magic, some Egyptians really thought they could bully their gods into submission. 'Once touching, always touching' is the idea

Figure 1.6: Hermod rides down to visit Hel on his eight-legged steed. Hel is depicted as a green deity, a kind of Earth Mother. Since there is no fertility in the land, as slain Baldr (god of the returning spring) is stuck down there, she eats from a bowl of starvation. (Icelandic manuscript, NKS 1867 4to.)

Figure 1.7: Horned and bound Loki. This is from the Kirkby Stephen Stone.

Figure 1.8: Another aspect of Loki is that he can fly around. This is *Loki's flight to Jötunheim*, 1908, by W. G. Collingwood. In this respect he is a bit like the fabled phoenix. This bird gets burnt up, but then eventually emerges from the ashes and flies away, possibly from a cosmic egg sometimes associated with the pyramid. (See also fig. 5.14) Like Loki, it too is a kind of fire god.

behind sympathetic magic.

Now, since this was some kind of harvest mound, to create the harvest, the soils of the county or kingdom needed to be fertile, everywhere. The gods needed to know that all the land needed to be fertile. By ensuring that all the needed soil types were present, they would all be blessed or 'resurrected'. This was a fertility mound, built for fertility. Put all the soils in a mound reaching up to heaven, and the mother goddess is then pregnant with them, reaching up with her earth belly towards the sky god, who may choose to fertilise her. The concept of ancient peoples possibly creating an attractive sexual object for the sky god is fascinating.

The fact they also filled the mound with some very nicely shaped stones, presumably chosen from around the kingdom, makes the tomb similar to some other, much older 'tombs' I would visit in Ireland. These were tombs with altars. Perhaps 'sacrifices' occurred in spring. Subsequently in autumn, the fruits of the harvest were brought back to the mounds. Thence 'thanksgiving', one of the oldest rituals in the world. This closed the cycle, ensuring that it *was* a cycle.

The museum even suggested that the house had had thirty-four radii. This, it claimed, corresponded to the number of lords of Irish mythology. The mound is dated to 95 BC based on the surviving oak central totem pole. I get the feeling however, that with a construction base only just before the time of Christ, that it is rather 'recent'. It is as if they were trying to recapture the lost glories of the past, create a new sacred place for Loki to reside. The current stories we have about Loki date from the Irish Golden age, that is the ninth and tenth centuries. But they are much older.

There were some other ideas which began clicking. For instance, the earliest structures at Stonehenge, seem to have been simple poles, perhaps dating from the eight millennium BC. These are poles once found in Post hole A and Post hole B. It is possibly comparable to the huge Siberian totem pole, the Shigir Idol, of a similarly ridiculously old age, described as the 'oldest statue in the world'. Various mounds around Europe, which I would visit, also seem to have been found relatively recently, to have been built around a wooden central pole.

The interminable Irish rains had flooded out the stadium where a game of Irish Football was under-way nearby. I was fascinated by the people eagerly flocking off to the stadium. It is a very unique game which you cannot really see played elsewhere.

Armagh was a centre of Irish paganism and religion. It has some strange huge mounds around it and within it. It is a fascinating landscape. While exploring 'the other' St Patrick Cathedral, on a strange old huge mound in the centre of Armagh, where St Patrick (or Pater if there was some confusion), is said to lie, the heavens opened up, and I ran back to the hostel.

'I see you got drenched... they're gonna get utterly drowned today', said the hostel manager.

'Who is?'

'Them at the stadium.'

* * *

'Patrick's buried in Armagh!? Hah! The Free Staters say his remains are in Dublin!' This is what an Irish-Australian friend later told me. Perhaps he is really in both places. 'Patrick' is easily confused with Latin *pater*, or Father = God. Any ancient place of supreme religious significance therefore become associated with St 'Patrick.'

The legends are highly confused. But why else do we venerate 'Patrick'? Who was he? He was not even the first Christian monk

Figure 1.9: Loki's brood. Here we see *Hel, Fenrir,* and *Jörmungandr.* Painted by Emil Doepler.

in Ireland! An earlier Christian evangeliser was Palladius. Patrick also had a rival called St Declan of Ardmore, who is not really given any credit. Then we have the riddle about why the Irish say that Patrick killed all the snakes in Ireland. Clearly this was either a case of extremely comprehensive pest control or he is being associated with the action of a god who dealt firmly with what was later seen as the devil.

I later did some reading about Loki. He is part fire god, part Lucifer, part Prometheus, part Satan, part fool. He is also a very human figure, fallible rather than truly evil, and living here on earth, with us, rather than in the heavens. This was all part of the religion brought by the Vikings to Ireland. Yet he is not necessarily the snake of Eden. That seems to be one of his children! His three children are *Hel*, an underworld goddess, a wolf, *Fenrir*, and a snake, Jörmungandr, who may be associated with the great Midgard serpent that lines the Earth, the bulk of its body supposedly lying under every ocean.

In Ireland, I was quite surprised to find that the snake may have been an ancient god. The underworld gods would have been venerated because they helped to create mankind. I learned in the Book of Kells museum, at Trinity College, Dublin, that Jesus himself is traditionally associated (in Ireland) with a serpent! This is because a serpent can shed its skin, making it capable of re-incarnation or new life. Hence fertility.

Eventually, for his misdeeds, Loki is punished by being bound under a mountain and then another serpent, not his son, drips acid on him. It is known that snakes are associated with holy trees which in turn are associated with mounds. In this respect Loki as a knowledge god is confused with Odin a sky god, (a derivative of which may be Asian Buddha) who is also 'bound' or hanging from the world tree. (World trees were placed on top of mounds, which seem to have represented the underworld.)

One might surmise that Merlin is part Loki as well, because he is also imprisoned for eternity in a kind of cave or mound, seduced to be with the goddess, Nimue. He is also Prometheus-like, bestowing knowledge upon mankind. With regards to his providing help to build Stonehenge, in the medieval writings of Geoffrey of Monmouth, he is Britain's answer to Egyptian Imhotep, who helped to build 3rd-dynasty Saqqara. I increasingly find that it is as if gods are found to fit archetypal stories, rather than stories being made about gods.

As far as being a burial place for a religious figure, there are certain alternatives. For instance, if Patrick is associated with 'Pater', or father in Latin, then 'Pater' could have been Father Sky. There is an old sky god called 'Allfather'. Any Patrick shrine could have been a former Allfather shrine, to the sky god.

In Armagh we have these churches on large hills which were once no-doubt dedicated by pagan ritual to the old gods. I think that since another Pater or Patrick came along and established his church over these underworld representations of snake, or Loki's children, he 'slew the snakes of Ireland.' Placing a church over them destroyed their power.

Observing the setting sun on Sally Hill, I began to wonder what previous ancient temple might have existed here, when St Patrick had arrived. It was such a long time ago.

Sligo

There was a cantankerous old Australian traveller from Brisbane sleeping in the bed above me. He came in on the Royal Brunei airline via London. He voiced the opinion that Dublin is as rainy as Melbourne and expressed the belief that Melbourne is just as dismal!

'Certainly not!'

I told him it does not rain in Melbourne every day anymore, since the climate changed about fifteen years ago. He had came to Dublin to research family history. He expressed a favourable interest in reading my work on Robin Hood.

At 3 a.m. someone very European, possibly from the Netherlands came in. He switched the light on and started packing. Shuttle busses start to leave for the airport around 3:30 a.m.

From the bunk above me arose the broad Australian voice, typical of Queenslanders.

'Switch the bloody light off!'

'I'm very sorry I need to pack!'

'Do it in the morning... switch the bloody light off!'

'You don't understand. I have to go to the airport now!'

'Switch the light off!'

'I'm sorry, I must pack. I'm going to the airport! I need to be at reception in ten minutes!'

'Oh Christ... (tossing and turning) switch the thing off!'

'I'm very sorry, I'm packing, I have to go, OK?'

'Oh switch the light off why don't ya?'

'I can't! I have to leave now!!' He was getting increasingly hysterical now.

'Just go to sleep. You can do it in the morning!'

'I can't! I'm going to the airport. Just please, please... give me one minute!'

'Do it in the morning!'

'Please, a minute.'

'Switch the bloody light off!'

Etc.

The following morning we were discussing some aspects of history. I told him that I thought Stonehenge represents the surviving portion of a lost civilisation. Naturally all the organic components would have rotted away. Iron would have rusted. Only gold would remain, which could easily be re-melted. The greatest heaviest stones would be the only thing left.

'Oh...' he shuddered. 'I wouldn't go that far'.

'No?'

'No. Have you read Eric von Daniken? A lot of what he says, you can't trust it.'

'Really?'

He told me that his ancestor had came to Melbourne in the 1840s. Back then Melbourne was only a few years old. She had been an orphan in a nunnery and was forced to come because early Melbourne of only 30,000 people needed more women. It is ironic that Ireland was a source of so many ancient migrations towards it, as a safe haven, and then migrations away from it until the present day.

Ireland has a relatively low population. Deep in the Irish countryside, in about the centre of the island, I could only pick up four radio stations! The countryside is endless. In Germany, while travelling from Dortmund to Aachen by train, I jokingly asked whether there are any farms in Germany. The industrial Ruhrgebiet or Ruhr area is like a megacity. Here, in Ireland, it is the opposite. Each town is nothingness and does not carry any impact relative to the ever-present green grass fields.

On the way to Sligo, I had my own table on the train with Wi-Fi. I was chatting to a friend, online. Long after passing Athlone and other central areas on the way from Dublin, things started to change. The landscape and clouds became much more Gothic and strange. I wondered if I had been reading one of several neglected but excellent Bram Stoker novels. It all reminded me of the sacred hills in the vicinity of Stonehenge and especially Avebury, which looked truly spectacular. We were entering the holy landscape of the Irish romantics and dreamers. This was the remotest part of Ireland, where both archaeology and ancient myth have been preserved the longest. I began to write.

'The landscape is starting to get really weird around here!' It was taking on all sorts of strange mountainous and hilly shapes, quite unlike the flat plains of the interior.

Five minutes later: 'I just passed a step pyramid on top of that mountain!'

This was Ireland's sacred west, and last outpost of its pagan spiritualism.

Over here in Sligo, The population in Sligo is really Anglo Saxon-looking and a bit different from the Dubliners. I think that is possibly because one thousand years ago, the Vikings invading Dublin were narrowly defeated by Ireland's greatest king, Brian Boru. Elsewhere they would have possibly followed the usual pattern of marrying the local women and killing the men. That could well have been the case here and in Cork.

On the west side of Ireland, people speak a lot more Gaelic. The *Gaeltacht* areas are like a national park for their language. Most Irish understand a few words of Gaelic in a similar way to most Germans knowing a few words of English: they were forced to learn it at school. I did some huge shopping at Tesco. I saw a blonde Anglo-Saxon woman talking to the people working there, asking about a particular product. 'So, why is she speaking Italian?' I thought to myself. It definitely sounded quite Mediterranean. I also wondered 'Does she honestly expect the workers there to understand?'

I was even more shocked when one of the shelf stockers not only understood but replied in this lingo. Two tall men responded in this 'Italian' as well even though they were very English looking. Later it occurred to me that I had just heard my first proper Gaelic conversation. One does not hear that sort of thing in the larger cities. Later on in the evening I went by the bar and saw drunken Irish teens singing what sounded like folk songs, but with modern words. Amazing!

'It is worth going to Ireland, if only to talk to the Irish' my professor had told me. The more cantankerous older Irish have a funny way of talking and funny logic to accompany it. At a hostel I heard: 'I was at a five-star hotel but it was really a no-star hotel, and the only stars I saw were the stars in the sky!' I had just checked out of that hostel after breakfast, taking the train to Sligo on the other coast. It took three hours. It was a diesel train running not that fast. Trains do not need to run that fast in Ireland as it is not very big.

The movie *Close Encounters* featured a flat-top mountain in Colorado which is where the aliens land to make contact. There is one of those outside the town, but I saw no aliens. A nearby mountain, which is no less impressive, has a huge pyramid 'cairn' on top. It dates to 3500 BC or older. Even though it was eight kilometres away, one can still see it clearly looming up over the horizon from the town's streets. See fig. 1.16. There are other weird mountains all around the town! 'It's like *Jurassic Park*!' is what I wrote in my diary. The travel book I was using, meanwhile, said that these, called the Knocknarea and Benbullen mountain plateaus, look like something from the movie *The Lost World*, prehistoric life protected by steep cliffs on all sides.

It is an amazing little town, steeped in a history too primordial to fathom. In town itself, I saw the ruins of a monastery so went there. I stayed about two hours. Most tourists there were German. They are naturally a highly inquisitive people, and like the Japanese they love cameras. I waited patiently until they were done with various sections of the ruins, in order to take nice photos of them. It has some really ridiculously nice and creepy medieval carvings of Jesus.

As for the town itself, I was following one man and he said 'hi' to everyone and everyone said 'hi' to him, from across the street, waving, stopping and talking. Such is small-town life in a bucolic nation.

Late in the day I was studying the tourist map, on a sign, in town near the river. There was something called 'Grass Fort' up on a hill behind the town and away from the river, which was not on the paper tourist map. Nor was it mentioned in the *Lonely Planet*. This really aroused my curiosity. I went there expecting it to be children's play equipment. Instead I was surprised to stumble across what must have been some strange dark-age fortress absolutely covered in very tall grass! I was wondering why I was having such a hard time getting onto the darn thing, if it was merely a hill fort. It was not! It was a stone castle, buried in grass located on top of a hill fort, overlooking and behind the town, away from the river. There were sheer walls about ten feet tall in some instances, surrounded by a 'moat' which I took to be a grassy swamp!

The walls themselves are utterly invisible due to the superabundance of long grass and thorns and so much greenery that it can only be described as a jungle! Rather than being merely a castle made of turf, hence 'grass fort', it may have been made of turf as well as stone. It also seems never to have been excavated. Archaeologists are addicted to Egypt or Stonehenge, but who wants to go to dig in rainy Ireland!

To actually get onto the darn thing, one fords a little swamp with grass around one's chest, and then a little scramble up to the top around the swamp to get up the invisible (due to the grass) steep wall that one otherwise crashes into, rather than walks up. There is such an incredible view from up there of the whole town, the river, the bizarre 'Jurassic' mountains behind, formed early in Earth's history. It is truly a magical place. About the castle, it has four towers, like a kind of Napoleonic configuration, with what looks like a 'crater' in the middle. The castle itself however is on top of a true huge ancient hill fort. The moat on top however, around the castle up top is invisible, as it is covered by jungle, brambles, berries and grass.

It all reminded me of the Lovecraft story *The Outsider*. In that story, a creature is living deep in the bowels of an underground castle.

Figure 1.10: This spectacular landscape near Sligo is the home of some of Ireland's oldest mythology. We see a cairn-like outcrop on top of this mountain.

It has no idea who or what it is. One day it climbs out and visits a church on the surface. It scares everyone and then looks in a mirror. It itself gets a shock and goes back into its abode.

I wished that I could really investigate the area for weeks. In addition to this place in the west, not too far from where some of the gold jewellery was found, there are incredible ancient roads called green roads which I would one day love to walk. The city feels more isolated than Ardmore, a small village on the south east coast. Eventually there were only about seven people, maximum, in the hostel, despite it being tourist season, so I had the room to myself for three days.

The following day I had a choice of one of two things that I had really come to Sligo for.

Carrowmore Megalithic Cemetery

'If you're from Australia, what are you doing in Ireland?'

I laughed.

'I don't know,' I truthfully replied, to the hosteler's query. I seemed to have been compelled there. I would have actually rather gone to Scotland but something drew me, some unknown force. It is fortunate to listen to intuition, as a person can have some of the best experiences of one's life. Since quantum mechanics seems to suggest temporal event-mechanics are interchangeable in either direction (in the sharemarket, waves look the same going in either direction. In other words, they can grow organically from either time direction and if one turns the graph upside down one, almost surprisingly, cannot tell from waves which way time is going), I put it down to something in my future.

On the third day of Sligo, I was assailed by one guest with the thickest Irish accent I have ever heard. The man's accent in the lounge of the hostel, after the long day, was so thick that I kept asking him to repeat. He had his eye on my tablet computer. Despite the fact the screen was almost gone he wanted to swap it for his netbook, with me adding a little cash. Without me wanting it, he kept lowering the offer price. I eventually decided to hide upstairs in my room so he would not try to keep working on improving my friendly refusals. I had an early night and a great sleep. There are not many tourists in Sligo, so one can have a room to oneself in a Sligo hostel, even in tourist season! Eventually I was told the particular notebook he was selling was a lemon, which crashed all the time.

The cairns or 'pyramids,' which is what they seem to be, close to the Atlantic are amongst the oldest in the world. The fact they happen to be located among the most sparsely populated parts of regional Ireland perhaps ensured their survival. The most fascinating tomb at Carrowmore is 'Listoghil'. If this was in Egypt it would be a 'mastaba' which is the Arab word for 'tomb'. Yet this could be a thousand years earlier, or more. Carbon dating results from the past decade or so seem to indicate dates of around 5000 BC. These could well be some of the oldest pyramids in the world, even if they are not called 'pyramids.' I think they should be.

The written information in the museum, back at Navan Fort, stated that Loki was trapped in the mountain. If I could find out about Loki, I guessed I would also find out about this mysterious deity which men everywhere were creating inside mountains, even making artificial mountains to situate their god wherever they pleased, or where an early population centre was. It all seemed very odd indeed. This god Loki was actually a part of Germanic mythology, from Scandinavia, original home of the Germans, but based upon a much earlier mythology of unknown peoples.

'Well I have a lot to write'. It is how I began daily reports to friends! I walked five kilometres out of Sligo (no bike rental in town and I do not like hitching when on a holiday) to the Carrowmore Megalithic Cemetery. It was a challenge just to find the tourist information office, as it had shifted around a bit in a last few years, with signs in wrong directions, etc.

Eventually I got there.

'There is no foot access?' I queried. There are no footpaths on Irish country roads. I had been looking at google earth, back in Australia, and wondering how I would get to some of these sites, without being run down by a lorry.

'Oh it's fine to walk along the road, people do it all the time'.

This was one of the two main reasons for the ancient historian to come to Sligo. Imagine thirty megalithic tombs, all in one place! Furthermore, it only cost one Euro to get in! More than ninety percent of the tourists seemed to be retired and simply arrived by tour bus. There were lot of Americans. I took the tripod and so made lots of good photos. I raced over to the good tombs in the breaks in between tour buses.

Here is how the site seems to work. All the tombs are satellite tombs of one main tomb which is called Listoghil. This makes it similar to Stonehenge, which is a temple with tombs all around. This made me wonder whether the central pyramid-tomb was for a god, or for men. Various large tombs could well have been for communal burials. Long Barrows, a proto-Germanic invention, were used as a kind of church, where people could go to meet the ancestors, placing bones inside. These were inevitably covered over after a generation or so.

What is Listoghil? It is a grey circular flat-topped pyramid made of lots of grey stones. Disappointingly it is not at all original, but reconstructed. The whole cemetery seems to have been plundered many times over. How old is this cemetery? Oh... it only dates to about 5400 to 3500 BC! It is so old that it seems the Neolithic spiral carving, seen on the entrances to other tombs, had not even been invented yet, when these tombs were made. I found it nowhere. There are no spirals or other carvings at all, and yet Listoghil is very similar to Newgrange. It is much the same, or a version on a smaller scale.

Fig. 1.12 is interesting. The late Philip Coppens wrote in *The New Pyramid Age* that several pyramids in America seem to have been built to look like the mountains behind them. He drew attention to a remark-

Figure 1.11: A side view of the rebuilt Listoghil, with people to the right. Like Newgrange, I think it was probably originally covered by soil.

able phenomenon. When one stands at the Huaca del Luna pyramid, in Peru for instance, the Huaca del Sol greatly resembles the mountain behind it, Cerra Blanco. Similarly if one stands where the Pyramid of the Moon is, at Teotihuacan, the Pyramid of the Sun resembles the shape of the mountain behind that. With this in mind, I thought of this curious perspective that I had photographed in Ireland, in which the 'restored' Listoghil seems to replicate Knocknarea behind it. I do not think Coppens knew about this example, where much the same thing may have been going on. Perhaps this was a case of 'as above, so below.' In order to bring the mountain gods into human life, one makes a representation of it on Earth. Unaware of geological layers and great time periods, what did ancients think a mountain was? Mountains are also sacred as such scenery is heavenly.

Listoghil is an uncovered tomb, at least in its present manifestation, which I very much doubt is original to the structure. You walk right in, instead of squeezing through narrow confines, like at every other tomb. Cyclone wire holds stones in their 'correct' configuration. There is a four-poster dolmen in the middle, underneath which would have

Figure 1.12: This is Listoghil restored. It used to be known as a 'cave' and the top was covered over, probably at least with topsoil. When it was new it may have looked even more like that mountain behind it, Knocknarea, which has its own pyramid/mound on top. It is perhaps no coincidence that this perspective is possible.

been the burial. Three hundred years ago, this place was described as a cave. Listoghil is itself a satellite tomb of the much larger Queen Medb's tomb which seems to tower over everything for thirty kilometres around. This is a landscape straight out of *Conan the Barbarian*, I thought to myself. I wondered which tomb Conan had plundered to secure his sacred sword.

Queen Medb's tomb, far away in the distance, also looks like a huge Listoghil or Newgrange. It is a huge grey flat-topped pyramid or cairn on top of a nearby mountain. Obviously it was built in order to awe all the Neolithic farmers. If it was not, then it would certainly have that effect. It is far off, almost in another place, another world. Aweing the people is one reason why pyramids and ziggurats of Sumer were built, at about the same time.

It occurred to me there might have been one of these pyramids on Glastonbury Tor as well, at Glastonbury, in England, but we will get to that later. It could have been replaced by the church which is currently

Figure 1.13: Close to Listoghil.

Figure 1.14: A frontal aspect of Listoghil with the author.

Figure 1.15: Inside Listoghil we have a tomb. All has been reconstructed from a ruin. The tomb looks nothing like it once did. It would once have had a closed roof, perhaps along the lines of fig. 1.56.

up there. At any rate, *something* pagan and sacred caused a church to be built up there, upon that strange sculpted hill.

I had the idea that perhaps these round conical pyramids might even have been replaced with the famed round towers, built during the waning years of the Irish golden age, from about the eighth to the twelfth or thirteenth centuries. There is a recurring British pagan legend of a church built on a mountain or hill. Then the devil removes it to the valley. What on Earth is that all about? I had thought that it was perhaps a shift from the veneration of the sky god to that of the water god, but who can say for sure? Nobody.

I wrote some speculations in my diary while I was at Carrowmore.

> Just sitting on dolmen #48 now. I think the reason they went to such ridiculous efforts to raise a dolmen for the dead, is due to the permanence of stone: a sort of soul communication, particularly as the body is surrounded by stone. Stone might be required to transmute the dead, from animal, to mineral, and thence immortality.

Figure 1.16: As can be seen, Medb's four-thousand-year-old tomb towers ridiculously, like Dracula's castle, over the town of Sligo. In the old days, people would have been suspicious of the dark forces associated. Some still are.

That Knocknarea up there is a true pilgrimage site. It looks incredible! The central tomb here is called *Listoghil.* Surrounded by satellites, it itself is a satellite of the much greater *Medb* tomb up there, (5km distant) that massive thing on the hill! One hill I walked up here at Carrowmore, itself seems to be a pyramid/mound with stones on top, like Navan fort, but may not be recognised as such.

Listoghil is not just a tomb, but a temple with bones in it. I think this culture spread its pyramids to South America. The first structures at Tiwanaku are also very early. In Ireland, it can be hot, and suddenly cold. The inquisitive Irish would have been curious where the warmth came from, and some of them may have found out! The pyramids seem to have flat tops and are circular, like cones. They remind me of Egyptian mastabas and were built at about the same time.

In Britain there is a persistent legend about churches once being built on top of hills, but then knocked down by the devil and built in valleys. This may be due to the fact that after the unstable Iron Age, towns moved down from hilltops. So did temples. There was also perhaps a conflict between the newer religion of the 'temple in town', and the older religion on the mountain, designed in massive-style, to awe the people below. It's clear the Knocknarea cairn (Medb's cairn) was designed to awe all surrounding farmers into submission for many miles around! It was a centre of religion, but also a centre of control.

These hilltop temples could be based upon those ideas. Queen Mab's tomb is ridiculous. It can surely be seen from fifty kilometres in almost every direction. From a distance anyway, it looks very much like a Central-American pyramid!

There must have been one of these on Glastonbury Tor as well, taken down and replaced by a church, with the centre of religion thence shifting to the town, rather than the dominating hilltop!

The pyramid-on-the-mountain religion *was* replaced by the church-in-the-town religion, though the latter was not a direct successor. The distant Queen Medb's ('Maeve's') tomb, which towers on a mountain in the distance, and which I did not visit on this particular day, looks, at least from a great distance, in profile, like a Mesoamerican pyramid. So does Listoghil. It is about the same ratio of height to width. I snapped a picture of them together on the same photo. (See front cover) I do not suppose Thor Heyerdahl ever considered that the fabulous 'Long Ears' or *Viracochas* of Native American legend came over in a boat from Ireland, of all places. He does not seem to have mentioned the possibility.

Interestingly Medb's tomb is also locally known as 'Medb's pap', as it resembles a breast, to some. This seems to be some sort of Earth-Mother material, implying that the goddess of the mound is female.

Pyramids must have diffused in some way, but we really do not know when or how. Due to the great antiquity of the pyramids on the west coast of Ireland (they seem to be among the oldest on Earth) and the proximity to the trade winds to America, this is the perfect spot!

Trade seems the most likely explanation but our conception of the immense size of the Pacific and Atlantic Oceans get in the way of our conceptions of what an ancient boat can do. It did not take the Polynesians very much in terms of sophistication, however, to migrate over the Pacific, taking pyramid building to Tonga for instance. Huge ships are not necessary if we are talking about the migration of small populations, and if these populations have a long time to migrate, over many generations. Clearly they have had that time available.

As mentioned, the Egyptians also made flat-topped 'mastabas' (tombs) at about the same 'pre-dynastic' time of just prior to 3000 BC, which look vaguely like the Irish versions, but it needs to be said that the Irish versions are heaps of rubble by comparison. These tombs on the west coast of Ireland date from about 5-4000 BC, and are nevertheless very different to the ones found in Egypt.

Neolithic long barrow tombs, arising from a Central European culture of longhouse builders, are much like churches (many barrows even have cross-shaped interiors). They were used for several generations for people to go inside and place there the bones or ashes of their recently deceased. Presumably prayers would have been offered. Eventually the long barrows contained the ancestral memory of a community. It contained all the memories of the good times, which included the thoughts and deeds of the wise ones. All were all sealed up together into this spiritual edifice, and the entrance was covered up. Many tombs are even cross-shaped inside with an entrance and then short passageways in three directions, ahead and to the sides, leading to chambers.

Carrowmore might be a megalithic cemetery but it is a plundered

Figure 1.17: Here, in Carrowmore, we have the ruins of, essentially a conical cairn. The same layout of stones graces the circumference of Newgrange and various places elsewhere. It is a sign of extreme antiquity, of a tomb dating to before 3000 BC. Since there are lots of these cairns in Carrowmore, they were probably used for people rather than gods. After many generations, however the two concepts might become indistinguishable.

one. Listoghil has satellite tombs. All these were plundered and destroyed many times over so that not much survives. There are very nice dolmens however. Carrowmore was used down the generations. This is evidenced by the presence of a bronze-age ring barrow, which is basically a short hill with a ditch around it. One picturesque dolmen even contained Roman artefacts! It is clearly a good place for a pastoral love affair on a sunny afternoon where the lovers, having received precious trade goods from Roman Britain, decided to place them in the mound as a fitting gesture.

Weather changes fast near the Atlantic. It was very hot in the morning and later on a hot Sun and cold wind. Would not the ancient Irish have wanted to explore where on Earth this heat came from, which could change so rapidly? Why were the winds, for instance, from the south and west warmer?

Figure 1.18: Carrowmore is a beautiful place. Using the people in the centre as a rough scale, one can see there would have been a cairn to the right, of about sixteen metres in diameter and several metres in height. Now only the outlier stones are visible. Mount Knocknarea is in the background with its two faces, green towards land, as shown here, but also with a rocky face towards the sea.

After a wonderful afternoon taking a million photos, it came time to get back my two euro which I had exchanged for a laminated map of the complex.

The woman behind the desk looked me up and saw that I had checked in that morning. She did a double take, and was both shocked and pleased.

'You've been here for over four hours!'

'Well, I'm not coming here for five minutes.'

'We really like when people stay longer.'

'Yes, we do!' chimed in the extremely attractive lady I saw earlier.

'I've come from Australia and just walked three miles from Silgo. This isn't a pleasure trip!'

Most people to the place come and look at the big tomb on the tourist bus before leaving, but you really need to stay and investigate things since there are over thirty megalithic tombs, in order to understand what's going on, and try to work everything out.

Back in the hostel I was talking to an Irish man. We were watching *Top Gear.*

'I've never owned a car, only vans. Wonder what it's like.'

'What are the shows which are shown on both English and Irish TV?'

'I don't know, because I'm not English,' I said.

Queen Medb's tomb on Knocknarea obviously seems rather large. It is a large flat-topped thing. I zoomed into it with the telephoto lens. It would be a fun experience to go up there.

I told him I was going to Medb's tomb tomorrow.

'Is that that big thing on the hill?' He had lived half his life in Sligo but it was just part of the scenery for him, as it is for most in Ireland. Apparently it is no big deal for the horizon to be dominated by a huge hill with someone's huge tomb on it. I told him that there were forty thousand tonnes of rocks up there.

'I wonder how they got all them huge rocks up there? It must have been a ridiculous thing to do?' He was shaking his head.

I would find out tomorrow that there was in fact a 'ramp' or causeway carved in the hill, perhaps in stone-age times, which may have assisted in the building of the tomb.

Knocknarea, West Ireland's main pyramid

I was going to visit a pyramid/cairn which was infinitely older than the mound at Navan Fort which was a mere 2100 years of age. This one would be more than double that. The name of the cairn is Medb's tomb but everyone refers to the woman supposedly buried there as 'Queen 'Meeeve''. She was an ancient warrior queen of whom there are associated legends. She was a cattle raider. In those days cattle were a store of wealth. She also hated Ulster, a region corresponding roughly to Northern Ireland. She was allegedly buried in this tomb, standing up and facing Ulster, ever watchful, protecting her homeland, as it were.

It was another spectacularly sunny day. I was starting to think I must have been blessed with some exceptional weather. If the two days had been washed out, the trip to Sligo would have been wasted, because there is little to do here except see the countryside!

The tourist information lady said that to get closer to Mount Knocknarea which has the 'pyramid'/cairn on top, I could simply take a bus to Strandhill, and then walk it. Strandhill is a small town about nine

Figure 1.19: Despite having some of the oldest pyramid/cairns in the world, dating to 5000 BC, Carrowmore also has this much more recent burial. Dating to about 2-3000 years younger, It is a ring barrow, that I am standing inside. This is something of a 'successor' to the pyramid. I say that quite loosely as some circular barrows are also in fact very old. Therefore rather than speaking of successors or predecessors we could be talking about rival burial-mound traditions. I believe it may have belonged to the tradition of another tribe. The stone barrow is something from the south, possibly North Africa, or Libya which has a genetic link to the north. The henge, however seems to originate from central Europe and possibly represents a moat for cosmic waters. These are part of the pyramid tradition at Silbury Hill and elsewhere.

kilometres from Sligo. Going there shortens the walk by a couple of miles.

Strandhill has a thousand people. Its on the beach. It was warm, and for the first time since I had arrived, there were nice spring-time smells, so much so that it felt like I was back in Australia!

I popped into the tourist information at Strandhill and asked for a map. This tourist information is also a bicycle shop with about a hundred brand new bicycles for rent, which seems to be the main business. The man behind the desk looked like he would have been a Californian 'surfer dude' in another universe, and this was indeed a surfing town. He spoke like the Irish equivalent.

'Six kilometres... a long walk!' He was nodding.

I looked over at the bicycles. On the one hand they would save time, but I do not travel to save time. In addition, I wanted to *absorb* the experience by taking longer, and making it more satisfying to just walk up to the top from sea level. I wanted to soak myself into the surroundings.

'I... think I'll walk it.'

It was a 6km walk, that felt a lot longer. I eventually regretted not taking the bike, especially because one has to push oneself into the nettles and bracken when cars go past. I found out that there was other stuff to see in this village, such as a couple ruins, but I simply had no time for it.

There were not many other tourists, only a few driving up to the hill's carpark. Most motorists were on the road back to Dublin. I stuck to the edge of the road, flattening myself against it when cars went past, my hands perpetually brushing against the stinging nettles which are, along with blackberries, one of the primary weeds of Europe. I was getting rather exhausted when a car pulled up next to me.

'Ah see he has a map!' It was Americans asking for directions. I was not sure if they were going up the mountain or going to Dublin. I told them how to get up the mountain.

I really wanted a lift up the rest of the way, but was too worn out to say so. Their back seats looked really cluttered anyway.

'Well, I'd offer you a lift, but I see you're very determined to make it so I don't want to spoil the experience.'

'Er... OK!'

I finally got to the top, overtook the Americans on the way up, and made some discoveries. The hill is huge and itself kind of flat-topped. It is covered in ruinous rubble. Walls have been built nearby using

Figure 1.20: While walking up Knocknarea, around it, to get to an ascending path, I noticed a curious recurring feature. There were streams coming out of the mountain and pouring down onto the road. This was most likely underground water, sources for ancient spring water. In Germanic myth, the three Norns live underneath the location of Yggdrasil (which is on the world mountain), which is placed at the centre of the world. These Norns are essentially the triple goddess, a truly ancient deity found all over, and precursor of the Holy Trinity. I would notice the same phenomenon at Cave Hill in Belfast. 'Norns' (1832), *Die Helden und Götter des Nordens, oder das Buch der Sagen.*

rubble taken directly from the pyramid. One can see where it has been taken away. The walls themselves are ruinous.

Then I noticed that there was not just one huge tomb but a whole host of them! I would explore them all. All the tombs had been sacked by people looking for gold, all except Medb's. That gave me the idea that this tomb was not a normal tomb for a human, but for a goddess. Sacking it would perhaps put a curse upon whomever dared to disturb it.

In fig. 1.23 we have an image of what it is like to stand on the Plateau, looking at what can only be described as a pyramid, but in Ireland. It is interesting that while the Giza plateau is (or was, until revolutionary unrest) packed with overheated tourists, bus fumes, boys selling 'pyramid water,' and tour guides, I had this much higher and unknown pyramid plateau (people think it is just another 'cairn', of which Ireland has thousands) to myself, for several hours, the way Giza was about three centuries ago!

Dramatic Medb's tomb is officially, about 60 metres wide by 11 metres high. It is not quite circular however and I counted more than 60 metres at its widest point, perhaps approaching 70 or even more if you follow the rubble pile. (It overlooks the sea and countryside. The elevation is 327 m on the top of distinctive Knocknarea. This stone version of Silbury Hill, with a flat top, is surrounded by several altars, which are not mentioned in any description I had read. It is built on the highest point of the hill, overlooking both land and sea (perhaps as Giza overlooks desert and river on different sides). It is built as close to the sky as possible. Is this a vestige of what was remembered as the Babel religion? The stones in the foreground, to the left, in fig. 1.23 represent a ruined smaller mound, with the path to the right. Listoghil, closer to sea level, below Knocknarea (front cover), does get bus-loads of retired American tourists.

All the tombs are well and truly 'Stone Age', and possibly several millennia older than Stonehenge. Easy to work with, gold is the only metal the diggers would have found, though I am sure they would not have complained. These tomb people were possibly even pre-Copper Age! I think there would have still perhaps have been mammoths roaming around somewhere on Earth back then, though perhaps not in Ireland.

Gold is easy to work and is excellent for jewellery. Apart from that, if the tomb robbers failed to find gold, they would instead have simply found bones, antler needles and stone or amber beads. They

Figure 1.21: Knocknarea from Stranhill, a village on the coast. Look carefully at the mountain. On the left side, we can see naturally-sculpted folds on the mountain, according with its appearance in fig. 1.12, which remind one of a terraced structure, perhaps a stairway to heaven. This is the side that faces towards the land. It reminds one of a hill fort or of similar features at Glastonbury Tor. On the right, however, we see that the mountain has a different colour and structure. This windblown side of Knocknarea, facing the beach and sea is rocky, with grey rocks. It is therefore a sort of meeting place of two forces, states of 'matter.' It is a mixing place, a creation place, from where water flows. This plateau, like the Giza plateau, is the home to a large ancient burial complex, as well as cave system, partly artificial, whose builders required a dramatic view of both sea and land.

Figure 1.22: One 'magical' thing about Knocknarea, is that it is round, but has two sides, two faces of the goddess. These are possibly Earth and Moon. This combined deity is a goddess that was perhaps very sacred to the proto-pyramid (Stone-Age) people. This may have come about by knowledge of both Earth and Moon being illuminated by the Sun, in a kind of divine sisterhood. The hill also is made of grey 'moon-colour' (from Earth) rocks as well as topsoil. We see a similar pattern at Newgrange, with about half the mound white stone, like a crescent moon, and half the mound Earth and grass. See fig. 6.3. As for etymologies for the Irish *Cnoc na Riabh*, we have the popular 'Hill of the stripes'. There are other possibilities however. *Cnoc na Ré*, or Hill of the Moon has also been suggested. I like this one, for the above reason, but it does not have to be this. There are other suggestions, including 'hill of executions', which is another possibility, due to the fact Medb is an object of dread in myth. We will never really know.

Figure 1.23: On top of the Knocknarea plateau.

may have found some pottery and perhaps some ivory combs, as well
as flints for weapons in the afterlife. That is about it. I noticed that
like the tombs in the Carrowmore cemetery, below the mountain, these
tombs do *not* have spirals in them. The implication is clear: they are
exceedingly ancient, and would possibly pre-date 3000 BC. The dates
we are talking about are 5000-3000 BC. Who is to say Medb's pyramid
is not seven thousand years old? I am not aware that any dating has
taken place. Nearby Carrowmore seems to date from that time.

The more ancient the monument, the greater the difference in mythology between what we think we know about ancient beliefs, and actual
beliefs in that time. God only knows the bizarre and unclear rituals
that took place here. The murky origins of the pyramid religion may
well have been old and forgotten when Khufu built or renovated his
pyramid in about the *c.* 2600s BC.

Although it is clear that tomb-robbers do not seem to have entered,
one can see where they might have tried. Medb's tomb has one side
which is semi-demolished. The Medb pyramid or cairn as they call it,
seems to be about fifty five metres wide and about ten or eleven metres
high. It is really a huge amount of stone. Shepherds could see it for
thirty kilometres or more, sitting there on top of the 371 metre-tall

Figure 1.24: A silhouette of the cairn/pyramid with local people walking a dog, which is the little spec to the right of the fourth person, on the right. They mentioned that the hill is used for making wishes.

mountain, for the last five or six or more thousand years.

I found other ruined pyramids up there, not mentioned in the *Lonely Planet*: at least six other ruined tombs. (Roger Walker, a 19th-century antiquary and landowner could have been responsible for some of the pillage. Apparently he had plans to tackle Medb's tomb as well, but his death prevented it.) All were plundered for stones a very long time ago. I think a lot of this was long before Roger Walker, for the stones are not just pushed aside in many cases, but absolutely gone, and perhaps used in walls nearby.

One mound with a truly great view of the Atlantic Ocean has only the central-tomb area left standing, with only small indications of the cairn which once surrounded it. This 'pyramid' is about twenty metres wide. Another, even more ruined, which has almost all trace obliterated, lies in between it and Medb's pyramid. This is about fifteen metres wide. I got excited as I was reminded of the three pyramids of Giza, as these seem to be the three 'big ones' on the site. Then again, there are several more of similar dimension, so any attempt at comparison might be a mistake.

Figure 1.25: A notch where tomb robbers perhaps wanted to get into Medb's tomb. The results are apparent. The sign warns people not to interfere with the structure.

Medb's pyramid is essentially part of a strange pyramid/cairn complex. Afterwards, I found out that there are even strange tunnels or caves on Knocknarea, possibly partly man made, on the north side of the hill. I had no time to explore or even find any. In *The New Pyramid Age*, Philip Coppens wrote that many pyramid sites, such as Giza, or the Pyramid of the Sun at Teotihuacan, seem to incorporate natural caves into the design. I would travel to more strange plateau sites with caves later on, which have a deeply ancient religious connection to the underworld.

My guide book stated that forty thousand tonnes of stone went into the building of Medb's pyramid. How did they get it up there? On the way up, I found the causeway they perhaps used which may have helped. It seems to have been a ramp cut into the hill with some stones now embedded in the grass. It needs to be said however that the archaeologist Stefan Bergh has studied the site and suggests a nearby depression near the top of the hill was a limestone quarry for the stones. (There goes the causeway theory!) One takes various ancient and long pathways over the top of the hills and one can visit this depression. It

Figure 1.26: It appears part of the pyramid was used to build a wall which emerges out of it, in various directions, before disappearing off into the distance. It was thus used as a quarry for farmers to divide up land.

Figure 1.27: The author sits amidst the central chamber of a stone satellite barrow. All the smaller covering stones have been removed, possibly by farmers for use in nearby walls, as well as treasure-seeking antiquarians of the past. This may have been an upright burial as it is rather cramped.

looked like a strange Lost World-type hidden valley to me, but I did not have time to explore it. Bergh has also suggested that much of the hill was utilised as a kind of huge complex. It certainly seems that way. It is wonderful to stumble across such incredible, at least five thousand year old ruins that almost no-one knows about.

One of the biggest surprises of the whole site, were three sacrificial altars surrounding the main pyramid/cairn!

Why might these be sacrificial altars? One of them had cup marks on the top. I guess this would have been for the blood. One altar is big enough and low enough to dump a cow on, and why not? In the *Iliad*, which purports to describe rituals of about 1180 BC, the men eat beef around a fire, wrapping fat around the bones, and then burning this so that the sky god could eat as well. Then again, in the Bible, Abraham takes his son up the mountain for a possible sacrifice which is averted. What was at the top of Abraham's mountain? Isaac was bound to an 'altar' on the now-unknown Mount Moriah, but there is no mention of

Figure 1.28: This is a large and utterly ruined satellite tomb close to Medb's cairn, of about 25 metres diameter. There seem to be at least three large tombs on top of Knocknarea, and possibly a few more of slightly smaller size. In addition, the rest which surround, are generally far smaller, satellite tombs. Perhaps they were for minor royalty. The tomb clearly had to have a good view for eternity, as well as having to be seen from a great distance. Given this, the builders were obviously not too worried about hiding a tomb in case of grave robberies. Why? Since pyramids seem to go in pairs or triples (this plateau seems to have two very large ones, and a smaller one in between them, with many little burials around them), this here is what I romantically called 'The Queen's pyramid.' I have no evidence or rationale for this declaration. It was just a passing fancy based upon the lesser satellite pyramids at Giza.

Figure 1.29: A plundered sattelite tomb. Utterly denuded of surrounding rubble, only a few barren central stones remain. The rest may have been used for the nearby farmers' walls. A sobering thought is that Ireland is utterly full of loose stone walls.

any mound. The mountain is also a place where Moses goes to talk to God.

After two hours, I no longer had the whole site to myself, because some locals walked a dog up there and they talked about making wishes. That caught my attention. They said that it was indeed a sacred wishing site, but that Medb's tomb was for the wishes. Well why not? It is the closest in terms of altitude that one can get to the sky god, in the vicinity. Their dog was racing up and down the pyramid. The stones made scattering noises as this occurred.

'Now now, down off there, down boy', its owner said.

'Has this thing really been here for five thousand years?' I wondered. It was being destroyed before my eyes, but I guess people might have re-stacked stones upon it in the past. That simply must have occurred, or there would long have been nothing left. It occurred for a reason.

I think it is clear that the whole site, with its main tomb, and satellite tombs, was for a royal family. These are not the communal long barrows of Neolithic farmers, as found in England and Northern Eu-

Figure 1.30: A causeway going up the mountain, possibly 'paved' with small stones to prevent erosion, lies adjacent to a pathway leading to the top (bottom left). It could have been used to drive sacrificial cattle to the top, as well as to help build the structure. It does not seem to be a relic of a farmer's wall, for it awkwardly goes straight up the mountain, directly to the top. Since it is rather steep, I wonder if it was not once a staircase.

rope. Therefore we are talking about at least a kind of proto-civilisation in Ireland. Why does Mesopotamia need to have all the glory? I guess the main reason is that they seem to have had a larger, certainly civic and farming population, with a clear instance of writing, so it is much easier to give them that title.

To me, Medb's tomb is *not* similar to Newgrange, as was written in the guide book. Rather it seems to be a mere hill covered with stones to make it hard for people to get in. There must have been a superstition protecting Medb's tomb, which may have endured until present times. The superstition did not extend to the lesser tombs.

I wrote this in my diary while I was up there:

> It is overlooking Sligo Bay. Was this really for Maeve the warrior queen, or is this the same pattern as the round tower overlooking the bay at Ardmore, also built on a hill?

Did the Irish round towers (some of which are on hills, but
most aren't) replace the idea of a round pyramid/cairn?
They also seem to be mysterious tombs, tombs for no-body
in particular.

There are the ruins of another large pyramid nearby,
about half the diameter of Medb's tomb. It's a little closer
to the bay, looking more upon it than upon the countryside,
as Medb's tomb does. In between both these structures
are the ruins of a third pyramid, again destroyed, with the
central burial area visible. This is about 40% the size of
the larger ruined tomb, or maybe less than a quarter of
the size of Medb's tomb. These three form an alignment
which reminds me of the three pyramids at Giza, though the
alignment may be disrupted by other tombs about, although
they seem to be smaller.

I think Medb's tomb may even have been once covered
with casing stones. Otherwise why are the stones still on it?
It feels so barren here. One can feel the eons of emptiness,
even if birds nearby are tweeting! Some sort of funny altar
is in front of Medb's tomb, and weird stone circles, the
remnants of destroyed tombs surround it.

One strange idea: did the Irish pyramids used to have casing stones?
Newgrange has a 'facade' which is held together on a near-vertical angle. But this is a modern 'reconstruction'. In order to reconstruct the
Listoghil tomb that I had seen the previous day, *cyclone wire* was used
to hold the stones in place. Now if that is the shape it is supposed to be,
and one needs cyclone wire to hold it together, then something is possibly wrong with our vision of what the tomb should have looked like.
Why not allow the possibility that some type of white casing stones
were perhaps once used, like in Egypt? These fashionable stones may
have been plundered to build houses and walls, by impoverished later
generations, as in Egypt. I saw 'casing' stones on the front facade of
the Tomb of Hostages at Tara, fig. 1.53. These tidy up the huge holes
between megalithic stones in the middle.

The longer you stay, the more you realise that every little pile of
stones was once a little satellite tomb of the great Medb structure. I
wonder if the famous Irish round towers of a thousand years ago were
not a more modern replacement for these pyramids. (a topic for another
exploration book!) The problem with my 'three pyramids' theory in
this case (I use it later), is that the middle mound (in between what

Figure 1.31: This is Medb's pyramid with altar. It is big enough to lay a cow upon. The pile of stones in the background is eleven metres tall.

I call the Queens and Kings pyramids) is not that much bigger than certain other mounds on nearby hills and also around the structure. Nevertheless, it forms part of a linear pattern of three on the highest peak. Since I noticed it without looking for it, not being aware I would develop a theory of pyramids as a representation of a sacred number, there might be something to it.

I was sad to leave the mound and the hill itself. I said goodbye to it, turned and left. Going back down the mountain was such a disappointing anti-climax, but it had to be done.

Antrim and the motte

I began all my daily dairy emails with the phrase: 'I have more to write than I can write.'

I was in Belfast, It was a nice sunny day. There had been torrential rain in between bouts of sunshine in the morning but finally it had decided to stay sunny for, at least the middle half of the day. Very strange weather!

Figure 1.32: A view from Medb's pyramid, of the bay. Pyramids seem to always need close proximity to water as if they were living creatures. In fact destroying a stupa (Asian mound) is comparable to murder, taking the life of a creature, in the eyes of some.

Figure 1.33: The great view from the other side the Medb mound. It was made to be seen from a great distance.

There is one thing weather-related that I noticed in the British Isles, which you don't get in Australia. You take off your jumper from intense Sun, which suddenly threatens to give you a good warm sunny day. Then you have to put it back on in a few minutes because it is raining somewhere far away and the cold wind blowing up from that place really gets you.

The Belfast hostel is in a protestant area. The nearby streets have the red white and blue of the Union Jack painted on the kerbstones. There are also some murals of various sufferings. The Irish call the last forty years 'the troubles', a term I heard used on the radio.

One reason for 'the troubles' in Northern Ireland was that the North was the most recently part to have been colonised by the English. In fact, about half of Ireland was an English colony for the past 800 years. This I suppose is the main reason why everyone speaks English in Ireland. These English colonists blended into the population and became Irish. The north however, was colonised just before the age of nationalism and this still lingers. The English and Scots did not blend with the Irish in the north. The north was sparsely populated and it was hoped that the Irish could be worked to extermination. Later it was found

Figure 1.34: I was wondering about this hidden valley on the summit. One author suggests that it is possibly a quarry from where the pyramid blocks were excavated by its builders.

that there were simply not enough English settlers to replace them, so they had to stay.

I hopped on the bus to Antrim town. This nice town of less than twenty thousand has many beautiful ruins. The main reason I went was a round tower which is twenty seven metres tall. We passed it on the bus near the centre so I walked back to it. It is the last remaining remnant of a monastic settlement. Everything else is gone. The peaceful solitary tower, surrounded by beautiful trees, is inhabited by pigeons and crows. The rest is an empty field with more trees.

The name Antrim itself comes from 'ein' tribe, one tribe. (Viking Scandinavia is the original home of the Germanics). Near the tower is a huge pagan altar. Perhaps this was used by the early Christians as well, but only if it was kept inside. It has two deep cup markings carved into it. In one the water is so stagnant that it could not be used as holy water. It is more for putting liquid *into* it, i.e. spilling blood on the stone. It is called the Witches' Stone. Apparently the witch was so upset the tower was built, that she jumped out the top window and made the elbow or cup marks in the stone when she landed. Since we have a medieval round tower associated with an altar, and pyramids associated with altars, with similar marks, I wondered at the connection.

Later I walked to the castle gardens. Incredible! A castle was burnt down here in 1922. Of the castle, one castle tower and some ruins remain. There is a 'modern-art' doorway now standing where the original door was. The extensive lands contain some highly ambitious gardens which reminded me of something the Sun King would design for himself, and dating from about the same era. The gardens are so ambitious that the current local authorities are unable to maintain all of them and some are left to wilderness.

There is a huge circular geometric garden of era 1660-1720s, with a neighbouring huge garden with geometric paths everywhere. There is a glorious hedged entrance, yet the trees are all huge and wild like in the 19th-century garden style. In the 'Versailles' era, the palaces had huge long rectangular pools called canals, so there are two of these. These were designed in order to demonstrate conquest over nature, and the economic power of the owner. It looks like the former lords had more money to look after the gardens back then, than the city does today. There are also huge circular pools surrounded by trees. The information boards stated that these are built such that one may look into the reflection, seeing the larger surrounding trees.

Figure 1.35: A photograph of the strange mound at Antrim castle grounds. Apparently it is a Norman motte, but any attacking army would be up and over in a few bounds. I would suspect it is older. The ruins are just about all that is left of the castle.

The garden also contained a 'pleasure garden'. This is a phenomenon of the great houses. It is typically a garden with mini hills and secret rainforest areas with fake ancient ruins and arches to walk through and little bridges to cross streams. It ticked all the boxes in this case. After that I walked off to Lough Neage, which is the biggest lake in the British Isles. It is so huge that it has beach areas which look like the seaside. Looking towards the opposite side, one cannot see the horizon! It really does look like a small ocean.

The main attraction so far as pyramids are concerned, was quite unexpected! There appeared to be this small harvest hill, surrounded by a fence, and covered in trees. Officially it is a Norman motte so it goes with the nearby castle ruins. The problem is it is obviously not big enough to be a Norman motte. Nor is it really a decent size for a mere watch tower! It really looks like a miniature Silbury Hill, which is the the greatest mound in Europe. The first thought was that this was basically an Irish equivalent to Merlin's Mount, also known as the Marlborough Mount, see fig. 4.4. The mount may have given

Figure 1.36: This was about as far as I got into the 'Antrim motte' before a man in a space suit came around the corner spraying a nasty green substance. 'Sorry mate it's closed today.'

*Marl*borough its name. That is, Marl-*bury* or a place where Merlin was buried. It could be the place Merlin was supposedly imprisoned by Nimue.

Merlin's Mount in Wiltshire has a step-pyramid structure, is also covered in trees, was also part of an aristocrat's gardens, and was thought to have been a Norman motte as well. Several years ago it was found to date from 2400 BC. As for the Antrim mount, God knows! Ireland is not a favourite destination for archaeologists.

Cave Hill, Belfast

'Jack... the Riperrrr!' is what the drunken man shouted at us.

'OK, I thought we should move over here rather than catch another earful.'

'Jack the Ripperrr!'

'And this is where he stood while...'

'Arrrrrgh! Jack the Ripperrrrr!'

I was on a ghost walking tour. We walked down the alleyways of central Belfast, in the solstice daylight of very late evening. It was a young woman guide and a fat Belfast man who was a trainee guide, who did the other half of the talking, a bit more nervously, while taking a long time to get to the point. Nevertheless they were a fantastic pair. It was a great tour and the stories will stay with me.

One of them was this. They took us to an alleyway where a lord who started the Ritz hotel chain, possibly César Ritz, had stayed, over one hundred years ago. He allegedly woke up sweating, and with heart racing. He dashed to the window for some air. Directly below in the alleyway was a black hooded figure, with a coffin next to him.

'Room for one more, sir?' The figure asked, looking up.

The man staggered back and when he composed himself enough to return to the window, the figure was gone. He was so sure that the incident had taken place that he wrote it in his diary. Years later he was building the Ritz hotel with all the modern electrics being incorporated. He was about to step in to a hotel elevator when the elevator boy made a fateful remark.

'Room for one more, sir?'

This must have triggered flashbacks. He recoiled from the elevator as if from a crazed lion. The dazed hotelier could only stop and stare as the lift left without him. He then could only listen as there was a loud noise and a crashing, snapping sound, as the cable broke and everyone in that lift plummeted to their doom.

In this way the earlier apparition, which may have simply been a dream, was so much like a metaphor of the future, a kind of telepathy. I wondered about the shamans of old and their hill tops. They may have drunk a cup of Soma, before falling into heavenly dreams, wrapped in warm furs, before their mountain pyramids. Like Moses of the Bible, they perhaps only came down half-starved, when the laws of a god, the dreams they had received, had been made clear.

The guide pointed out a corner the alleyway. A hundred years ago a man had been lying there. They found he had two sharp knives with him and was subsequently arrested on suspicion of being Jack the Ripper. For the three weeks they held him in October, there were no Whitechapel murders in London. We then went to another part of town. We were standing outside one pub. There was one fancily-dressed short Irishman who looked like the young Eric Burdon from *The Animals,* doing a lot of talking and later he was listening to the story. Meanwhile another drunk realised these were spooky laneway stories going on, so he kept saying one phrase over and over.

'Jack the ripper!'

Later I offered a suggestion. 'Maybe he knows something we don't? You should hire him to do the tours!'

They told some absolutely awful but funny stories. The guides showed where the gallows used to be for public executions. They showed us one narrow alleyway where eight years ago, two workers installing the extractor fans we heard running, were blown out onto the sidewalk and dazed by a supernatural wind. They subsequently refused to return to the site, simply a few metres off the main road. The wind was allegedly caused by the fact there is a mass grave of cholera victims underneath the street.

'We've got a great view of this thing called Napoleon's nose, I bet there are tombs up there.' I asked, hesitantly, pointing up at the mountain, known as Cave Hill.

'Any spooky stories?'

'Not that I'm aware!'

'But there is a big round cave entrance there, pirates might have put treasure inside! I'm going there tomorrow to take a look!'

The next day I went to this 'cave hill' On cave hill, Belfast, we seem to have an abode of the mountain religion. This is five kilometres by convenient bus from the centre of Belfast. On the way I must have passed through a Catholic area with free state flags and one graffito stating: 'prods not welcome'.

Cave Hill is basically the huge hill overlooking the town. Hill overlooking a town? It seemed to be looking over the bay as well. Would it have more little pyramids and cairns on it? It did, but more on that later. It has the so-called 'Napoleon's Nose' on it. When I got up to it, this nose actually turned out to be an Iron Age fort sticking out of the top.

My travel book did not say so, but this hill and surrounding ones are full of tombs, which I was happy to go off the little tourist trail to examine. They overlook Belfast, just as the tombs on other hills overlook Sligo and Galway.

'Belfast' supposedly comes from 'river mouth of the sandbar/ford'. But why not Baal's 'fortress?' (Just a suggestion which could easily be wrong). That is what 'fast' often means, in Scotland at least. There is definitely a fortress up there overlooking it, directly on the mountain! Rather than making a connection to a god who is not even Irish, however, we could use a Germanic equivalent. There is a bleeding/resurrection god in Beowulf called *Bealdor*, another form of Baldr. Like Baal, which means 'Lord', Bealdor means the same thing. He is a shining young man who is killed by the mistletoe branch. It is perhaps similar to how Jesus is bled to death on the cross with Longinus' spear and a crown of thorns. Like the Abrahamic religions, converts are demanded, for it is said that the only way to bring back Baldr, and thus ensure continuity of the land's fertility, is if absolutely everyone weeps for him.

The impression I got is that the whole of Cave Hill could actually be the original Belfast settlement, rather than that which is currently down by the river and bay. Back in the Iron Age, settlements and fortresses were often placed on tops of hills, as my later visit to Poland would reveal. Since it is a huge hill overlooking a bay, it can also be used for sea trade.

Leave the path up to the fort (Napoleon's nose) and go right up to the windy top. I personally cannot call the structure found there a 'pyramid' like the others as it is simply not big enough. Its placement, however indicates something quite peculiar about the pyramid religion. Right at the top-most part of the hill, 370 metres above sea level, there is a ruined flat-top cairn. It is called 'The Ballyaghagan Cairn'. One can almost, but not quite call this a terraced structure. There is another terrace you go over to get to it. I think originally it may have been a kind of step pyramid, or at least a conical pyramid of greater dimension, probably covered in stones, but it has been truly obliterated.

All the pyramids I have seen in Ireland have made me think of the structures in America. Back in Derry, a guide for a walking tour told us that he has no doubt that the Irish are the greatest travellers in the world. There is an Irish pub in every country, so why couldn't they have gone to America and helped built pyramids there, or at least carry the idea along? The Irish are around half ancient Spanish and half Viking. The 'Solutrean' hypothesis proposed in 1999 by Dennis Standford suggests that the Clovis (Among the earliest peoples on America) arose from the Solutrean people who inhabited southern Europe 21,000 to 15,000 years ago. The reason for this proposition is that the tool technology seems to be almost identical. If they were building mounds that early, part of their culture may have diffused to Ireland. Part may have diffused to the Americas. Critics of the hypothesis point to the difficulties of ocean crossing, slight differences in the tools and lack of cave art among the Clovis in America. Some of the pyramids/mounds in the Carrowmore cemetery area test to 5000 BC, the earliest that I am aware of in Europe. If so, they could well be 'post-Clovis, with 'only' four millennia separating them from the migration of Clovis to America. This would be a common link or common origin with America.

There may have been an Ice-Age pyramid-building polity or proto-civilisation (or even a collection of pyramid-building Neolithic hunter-gatherers relying upon a proto-agricultural permaculture) existing somewhere in the Mediterranean in this deeply ancestral period. The pyramids may have been erased later on when the rocks were required to build houses, as has partly happened in the case of Khufu's pyramid. Mounds may even have been re-used at a later stage, subsequently muddled with the newer, dead inhabitants (intrusive burials). As is usually the case, we do not know one way or the other about any of this, but it is a possibility.

From the top of Cave Hill, you have an awesome view of most of Belfast. You can see all of Belfast harbour, including the docks where the Titanic was built. Across on the other side of the harbour is a hill with a church on top. That *was* interesting! It could be another replacement for some Yggdrasil temple or cairn which may have once resided there. Clearly, these hill forts and pyramids were for pilgrimage. This was the old religion related to the legend of the Tower of Babel. It is a far older legend than Babel or Babylon or even than the building period of the Sumerian Ziggurats would suggest, for stories of the spread of languages following the building of the enormous tower to heaven (without mentioning Babel), dotted the pre-Colombian Americas, much to the surprise of early scholarly priests and conquistadors, who interrogated the natives. That story may also be mixed in with ideas about a primordial mound, from whence everyone emerged.

As is clear from the placement of the cairn on the very top of Cave Hill, it certainly resonates with the Biblical idea, told several millennia later, of a tower as close to heaven as possible. Yet the (much larger) cairns or pyramids as I like to call them, are always looking on over the city (or over water). It seems the cities have not really moved around very much in five thousand years. A modern analogy would be the pyramids watching over Cairo! (Silbury hill in England appears to be in the middle of nowhere, but in 2007 a Roman town was discovered adjacent to it). The ancestors still like to watch over and control the affairs of Earth, as they lie close to heaven. They are the link between man and the gods. Looking to the nearby hills from the top of Cave Hill, it is apparent that they are full of tombs and mobile phone towers. (These are a modern thing placed on the top of hills, and are placed as close to heaven as possible, but for scientific reasons). I wonder how many ancient sites dedicated to the pyramid or mountain religion have been ruined in the last ten years by these things. Probably quite a few, because every time I went to the top of any hill it was hard not to trip over ruins. Ancient people did not have mobile phones. They believed in spiritual forces of communication, through meditation or shamanic means like drugs and dreams.

I walked around the whole park of which Cave Hill is a part. Next to this tomb/pyramid called Ballyaghagan cairn is McArt's Fort. This fort is henged off by a ditch, and has a circular Iron-Age storage pit. A sign says that metal detectors are illegal and anything found must be taken to the Ulster Museum. This is the Napoleon's nose bit of the mountain. You have to be careful you don't fall off because this 'fortress' is actually a small little rocky outcrop on the edge of a cliff, but it does not look like it while you are up on it! On top of the fort is a cairn with a carved hole with water in it. I put some on my forehead because the thought occurred to me that if I did, it would open my third eye. I imagine that ancient peoples, as well as modern ones, did much the same thing. Travel has indeed broadened things considerably so I guess the operation was a success. My 'third eye' has indeed been opened.

Commanding a solid view of Belfast, I am guessing that this hill site is indeed part of an incredibly old town. One side of McArt's fort has a recessed room within the two-metre thick outer walls. There is another room opposite on the outside. There are oaks growing around and inside it. The storage pit would be an excellent place to drink beer at midnight and then stand up to look at the city lights. Not that I heard any rumours about it, but I wonder how many young people have drunkenly fallen off. It must be an incredibly popular place at night time, for teenagers to drink. Cave Hill would unfortunately be a good place to go for a 'dare'.

This so-called fort with megalith is right on the edge of a huge three hundred metre-tall cliff. You could walk right off the edge very easily. In Australia it would all have been fenced off. The dolmen with the water pond is *right* on the edge. It would be interesting to speculate that the dolmen and the tombs on the hill are a linked communal religious site. In that case, perhaps in ancient times, one goes to the edge of the cliff for a little 'trial of fear'. What if they used to blindfold people, lead them in blind faith to the edge of the cliff, and then baptise them with water from the dolmen? You need to trust your peers to allow that to happen. Afterwards you are all brothers. Alternately, or afterwards, they could go fifty metres up to the middle of the hill to worship at the graves of the ancestors. They could even sleep there in summer and have communicative dreams with the Gods.

The reason the whole hill is called Cave Hill becomes apparent when you see a spectacular cave in the side which looks like the perfect place to store a pirates' treasure. (assuming the place was a little more deserted!) Unfortunately the cave is too high up the cliff to get in without some kind of ladder or rope. There is huge round valley in front of it called the 'Devil's Punchbowl', which may have looked artificial to ancient people, resembling a bizarre interior of an enormous cocktail glass. They hid valuable stuff in the cave in WWII here, because Belfast was heavily bombed by the Germans.

There is amazing scenery. I wandered right through the park and on the other side finally found the Iron-Age ring fort which the map, but not the tourist book mentioned. One can only see the foundations really, in a field with no sign. It is about eighty metres across or more, with a 'moat' on the approaching side coming uphill. Is this early Belfast, right here?

Figure 1.37: The Ballyaghagan Cairn. It is found at the highest point of Cave hill, where it is very windy indeed! It was/is either a flat-topped pyramid, or it simply looks like that because it has basically been dug up and stripped bare, with the remainder covered in earth. It appears to have been a burial. If this were located in remote North Western Ireland, rather than looming above Belfast, a city of 200,000 lurking below, it would perhaps still be largely intact.

Figure 1.38: From the top of the Ballyaghagan cairn. Clearly the afterlife denizen needs a good view.

Figure 1.39: Standing on top of the Ballyaghagan Cairn, looking in the other direction now, the view is superlative. We can see all of nearby McArt's fort, (Napoleon's Nose) as well as Belfast below. This is the highest part of the hill. It is representative of where the dead wished to be buried, as well as the sky religion. It is not just a convenient place. It is hardly simply a pleasant 'hill by the seaside' due to high winds. It is also on the highest part of the hill possible. This implies the input of the sky religion into the decision-making process of where this cairn should have been situated.

Figure 1.40: A Stunning picture of the view over Belfast, from under McArt's fort. This old religion needed to be situated as high as possible.

Figure 1.41: From up here, they could spot any ship in the harbour. In the centre, on the other side of the harbour, but barely visible in this photo, is a large hill with a church on top. It would have replaced a shrine at yet another site of pilgrimage.

Newgrange

Dublin has green letterboxes. When the Irish took over from the British in the 1920s, it was easier to simply splash green paint on the red letterboxes, than to rip them out and put new ones in. I used one to send some postcards, and then it was time for the tour bus!

I went to the meeting place for a bus tour. It would go to the Hill of Tara and Newgrange!

Exiting Dublin, on the motorway, one can drive to 120 km/h, but then one has to come to a stop on the road, at a toll booth. One of the reasons Ireland has a reputation for being so green becomes obvious with a drive in the countryside. Green, green, green. Where is the wheat? Not a single ear of it! Pretty much the main crop that farmers grow is grass for cows.

Initially I thought: 'Why has this island maintained its stone walls and sheep fields which surely date from the Middle Ages, when the rest of Europe is farming crops?' Actually, this is a pattern which goes way back. There is some medieval anti-Irish propaganda from the Anglo Normans. It basically states that the Irish are primitive since they have no agriculture, and are a nation of shepherds. However, there was also a medieval description of Ireland, stating that snow never lies on the ground for more than three days. It is really warmed by water from the Caribbean. The use of land all year, feeding animals with grass perhaps makes more sense. The other thing is that rain kills the crops.

Unfortunately the tendency for Ireland to specialise in particular crops is one of the reasons why the Potato Famine was so bad. Until the 1840s, Ireland was an up and coming great power with a large population. After that it all went to hell and Ireland has been shrinking. Apparently the famine occurred in other European countries as well, but in Ireland, all the cows and animals also died from plague and even the apple trees died. Another explanation I got from someone else is that no, only potatoes were affected, and furthermore, there was *no* general crop failure at all! Rather, it was the English landlords who exported literally everything non-potato and therefore left the people to starve. After that everyone has been fleeing Ireland for a hundred and fifty years, or at least until the 'Celtic Tiger' economy of the 90s brought foreign investment and jobs.

The tour guide said that while other countries had experienced a Dark Ages, between the collapse of the Roman Empire and about the year 1000, this period was Ireland's Golden Age! They established Irish monasteries all over Italy in this time and intellectuals from everywhere went to study there. This was perhaps an important time for the preservation of ancient Irish history. This is something which did not occur in most other European countries.

What am I on about? An excellent book is *Exodus to Arthur*, by Mike Baillie, a dendrochronologist. It seems that Irish historic record goes back almost as far as the days of Newgrange itself, a huge communal tomb or worship mound which guides say is 'older than the pyramids.' No other civilisation except maybe the Chinese have history stretching back this far. In papers for *Archaeology Ireland*, as well as *Emania*, Richard Warner claims that one of the narrowest tree-ring events on record (indicating a year of bad weather) occurred in the ring for the year 2345 BC. Meanwhile, some of the first entries in ancient Irish chronicles refer to various loughs (*lough* is the Irish word for loch, or lake) which 'broke out' or erupted (flooding perhaps). They mention that one erupts in about 2341 BC. The implication is that the chronicler of later times recorded a natural disaster, which would possibly be the Hekla 4 Volcanic eruption in Iceland, associated with narrow tree rings of the period 2353-2345 BC. He either recorded it based upon a written or oral tradition. An implication is that someone in unrecorded antiquity sat down with one of the last surviving druids, who carried on the oral traditions, and took it all down! Baillie speculates that the infamous Irish antiquarian, Bishop James Ussher, of the seventeenth century, calculated the flood to have occurred in about 2349 BC based on Irish chronicles.

This is not the only date either. Imagine if they recorded the eruption of Santorini? This decimated the earlier Minoan Empire around 1627 BC, according to tree ring evidence. (The late Bronze Age Trojan war supposedly occurred about five centuries later). It caused a geo-political catastrophe for nations. Trade was cut off, crops failed and tribes migrated. The Bible appears to remember the time as the Hyksos invasion of Egypt. Irish history or mythology, depending on your point of view, recalls it as the time when king Tigernmas died, along with three quarters of the men of Ireland. After this Ireland was seven years without a king.

The implications of the sheer length of Irish history are staggering. Ireland has an 'uninterrupted' history based upon oral or written sources dating back millennia! Invasion, plague or genocide seem not to have utterly obliterated the ancient Irish history, as in most of the rest of the world! A further implication is that Ireland was an educated and decent society in perhaps the time of Newgrange with at least an educated class of men, or even women who took steps to pass down an oral tradition. Perhaps we need to look past ideas of mere 'Neolithic farmers' building various monuments in their part time and start to re-consider what we really mean when we call a society a civilisation. This was a society of kings, queens and princes. It endured in one form or another down the ages, passing on the old ideas and traditions.

In summary, Ireland is old, very old.

'Egypt has the pyramids... Ireland has Newgrange,' the tour guide said.

He added that Newgrange is five hundred years older than the pyramids of Giza, and a thousand years older than Stonehenge. It dates from about 3200 BC. What a place! It was a real highlight to visit. I was dwarfed by the white quartz walls of the front facade, which are about 4.5 metres high! It is a huge communal temple/tomb on top of a hill. Dare we call it a pyramid? Perhaps in former religion, but not really in looks. The view from Newgrange itself is amazing and it was designed to be seen from quite a distance! From the hill on which it is situated, we see a huge sweeping valley on each side of the structure. This place was indeed chosen well, 5000 years ago! I was so amazed to be there.

Anyone can feel like Indiana Jones at Newgrange because it is quite interesting to go and squeeze along the passageway inside! First we had a guided talk. Very few visitors are allowed in because of some 'mould' which we were told has developed inside. Half the people waiting went inside and the other half could just walk around it and explore and look at the view.

The mound is very similar to mounds I would later see in Poland, but it is surrounded by horizontal megaliths which look about the size and colour of Stonehenge rocks. I was starting to develop the idea that Stonehenge really may have been conceived and built in Ireland, just as Medieval chronicler Geoffrey of Monmouth stated, before being shifted to Britain by the guidance of 'Merlin.'

Some stones (fig. 1.45) have spirals carved in them as well as wave carvings. Every place has its own unique environmental and magnetic 'vibration' which the brain interprets in its own way. In Fred Hoyle's view, the increasing complexity of the life and universe with time result in a vast complex intellect residing in the future, directing quantum signals back towards the past.

I listened and tuned in to see what the feel was in the place. The

Figure 1.42: The front of Newgrange. Personally, I am reminded of Stonehenge. That large rough stone at the front is like Stonehenge's Heel stone, obscuring incoming light. The cut and shaped stones around the base remind one of the Sarsen circle. We could be looking at a very similar religion. Stonehenge is in the open, by comparison, so a huge audience could actually see the fertility ritual which once occurred. Since Pater/Patrick/Peter dominates the religious landscape, I wonder: are these the original Pearly Gates?

Figure 1.43: Walking around to the right of Newgrange, from the front. The huge stones were allegedly brought twenty kilometres, from a valley below. This was a terrific project.

Figure 1.44: The back of Newgrange basically looks like a regular large mound.

Figure 1.45: Here is a huge base stone, from around the side of Newgrange.

vibe was instantly 'talking' and pulling at the chakras, especially the one under the heart, which may have been what some refer to as the 'Solar Plexus.' However the message was all babble. There were lots of whispers which were too eager and enthusiastic to form a coherent message. Unlike Stonehenge where the vibe is something which is 'sleeping' (lots of visitors to Stonehenge actually say it has a has a bad vibe. It feels like it has little to say, whilst insidiously plotting to keep something an enormous secret!) this place is more than alive. Firstly, there was a feeling of true joy: a true place of power! Spiritually, it felt like it was telling me that it welcomes me wholeheartedly, and that it considered me very nice and all sorts of stuff of that order! I get the feeling lots of these places really want to tell a story but they cannot because human and mineral have severe communication issues, even if we are all vibrating energy.

Newgrange was used for two hundred years, and then gradually turned into a hill for the next 5000 years until 1699 when the advancing population rediscovered it. A nobleman started to use it as a quarry since God had obviously conveniently left a huge heap of stones on top of the hill for them to use. It was then that they discovered it was a huge ancient structure.

The front of the monument has a second narrow entrance above the door. It was used to let light in. Newgrange is really a light receptacle. It is a mound on top of a much larger mound: a hill, which is being used to absorb light. It is firstly reflected by the white quartz stones of its facade, giving a stunning appearance at sunrise or sunset. Secondly it allows the light into its interior, via a light box, for ritual purposes.

We finally got to go inside as the first group was now emerging. No photos were allowed of the interior. I was nearly the last one in, but two Americans and one Australian woman made sure that they stayed behind me as they were claustrophobic, as the guide had warned us about possible claustrophobia. First you bend down to go under one section, the doorway and passage being about four feet tall. Then suddenly the passageway is tall again. You squeeze a little or walk sideways between rocks which are assembled along the passageway like soldiers on each side. Death was seen as a kind of rebirth so it is like a birth canal. I noticed the passageway winds like a snake as well! This represents the passage of life to death. The snake is a metaphor for the winding random turns of life!

It appeared that the passageway was sloping upwards. It is actually two metres higher in the central 'tomb area', than at the entrance. I noted that the Great Pyramid of Egypt has an upward sloping passage as well. All the others slope down for an alleged burial underneath the pyramid, which often did not occur.

Finally, after a few more metres, one gets to the tomb-area itself, if it can be called that! There are strange notches carved into the rocks. Above us is a kind of dome of rocks held against each other which is like a primitive proto-beehive tomb-like structure. It was sensational! Let me describe the rest. Facing inwards, in front of you and to each side are doorways with huge carved stone basins on the floor. One is in each niche. These would have been used for putting ritual objects in. The basins are smooth and well shaped. They are separate from the tomb structure and less than a metre in diameter.

'The basins are egg-shaped. This could be related to a myth of the birth from the cosmic egg,' I interjected.

'That's a good point,' the guide said.

In mounds or pyramids, I have noticed that birth or rebirth is suggested by cosmic waters, or some cosmic egg, in the stone-age religion, in whatever country it is to be found. The cosmic egg either gives birth to the universe, or it might give birth to a Loki-like joker figure, like the stone monkey of Asian lore. This figure would be a benefactor to mankind, allowing him supremacy over the other animals of Earth, a hidden advantage which the greater gods would not like: for man was perhaps never predicted, never feted to conquer Earth. Too much was arrayed against him in this path. He needed a benefactor, an unpopular and dark benefactor. There is another myth, an Egyptian one. In this the cosmic egg is carried to the primeval mound at Hermopolis (now at an unknown location) by Thoth, an Ibis and god of knowledge. Once at the mound there was a rebirth of the Sun. This would be similar to the rebirth of Nordic Baldr, the shining youth god, from the underworld, every year.

Above the basin of the right-most recess are spirals, carved on the ceiling. These symbolise the universe, or the unknown, or the rebirth of fertility, or the mysterious repetition or pattern of life.

The guide began to speak. 'OK, we're switching the lights off, if the kids are OK with that?'

'Sure no problem,' a five year old girl said.

'OK no problem for the kids, but maybe for the adults there might be a problem.'

The claustrophobics in the back grinned, nervously. All was dark except for a very modest light coming through a crack.

'This is a simulation of what happens on the winter solstice.'

She switched a light on which represented the red sunlight emerging along the floor. Sunlight is supposed to come in via a light through the light box above the front door but since the tomb is two metres higher than the door, the light only fingers along the floor, slowly, from the entrance, towards the back, until it touches the rear basin (this was smashed up by treasure hunters one hundred years ago, but the huge fragments are still there. The other basins are intact). Presumably sacrificial goods would have been placed in the rear basin for the sunlight to bathe over!

Then the colour of the 'sunlight' turned orange.

'The change in colour represents the Sun turning golden as it rises.' The light stayed where it was, a finger-width beam along the floor, now getting brighter. The whole spectacle is supposed to last seventeen minutes. Outside I had noticed a huge stone about twenty metres from the front, probably designed to block further solar light, so the spectacle could only be very short. One of the reasons I mention and later discuss Stonehenge in this book is that Stonehenge has almost precisely the same mechanism, with a 'heel stone' used to block out certain sections of the morning light, which would have washed over the white 'Altar Stone' (perhaps symbolising what Robert Graves referred to as the 'white goddess'), which now lies underneath a fallen trilithon. (Stonehenge is a kind of uncovered version of a tomb.) This was worked out in the 80s in a sensational book called *Stonehenge Solved* by George Terance Meaden. I was very eager to ask questions of the guide, so I piped up.

'Presumably the Sun reaches in at midwinter to fertilise whatever liquid is inside the basins, presumably cow blood, since cows were sacrificed in the *Iliad*?'

'Uh well, could be!'

She did not like the sound of that, but tended to agree that it was possible. In fact she pointed out that one of the basins had its own hemispherical egg-like recess.

As soon as the guide finished talking and the talk was over, I turned to look at the claustrophobics, and was greeted by an empty space. They had already retreated about three metres back down the passage, relative to their previously observed position, inside the chamber, several seconds earlier.

The guide said that Newgrange is so well built that no drop of water ever enters! The whole hill is artificial. It is an amazing achievement.

Something like this was really a communal tomb or church. One goes inside and prays to the ancestors. Some bones would have been in there as well. The tombs were originally left open back then in the stone age, before being covered and abandoned after a few generations, when the ancestors and stories surrounding them were perhaps forgotten and were no-longer relevant.

There are two other mounds nearby which seem to be similar to Newgrange. These are Knowth (67 metres wide by 12 high), which is aligned to the equinoxes, and Dowth (85 metres wide by 15 high), aligned to midwinter sunsets. Dowth in particular puts on a dramatic light show. During the winter solstice, the light is reflected by a convex stone onto a stone bearing cosmic patterns. It appears the huge mounds (or do we call them pyramids?) were built to immortalise astronomical knowledge. It was a useful knowledge of Sun and seasons which helped them to survive.

Mythology is a little sketchy. Firstly, the entire Brú na Bóinne, bend in the Boyne, or Boyne Valley, which includes other tombs of Loughcrew, is a huge World Heritage area. Apparently, firstly there was one druid living in the area. Subsequently, giants moved in, represented in mythology by Dagda entering. Dagda is a huge brown man with an enormous club which can kill nine men with one sweep. He is not brown because he is African, but because he is the giant who lives under the Earth. Rodney Castleden, whom I greatly admire, wrote a book called *The Cerne Giant* about a huge man with phallus and club carved in chalk at Cerne in southern England. He suggests, as do others subsequent, that the giant is Helis, a Welsh god, or Hercules, who holds a club and lion skin. In fact I think Hercules is not the best comparison, despite it being a current favourite. I think the Cerne Giant is rather the equivalent of Greek Orion, an enormous primordial hunter bearing a club. An even better geographical solution would in fact be Irish Dagda, (suggested many decades ago but never fully accepted) who is much the same, but who has an enormous phallus which drags along the ground after him. I have seen images of Dagda carved into centuries-old buildings in old towns in Germany and Poland, a memory of early Celtic tradition, so his memory was rather widespread. I think he must even be related to the black knight of Arthurian tradition, a huge giant of a man. He is the giant of the underworld, the dark furnace below. He is known as the 'all-father' and is skilled, and is also called 'the horned one'. He is in essence, Loki, or Lucifer. It is a bit more complex than this, however, as aspects of him also refer to the great sky father, possibly because he was a great male deity. Hercules on the other hand does have aspects of Orion, but is also mixed up with at least one historical figure from the Mycenaean period. Dagda and Orion are more primordial.

In the Boyne Valley mythology, this giant, Dagda takes over the whole valley. Eventually he is replaced by his son, essentially a Baldr-like figure, a shining young god, called Aongus Og. This might be mixed up with a memory of the coming of Christianity, or something preceding Christianity. This also gives us a clue in terms of associations with Nordic tradition. As an underworld giant, Loki and Baldr are inseparable. Without Baldr, Loki would not have his place in the underworld. Without Loki, Baldr would not have been able to reincarnate every year to bring back the fertility season and mankind would suffer an eternal winter. It is one reason why the fire god Loki is not really seen as evil in the old days.

Overall the Newgrange experience was amazing. The whole time the guide was talking, an old lady was sitting in the lotus position in the corner meditating. As the chamber began to empty, she was still sitting there, with eyes closed, taking it all in. Outside I noticed a woman in front of the mound, making a water-colour drawing of the white edifice of the structure. In five millennia, Newgrange has not lost its spiritual charm! One thing I noticed was that the number three seems to be very sacred at Newgrange as well. For instance, there are three spirals on the entrance gate stone, as well as three chambers with basins on the inside. It might be said that the Great pyramid has three burial chambers as well. (But that's really stretching it!)

Tara, another sacred place, was once part of some wider city. I would guess that Newgrange must have been built beside a town as well, just as it seems there was once a city around Stonehenge. Ireland has lots of monastic ruins apparently in the middle of nowhere, but they once had thriving communities around them.

Tara, trash trees and more tombs

'Thanks Angela Merkel for building these roads in Ireland,' the tour driver said. (Germany provides a huge chunk of the European Union's economic funding by itself). The driver was really paranoid about the toll booths on the motorway. He paused about a hundred metres before the toll booth and asked passengers which box had a hand sticking out. He selected one and then panicked when the man in the box disappeared

Figure 1.46: Currently associated with Hercules, this chalk hill giant of the southern coast of England, south of London, falls short of the heroic ideal. He is more likely related to Irish Dagda, whose Greek version would be 'Orion', a cleaner fit. Irish Dagda is a great father of knowledge, but is portrayed as crude and comical in legend. A possible Roman temple was placed nearby, seen above the giant, and there was a holy fountain as well. In Egyptian myth, Osiris, who is an Earth father, and possible equivalent of Dagda in some respects, has relations with Isis. The product of the union is Horus, a sky god. Osiris then goes to heaven to become Orion. Orion himself is a man with a huge club. 'Osiris' is the Egyptian Orion.

Figure 1.47: The entrance to Newgrange. One can see the light box above the doorway. This is at ground level at the centre of the mound. When the season is right, one can stand in the centre (if one wins a special Newgrange lottery), and see the solar rays entering at dawn, via the light box. They slowly advance along the ground like a solar (water) tide coming in, to light up and possibly 'acknowledge' whatever offerings are placed in a large bowl in a recess.

Figure 1.48: Newgrange. Older than the pyramids, this resembles the Giza pyramids, as well as early Silbury Hill, because it was designed to have a white facade. The white facade is a circular slither around part of the mound that is Newgrange. In the image, the white facade is here mixed with darker stones. It peters out into a penumbra of darkness on this side, as well as on the other side of the 'crescent.' This seems to be a representation of the *crescent* moon! Newgrange itself is a mound on top of a windy hill.

so he could not get the bus through, and went somewhere else to pay. On the way back from the tour, instead of just looking at which lanes have a green arrow, he pulled over for a few minutes. He had to make sure the lane he wanted to be in had someone at the box.

It looks like people in Cork, the second city in Ireland on the south coast, have a reputation in Dublin for thinking too much of themselves. The bus driver tried a joke.

'Did you hear of the Cork man with the inferiority complex?'

'He only thought he was as good as everyone else.'

We reached the Hill of Tara. This is Ireland's 'Camelot', although nothing really remains today. It is such a tall hill that one can see most of Ireland from the top, where it is extremely windy. This itself, the driver pointed out, made it unlikely it would have actually been used as a royal residence, despite its reputation. Anyone taking a hostile army up here, however, would require quite a breather.

It was quite cold as well.

'This is, believe it or not, a very good day. You should be up here during a storm!'

Anyway, there were not many people at the hill of Tara, and one can just go in and walk around, no fee required. It is best seen from the air, however. From the ground it is like being on a small surface of a huge hemisphere, or egg. One cannot really see the layout.

One walks past a church (it must have been built to replace a pagan temple), which is itself next to some earlier strange wall of a ruin. Then one enters the main part of the hill itself.

I was racing up and down the embankments, attempting to explore it as quickly as possible with the time allowed. Apparently it was a royal seat. They know precisely what buildings were once there, as Irish chronicles talk about it! It is a bit of an indication just how far back the chronicles go. Other than that information, the hill is prehistoric.

What they call a 'banquet hall', if it had occurred in Britain, might really be called a 'cursus', or a huge linear earthwork. It is a bit of a long avenue leading to a henge (circular ditch) or is that another former house? While I was wandering around, I noticed the stone walls just beneath the turf. It was just like at the Krakus Mound in Poland, which I would later visit. Dark-age ruins! I had never read about any stone walls up here. People simply do not like to talk about it, or do not know. Then I discovered more stuff. There were lots of loose stones, so I picked up one huge chunk from the wall and it had right angles! One

Figure 1.49: An interesting ground-down stone found cast aside on the Tara hill. Since it was not attached to anything, an implication is there might have been more structures up here, presumably more mounds, or tombs, subsequently destroyed.

side was clearly and methodically ground down totally flat, rather than split! My guess is this was from some earlier monumental structure. It was subsequently ruined centuries or millennia ago by a farmer when it was time to build a wall. This seems to be evident because the stones on the facade of the tomb of the Hostages also have right angles.

'You can see two thirds of Ireland from the summit,' the driver pointed out. We had a very good view of that. He proceeded to point and count off the different counties.

The stone wall around the hill followed a natural circular embankment which would have defended the Tara fortress. Tara was in fact the centre of a huge Iron-Age city, even if the hill itself seems very chilly, which is a bit of a mystery! Ireland has unfortunately experienced depopulation many many times in its history, so these cities are gone, leaving ruins in the middle of nowhere. As for the 'current' or modern depopulation, the guide said that in the 1940s, it had been calculated that if emigration continued at the then-current levels, there would only have been 200,000 people left in Ireland by the year 2000.

Emigration really stopped when the multinationals moved to Ireland to provide employment in the 90s.

It was lucky that I came back to the Hill of Tara for a second visit. What I thought, on the previous visit, was simply a silly tree with decorations on it placed there by hippies and dolphin lovers, turned out to be something quite different.

I had been interested in the Yggdrasil, the Germanic tree of knowledge and life: basically much the same thing as the story in the Old Testament, the one God warned us about, responsible for the original sin of mankind. They seem to have been planted on high hills or close to heaven. Examples seem to be found everywhere. If we look at an Asian pyramid, or *stupa*, for instance, they have this umbrella-like structure on top which much resembles a classical Christmas tree or conifer. In addition the tree of life is connected with Asian stupa ritual, with coloured ribbons being sometimes attached. The stupas, which are characteristically hemispherical mounds, themselves represent water in their old religions.

The hills, pyramids and mounds of Europe, and in particular the Celtic mounds from about the time of Christ, seem to be European versions of the stupas of Asia. In those the wise man Buddha was buried. In Europe the wise man Odin was hung from the tree of knowledge. In this way it may have been related to a place of execution. This old knowledge of the tree as a possible place of execution may have been one reason, re: the Christian cross, for the uptake of Christianity in the north. I noticed that old sources about Christ in medieval English Robin Hood ballads call him something like '*Hym that died on tre*', (him that died on the tree). Christianity itself, not to mention the Old Testament, written during the Babylonian exile, seems to be filled with deeply ancient Indo-European themes.

In fig. 1.50, we have an image which encapsulates the world mountain mythos. In this image we see tree, bird on top, snake on the bottom, mountain and water. I believe these are key elements of the mountain or pyramid religion. Compare, for instance, the mythological image with a photo of Silbury Hill and its moat, fig. 4.6, which may have been built as a pyramid or world mound, which should be in the centre of the universe. There are three worlds in this mythology. We occupy a world for which the ancients, may have been a kind of 'flatland.' Below there was the great unknown, an underworld, of which we only knew geological forces. Above was a great cold land of glorious patterns of clouds and sunsets, Asgard. When one climbs a mountain,

Figure 1.50: A picture of Yggdrasil on world mountain. This is the centre of all creation. *Asgard and the Gods*, by Friedrich Wilhelm Heine 1845-1921.

the climate and vegetation changes, as if one were approaching towards ninety degrees latitude on the globe. Just a little elevation and everything gets colder and windier. The mountain is therefore a gateway, poking into Asgard, and why should it do that? (A plateau is even better than a mountain peak as it suggests a whole new plane of existence which one may survive upon.) Why would Earth Mother want to push herself up towards the sky father?

What was very remarkable is that this 'tree of Eden' religion still lives in Ireland! This was possibly the Indo-European competitor of Yahweh worship which is possibly the reason Yahweh forbade it. He is a 'jealous God' according to the Bible. This unspoken religion seemed to be very strong in at least two areas I found on the day of my Tara visit, Tara and Loughcrew!

I thought nothing of the tree full of ribbons on my first visit to Tara, thinking it was some recent festival. But with a different tour guide to show us around the site, one always gets new information! It may not be always correct, but it is new information nonetheless!

'Do you see that tree over there with the trash on it? Lets go over to it,' he said.

Bear in mind the hill of Tara was a seat of kings, at a high elevation. There are several Hawthorn trees, not quite on the highest point, but not too far off. The tree we approached had all sorts of things dangling on it, which convinced me that the presumably local people who had attached them were not just weekend pagans who had attached a handful of party ribbons they had bought from the supermarket. No. You could see at once that these people were utterly and deadly serious about their practice. They were traditionalists.

With the amount of superstitious fable I heard espoused in the Irish countryside, told as if it were true beyond any question, truer than one's hand in front of one's face, it is not hard to believe how much in earnest these people are. Of course, some will not believe and regard the stories with the same curious humour as you or I. Nevertheless even sceptics will not mess with a sacred site. For others, it is easier to believe that a cow has gone around the moon than that there is any possibility the stories of what has happened to men who have dared cross the 'little people' are wrong. These beliefs are impregnated from early childhood. The combination of the fear of an ancestral curse powerful enough to ruin a life, as well as a healthy and noble respect for the dead, unmatched in other countries, still keep people away from disturbing sacred areas and burial sites. The ever-changing Irish dream-

Figure 1.51: The Trash Tree at Tara, centre of a hill religion which survives to this day, though in perhaps a different form to the original intention. Is this where the Christmas tree religion comes from, or a later variant? Certain places in England do this as well (I am unsure if this was imported from Ireland in modern times). China also seems to do this with red ribbons, as a survival of a truly widespread ancient tradition.

like landscape makes it easier to believe that the gods are closer than we can imagine.

Attached to the tree, and others like it all around the countryside, especially on sacred hills, there were baby boots, all sorts of clothes, bras, panties, all sorts of nonsense. It looked like a junk yard in the branches! What is the purpose? These are magical wishes! In essence, 'God(s), look at my baby. My child is sick. Protect us.' The sacred hill fort on which the tree exists was both practical and religious because it often contains tombs of ancestral demi-gods. They had powerful magic stored up for millennia. The guide pointed to some bras.

'This is people wishing for breast enlargements... or reductions.'

The tour driver, who grew up in Dublin, said that in the 70s, road workers refused to cut down the hawthorn trees. That is apparently why many roads today were built in squiggly lines around the trees!

Figure 1.52: A sign at the Fairy tree at Tara tells us that the attachments are 'thoughts'. 'Please tie thoughts loosely so they can fly, and the trees can survive.'

Figure 1.53: The tomb of the hostages at Tara. This stone brickwork
is perhaps four thousand years old, or even older. The right angles of
the stones are apparent.

Something I did not notice at Tara on the first visit, but did on the
second, is something which is known as the 'Tomb of the Hostages'.
It is a mound with a neolithic entrance, fig. 1.53. In the old days,
kings took families of some of their nobles hostage, just to make sure.
Somehow this idea became associated with the tomb. The facade on the
tomb is composed of nicely stacked right-angle stones. One can point
the camera inside the grating to look at the swirly patterns inside,
representing eternity and the universe (fig. 1.54). Looking at the newer
stone walls all around the tomb, on various properties, I realised that
maybe half of those stones could be from old tombs! It is hard to say.

There is also a church on top of this hill, to one side, implying there
was a religious spot here. Again, where would they have got the stones
to build that church on that hill? Surely it would have been easier to
plunder some old tombs they did not care about, than to bring in fresh
stones from somewhere else?

The church could be adjacent to where an original Yggdrasil or pillar
or shine once was. Why place a church up there on the windy hill if
it was not to detract attention away from an old pagan shrine? Next

Figure 1.54: Inside the Tomb of Hostages. I got the feeling later that humans would not have been kept in there. Rather the hostages would have been mythological ones. These would have been Loki and his infamous family, as well as the three Norns or witches. These are the weavers of man's fete. They have survived in English lore in Shakespeare's Macbeth, stirring up toil and trouble on Earth. This tomb, for ancients, may have been seen as the centre of the Earth, and place of the hostages of Thor. Then again it is rather small and could have been a mere tomb for a king and nothing more.

to the church is a huge and bizarre lump of rocks which appears to be a wall, partly melted together, from the earlier church. Who knows how old it is or why it would have been left there like that. The 'tomb of the hostages' dates from 3500 BC. Is that how long people have been hanging up stuff on trees? Since the tree religion was seemingly universal in Eurasia, the religion is probably much older.

Next, we were off to 'Jumping Church'. According to legend three people were buried together, two priests and a sinner. In the afterlife the priests said to each other: 'why are we buried next to a sinner?' Using their powers, they pushed the church six feet away from the sinner, so that he was now buried outside church grounds. What could have inspired the legend? Perhaps there were earlier failed plans to build a church on top of a pagan site, rather than say, six feet next to it? The Irish remain a superstitious folk. The guide told us that to this day people do not look at the Jumping Church when they pass it. They feed the sheep instead, or simply look at them to distract them from the church. Something awful must have happened there. It was so bad that people did not talk about it for so many generations, that no-one even knows what it was! That is real fear, increased by the spectre of the unknown.

After that it was off to an awesome ruined castle which would have belonged to a knight or baron. I took plenty of photos. One can see huge chimneys reaching up several levels to the sky, with no fireplace under them! One could also clamber up certain rocks to walk on the first floor in one area. In another area there was a tower reaching towards the sky. I followed the spiral staircase up but then it was blocked at the ceiling after one floor.

Next we went to Trim Castle which is Ireland's largest Norman castle. All day we were just driving between archaeological attractions in the Boyne Valley. This large valley near Dublin was always one of the richest parts of Ireland due to its proximity to England. Trim castle has amazing walls, hundreds of arrow slits, as well as a fantastic keep, which we did not enter. The place has excellent vibes. Both these castles are next to rivers, and presumably, possibly former sacred sites. The driver said that Ireland never had an industrial revolution so the rivers are pristine. It is awesome to drink from a good river.

The Irish countryside is extremely beautiful with puffy white clouds scudding low above fluorescent green grass when the sun is at the right angle. Against this scenery, the black and white cows provide a little transient contrast, to prevent the viewer from slipping into the delusion

Figure 1.55: Ascending the hill to Loughcrew. There are tombs on top of all the nearby hills. It can be seen that the people walk through a series of hill-fort embankments on the way up. This place was used for defence as well as religion. Or are they sacred embankments, like at Stonehenge?

that he is in Elysium.

Loughcrew

We later went to the Loughcrew Portal tomb, which was truly the highlight of the day! The reason for this is it is just like Newgrange. It was built by the same ancient cult, to a very similar specification, yet is a mini version. It has had a lot less or no restoration work done on it. Because it is a bit shoddier, however, no-one goes there. A few factors keep the tourists away. It is on top of a farmer's hill, so a tour guide would have to walk his group up there. It is not sign-posted that well either. The benefits of the place however, are enormous. One can take pictures inside and stay basically as long as one wishes! One can get the key to open the gate to the tomb from the local pub, and then climb the massive hill and get inside. A local woman got the key and

Figure 1.56: Loughcrew.

we walked up with the tour group.

The tomb itself looks like a huge pile of rubble, a pyramid essentially on top of a large hill. The hill is so tall that one can literally see half of Ireland. The guide was pointing out all the counties. That is another clue to what was going on in the ancestors' minds. There is invariably a good view where the mountain or pyramid religion seems to have concerned itself. As I travelled around, it was becoming rather obvious to me that they wanted the tomb close to heaven, but also where it could be seen so that the building potential of the hierarchy, the power to command men on a large scale, could be demonstrated to all. People would grow up knowing that there was power in heaven, and also on Earth. We approached the large cairn.

'This is the burial place of Queen Mab,' (Medb) the guide said.

'Hang on, isn't Queen Mab buried in that cairn up near Sligo on Knocknarea?'

'Ah yes, she is as well! You been there have you? Yes, I've heard about that.'

'Yes. It seems to be Ireland's greatest stone pyramid,' I said.

'Is it indeed?'

It appears that many of these mounds on tops of hills are named

Figure 1.57: Next to the Loughcrew mound is this ominous altar. A fanatic has carved a cross into it. Who knows when? Ironically the cross is also a pagan symbol deriving from a tree so the ancients may not have minded.

after the primordial witch-queen Medb. Perhaps it is little wonder that the mound has not been destroyed (that much) by tomb robbers. They might have been terrified of her. Still, she cannot be buried everywhere, under every hill. A similar legend exists about Buddha, who is purportedly buried under various stupas throughout India.

'The age of the tomb, and the fact it is still intact, always blows me away, and I've been taking people here for a few years now,' the guide said.

We all walked around the outside of the tomb. Someone pointed at an object.

'Oh! Is that what I think it is?'

'What is?'

'An altar?'

'Sure looks like it, doesn't it!' (fig. 1.57)

The 'altar' was right up against the pyramid/cairn and looked like it was designed for sacrificing small animals at the very least. This meant the cairn was not just a tomb, but had a ritual purpose. It was a darn-proper pyramid... Aztec style!

The tomb looks like a scaled-down but otherwise carbon copy of Queen Medb's grave near Sligo. Both these tombs have the same legend attached. Seven people were going in at a time and you can take as many photos as you wish. I took millions. There are lots of spirals there carved in the rocks, as well as dots. Inside it is much the same as at Newgrange. After entering and a little squeeze symbolising birth, you get to the end and there is a proto-beehive chamber and three niches, two to each side and one in front. In the niche on the right the guide pointed out a tree carving. It looked more like a huge leaf to me. He said this might relate to the tree religion. It certainly makes sense! Walking up this massive hill from which there is a fantastic view of half of Ireland's lavish greenness, is another Hawthorn tree covered with various wishes and offerings.

The hill is also defensive. I saw a wall and two ramparts on the way up. An American back at Tara was asking if they were defensive ditches and the guide said no, the British Israelites, a curious group from the 19th century were digging for the Ark of the Covenant and they really made a mess of things. While that is the official tour-guide story however, clearly, both Tara and Loughcrew are huge hill forts with tombs on them, and many surrounding defences.

Next door to the Queen Mab/Medb tomb (not the same as the one at Sligo on the other side of the island!) are two smaller tombs. You can simply get into both from the top since people destroyed them looking for treasure. See fig. 1.64. There are lots of nice spirals and other engravings inside. This places them after about 3000 BC, in construction.

We had lunch at a bar. Surprisingly they did not have any local Irish beer except for Guinness. The Irish do not seem very big on brewing. They are more about distilling. The guide said he has been in Dublin all his life but has never been to the Guinness brewery which is the top tourist attraction. He said it is the same in Paris. Parisians have never been to the Eiffel tower and an American chimed in that Washingtonians never go to the Washington Monument.

After that we went to Monasterboice. It is hard to get to, so only one other car was there. There is a very good round tower, plus the tallest Celtic high cross in Ireland as well. In addition Monasterboice also has the best-preserved Celtic high cross in Ireland! The round towers are an enormous mystery. Why did the Irish put so much trouble and effort into making a tower which cost more work than the church which adjoined it? The tower itself is not really suitable for defence and seems more symbolic.

These towers are thousand year old skyscrapers. They are the last gasp of the Irish Golden Age, which coincided with the Dark Age of the rest of Europe. At about six metres wide at the base, and two hundred feet tall, the thing is enormous, and one of the larger round towers. The guide told us something very interesting about them. Traditionally they are supposedly and spuriously meant to have protected people from Vikings. However, the guide said he thinks they were used for travellers, in order to see above the now-extinct tree line! I thought this was similar, but not quite the same as the old idea of ley lines, which were often made up of prominent hills. I think you need to travel to a high location to be presented with a menu of nearby artificial hills or directions. I think the myth of the straightness of the ley line may simply be an illusion caused by two cities, both aligned to the astronomically determined compass points of the Etruscan Discipline (Roman city design), not too far apart.

With both of the cities subsequently ruined, one can align churches and other monuments along a 'straight line' which is really meaningless. Alternatively 'leys' might have been traced along former roads between a military camp and a town, which would have been straight but no longer need to be. This could have caused misconceptions to arise. Ley lines did not need to be straight to be used for navigation, what their inventor, Alfred Watkins, considered them to have been for.

We know that Christian sites were built on pagan sites, so what did the round towers, if anything, *replace*? Although they are not usually placed on hilltops, some of them are. As skyscrapers they are clearly meant to be seen from a distance. If you get close enough to them they all seem to be definitely leaning. Are they visual beacons? The most prominent of the hilltop beacons was a sort of Irish cairn or pyramid, as I would refer to Medb's 'tomb' in Sligo. Since that has altars around it, it was clearly a religious site used for sacrifice. What used to be on Cashel hill, now occupied by a round tower and monastery, before it was built?

After that we went off to the town of Drogheda to look at a church for a saint who was killed by the English. Irish churches are very fragrant and smoky with lots of incense burning. It was amazing, but not very medieval. I am not religious, but gave thanks to God there. After that we walked around the town. I realised there was really nothing in the town, save for the fact it was one of the oldest towns on Earth, due

Figure 1.58: Entering Loughcrew. The entrance is constricted, to possibly resemble birth. Let us go explore a pyramid!

Figure 1.59: There are some strange symbols in here. This stone is near the entrance.

Figure 1.60: We reach the middle. It looks almost like a Tholos tomb from Greece, but by comparison, this version would have been considered to have been put together by amateurs. It is however, well built! Apparently, until they put the grating, and hole up there, to open it up, not a single drop of water reached the chamber.

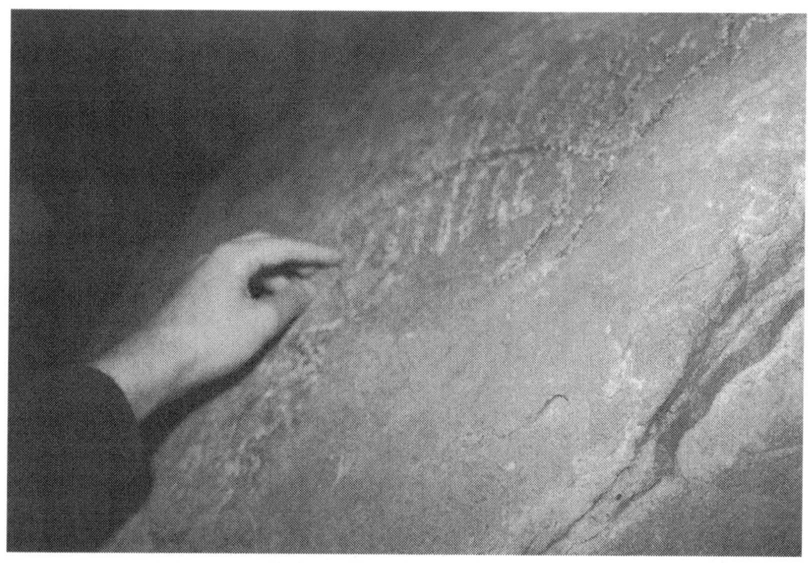

Figure 1.61: Inside the right niche, at the centre of the Loughcrew Cairn, there appears to be a carving of a leaf or tree. Here, possibly, is a representation of the old tree-on-the-hill religion.

Figure 1.62: A wheel or flower symbol from about 3000 BC. It could represent a weather or astronomical cycle.

to its closeness to the tombs. Drogheda is near Monasterboice. You need a bike or car, or a tour bus which is better still, although you cannot stay long enough. I walked to the end of the town and there was a Norman barbican. As in other cities in Europe, they demolished the walls and just kept the barbican! After that it was back to good old Dublin.

McCaffrey and Eaton, in *In Search of Ancient Ireland*, are told local stories even regarding the building of tombs at Loughcrew. Thirty tombs remain, scattered over three hilltops. Only one seems readily accessible. One story, told to them by an eighty-two year old, is that one site, the Hill of the Witches, or *Sliabh na Caillighe*, was built by a fairy queen. She apparently came flying in with an apron full of stones, dropping them on three hills to make the cairns. About to make another, she jumped off one hill and died. She herself was buried under a heap of stones. I heard a very similar story at Antrim. A witch in a round tower was so distressed with the fact it was built, she jumped off and made the cup marks with her elbows in a sacrificial altar nearby.

As to why the tombs have not been destroyed, some locals who have

Figure 1.63: Exiting the tomb.

Figure 1.64: The author searches for and examines spiral carvings amidst the satellite tombs of Loughcrew. The main cairn is in the background.

lived there their whole lives say they are haunted. They are quite firm in this belief and will not waver in it for anybody or any explanation. Mcaffrey and Eaton appear to discuss the altar I have mentioned and photographed, or a related one on another hill, when they quote a local telling them: 'This was the witches' chair. She was mistress of Ireland. She would sit and smoke her pipe and make laws for everyone. If they didn't do what she wanted, she would cast a spell on them and turn them into anything of her choosing.'

The 'anything of her choosing' sounds awfully like any arbitrary punishment of her choosing. Importantly, the authors suggest these tombs were not just tombs, but places of assembly and central to the tribal landscape. The dead looked down on the living and the living looked up to the dead. To convince the reader I am not totally going off the 'deep end' in comparing these structures to pyramids, the authors even suggest a similarity with Egypt. They suggest that like Egypt's pyramids, these were built to honour rulers or priests of great spiritual importance, whose power would protect the people for all time.

The authors suggest this was a relatively sophisticated culture.

They needed astronomers to know the solar calendar to align the pyramids to the sunrises at certain times of the year. They needed masons, engineers for ramps, artists for spirals, musicians, priests, cooks and healers. In other words, they needed something resembling a civilisation.

Golden Objects from the Stone Age

With a few hours to spare in Dublin, one might wander across the river and down to the National Archaeology Museum: admission free. My goodness! Ireland seems to have the best artistic work from Bronze Age Europe, which one can see in *any* museum. Does this mean it was once the most sophisticated civilisation of the Bronze Age? It could simply mean Ireland was harder to invade and people were very superstitious about looting old sites in the past. There appears to be an ongoing 'curse of the pyramids' in Ireland with lots of people staying well clear of 'fairy rings' which are old ring forts and henges.

The museum contains quite a fair amount of gold jewellery from 2000 BC. One simply does not see this in England, or on the continent! Ireland seems to have more 'crown jewels' from 2000 BC than most European countries do, from their own medieval periods. It seems there was an unknown Stone-Age culture which made lots of golden objects, from 2000-1500 BC. On view was also a Spanish Venus statue from the Iron Age.

The truly ancient jewellery has flat sun-wheel earrings with crosses on them. The more recent jewellery from a mere 2500 years ago has huge golden wheels for the ears as well as massive solid-gold necklaces. They are perhaps an imitation of the Egyptian or even 'Bronze Age' style, as there are similarities. There is amazing stuff surviving in Ireland which shows they were perhaps just as civilised back then, as Egypt or Sumer, but just with a smaller population.

There were strange hollow balls of gold, made for some necklace, so the information said. Some were ten centimetres in diameter! I joked that I was dreaming and looking at some strange treasure of Atlantis.

I saw one statue head from 1000 BC, which had three sides with one face on each side. I was thinking this must be related to Janus the two-face god. This is January who looks in one direction at the forthcoming year, and backwards at the previous one. Or was it a type of Hermes Trismegistus? What really surprised me was the realisation that no-one else was making stone statues back then except maybe

Figure 1.65: The Gold Jewellery of the kings and queens of 2000 BC. Owned by the pyramid or post-pyramid/cairn builders.

Sardinia and Egypt. Amazing!

I saw one exhibit from one hoard of the museum's which looked like pineapple grenades. These was described as 'objects' (Thanks!) and from 1000 BC. The workmanship was brilliant. They looked like they were made in the factory! They looked awfully like modern munitions or something with almost but not quite threaded grooves!

We have North American mounds, and more classic pyramids in Central and South America. I have to say that the Grave Creek mound in West Virginia clearly exhibits the influence of the same culture which once lived in Europe. The question is, did the Clovis migrate over from Spain recently enough to have done it? Probably not. I would say it is a related culture that made the similar golden ornaments, on both sides of the Atlantic.

Why does Ireland possess this royal gold jewellery from 2000 BC, yet other countries do not? Even Troy's jewellery is not of this age! Perhaps Ireland has always had a low population, so not enough people were around to dig it up until modern times? It is also on the edge of Europe, so Ireland suffered from fewer culture-changing invasions.

'Taranis' was the name of the god, which the Stone-Age re-enactment

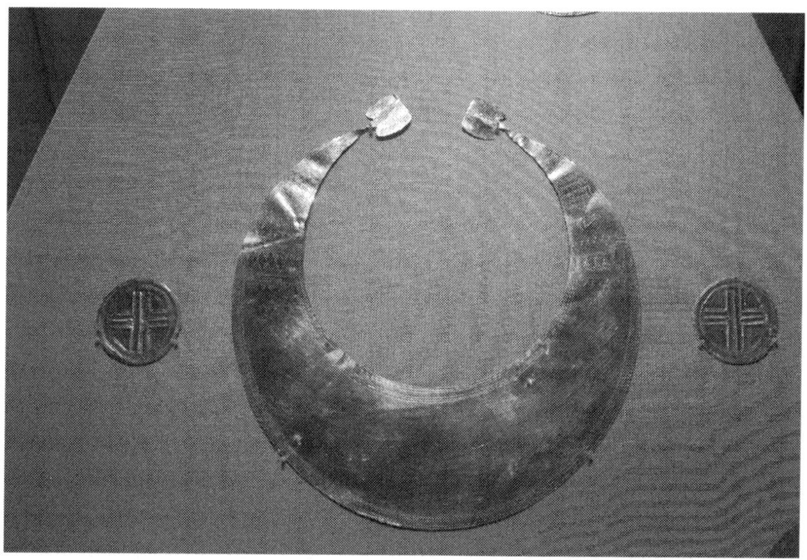

Figure 1.66: More gold jewellery from around 2000 BC. This is from perhaps a millennium or several centuries after the pyramids were built in Ireland.

women had told me about. I read it was a three-headed god on a pillar. I finally found an example in the museum. I thought it was perhaps a Roman 'Hermes Trismegistus', but that might actually be a kind of Greco-Roman equivalent of this. This example was probably an Irish one. The other Celtic names are Teutates and Esus. Whereas Janus' heads look in each direction, at 180 degrees from each other (he looked from the 'world' of one year to another, i.e. January), like a door, these heads are set at 120 degrees. By comparison, the one I call Brahma, in Poland, or Svetovit, as it is conventionally called, has heads at 90 degrees from each other. We shall get to that very soon.

Back at the Long Room at Trinity College, Dublin, they were celebrating the Irish national hero, Brian Boru, who united Ireland. There was his 'harp' (really a late-medieval harp), as well as paintings marking his achievements. The harp is on every coin. Irish history re-starts at the same time most European history does, such as Poland's, around 1000. Funnily enough Both Ireland and Poland also achieved their independence at about the same time in the 20th century. Boru was famous because he defended Ireland from a Viking invasion and won the Battle

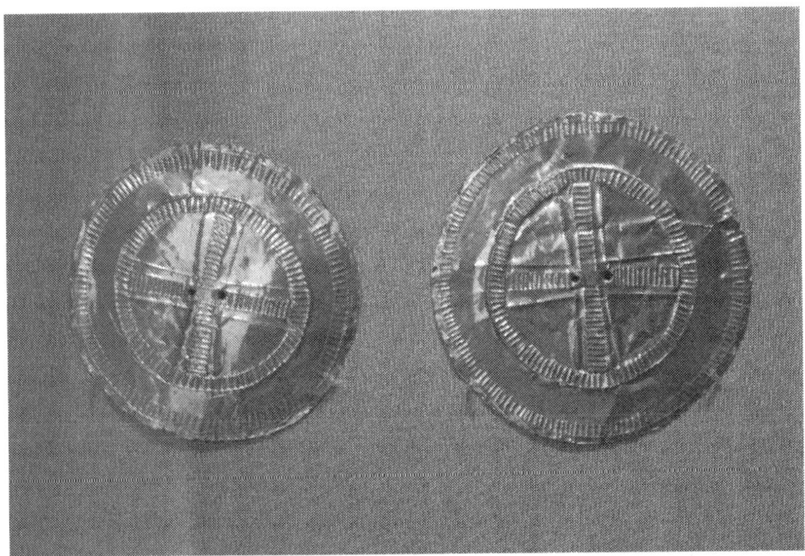

Figure 1.67: Other strange artefacts from this time. Earrings from 2000 BC.

of Clontarf (Dublin), but he was killed in battle, or afterwards in his tent.

Archaeologists do not necessarily actually like the historical or chronicled record, as it is so easy to romanticise it and fill it with errors, whilst their dug-up records, bricks and buildings, are obviously real and constitute solid primary evidence. There was an exhibit in the museum stating that our ideas about Brian Boru heroically defeating the Vikings and preserving a unified Ireland a thousand years ago, are a modern construction. The exhibit stated that actually Ireland had had Vikings living there for centuries anyway. Furthermore, some Irish even fought on the Viking side in that final battle for Dublin! Whilst a lot of this is true, it is also true that the Vikings, or at least proto-Vikings seem to have been pouring across to Ireland for many thousands of years. It is probably the reason why Taranis is so similar to Thor. We can have 'Indo-Germanic' mythology here even if it is not Germany.

In Ireland in the past, and to this day, the Celts are erroneously seen as a race. In fact they are a culture. The so-called 'Celtic' culture is really almost a Germanic one. (Of course it is not really a Germanic culture which links possibly worldwide pyramid ideas, but a much ear-

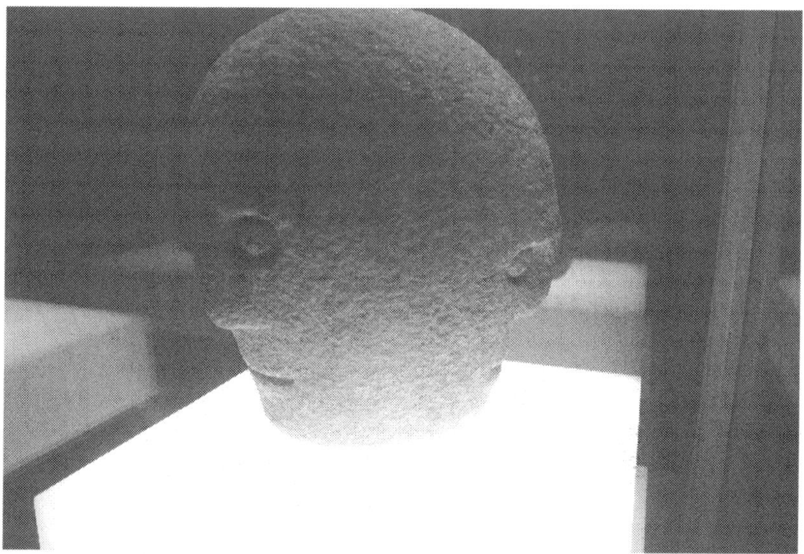

Figure 1.68: Taranis. This is the sky or world god himself, a god similar to Thor, who is a fertility god, but with perhaps more powers. He has three faces, so he was perhaps a kind of European version of Hermes Trismegistus. An eastern, Slavic version would be Triglav, a god with three goat heads, whose constituent deities vary from tribe to tribe. The attribution to Taranis is the author's: one great god with three aspects, like the Roman trinity. The description in the museum merely reads: 'Carved stone head, 1st century AD.'

lier culture known as Indo-Germanic. This began far to the east.) Like the Celtic culture, Indo-Germanic spread out to the periphery before dying in the middle, at its origin point. The pyramids/cairns of Ireland could be partly a relic of this Indo-Germanic or 'Aryan' (Ir-ish) or even Scythian (possibly 'proto-Scottish') culture, which originated on the plains of southern Russia.

The Scots themselves, constituting Northern Ireland and Scotland, are a bit of an anomaly in Western Europe. I noticed their eastern faces and heavy builds, moreso than the regular Irish. This is not really a feature in Western Europe. Their old kings also have eastern names, like 'Alexander,' which are found in places like Macedonia or Russia. The R1a1a haplogroup encompasses all of the east, from Scandinavia and Germany to India. France, England, Spain and Ireland proper are exceptions. Northern Ireland and Scotland, have this haplogroup. The countries exempt from this haplogroup may represent, in part, the Atlantic Megalithic culture.

The Celts, like the Indo-Germanics are not a race but a culture. They represent a wide area in ancient times. The later manifestation of the pyramid builders, at least in the west, was perhaps known as the Celtic culture. I would go to Poland, one of the early homes of the Celtic culture, to find out a great deal more about this extinct people, and their odd beliefs. Poland has more than a few instances of the old World Mountain, of its own. These are huge artificial hills, with a religious purpose, and with no-one found buried inside.

Cracow, Poland's former capital, is a city of pyramids.

Chapter 2

In Poland
(*and towards the Midgard Serpent*)

Torun is the city of Copernicus, and a wonderful place to visit. In the light of yellow lamps at night, with its lit up clock tower, and mysterious river, Torun looks like any excellent European capital. There are well-lit streets with lights in tasteful old gas lamps, like in one of those night-time Edward Munch paintings.

We were in Poland, partly to look for holy hills, the European version of a pyramid. Often, underneath a holy hill, a serpent is said to live, in Indo-European mythology. Unlike in Ireland, these hills in Poland no longer sport a holy tree, though they once did, according to legend. That religion appears to be more extinct in the rest of Europe than it is in Ireland. I usually travel by myself overseas, but for this trip my mother came along so we could meet her family, and she could help out with the language.

We walked down to the silent and wide Vistula river. It was a warm evening. There were lovers sitting around kissing and boats moored up. A mist had descended on the river and it looked incredibly mysterious! We walked the short distance back into town, stopping near the 'leaning tower,' one of the towers on the walls, which is at an incredibly odd angle. At another tower, at the centre of the town, there was a queue, which we joined. We climbed to the top and looked out at the night. The view of the small town on such a chilly and exciting night, was not that much different from that seen in the nineteenth century, and earlier more mysterious times, when Copernicus himself would climb the clock tower to view the stars.

To describe the view, on one side there is a huge void in the lights which is the wide Vistula. There never was a town built on the other side, so wide is the river. There is merely wilderness. Around one side of the tower there was an astronomer with a 4 inch reflector on equatorial mounting. He was explaining where the great bear was and we saw it through the mist. I thought it was the little bear initially when I saw it, but the little bear was actually invisible. It is hard to see in Europe, with all the light pollution.

A girl saw the moon with craters through the scope, which was not so very impressive a sight to one who has seen them before, and said 'oyoyoyoyoy!'

While we shivered, but were warmed by excitement, the astronomer guide explained the constellations.

'Ursa Major. In America they call it, Big Dipperrr, as if it were a spoon... or scoop'. He made a scooping motion and chuckled at this comparison, along with others. 'And for the Egyptians, it was a crocodile!'

We thanked him. They handed us a Polish amateur-astronomy magazine as we left.

I began to wonder. The crocodile was in some respects the river god of the ancient Egyptians. The old Europeans also had a green river god, perhaps similar to St Christopher, a kind of giant with a staff, like Little John, who carried Christ, or even Robin Hood, across the river. There were definitely some interlinking bits of mythology here, parts of a puzzle with all the rest of the pieces missing. One does not really know what the jigsaw is supposed to look like, as no-one lives long enough to assemble it. The pieces are also, not only scattered across time, slowly revealed by archaeological discoveries: they also disintegrate with time! Hunting the mythology of pyramid building is a supreme puzzle.

As for the Bear, Ursa, this was essentially the original 'King Arthur', as Arthur means bear in Welsh/Brythonic, a pre-Saxon language of Britain. These were gods of both Father Sky as they occurred in heaven, and Mother Earth, where they have their real representation. There is a link in bear worship between the Sami, among the oldest indigenous peoples of northern Europe, Japan's Ainu, and Native Americans, with few bear worshippers in between.

Mounds of the old city

Cracow has many mounds. One of the biggest is the natural mound, known as Wawel. Wawel, pronounced 'Vavel', is a castle situated on Wawel Hill, traditionally thought to be driven by a kind of 'dragon energy.' It supposedly once had a dragon living underneath, who used to eat virgins. (Please recall that Loki who lives underground is the 'roarer', or fire god). Either this is a myth about sacrifice or just a fairy tale.

The dragon under the mountain is the serpent which was said by legend (not known at Wawel) to have been imprisoned with Loki, perhaps under the mountain at the centre of the world. Wawel is one of those old world centres. It was also the centre of the Polish state itself, for six centuries. Wawel itself is a huge hill, a mound which has an almost gentle and artificial look to it, though it is totally natural. The effect is due to the outcrop being covered in topsoil.

Wawel is the 'original' early settlement of Cracow (or at least one of them as I was to discover). One of the reasons for coming here is to see the cave of the dragon. As well as being a possible son of Loki, the serpent may also be a possible variety of the Midgard serpent. This is a serpent which lives on our 'two dimensional' plane of existence, *Midgard*, but in legend is perhaps hiding just under the surface, or is lying under the oceans, and who is partly responsible for geological forces, with its movements. Wawel appears to be the Polish answer to Hohensyburg, or Wewelsburg in Germany (We will get to that later on). Like that place, Wawel is a huge natural hill, well fortified from immemorial times, and a capital city as well. It was also possibly the centre of a tree cult which had a widespread influence.

Cracow itself is fascinating. Climb a mound and one can see the other mounds. In this respect it is a lot like Rome or Bath, being built on seven hills. The hills were presumably required as a kind of refuge. Then there is the name Krakus, also known as Krak or Grakch, founder of the city in the last dark ages (the city is much older so there might be earlier legend mixed in). I discovered this is also an Etruscan name, though people resisting an interdisciplinary attitude do not mention it. For instance, there was Tiberius Gracchus, who lived in 163-133 BC. He had been a *populares* and sought, as tribune, to transfer agricultural wealth from the rich to the poor. For this he was murdered. The *Optimate* ('best ones') faction, who were the conservative faction, may have been complicit.

I had often thought that the Romans had had this acquisitive side

which is typical of the east in general and wonder if the name is a
Sarmatian influence from the old Asiatic Europeans: the old Aryans
who once flung their colonies to Japan, Korea and Northern China. The
characteristic Roman noses are certainly a Near-Eastern feature. The
free-spending Anglos I grew up with simply did not mesh with what I
knew about the Roman patricians, from Livy, Plutarch, and Gibbon.
The Romans were *not* an easygoing people like the Aryans in India,
or like people in Ireland. They were quick to offence, honourable and
loyal until the end, and with very eastern ideas of the consequences of
betrayal and the necessity for suicide when that honor had been lost.
Failing in battle for instance, or failing in a conspiracy was a sign of
ineptitude and caused great shame. One was simply not a man if one
could not conquer and overcome.

It occurred to me that here, with these mounds extending great
stretches into the distance, was a prehistoric highway selector. In an
era when men were too poor to build any roads, the only way to find
one's way around the vastly wooded countryside is to select hills. One
climbs one to get to another. One needs to do that to see where one
is, above the tree canopy. One can then see the whole scope of the
countryside. One would then take a bearing and head for another hill,
and it will take the traveller to yet another hill. This could be one
reason why Roman roads are pointed out as going straight up a hill
sometimes, especially in England.

I had been fascinated by the alleged existence of ley lines (perhaps
in 4000 BC, before roads, people built landmarks in alignments to nav-
igate, a tenuous idea) and the fact they supposedly occurred in straight
lines. I wondered if they might be real, though I doubted they were
as perfectly straight as their founder, Alfred Watkins (1855-1935) had
suggested. Several recent Ley Line theorists even say that they are
not straight. Why would they be? Every road needs twists and turns
somewhere. Additionally, one does not really build pagan sites around
a road. Rather it is the other way around. Roads are built between
pagan sites. Still, it seemed reasonable to suggest leys possibly went between pagan sites, later on replaced by churches, and that communities
once lived around these sites.

Watkins was not able to advertise his work in any archaeological
journal. That is fair enough. Ley lines are not archaeology. Archaeology is finding a site and publishing what is found in meticulous detail.
Archaeology is not about speculating what was going on in the mind
of an ancient merchant trying to find his way around the countryside.

That is probably the realm of psychology, ancient literature, geography, anthropology and even mythology.

Just because it is not archaeology does not mean that all the elements in the idea are wrong. It merely means that archaeology as a discipline is not equipped to deal with notions of ancient (or modern) geography. It is a different field. The emphasis that Watkins placed on straight lines of navigation was clearly misguided, as it implied an ancient race of great cartographers and precise measuring equipment, in every single case.

I think the possible hill-navigation system was a kind of primitive visual navigation aid in the days before roads. A primitive society or kingdom with a low population spread over a vast area clearly cannot build any roads. On the other hand it does not take that much extra effort to erect an obviously man-made mound above the treeline to show merchants where the iron-age town is located, not to mention assist in defence, as well as in religion.

Watkins thought that leys were for flint merchants navigating the landscape. Europe once had great flint mines and manufacturies whose tools were carried hundreds of kilometres. In the tree-lined woodscapes of 4000 BC, neither Britain nor Europe was the bucolic countryside of rolling hills that it is today, where one can simply see one's way from ground level. I would hazard the conclusion that one simply must ascend a mound or mountain in order to see how to find the next hill, and the next. A *pilgrim*, was by definition a traveller. He probably went from holy mound to holy mound, as tourists do today. Eventually the journey is done.

Krakus Mound

There are three huge artificial mounds in Cracow. These are the Pilsudski, Kosciuszko, and Krakus. Only the latter is ancient. It is very comparable to the 'Tomb of the Hostages' on the Hill of Tara and associated ruins. That is because this is a religious site on top of a hill fort. Or perhaps it is more comparable to the more recent religious mound on the Navan ring fort.

This is one of the unknown highlights to any trip to Cracow. As Poland's biggest mound, this is Poland's equivalent to Silbury Hill, and it is quite similar-looking too! Silbury Hill is the tallest man-made pyramid in Europe. According to legend King Sil was buried there on a golden horse, but nothing related was found there when they dug.

Figure 2.1: Cracow is truly a landscape for the imagination. This is a early nineteenth-century representation of its mounds. The modern Kosciuszko mound is in the foreground. The ancient mounds of Wanda and Krakus from left to right, are in the background. It is definitely not to scale. The Esterka mound is not visible. Kosciuszko, in the foreground, along with the Pilsudski mound (not shown), are modern mounds. However, they may well be located on once-sacred hills.

It is not a regular barrow. What was found were the deer antlers and bones used to dig it, implying it possibly precedes the metal-working ages.

Similarly King Krak was said to have been buried at Krak's mound near Cracow. But nothing was found. It supposedly dates from the 8th century due to Avar artefacts found there. There is another prehistoric mound, Wanda's mound, which he built for his daughter who killed herself. With this in mind we went to explore. We worked out how to get there and took a tram to Krak's mound.

What do we know about King Krak? He is first mentioned under the name *Grakch* in the chronicle *Chronica seu originale Regum et Principum Poloniae*, written 1190-1208. This was composed in four volumes by Wincenty Kadłubek. According to the mythological history within, King Krak defeated the Roman armies marching up from the south. The implication is he owned a kingdom possibly on the border of the Byzantine or East Roman Empire. He also founded Wawel castle, and as a peasant, defeated the 'dragon' there, becoming king. That sounds a bit like someone who laid siege to the hill. The word Krak also seems to mean something like *oak* or *sacred tree*. That certainly complicates matters.

'Excuse me how do we get to the Krakus Mound?'

'Hmm? Never heard of it!'

Mother kept asking confused pensioners at the tram stops how to get there and no-one really knew where it was. Finally someone knew and gave us the directions.

If one wants to buy tram tickets in Poland, one buys them from a ticket machine on the tram, or alternately a shop next to the train station. The tram stops are like train stations. Each one has a name and they are very far apart and have tiny, natty little kiosks next to them. Alternately, there is an alcohol shop across the road and you might buy your tram tickets there, since there is a tram stop outside. We got the tickets and got off at the right place. I wanted to see exactly what this huge burial mound was like!

It is next to a freeway. There was a huge long billboard of Polish history nearby. We found the mound in a park walking up an improvised access path which went up the Krakus hill fort, which is a kind of large hill. Finally, coming up above the crest, we saw the perfectly shaped hemisphere. It is more than just a burial mound. It is a burial mound on top of a mountain, a plateau, which reminded me of my experiences in Ireland! There was even more to remind me of Ireland. I had read that intensive archaeology carried out in 1934-8, revealed that the Krakus Mound was the focus point of a burial complex. In other words it had satellite tombs around it. I saw remnants of these, but they do not really seem to exist today. In fact a major clue regarding the nature of the site is that there is a modern cemetery behind a fence next door! That reminds me of Giza, which also has a modern cemetery. The conclusion of 20th-century archaeology studies was that the thing was built in the 8th to the 10th centuries. However, like every good pyramid worth its salt, *no burial was ever found* in the main central mound.

This is the start of an indication that this is not one of those mounds built for a normal king. Rather it is a mound built for an extremely exceptional king, or more likely for a god. For starters, to get to it, one must climb onto great big hill fort. The mound is therefore found in a sacred and royal area. Regarding the hill fort itself, we saw lots of levels to it, and bastions and even *old stone ruins*, in many locations which were hiding just beneath the ground! These ruins were like those I saw at Giecz (the original capital of Poland dating from the eight century) and Wawel, and perhaps were over a thousand years old, like the Irish ruins from their golden age.

The ramparts were fortified like some of the Dark-Age forts that I had seen pictures of, the Dark Age castles of Ireland. I was wondering why King Krak had *two* castles in Cracow? Apparently he killed the dragon at Wawel castle thus 'capturing' that, if that is what the garbled mythology is suggesting. This was king *Graccus* or *Krakkus*, or *Gracu*. Maybe it was the land of the 'two towers?' Krak's fortress is on the other side of the river to Wawel, so it was possibly a rival city, to guard the traffic on the Vistula, which is in part, the old amber road. Cracow is certainly a very old town. I heard that, in fact the Austrian Emperor on the other side of the river tried to bankrupt Cracow by building a rival city on the Krakus Mound-side of the river. History may very well repeat. There is also a link between Windsor and Cracow insofar as we have mounds on various sides of the river.

I identified aspects of the fort to mother. There were even ancient rubbish dump holes and food storage pits! Unbelievable, and so close to such a city! Think what a tourist attraction this could be! And no museum here, because Krak is just a legend, so it is *not* history.

Where history begins and myth or legends start however, has always been a problem for historians. History only begins with Prince Mieszko of Poland, deciding to become Christian in 966 to keep the Germans away, since that is recorded in administrative documents. In this situation, we can see that history and Christianity are more or less synonymous, presumably because of the burnings of old books and idols needed to convert everyone, a situation much like that which occurred in the Americas with the burning of pre-Colombian books and artefacts. The past was simply 'a bunch of pagan savages.'

The Polish people that I know often possess extensive libraries, and adore books, yet we shamefully seem to have no book from before 1000. There is a museum at the Giecz hill fort, because it is recorded as Poland's first capital. It has quite similar ruins. Wawel too has much the same ruins on its hill, which are cordoned off with little rope fences. Here, nothing! Perhaps no-one knows what went on here. As for Krak, well, this is all prehistory, mythology! Then there were all those dark-age migrations, including many Viking invasions, which

Figure 2.2: A stone wall and other ruins running under the grass. There was some palace or church up here on the Krakus fort long ago, next to the huge mound.

Figure 2.3: Former ruins of a church or palace lie under the ground adjoining the mound.

continually erased ancient history and knowledge.

Much of Europe has the same problem. In Ireland the problem was much reduced because of their island isolation, so they have a deep ancient history, corrupted by mythology. Even so, they too suffered destructive raids. We have a lot of material from Rome or Greece (there was once about a hundred or thousand times more). This is not because these peoples were more cultured than everyone else. (Everywhere one looks in Europe, and from North Africa to Arabia, there seems to have been an ancient alphabet, dating to the Stone Age) It is because the Romans destroyed everyone else, but saved the Greek material. It was their exotic sunny refuge of temples, islands and Odysseus. Rome conquered Greece, but the Greek culture certainly overwhelmed Rome.

We went higher and higher up the hill fort. Where on Earth was the mound? We reached the top of the hill fort, which is a levelled-out plain, a plateau! And on top of this plain is Krak's mound, a perfectly shaped ovoid thing of turf, maybe even shaped like a cosmic egg. And there it was, a perfect hemisphere, like an Asian stupa, enlarging as we passed the lip of the hill, a glorious testament to geometry. It was a hemisphere of the Earth itself, or the dome of the sky replicated on the ground. It looks quite superb. So you have this religious hill on top of a practical defensive, or larger religious hill, and with quite a view. This is therefore, Poland's answer to the Navan fort, or Knocknarea, which are also huge mounds on top of large hills, but here the mound was much bigger!

The mound was built in an unknown time, but an excavation in the 1930s revealed objects purportedly from the 8th to 10th centuries. Like Navan fort, it contains a solid wooden core. Being built around this 'totem', perhaps the buried centre of a house, its use remains a mystery.

I found stone ruins! No doubt these have been seen by others before. They are buried under the grass and turf but you can just see the outline of a palace, the same size and shape and wall thickness as the stone foundations inside the hillfort at Giecz which dates from 840 A.D. and is the first Polish capital. I saw the same type of ruins at Wawel hill inside the Wawel castle courtyard as well. There they were roped off. And why is there no museum here? Ramparts of turf and crumbled rock are everywhere. Then we climbed the hill for a wonderful view and picnic. It is not as big as Glastonbury Tor, or as dramatic, but still very good to visit. Because of this, we were wondering why there were not more tourists! People just do not know about this stuff. Mother suggested that this is because they have other tourist attractions in Cracow.

So it seems that Krak's mound is a religious site on top of a hill fort. I was thinking to myself, 'wow, this is the real first location of Cracow, not Wawel!' Judging by the ruins, people would have been living on this hill fort, and there would have been houses all over it, everywhere in Celtic times.

Cracow is something of a 'megalithic' city *in progress*. Halted millennia ago in other places, the pyramid religion is 'ongoing' here. Krak's mound was built in 8th century after his death and he was supposedly buried there. His daughter committed suicide for some reason and her mound was built about 20 km away, so the rising Sun of May Day rises over her mound, as viewed from Krak's mound. In other words she is the Green summer goddess! Then King Casimir built a mound for his lover in the 1300s whose remnants were bulldozed by the government in the 1950s, to make way for the football stadium. The next mound was made for General Kosciuszko 200 years ago, just after he died, since he defeated the Russians. That makes sense as Krak is supposed to have defeated the Romans so he got one, perhaps for that. Then one

Figure 2.4: Ascending the Krakus Mound

was made for Pilsudski, since he also defeated someone, the Russians, preserving Poland's independence in the 1920s. In other words, here, people are still raising 'megalithic' or cyclopean landscapes!

Megalithic cities were possibly being built up the same way in Britain. Stonehenge was tampered with and modified for two thousand years. I am not ruling out however, that the two later Cracow mounds are not modified or repaired earlier mounds simply named after new people. Perhaps even the Krak mound and Wanda Mound once went by another name.

Like any good pyramid complex there must be burials around it. In fact a whole modern cemetery is built on one descending face of the hill fort. It is huge! It is also interrupted by a quarry on one side, so the Krakus Mound is effectively on the edge of a cliff. (White limestone, what else?)

This makes it eerily familiar with the mound on Navan Fort. The Navan fort mound was small. This is much larger. Like the Navan fort mound, this Krakus Mound is on top of a hill fort which would have been the seat of kings, and similarly also next to a quarry! In other words, a high cliff-location was selected for the mound complex to be seen from a distance, in both instances. It had to be overlooking people

Figure 2.5: The Krakus Mound. A 6'2" human is on top for scale. Although there is no flowing water associated with the Krakus Mound, the wind blows the grass about in hypnotic ripples. Despite extensive excavation, no burial has ever been found.

in order to either control them, or in a high location for the priests to chat with the gods.

Back in Ireland now; there was a kind and enthusiastic man running the Navan fort museum (I was the only customer of that glorious museum for most of the day). I had told the man about the Krakus Mound and how it was so similar to Navan, to which he remarked: 'yes, lots of Celtic stuff started around there.'

On the mound itself, and at the risk of sounding like a synesthete, it would be prudent to remark upon what a wonderful green and red flowing energy there was felt to be coming out of the mound! Naturally this is not scientifically verifiable, (thank God ancient history is a soft science?) but places are spiritual for a reason. What that reason is, is bound to be very complex, and I will not speculate, but it is possibly driven by a mixture of enthusiasm, awareness and geomagnetics. Some sites are soft and feel dead, or creepy like Stonehenge. (In *Places of Power*, Devereux points out that testing reveals Stonehenge actually absorbs rather than emits energy.) Others seem to be more active, and

Figure 2.6: The top of the Krakus Mound, as like so many, many mounds, is perfectly flat.

living. I am willing to bet that most people would have similar feelings regarding various ancient sites, should a sort of study be undertaken. We were meditating on top, taking it all in. I had the 300mm telescoping lens out and was looking at the other mounds with the camera. Basically these are tiny humps you can barely see on the horizon.

It was a feminine 'mollycoddling' energy coming out of the mound which was very caring and warm. It was some kind of Earth mother! Krak's mound is done very well. People who know of the sixth sense will know exactly what I mean and those who do not will not.

After a rest, we went along to the free museum night. It is something similar to the White Night festivals around the world in various cities, except only for museums. We went to the archaeology museum first, and saw the statue of Svetovid. This was a fascinating creature indeed. I think it must be a version of Brahma. It is certainly the best of the ancient god sculptures we saw.

There were many strange Egyptian artefacts. I also saw Slavic god pictures and inscriptions with something looking like Phoenician characters. Maybe the Vandals left them.

Then we went to the Wawel castle state rooms which were free.

There was a huge queue. Mother was amazed. She had seen Wawel, but had not been in that particular section. On the outside there is a *Smok Wawelski* dragon statue, blazing gas fire out of its mouth, once every minute! Dragons in mountains may come from the ancient idea of dinosaur fossils found in geological columns. It is hard to say one way or the other where they come from.

As for the castle itself, the state rooms are very good. We saw the throne rooms and rooms with heads on ceilings and hundreds of tapestries with Biblical imagery. All very nice! It is all rather similar to Windsor Castle, except the wallpaper in this instance is over two hundred years old, and very dark and imperial-looking with gold on it. It is magnificent inside. British palaces have a fireplace in each room but in Poland they had some kind of hydronic heating with fire. They light the inside of a huge ceramic stove and warm their hands on it, and it heats the whole room! The stove is tiled with white decorated tiles to send the heat into the room, as light substances are insulators of heat and resist it. It is a nice smokeless heating source found in upper middle-class houses in Poland, Germany and elsewhere in the old days.

The museum was interesting. There were bits and pieces on human evolution. It seems humans in the area have been putting flint on the ends of spears for 70,000 years but only started making arrows 21,000 years ago: possibly the stone-age equivalent of the 'iPhone'.

The Wanda Mound

Let us go backward in the mists of time, to the eighth century AD. Naturally it was a time of princes, damsels and arranged marriages. Wanda (pronounced 'Vandah') was a young girl, who would become an early 'Polish' patriot. According to legend, Wanda was being forced to marry a German nobleman from presumably a neighbouring kingdom. Unable to leave her love, she threw herself into the Vistula (pronounced 'Vistwa') river and drowned. Her heartbroken father thence built her a mound, presumably over where she was buried. That is the mythology. There is a possibility, however that a more ancient tradition might have become mixed up with history before the story reaches us. One of the shops in the Cracow square had a postcard with a cartoonish pair of high-heeled legs sticking out of the water. A bird lands on her foot and asks, 'Wanda?'

Since we had had such a good time on the Krakus Mound during the Polish spring, and a nice picnic, it was time to see this other surviving early mound. Historically speaking, Krak, her alleged father (a Polish equivalent of King Arthur, in that we do not know when he lived), may have been of the Germanic 'Vandals' since his 'daughter's' name is 'Wanda'. That is, he may have been the father of the 'Wandals', rather than a person of that name. The mound, built by her father, in her honour, or the honour of the tribe, perhaps as a harvest hill, for fertility reasons, is fourteen metres tall. Like the Krakus Mound, there is a mystery as to when it was built. This will probably be resolved in the next few decades.

What do we know about Wanda? It seems there was a royal dynasty during the Dark Ages, or even far earlier, on this part of the Vistula. The name of the civilisation was '*Vistulanie*' in Polish, or the region of the Vistulans, to us. This is an extinct civilisation of the late Dark Ages. We know the names of no dukes who ruled it. It perhaps corresponds to the borders of what became known as 'Little Poland', an area of expansion from 'Great Poland' in the north-west. That mighty river, the Vistula, itself seems to be based upon a Germanic word, 'west'. It implies a German-speaking people lived to the east of it. This civilisation, under Krak, existed before regular 'Great Poland' had begun to emerge to the north west in the Poznan region, which perhaps back then had been ruled by legendary 'Lech'.

Poles, Czechs and Russians are told the story of Lech, Czech and Rus. All three brothers arrived in Poland. Czech said 'this place isn't right, I'm going further south!' 'As for me, I shall go east,' Rus said. 'I will stay here,' said Lech. To this day, Poland is referred to by the Turks as 'Lechistan'. I presume this was the name used by the Byzantines. 'Poland' is a bit of a mystery, but it may come from the east, brought over by invaders from the steppe. Since they were heading in a south-east direction, however, it would appear the three brothers were actually Scandinavians, proto-Vikings, rather than Slavs.

We finally got there. It is almost at the end of the tram line from Cracow and in industrial, yet beautiful countryside and forest. The small forested area is basically an extension to an old railyard. From the ground however it looks like one is at the start of a pleasant forest, despite the ever-present throbbing of industry. Perhaps that adds to the dynamic hypnotic flavour of the place.

A sign pointed the way off the main road, down a path. There was a bit of litter here and there, and a sign saying *Wanda Kopiec* (Mound). When I saw it, a thought occurred to me. 'Well it is certainly not of the same quality and cannot be made by the same people as the Krakus

Figure 2.7: Wanda Mound. This is where Wanda was supposedly buried after she killed herself. Or, is the mound actually related to virgin sacrifice, symbolic or real? It would have been easy for two different stories, retold down the generations, to become blurred.

Mound! It simply can't be!' The hill is not that good at all. It is rather uneven and dull and unspectacular in any way. The Krakus Mound is shaped like the bottom or wider rounded part of of an egg, almost a hemisphere! This, however, is hardly shaped at all, except from a distance. It is like some reluctant grumbling workers were forced at sword-point to come here on their day off and throw up some sort of mound. The construction was evidently completed when one of the workers dropped his shovel and said 'I've had enough!' Alternately, the mound may have been damaged by treasure hunters.

We climbed the mound and had a picnic. It is tastefully surrounded by trees, in its own little grove. From the top you can barely see the other mounds in the distance, around Cracow. To see the Krakus Mound from the top, one actually needs to look between the chimneys of the old socialist power station, *Nowa Huta*, which resembles a nuclear reactor!

Later on we detected what seemed to be 'energies'. It is pure scientific forces, that is electrics and strange gasses which seem invariably

Figure 2.8: The other side of the Wanda Mound. The top is graced
with a 19th-century statue dedicated to Wanda.

Figure 2.9: A further perspective of the Wanda Mound

to me mainly responsible for ghosting phenomena, though this is the subject for another book. As such, an industrial site, as this was, with its coils and strong magnetic fields, would be perfect for hauntings. The Wanda Mound is next to a semi-derelict train station behind a small wood, as well as other factories and electrics. There is a continuous electrical hum in the background. My brain received imagery of a girl playing, and later we walked in the nearby grove. To me, it was clearly haunted because I saw the fabled leprechaun-like movement which one does not see, if one looks twice, or directly. It is the sort of thing that surprises one, but the brain quickly dismisses it as having occurred, if it does not recur.

A thought arose 'out of the blue'. 'If I touch that tree, lean on it, I will feel utterly wonderful.'

I did so and it had an extraordinary effect which surpassed my wildest expectations. Dick Smith, a famous Australian entrepreneur once said that he finds great relief in hugging trees and feels wonderful from it. I have tried with the best of intentions in the past to replicate this experiment but it has always ended in dismal failure. I felt nothing.

This was different, for its effect was wonderment. Not only did I feel a definite energy (call it placebo if you want). There was huge placebo 'energy' surging out of this tree when I put my hand on it. Maybe this is why they chose this remote location for the mound? Mother and I realised we were starting to get hypnotised and would not want to leave! I find this is a common effect possibly relating to volcanism and magnetic fields. I have noticed similar effects in rocky gold-producing (volcanic) areas and near certain large lakes. We had to get out of there before we became hypnotised by love of this sacred site, and stuck in there forever like the characters in the epic Australian film *Picnic at Hanging Rock*!

From the top I detected a possible prehistoric navigation line. I cannot really use the word 'ley line' because that theory goes too far, or has been taken too far by various theorists into areas which archaeologists and others do not go, more into the metaphysical realm of pilot waves and some spiritual version of Gaia theory. There are a lot of 'black and white' assumptions out there which unfortunately either rule it in or rule it out. The archaeologists ruled it out from the beginning, as one does not often proceed in archaeology with an expansive theory, thence collecting evidence. One merely excavates his ruin for many years and slowly writes it up. This means that the people who talk about it are generally only those who are prepared to go too far in other areas.

(Paul Devereux, as well as talk on 'trackways' are exceptions. There
is perhaps merit in various other notions, but one cannot read everything!) The people who do not talk about it, simply ignore what is
there in the landscape. Any traveller knows that landmarks are clearly
used for navigation *now*, so why not in the past when we did not even
have the luxury of paper, or the map, or the phone? Where there are
people, there would hopefully be landmarks left behind by them.

I think of a 'ley line' not in the mystical sense (only insofar as it
relates to sacred sites), but rather in a practical sense, for navigation,
and it does *not* have to be straight. This was for the utility, as stated
by its discoverer, Alfred Watkins, of the communication system of a
civilisation, before the onset of roads. As mentioned, strangers, or
traders, perhaps used mounds sticking up above trees to see distant
aspects of the landscape form, or to see the landscape full stop, *even if
the mounds were not intended for that purpose.*

As also mentioned, due to widespread forests, it hit me that one
could only see the hill forts on which villages once resided, from *the
tops of other hill forts.* It is only huge-scale agriculture which has de-
pleted Europe of thick primal forest, allowing proper roads and making
mounds utterly unnecessary as navigational beacons (along with their
other uses), because one can actually now see past the trees. The
mound is aligned with Wawel in the distance and another fortress on
a mountain far behind that! It could just be a coincidence. The alignment is off by about half a degree or one degree. On an unrelated
tangent, the 360-degree measure could have been a truly ancient and
widespread system for the Indo-Europeans, and others, not just due to
the Sumerians who invented it. The reason is astronomy and the moon.
It is an interesting coincidence that the full moon takes up about half
a degree in the sky. The fact the spheres all travel in apparent circles,
gives rise to the possibility of the invention of the 360-degree system.
It does not necessarily come from days of the year, but the study of
the moon. On a flat Earth, the moon traverses 360 units, or twice 180
degrees from one side to the other; a system thence possibly retained
for a spherical Earth. In addition, the very old idea that there are
360 days in the year may very well come from the idea of a geocentric
system, with the Sun taking one year or 360 degrees to move around
it!

It is known that the mounds seem to have been placed according
to astronomical alignments. Their positions are therefore not necessarily random. Wanda Mound may have been used as a watchtower, or

placed in its more remote region in order to make sure there are some astronomical coincidences with the other mounds. It is known that the Wanda Mound combines with the Krakus Mound and two natural hills (Wawel hill included) to form an astronomical calendar. As stated earlier, stand on the Krakus Mound, and the Sun rises over the Wanda Mound on May day.

One may stand on Sikornik hill, where the enormous but modern Kosciuszko mound is. On November the first, Celtic New Year (half way between the Autumn equinox and Winter solstice), one will see the Sun rise over the Krakus Mound. The Sun will also rise over Wawel hill (where there may have been another mound) on the equinoxes. Of course this means that the enormous Kosciuszko mound, erected in the 19th century, built on Sikornik hill, may have been transformed out of an existing pagan sacred place, or harvest hill, or even a town or village. People would have played 'musical chairs' with the mounds of Cracow several times a year.

We were wondering how to buy a ticket to get back into the center, as the shops near the tram stop did not have one. The driver said there was a ticket machine on the tram. I started putting coins in. Well, I put in the coins and then I put in more coins than it was counting! I was fumbling with the smaller coins since we did not have enough change and it got impatient and spat them all out the bottom and reset, except it seemed to have permanently eaten 1zl. Using the 'change' from the machine I then tried to buy a 20 minute ticket instead of a 40 minute ticket which I could no longer afford.

'It's eating your money without registering it,' mum said.

'I'm out of coins,' I said.

'It seems to have eaten a lot more than you put in.'

'I've put in at least twice what it says!'

After pressing refund, I once again only held in my hand about half the coins that I actually put in the damn thing.

'Pressing refund doesn't seem to help.'

'I would have had enough money if it hadn't eaten it!'

'It does not seem to notice small coins.'

The pattern continued. We got off after three stops and went to a nearby shop to get 20 minute tickets. We went everywhere but everyone seemed to have run out, only selling 40 minute tickets. 'That's all I have, what can I do?' 'That's OK, it's still better than the smartcards in Melbourne!'

Back in the centre we saw Wawel castle. Walking past it, it seems

Figure 2.10: Wawel castle, Cracow. It is not only the medieval capital of Poland, but the hill itself is home to an earlier Iron-Age capital and religious site well before that. There are legends of lots of strange caves underneath, leading towards the town.

to be either Italian Renaissance or Ancient Rome or a medieval hunting Henry-the-eighth-style lodge! Or is that bit of it like a Georgian apartment block. It is utterly ridiculous! They took the best of everything and smacked it together into a phantasmagoric creation. The castle it reminded me of the most, would be Windsor castle, also a mix of styles.

Underneath the castle is the dragons' cave. This is part natural, part artificial, being enlarged in modern times. We watched countless hordes rushing through it, almost wasting their opportunity, after spending so much valuable time descending a long winding staircase in order to get to it. We stayed for hours. It was an amazing, incredible experience, with the dripping stalactites, to be in the home of Loki, and the serpent who drips acid on him.

In J.R.R. Tolkien's universe, which is basically Germanic mythology, there is a dragon under the mountain guarding lots of gold. The gold may as well be the treasure of the dead kings who have been entombed in the mound. The dragon perhaps represents geological forces, earthquake energy. As for gold, stupa mounds in Thailand are made of gold, but I know of little further relation.

A trip to the museum

One day, we went to a gallery in the basement of an almost abandoned building run by trendy art-intellectual people dressed in black. It was next to a cafe, but in a basement area. The contents of the gallery were some modern art performance which we watched on a cinema screen. It did not capture my imagination. Nor did the other modern art we saw around town. Mother said 'they do any old thing, and then they think it is a Picasso'!

Then we went under the market square. There had been huge excavations and building works in 2006 and we now saw the results. There is now a brilliant museum down there! One looks down into the museum from the square through a glass pyramid (in emulation of Paris). While down there, one can see a cross-section of a thousand years of the city! One can see that they started building with bricks in about the 1400s, but before that it is all stonework from quarries. About five metres below the surface is the medieval market square. One can actually see the cobble-stone roads, the shops, the remnants of the guildhalls. The museum is brilliantly done.

One can walk past all the shops from the days of Christopher Columbus, just recesses in the stone walls. I touched the oldest wall, from about the thirteenth century, or time of Robin hood. I felt like it was asking me more questions, like it simply wanted to feel 'my' energy, or find out about me, so it did not really give me anything in the way of ideas that my mind could rationalise into imagery. It is a spiritual place.

Documentaries in the museum were explaining how Cracow was once part of the Hanseatic league. Back then, before the age of nationalism, they did not care about 'nation' but about lineage and ability. Countries were more about 'property' and title than 'nation' and a sense of belonging to a certain culture. At the time, Cracow had a salt monopoly, and a kilo of salt was allegedly worth half a kilo of gold!

The documentaries were brilliant. These included one about the founding of Cracow. Before the existence of the 'Kingdom of Poland', in the west, there was another kingdom which may have been Polish-speaking. In the south-east, there was 'Vistula land.' The ruler of this place was the 'King of the Vistula'. It is presumed that the capital of this nation was Cracow, because archaeologists discovered the biggest ever Polish Dark-Ages treasure here. They found something similar to ancient 'talents' and still debate if they were currency or not. These were basically a large number of axe heads. Talents everywhere in ancient times were also in the shape of axe heads so it may well have been ancient currency, but I suppose such currency was pre-coin and went back to the Bronze Age. In other words we are dealing with a very ancient past, despite the destruction of history up till one thousand years ago.

The west part of Poland was simply under too much threat from the German states, as well as from the Czechs. This could be why Poland shifted their capital here after Gniezno was destroyed. Cracow, however, was an ancient nation on a huge trade route which went in various directions. It seems to have had strong historical precedent as a capital in ancient tradition. It was well defended. The current capital, Warsaw ('Varshava') was simply chosen as there was a fire at Wawel in the time of King Sigismund, so he packed up and headed to the comparative countryside of Moravia, an impoverished region which looks like a flat desert. Warsaw is kind of in a horrible location, reflecting Versailles, and yet it became a capital. I would call it the 'Polish Versailles' for this reason alone. It was not really on a trade route, except of course for the Vistula, and its position may have reflected the growing importance of trade with Russia.

So it appears that in ancient times, there was one version of Poland around Gniezno/Poznan (Great Poland) in the west. There was another nation centred on Cracow. Maybe that is why they call the Cracow area 'Small Poland', even if it later on had the capital within it. They both joined up and became 'Poland' around the year 966.

The museum under the market square had a number of televisions on display in various booths. One showed a brilliant documentary about paganism, with pagans dancing around that famous statue of a funny statue called 'Svetovid,' a central-European totem pole. Apparently, the Slavs burned their dead, to turn it all into a substance, gas and smoke, so it could float up to heaven. It looked like some druid ceremony in the museum video: a bunch of grim reapers chanting in front of a large fire with an animal-headed shaman in command.

Most fascinatingly of all, and something which at the time made the cog-wheels start to turn, and later became, for me, a key to the link between pyramids and mountain worship, was a fact which was next revealed in the video. The documentary stated that on top of the Krakus Mound, where they perhaps put King Krak's ashes, (no body or burial was ever found) they *planted an oak tree*. Fair enough! They plant an oak. So what? It is still done today. According to legend, this was a mighty oak tree. Furthermore, *it was cut down by Christians in the year 1000*. Centuries later a cross was seen on top of the hill and drawn in by artists.

That is highly suspicious! Why did Christians not want this tree on top of the hill? Its roots were found in the 1930s, while excavating. Was this an Yggdrasil, a world tree, upon which Odin hung? Back then, they determined the mound was of about the eighth century. Of course that was before even the primitive attempts at carbon dating. Now we have other techniques, but they do not appear to have yet been applied to the mystery of the Krakus Mound. I would later find out that this tree-on-the-hill religion goes back to perhaps the beginnings of agriculture, or earlier. It is one of the easiest ways to build a shrine, which is also a landmark.

The documentary also stated that the early design of the layout of Cracow and its churches, bizarrely, seems to be a carbon copy of the layout of Aachen in Germany. This was Charlemagne's capital in the 800s. To me, that would suggest that Cracow was attempting to model itself in the imperial fashion within a century or so of Charlemagne. Either they wanted to rival Achen (kind of like a Rome of the East—before Moscow achieved that designation), or it was a religious layout also followed elsewhere, and we do not know about it yet. They possibly thought they were living in a kind of 'Rome' with their holy hills.

The Romans themselves used a religious layout for their cities. The whole grid was aligned to the compass points and then divided into quadrants. Temples to certain gods had to be located in certain locations. This science was called the Etruscan Discipline. One can therefore look at a plan of the centre of any old Roman town in England or elsewhere and note down where the churches currently are. Based on the quadrant system, one can simply look at the positions and see which ones would have been originally pagan temples dedicated to specific gods, simply based upon the quadrant layout.

A fascinating thing we learned about Medieval Cracow was the Magdeburg law. This means that if you stole, they would cut your hair off, hit you with sticks, or even cut your fingers or ears off. If you stole too much they would have executed you! This Magdeburg law of about the 1250s changed the layout of Cracow and made it merchant-oriented. A huge *rynek* (market square) in the middle was made for big business, the cloth traders. A small rynek was set up where they moved the bread sellers over to. (small business) There was a small documentary film about this too, in the museum, with a merchant telling a bread woman with a basket, to 'get out of here, go to the small rynek!'

Cracow

After an interlude, it was time for a second visit to Cracow.

It is one of those trains you would expect in an Agatha Christie film, with seating compartments and corridors. Between Wroclaw and Cracow, it takes five and a half hours through the coal-mining countryside of industrial southern Poland. All the industry is in the south, and so is the population. I noticed that in the forests in the south, (Little Poland) the trees are more spindly and tightly packed, like Australian forests. In the north (Great Poland and Pomerania) they are more majestic, and the population is far more sparse.

The hostel we went to, 'Goodbye Lenin,' had a very good free breakfast, the best from any hostel I have experienced anywhere. We could take as much as we wanted! I had four cucumber sandwiches. You add what you want, mayonnaise, cheese spread, mustard, ham, etc. It is a typical central-north-European breakfast, not really known in the west.

We walked out of the massive town square, which is the biggest medieval market square in Europe, towards Wawel hill. The first thing we did was walk around this enormous hill. It reminds me of the Windsor Castle hill. Cracow was Poland's capital for centuries so everything is up here! One walks around inside the courtyards of the castle, and then one looks over the edge, and it is fifty metres down! The castle is built upon an ancient massive hill fort. Looking at an old map of Wawel, one can actually see that the Wawel castle walls, were pretty much the walls of the old town. The Iron Age was a shaky time and one often sees settlements on hilltops.

Perhaps since the original town was inside the castle, there is actually a clock tower in there as well. In addition, one can see foundations of the original stone fortress from a thousand years ago, which are much smaller. They looked just like the ruins inside the hill fort at Giecz, which I also visited, which was Poland's capital in 840 AD. Most Polish people seem to be unaware of this, but there is a nice museum there. I would see very similar ruins upon the Krakus Mound. We saw the 'chicken legs' tower which was possibly the laboratory of the great alchemist Michael Sendivogius and I suppose John Dee might have lived there as well when he came over for a visit. Dee was Queen Elizabeth's chief alchemist but spent several years in Poland and central Europe.

Next to Wawel, a nice grass area outside the city walls, on the royal promenade, is a place where the tourist busses pull up, between the castle and old town. Partly concealed under a tree, stands a full-size replica of Poland's best-known pagan monument. This is Svetovid. The original is nearby, in the Cracow Archaeology Museum.

I recalled that I once saw this in a book on Polish archaeology. It is the four headed God. But who *is* he? Underneath the four heads looking out towards the compass points, are various carvings on each side. On different levels (of the world?) there are various figures or faces with blank and timeless expressions holding up the floor. One of the four faces on top is holding a ring between his fingers, fig. 2.18. This links him to Germanic mythology. Norse *Völundr*, known as *Wayland* in England, sculpted various rings. He was wrongly imprisoned on an island for the false charge of having stolen one, and wreaked havoc in his vengeance. He is a Loki-like figure, an artificer who could also fly. I suppose that Christians of the day, a thousand years ago, might have thought him a demon, and hence threw the idol into a swamp. This action ironically preserved it.

We sat around Svetovid for a while and I wrote about it in my diary. I think it is clearly a picture of the universe. There are gods of the lower levels holding up the floor for humans above to walk upon. Phoenicians had similar pillar gods whom they called *Baal* or Lord, and I wonder if there is not a connection. Poland is truly ancient, for there actually does seem to be a *Phoenician* city near Cracow, at least according to that town's website. The Phoenicians were a great trading empire from Lebanon. The height of their civilisation was achieved several centuries after the Trojan war. The name of this town is *Olkucz*, perhaps based upon 'El Khuds', 'to chisel', as it is a silver and lead town. Unfortunately, we did not really have time to follow up that lead.

Next to the four-faced god, there was a melted candle and flowers, plucked from the tree, and laid beside the pillar, reverently. There are some still around with a healthy respect for the old religion! Mother picked some more flowers to lay next to it, which was a nice gesture. We really liked this statue. Later I touched the walls of Wawel. I was searching for the New Age energy source known as the Wawel Chakra.

What is this Wawel Chakra? It is essentially the Polish version of 'pyramid energy'. In the 1930s, it seems two mysterious Indians went journeying around the world and claimed that the Eighth Chakra of the World was at Wawel. I wanted to know if there was anything to this legend at all. Every tourist here does, who is aware of the phenomenon. Fascinatingly enough, the chakra is at the highest point of the hill. 'That is a bit odd,' I thought. The Irish of 3000-2000 BC seem to have been very determined that their tombs and sacrificial pyramids should be at the very highest points of various hills as well.

There has been an awful lot of research into the Wawel chakra, unfortunately not available in English. The geomanticist Leszek Matela has measured the chakra radiation as being 120,000 points on the Bovis-Simenoton-Matela scale. The human body supposedly only clocks in at 6500 units. The Polish book is called *Tajemnice Czakramu Wawelskiego i sekrety Krakowa* (Secrets of the Wawel Chakra and Mysteries of Cracow). Polish theosophy also has a long tradition of speculation, including that the radiative powers were discovered by no less than Apollonius of Tyana, sometimes associated with Jesus, during one of his great journeys. He supposedly placed a talisman there, to realise the full potential of the energies. It is a great pity that certain Polish books about the old lore of Wawel, as well as the alignments between various mounds of Cracow, (which reflect ideas of mound solar/lunar alignments at Glastonbury) are not available in the English language. Their contents would surprise many geomantic investigators in England, as these lands of Poland are among the original Celtic lands. National boundaries as we understand them did not really exist in the Stone, through to Iron Ages. They were more like cultural boundaries.

One cannot actually access the chakra, which I found was in a sort of enclosure which is off limits. This is at the highest point of the hill. An area which one may actually touch is a wall, behind which the chakra exists. This area is roped off, presumably to prevent new agers from congregating and eroding the wall in question, which is rather dirty-looking from people having pressed themselves up against it. One can easily sit nearby however. The result: I could not feel a thing, in light of anything transcendental or life-changing! In fact the opposite. It seems to drain energy! However I felt a huge underground 'movement', which is to say an almost disconcerting feeling.

There is a legendary dragon said to be living under the castle as well. Its name is *Smok Wawelsky*. Ideas of dragons in mountains could be related to mythological ideas inspired by geological forces. Later, walking around the castle, I felt the energy chakra. It was swirling considerably like a fan or vortex. Waves were hitting my body and they felt like joy or love, but it was choppy and irregular like a slow

Figure 2.11: The author sitting near the Wawel Chakra at night time, close to the highest point of Wawel hill.

fan. I think there is something geomagnetic under the castle.

Personal feelings are subjective and not really quantifiable. For a scientific spin on such earth mysteries, I would recommend the books of Paul Devereux, in particular *Earthlights* as well as *Places of Power*, which provide scientific rather than mystical explanations for these 'shamanic' phenomena. I felt something as well on the train into Cracow. It was an upwelling of energy, possibly some geomagnetic disturbance, from under the ground, which felt quite pleasant. There is a great view from Wawel and there may be considerable geomagnetic phenomena at work. This could be related to the substructure of rocks beneath the ground. The north of Poland is a vast empty plain. The south is where the population live. It is more hilly and industrial and polluted. Cracow is built on salt mines. It is far from impossible that different subsurface crystalline consistencies induce subtle variations in our perceptions, affecting moods and behaviour as we go from one area to another. A fascinating work on a similar subject is *Circles of Silence*, by Don Robins, which had me enthralled and spellbound as a child.

I mention this New-Age claptrap because our ancestors were neither materialists nor atheists, at least not all of them. As today, they could be rather religious. Priests were the educated class. It would be fascinating to investigate in great detail the psychological effects, in terms of personal feeling, that sacred sites induce, and plot these according to a population sample. Since the ideas regarding this are so hard to measure electronically (noble attempts have been made), we can simply use our own minds, as we visit these sites, to perceive the possible original effect, first hand.

I have my own idea regarding the Wawel Chakra. As it is at the highest point of the hill, it relates very much to the positioning of an Yggdrasil, the centre of the universe. The two Indians who visited Wawel hill long ago, perhaps recognised it as an old sacred hill or harvest hill, in their old Aryan traditions, but since it was such an enormous hill of unprecedented size, claimed it was one of the eight great chakra centres of the world.

They may have been talking about something similar to the old Yggdrasil legend because that legend speaks of the world tree on a mountain at the centre of the world. There can only be a certain number of these 'centres' or chakras. Obviously these world trees were found all over the place, but some were more esteemed than others. If there was a tree (we know there was one on the nearby Krakus Mound), then this was seen by devotees of the mountain/pyramid religion as the closest place to heaven, and the point of focus of earth energies reaching heaven. I found it fascinating that the idea itself is so buried within the human psyche that so many think the idea of the chakra is true, and even override, in their own minds, the presence of the castle itself, treating the hill as a religious centre.

The Polish language has changed since mother's Poland of the 1970s. They now say *dobra*, which used to mean nice woman, but which is now used to mean 'good'. The word for good generally used to be *dobrze*. *Dobra* seems a rather useless word to use, now fashionable. Also they say *Dien Dobry* at any time of day. Someone wished us *Dien Dobry* at night time, to which mum said 'it's night and they said good day! It's changed!'

Later, we decided to go to Kazimierz. This was a Jewish town south of Wawel, which is to the south of Cracow. Well, it looked like a ghetto. This was the town which was cleared of Jews in the *Schindler's List* movie, as well as in real life. The Old Jewish cemetery has long uncut grass, presumably because all the owners and their friends were murdered. This town was established by Casimir the Great in the fourteenth century, as he had wanted to develop Poland's economy. There are certain links between Christianity in the Middle Ages and Islam today, as Christians were not really allowed to lend money. Jews controlled part of the banking trade, so they were a stimulus to the economy. There was in fact once a mound around here. It may have been that Kazimierz was built on the former site of an older city. It was as if Casimir was thinking: 'well there are ancient traces here... let us redevelop the darn thing.' Lacking finances he perhaps invited the Jews to help do so.

The guide of a walking tour said that if one went down to Kazimierz in the 80s at night one would walk out missing a wallet, since the socialist government settled criminals there. Then it was settled by students and starving artists, such that many pubs sprang up. Now it is the pub capital of Cracow. The guide told us also that there are rumours of secret tunnels underground, leading between Wawel and Cracow. That might of course tie in with old Germanic legends about the Norns living under the tree of Yggdrasil, and various other nefarious underworld creatures. I have read books about secret tunnels in Tibet, but never anything regarding tunnels in Poland. The exotic east fascinates the west, but Poland or even Germany are clearly not east enough, despite there being a large ancient 'Buddhist' stupa, or mound in town. Is that so? Yes, it seems to be (the Krakus Mound), but the Buddhist usage needs clarification which I will provide later, as I apply it to a Stone-Age religion once shared with Asia. Cracow is definitely very ancient, however and there is something funny going on underground, with rumours of tunnels in different directions. In addition to being based upon memories of the Midgard serpent, it could also be based on Cracow's history of salt mining.

The pubs of Kazimierz are very trendy. One pub is called 'Narnia'. Inside, one must go through a nice wardrobe to get to the smoking room.

We come now to Esterka's mound. This *was* located three kilometres north west of Wawel hill in the grounds of Lobzow palace. King Casimir (Kazimierz) the Great was ruler of Poland from 1333-70. Betrayed by him, his lover Ester committed suicide. He threw up a mound in her honour. That is what the myth says.

Looking at the location, we see it is near water. Esterka's mound was on the Rudawa river. Since it was within the grounds of a royal palace, it was perhaps being used as part of a pleasure garden as the mound in the Antrim castle gardens. It was excavated by King Poniatowski in the late 1700s. He was obviously an inquisitive chap, as well as being Poland's last independent monarch. He had expected to find the fabled grave of Casimirez' lost lover. Guess what, it was empty! The mound could be Bronze or Iron age like all the others. The story about a lost love and a mound sounds a lot like King Krak and Wanda as well. I would suggest it was an *earlier* 'Casimir' or even 'great' king which the story relates to, some forgotten Arthurian-type figure of deep antiquity.

Esterka was not a very well documented mound. A strange local legend claims that it 'melted', which might imply that it suffered an implosion similar to that suffered by the Hatfield barrow in England, which was destroyed by proto-archaeologists in their quest for a burial in the early 1800s. (Nothing was found) The possible incomplete nature of the Esterka mound could be one reason town planners simply decided to level it.

Presently we see an old drawing of the palace and gardens surrounding the lost mound. This mound, was supposedly dedicated to Esterka or Esther who, betrayed by Casimir, committed suicide. After initial damage, it was further allegedly partly destroyed in the 1940s to make way for a barracks. It was conclusively obliterated in the 50s to make way for a stadium. Who knows, it might have been of the Bronze Age! Here it is shown in an old picture, as having been part of the palace

Figure 2.12: The lost cone pyramid, with a flat top, allegedly built by Casimir for his lost love, can be seen to the lower left.

pleasure gardens. Like seemingly all European pyramids, it was flat topped.

Esterka is associated with Casimir the Great perhaps because of his policy of benevolence and welcoming towards the Jews, expelled from elsewhere in Europe. Otherwise, mound building does not seem to have been part of the medieval tradition, so the story is curious. It would have been too sad to visit the sports stadium where the mound once stood, so we wandered into the old Jewish Quarter, Kazimierz, on a guided tour. We even went to Schindler's factory and the tour guide pointed out some inaccuracies with the famous movie. He said that Oscar Schindler only looked after the Jews after he saw the war was lost. Then he needed to keep his witnesses alive so he resettled them in the countryside in what he assured the authorities was a factory. Furthermore, one had to pay out heaps to get onto his list. All the other Jews were taken out of Kazimierz and put in a ghetto. This ghetto was formerly a town established by the Austrian Emperor. The Austrian empire was on the other side of the river in those days, and he wanted to destroy Cracow's economy by building a city on the other side called Underhill, but it did not take off. It reminded me of the fact that ancient Cracow also seems to have been similarly divided, a twin city, dominated by fortress-mounds on each side of the river, like Buda-Pest. Now it is one city.

On the Schindler factory there is a Jewish motto engraved: 'Saving one life, you save the whole world'. If only the ancient pyramid builders had had this philosophy. I do not think they did. They generally took a life, or two, to build a pyramid to perhaps save the world! The guide further added that the movie was inaccurate in other respects because Oscar says: 'Why did I keep the car, I could have saved five lives?' He needed the car to escape the Russians.

The great Polish tradition of tolerance continued amidst the turmoil of the Second World War. The guide said that people could not really help the Jews, as they and their families and even their neighbours as well, would have been executed instantly for it. The guide took us to a sewer through which one Jew managed to escape. He showed a wall the Nazis built when they established the ghetto. It had rounded crenels on top and he said that this was either to reassure the Jews or scare the hell out of them, because it looked much like their tombstones. The energy in these places felt like: 'OK, we're being rushed and have to do stuff,' but that might have simply been due to the tour. At the time the Jews were informed that they were being put on trains towards

Ukraine, where there were health resorts waiting for them.

A Mystery at Golub-Dobrzyń

One day we were away from Cracow, near Torun. We went off to the bus station and took a coach to Golub-Dobrzyń, a 49 km trip from that city, according to the tickets which were only 8.4zl each. About three bucks. Off we went across the countryside! Polish people are all very nice, kind and gentlemanly. Poles also seem to say 'sorry' a lot (*'pzesprasham'*) just like the English and Irish. This could be because they had a possible influx of Ynglings, related to the English, in ancient times. Mother asked the driver if they give a pensioner discount and he kindly said that she does not look like a pensioner, but also that they do not give them anyway.

We arrived at the Golub-Dobrzyń bus terminal. It lay on one side of a long road which must have once been related to a major road into the town. As we started walking towards the centre, we saw it was along the line of site of the enormous Zamek (castle) in the distance. This is the 'Golub Castle.' The castle has the appearance of being enormous, as it is on a great partly-artificial mound, on top of a hill. The mound however cannot be seen unless one is also on top of the hill, so the castle is smaller than it needs to be, in order to create this tricky little effect! See fig. 2.13. When the Teutonic knights built this, they deliberately placed it on top of that mound on top of the hill. They placed it right on the very edge of this mound, towards the town, so the lip of the much larger hill underneath would not obscure the castle's view. I found this most curious and wondered where I had seen it before. (Hint, pyramids on plateaus) Everyone in town clearly needed to know where the true power lay!

We walked along this industrial road, a considerable journey in heavy pollution, till we reached the town centre. There seems to have been a dust and pollution storm or sandstorm going on. To understand what I am talking about, I need to explain about the geological situation which seems to be going on in Poland, and the east in general. If one reads reports from German soldiers in Russia during WW2, they inevitably talk about the fact that in summer there was this fine dust everywhere which got into everything, along with the mosquitoes. By autumn however, this dust turned to mud and slush, which literally bogged down the blitzkrieg. This 'steppe' dust seems to be present in Poland as well as Russia, and some parts of Germany.

The etymology of Poland or 'Pl-land' is 'Plane Land'. Polish are therefore, 'people of the plains.' Since 'Aryan', one of the major European tribes, seems to mean something like 'farmer', this seems different to 'plain' which would refer to the Asiatic steppe, upon which farming does not really work. Sarmatian nomads, possibly a mixture of Indo-European and Asiatic, may have come over and conquered the land in ancient times. It would have happened many times, obliterating past histories. No-one really knows a thing about the mythologies or old mounds of migration corridors.

Dust from the Asiatic steppe was now covering and filling the gutters on the street! Everywhere they are packed with sand. The footpaths sometimes are half buried in sand wherever you go! In Poznan, people are on the street shovelling the sand out of the gutters and sweeping it up. Its gets worse in the country towns where they do not even sweep it up. The effect is this. If people stopped using the infrastructure, in a few weeks of dust season, I think all the streets would vanish underground, to be slowly replaced by green fields. Is this why there is no Stonehenge in Poland? Poland's oldest surviving settlement, Biskupin, an Iron-Age town of logs and longhouses, build on top of a river, was discovered as logs sticking out of a river, rather than somewhere out in an open field.

Poland is trying to turn the cities back into a plain! It is trying to bury them every day. Perhaps this is one reason why people built pyramids, especially in Egypt. They realised that with the decline of civilisation, the dust would take over, covering anything which was not too massive to be destroyed, to be removed from the memory of man. On this particular day, there was something of a sandstorm going on, although obviously not as bad as in Arabia. It is like the plot of a Ballard novel, *The Wind From Nowhere*, where a wind accelerates around the globe sweeping everything away, every structure on Earth, before subsiding. It is kind of a 'civilisation reset' concept which many New Age authors think was a fear in the ancient consciousness. I have my doubts. The most pressing need was food, marriage, children, not old tales from the Dreamtime.

Dust is not the only thing sweeping into Poland from the Steppe. Throughout its history, nomads would arrive, conquering the land and imposing their will. Many Polish cities would have been built on mounds. A traditional fighting style of Asiatic invaders is to attack with arrows from horseback, and then flee, before attacking again and again, to wear out an opponent. It would have been easier to simply

Figure 2.13: The castle at Golub-Dobrzyń looms impressively over the town, dominating it utterly from a great distance. From here, we see it on a natural hill. In this photo one cannot see the strange mound it rests upon. It may have been representative of the mound-on-the-plateau/hill religion, that one sees time and again. Mounds needed to be close to heaven, and god. When I saw this, I was reminded of religion.

close the gates and live up on a safe hill and hunker down for a while. Such a hill exists here at Golub-Dobrzyń.

We had a great view of the town! A motorcycle gang arrived consisting of the usual weekend middle-class motorcyclists. They wore chains and a uniform which said 'Nine Six' in English. One had a Honda gull wing. They asked me to take pictures of them in front of the castle so I said 'OK ras dwa trzy'. (one, two three). I got a 'Thenk you' in English because people in Poland are more desperate to try out their English than they are willing to let you try out your Polish. The vantage-point from where we took photos was even higher than the base of the castle. This revealed at once that something was terribly amiss! The artificial mound, if that is what it was, is much bigger than the castle! It would have posed a terrible security hazard should an enemy army manage to get siege equipment up there. This did not sit right with me at all.

Figure 2.14: The mound on top of the hill is no longer used for pagan pilgrimage, assuming it once was. Perhaps sacrifices once took place on top, to be fittingly replaced by the torture instruments of the Teutonic Knights. The mound is mainly natural and was not simply built for purposes of the castle, or even a prior wooden fort. It is much larger than the castle, once posing a security hazard for the castle itself should an enemy army find its way up there. Of note is that it is on the extreme edge of its plateau. There is a good deal more levelled-out hill behind it, which frankly puzzled me. Such an outcrop as this was incorporated into the Great Pyramid at Giza. The highest point of a hill is most sacred.

We found the tourist information in town.

'Oh come in!'

'You're from Australia. Come into my office then, and sit down!'

He handed us multiple copies of every brochure he had, but could not tell us that much about the history of the castle. With his prodigious billowing grey moustache and blonde hair, he looked like a refined Germanic scholar, or serious school teacher.

He gave us lots of pamphlets about this highly polluted town with cement dust, sand and other carboniferous gasses blowing around everywhere. I wondered how he could stand it. Did he not know that other cities were not like this? I had come from a backwater place, no major cities or industry around, to here, the heart of Europe, the heart of the smoggy industrial dragon.

'We've come for the castle,' I said.

'Please come back later, after the castle and you can sit here and relax!'

'If I wasn't here they would demolish this house, which is 200 years old,' he added.

Climbing up to the town's castle, we saw it was rather a poor place. In fact the entire town seemed rather despondent. Most of the town's people had an eastern look about them, Ukrainians brought in to replace Germans, when Poland's borders shifted after the war. Poor children were kicking a ball around, instead of going to the nearby school, which appeared to be run by nuns. A woman, sitting on a doorstep, stared at us, and everything going by, hardly moving.

This is a very strange town, an ancient merger of Golub and Dobrzyń, a later settlement on the other side of the river. The old German coat of arms was a Teutonic knight with a sword symbolising a cross (now a white lady with a sword). She stands between two trees, denuded of branches, each crowned by a dove. The coat of arms seemed like a merger of an older religion with the new Christian religion.

The castle is a strange thing, a square red brick fortress on a huge mound which looks artificial but is too big for that. The whole hill is a kind of plateau. It is much bigger than the castle. This would have once been the home of the settlement itself, especially in the crisis-ridden Iron Age. It occurred to me that such outcrops, natural or unnatural are literally all over the place. Often they have existing castles on top. I still could not fathom why the castle had to be edged right against its particular mound. The Teutonic knights who built the castle were crusaders in the East. They were hard workers, busily converting the Poles and other Slavs to Roman Catholicism, seeking to save their own souls and win a place close to Christ. Since Poland was already Catholic, that was also an excuse for a land grab. They may have been disgusted at an existing structure looming on the edge of the precipice, overlooking the town, or it may simply have been an older castle. Still, it is religious sites which often go on the mountain or mound. The motte, used for a castle is not much different to the mound or harvest hill.

To summarise, I was absolutely astounded at why the top of the hill was so levelled out, well behind the castle. I have simply not seen this at other medieval castles. It reminded me of the levelling out which had been done at Giza, prior to the building of the Great Pyramid. It is as if the castle is a much newer component of a very ancient sacred area, which once contained another, fascinating and unknown structure.

Presently, we have an old plan of the complex. On top, is the castle. On the bottom, is a strange rectangular field, perfectly levelled, currently used for mock joustings. It is on the same level as the castle. It may have once been a palisaded accompanying village. To my surprise, both the castle and field had a pyramid-like alignment to the compass points, but not quite. I have never seen the like before. There was a possible interest in magnetic north here. Since there is an upper 'corner' missing, caused by the slope of the hill, the field seems to have been a compromise between an alignment towards the north, and a compass or stellar alignment. From the field to the castle, the alignment is towards the rising Sun. The religious value of the outcrop may not have been unnoticed by ancient peoples seeking to create a world mound here.

While leaving, walking down the hill, the woman who was sitting on the doorstep was still there, looking without looking, her place unchanged, staring with neutral intent. It is an ambivalence borne of finding small pleasures in seeing small changes, in an unchanging world.

Svetovid

Did average folk in ancient times have a 'Pantheon' of the gods? The word is associated with elaborate Greek plays and supernatural intrigue. A pantheon of the gods seems to be the idealistic fancy of someone with the time and resources to devote to working out familial inter-relationships. Perhaps they had only two or three gods, which they really took an interest in. Everything else were minor spirits, in-

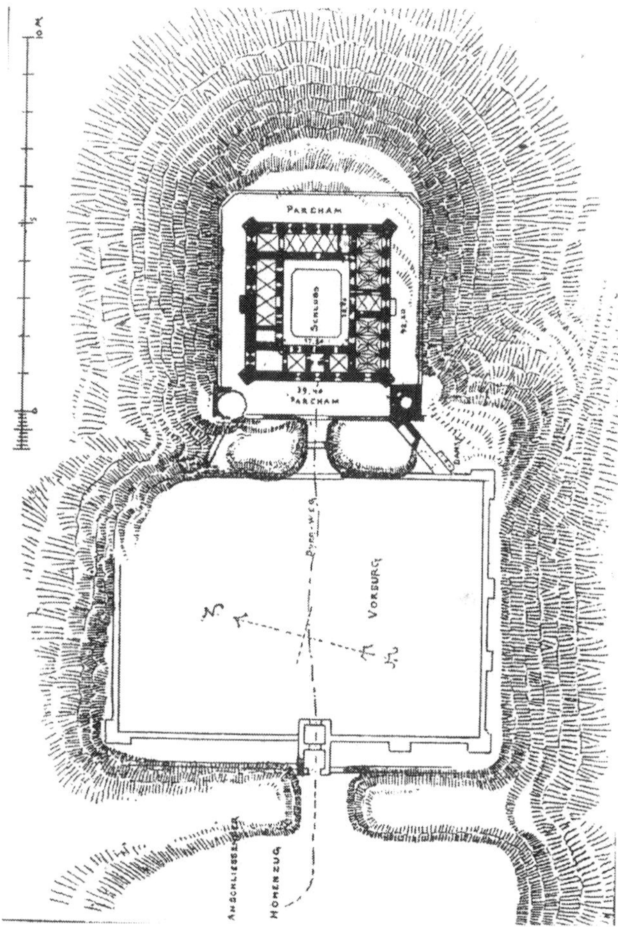

Figure 2.15: Later on I was to examine what I had seen at the castle. This plan, from 1890, shows the plan of the outcrop. The leveled field is shown on the bottom half of the map, with compass superimposed.

cluding household gods. Perhaps the idea of a pantheon is an idealised version of reality in which every person is aware of who he himself should worship, personally, to activate a specific wish.

Consider this hypothetical and fictional scenario: humans have *always* been monotheistic. Furthermore, tribes migrate and mix. Each tribe maintains a monotheism. There is always one great god, with a female, or male counterpart to balance the universe out and stop it collapsing in on itself. The rest are mere spirits. During the mixing and trade phase, gods are exchanged, as well as humans. Tribes must sometimes unite to survive. What are these early monotheistic gods? They would have been figures such as Uranus, the whole world, encapsulating space and time dimensions. They would be the Earth Mother, which nourishes everything. They would also be Father Sky, a strange mysterious dome-like firmament up there, a true heaven of fluffy clouds, strangeness, and wonder. Are these not early monotheisms? We cannot claim Akhenaten as the first monotheist, as some do. He merely got a lot of 20th-century attention due to the fantastic discoveries made in Egypt.

There are different Greek goddesses. There are Athena, Artemis, Demeter and Hera. They all have rather similar or inter-related roles. The Earth Mother 'Demeter' is not exactly a 'mistress of beasts' like Artemis. They may all have been Earth mothers, but from different tribes, acquiring various symbolic roles as civilisation advanced away from the hunter age.

In these old days, the most sacred ritual was perhaps the union of Mother Earth and Father Sky. This is the fertilisation myth common in several world religions.

The gods of any pantheon were not necessarily such discreet entities as is made out. Rather they were each an assortment of various ideas, grouped into different human-like characters, but based upon natural disasters, Ice-Age, geological, ecological and metamorphosis phenomena.

In Ireland, I saw a strange three headed stone thing which looked good enough like a universal Father-Sky type figure. I later found out that that was Taranis that the Stone-Age living history people were talking about. The Slavs (or mixture of Sarmatian/Scythian/Tocharians/Aryans?) who inhabited central Asia, have been a kind of Indo-European 'cultural bridge' through which ideas of the pyramid and its religion spread to Japan, and south-east Asia. They had their own many-headed gods.

I was happy to encounter 'Svetovid' in a museum in Cracow. There is a replica outside Wawel.

We presently see an image of Svetovid. It is perhaps one of Poland's greatest pagan national treasures. The following is my interpretation of this image. I am unsure if some of the following is discussed in the literature, probably mainly in Polish, but I imagine it would be. This aspect of Svetovid is clearly an early 'Lord of the Ring'. J.R.R. Tolkien clearly based his novels on Germanic mythology. In one Norse tale, *Völundr*, a Loki-like character and also a hunter, is leading a reasonably happy existence, but he laments at lost love.

He has made himself some cunningly made rings, one of which is for his lover. Nidud, lord of Niars has heard about this and when Völundr is alone Nidud's riders rob him and take one lover's ring. Völundr imagines his lover has come back for it, and is happy. Perhaps wanting more loot, Völundr is later hauled before Nidud and accused of stealing his gold. Völundr is hamstrung and kept prisoner, forced to make rings with his forge for his overlord on a small prison island offshore. He never sleeps but plots revenge, banging away with his forge. No-one however, should mess with a trickster, for it all goes quite *Titus Andronicus* in the end.

One day Nidud's sons sneak onto the island, demanding to see Völundr's treasures. Völundr kills them and then begins making jewellery out of their eyeballs and skulls as a gift for their parents. The fact he can make a jewel out of an eyeball suggests these characters are geological underworld spirits. The daughter of Nidud, Bodvild, who had received the stolen ring from her father is intrigued by a gift of jewelled teeth from him, and visits the island, upon which Völundr violates her. Declaring his revenge complete, he turns into a bird and flees. Loki also could turn into a bird. Since Loki/Lucifer is a kind of 'devil' (not some shocking supreme figure like the Abrahamic one), one might even envisage the old idea of bats as vampire spirits being a related tale. There is a lot of overlap in the old religions between gods. Different bards in different areas had various ideas, as well as names, regarding who did what. In the image above, we perhaps have someone similar to Völundr, the overcomer god, as well as fire god, holding out his ring and awaiting his lost love.

Svetovid seems to be merely a Slav name for a much older God which finds its Aryan name in India as Brahma. The Aryans may have been an earlier tribe than the Slavs, who emerged out of the Indo-European mixing pot stretching from the Black Sea to central Asia.

Figure 2.16: Svetovid. Is he related to Brahma? This is a replica standing outside Wawel. It is interesting to note that lots of gods are placed together, incorporated into one image. The underworld and above world held a collection of deities, representing unified forces which might blow in different directions depending upon the laws of fate.

Figure 2.17: The original Zbruch Idol of supposedly 'Svetovid', found in the Ukraine. This is merely one of the possible names of the four-face god. He was active from India (as Brahma) to Egypt (I found a reference in one text to an obscure storm god with four faces). The top level is Asgard, home of gods. Midgard is in the middle, where man resides. *Hel* is below, showing a huge giant, possibly related to Loki, holding up the world. His mouth is open as he groans. Its location, when found in the Ukraine, shows part of former reach and veneration of Indo-Germanic mythology.

Figure 2.18: Another museum original of Svetovid.

Figure 2.19: In Germanic mythology, Völundr was hamstrung and marooned on a small island off the shore, where he worked his metal craft. Völundr is a Loki-like figure, a lord of the underworld and forge. He is a crafter. A St Michael's mount is typically an island with a hill, found slightly offshore. It is obviously associated with St Michael who vanquished the devil, in a war in heaven, flinging him to Earth. This one is in Cornwall. Völundr presumably resided here for eternity, working away in his geological forge, making jewels beneath the Earth.

They are an early tribe, as their name survives on the peripheries, Iran, Ire-land, and as Ary-ans in India. The expansion of Slavs over the former cultural bridge of the Aryans, wiped out some of the latter's tracks, but an older god was incorporated into a newer religion.

As mentioned, Svetovid has characteristics of Brahma (a.k.a. Ouranos), a world god of the Aryans, said to have been a four faced God. Like Brahma, this statue certainly seems to represent 'world' as it contains representations of levels of heaven and Earth held up on the shoulders of various 'people' on each side. However, these are not people, but really layers of the world, the three primordial levels. Other gods? Or are they buried within the Earth? Are these the images of Prometheus or the Loki, or Odin/Buddha, or the Gods in the pyramids or mounds?

This 'Zbruch Idol' deity was dug out of a swamp in what is now Ukraine. Svetovid was said to have two faces looking backward, two forward. It looks to the four corners of heaven, and is therefore an all-seeing god like Osiris. Like Brahma, this statue certainly seems to represent 'world' as it contains representations of levels of heaven and Earth, held up on the shoulders of various people on each side. It also has representations of a horse and sword, possibly making it a war god. These were the symbols of power in Central Asia. The horse and sword show that this was the god which was spread over large distances. It is only by means of the horse that these ancient tribes lived their particular lifestyles.

There are also similarities with Shiva worship in that it is a stone lingam. Svetovid is a penis-shaped God. (Presumably the universe seen as a huge penis?) He is the father, or presumably father sky. There is more going up there in the sky than we can see on Earth around us. We can see further by looking up, than we can by looking down. Up is the direction of the universe. He is perhaps the 'world god' which the World Mound and World Tree are designed for, but we can't be sure.

The giant holding up the world on the idol, and therefore supporting the whole thing, would seem to be a representation of Loki, also a giant, and imprisoned in the underworld, for killing off the bleeding man, (related to the wounded king of Arthurian lore) Balder. (A mixture of Baal and Thor?)

The fact there is an underground god (of earthquakes?), or 'Loki' on the idol, is all rather interesting.

There are other mounds/pyramids in Poland! I recommend the hard to find *The Archaeology of Early Medieval Poland* by Andrzej Buko, which is a brilliant book. There are another eight more mounds scat-

Figure 2.20: Another figure of Svetovid. The figure on the bottom with the huge mask-like face holding up a level of the world, might well be the giant Loki, the trickster who is imprisoned in the underworld for his crimes. He is a sort of pagan Lucifer, and may in fact be much the same god. In some respects, he is a kind of Hephaestus, a crafty god and a metalworker. He is a god of fire as well as of foolishness. Above the giant Loki are smaller creatures who may be humans. Above this is the largest god, the four faced 'world god', Brahma, or Svetovid. Thus is represented Germanic 'Hel' below, humans in the middle ('Middle Earth'), and the sky god or more likely the world god on top.

tered over Little Poland (South East Poland) alone. One, at Husynne, is called the 'moon grave'. I recall that Sumerian Ziggurats were built for the lunar goddess. We also have a 'pyramid of the moon' over in central America. It is fascinating stuff!

It is time for a conclusion. We have touched on the subject of buried spirits of gods inside pyramids. The dragon at Wawel might be a more modern interpretation of a strange ancient force, a type of mountain god. The dragon may also be a memory of the Midgard Serpent god, which once guarded an Yggdrasil-like tree. The Midgard serpent is also a kind of child of Loki, who is the king under the mountain. This is all rather compelling stuff.

Since Germanic mythology kept popping up as a basis for the extinct mound or mountain or sky religion, it seemed prudent to go 'back to where it all began.'

Chapter 3

To Germany
(*and to the 'Mountain of the Gods'*)

'Dortmund is not really the part of Germany I would go for a holiday. We have better cities', said the very serious German hiker in my dorm.

'I'm not going because of the scenery. I'm going because I have friends there.'

Incidentally I was to do day trips to both Cologne and Aachen, regardless, two of the more famous tourist destinations. Bless Europe for having everything so close together!

Flying in from Ireland, once past the Netherlands, the plane puts its flaps on and starts circling in order to reduce speed for landing. One can see the smokestacks of the most industrialised part of Europe popping up high above the clouds, obscuring everything below.

I was in Germany, the industrial zone called the Ruhrgebiet, or Ruhr area. This is really a nine-fold megacity of around ten million people. It is Germany's most densely populated area. It also seems to be the most polluted as well, as well as an area with one of the longest traditions of multiculturalism in Germany (lots of migrants from the east/Poland in the 19th century). What I really wanted to see was some kind of cyberpunk futurism. Aside from the power station belching dust and smoke, and the asthma which I never really knew I had before, the industry seemed more a product of the past than of the future. Things were cleaning up. The power station would be shut down. The old coal mine with its Malakow Turm, or primitive elevator tower, was now a technical college.

German people are shorter than London people, but often of heavier build, or the big ones anyway, as there are no typical Germans. I did notice bigger, wider heads, bigger muscles, solid builds. I would not call them fat. They are born that way. The children are like that too. They are huge. In Australia I am considered tall, but in North-central Europe I am quite normal sized.

I really preferred German supermarkets to Irish ones. Irish supermarkets actually have more meat than the German ones, but it is more a international food being sold. German supermarkets, meanwhile, are full of millions of types of herring. Personally, I love herring. In Germany they have salty Dutch herring, herring in gelatine, and all sorts. In Ireland, I never saw any tinned or other herring until I visited a larger supermarket. They had herring in tomato sauce, and that's it.

Germany was really amazing. The buses and trains have electronic Germanic monotone voices, really accentuating the longer vowels as Germans do. On the trains, in addition to an announcement of the next stop, one is also told to alight on either the right or the left. (In some countries one can open doors on both sides of the train, so people walk out onto the tracks). In the Ruhrgebiet one can travel on the S-Bahn, a regular city train but with huge carriages, or the U-Bahn, a light rail.

The best thing about the Ruhrgebiet is of course, the cheap beer. Prices are the lowest in Germany. Beer goes in what Australians would call a milk crate. With a box full of beer, I had fifty euro out waiting to pay, and was asked if I had something smaller. To my shock, the cash register only required 11.50 euro. Plus you get some back if you return the bottles! It seems the cheap places for beer in Europe, are Germany, and Eastern Europe.

I was told, 'foreigners only know a few things of Germany... Oktoberfest, Neuschwanstein (New Swanston) Castle, that's it!' It was a good insight and it is true. Thankfully this makes it easy for the tourist to see things in Germany without too many (or any) tourists getting in the way! On the weekend, a good English castle is swamped with tourists from all over the world. There are Japanese, Chinese, and representatives from Western Europe as well as a few Russians. A good German castle meanwhile only has German tourists, and not that many. Generally only younger Germans speak English. I noticed about that about half of Germans can speak *some* level of English, but usually not that much. Older museum staff were often unable to speak to me in English, with my German being pretty vacuous. As soon as I gave an 'Ich kein Deutsch' ('I can't German!'), the conversation was basically over. Lots of Germans tended to agree that Germany was not a tourist country. Nevertheless, for a true traveller, this makes it even better than a tourist country, as there is more to 'discover', rather than simply visit, in a controlled environment.

What I really wanted to find was the old Germany. I wanted to see something from the 80s. A nice dystopian reality. People choking on pollution, toxic barrels of nuclear waste on the sides of the street with fires burning in them and people struggling to keep warm, and fights pouring out of a disco with punks dressed in all shiny black leather making a fast getaway on futuristic modified Harleys. I also wanted to see a bit of Inspector Rex and people tearing down concrete walls or painting re-unification graffiti in East Berlin to the tune of *Wind of Change* by The Scorpions.

'You've been watching too many movies', is what I was told. I was also told that a town which closely resembled my technocratic 1984-ish vision of a blend of industry and factory, was possibly Hagen. I also really wanted to stop in a place called Wuppertal, which has a century old *Schwebebahn*, a type of 'steampunk' skytrain. Maybe next time. I saw some glorious green-painted huge steelworks and chemical industries but the high-tech was only really present in the cars.

What I found in the Ruhrgebiet was a nation somewhat poorer than most of what I had seen in England. Bars are everywhere but most seem to have just one customer. One old saying in Germany is 'if you don't have a career, open a bar.' Unlike in Australia, the 1940s and 50s hairstyle was in vogue. Long on the top and short on the sides, but I also heard it was more the Turks who were engaged in this trend. It is in their blood. In 588 AD the riots in Byzantium were held between two opposing groups of chariot team fans with different hairstyles. Back then, it was perhaps a little bit like a Dr Seuss book where the characters with the buttered side up go to war with those with the buttered side down.

The hair style, when I visited was more Elvis than punk. In Poland, in 2013, the style is very much returning to the punk of the 70s whereas in Germany it is the Elvis of the 50s, with a bit of a swirl on top in some cases, like Tintin, or the first rock and rollers.

Frankly, lots of housewives in the Ruhrgebiet dress like men. Short hair, glasses, not much to be attracted too as they take out an ecigarette to puff away and then quickly replace it, anxious to get somewhere with minimum disturbance. I was told that that Adolf Hitler had disapproved of makeup and the minimalist fashion remained in some cases. A German woman was a proper woman, an equal to man on many levels, and to be taken seriously, so they do not doll themselves up. The ones who do, are often said to be 'from the east.'

Germans are mechanical, seemingly unfeeling. That is the stereotype, but this is an absolute illusion. One behavioural trait typical of Germanics is the gaze. They can momentarily gaze intently and suspiciously before looking away to gaze anew at another object or person, with the same cold reptile expression. Germans can be a shy and suspicious people, but a wonderful people as well.

They do not talk a lot in train stations. The Germans are too preoccupied for small talk between strangers. I felt they had too much poetic prose, engineering designs, and architectural fantasies going on in their superlative skulls to bother around with that. One thing they will never be is 'standoffish' when one actually begs their assistance. They will always be ready to help (with directions at least) and assist if the need truly arises. Their shyness gives the illusion that they would be unwilling to do so, but it is simply that, an illusion.

I met my colleague, local antiquary Sylvia Joiko, who has developed a fascinating theory on what she tells me is the original location of that great tree that is a variety of the Tree of Eden, also known as *Yggdrasil* or the World Tree, a proto-Indo-Germanic/European myth which is perhaps over ten thousand years old. This is something which had fascinated me, as it relates to the pyramid religion. The tree seemed to have been a fundamental part of it, in the old lore.

I like to think of the Germanic mythological world as three dinner plates on top of each other, with a pole stuck through the middle of each one. Think of Svetovid. The three dinner plates are now hanging in space. The one in the middle, *Midgard* (perhaps Tolkien's 'Middle Earth'), is the world of man.

In Germanic myth, Odin is hung from the world tree, suffering, but in doing so he acquires knowledge. The tree where this happens is Yggdrasil, located in the middle of both original, and ongoing creation.

We spent a few days just walking around an amazing local forest, exploring for ruins. Basically it is a huge beach-tree forest, looking in the summertime, like a true 'greenwood'. Sylvia was telling me there is prehistoric stuff around, ruins, a possible barrow, as well as a possible cursus. I also 'discovered' a prehistoric hill fort (they are on every hill really!). There were the ramparts, the dykes. There was even a driveway which would have led to the former palisade castle. Based on ground markings, it seemed that it would once have had a triple-gate entrance. I doubt that any archaeologist has investigated. It is hard to see it all due to so many trees.

A sacred place: Wewelsburg

We hired a car and drove out to various places. One day we drove out to the beautiful village of Soest with its traditional German houses of black oak beams and white plaster which are centuries old. Somehow spared from the bombings of the war, this village has endured, preserving its medieval city walls.

It is great fun to drive on the German autobahns with their gentle curves. The *Smart Fortwo* was rather cheap to rent: a third of the price of a Mercedes sedan. The car was maxing out at 144 km/h. (Top speed is 145). On the third day of driving on the autobahns, on a slight downward gradient, the car finally found another gear I did not know was there, and so I was able to take the one liter engined car to its top speed of 164km/h. With these new engine technologies, who needs a Ferrari? A decent standard sedan of today can confidently beat the former supercars of the 80s, which once adorned every male teenager's bedroom wall. The old cars still look better, though.

Altena Castle is just plain creepy and ghoulish. It loomed like Dracula's castle over the river valley in the dying Sun and felt just as gothic, creepy and ridiculous. The town is nice, but quiet. People do not go to Germany for tourism, not even Germans.

Wewelsburg, by contrast is a Cinderella-like castle built upon what would once have been a sacred hill, back in the 1600s. One of the star attractions is the magnificent view it affords over the rolling hills and fields of cows. Wewelsburg was supposed to be a place for the Nazi religion, a point of focus. This was to have been the spiritual heart of the National Socialist empire, but the project was Himmler's, with Hitler really concentrating on the post-war future of Berlin, which would have been renamed to *Germania*. With its supreme views, Wewelsburg castle makes a good home for the old mountain religion. Perhaps once, in ancient times there was a temple up here, but nothing of that order has been found.

Closed until 2009, the Himmler room is now open for tourists. There was a sign pointing upstairs to 'Hall of the Supreme SS leaders.' It was a pleasant surprise to be allowed inside since we were not aware of the recent opening. There was no-one else in the room. One can stand on the 'Black Sun' (which is actually green), which was where Himmler's version of the 'knights of the round table' was to be. This presumably was supposed to be the omphalos, or centre of creation by which ideas of dark and divine inspiration would leach into the heads of assembled dignitaries, in Himmler's mind anyway. The Black Sun is two swastikas superimposed such that the resulting 'Sun' has eight arms, and looks like a sunwheel. There are views from the windows, in that fairy-tale room, of the fairy-tale countryside.

With all its dark history, one would have expected the castle and hill to give off a creepy feel of oppressed slaves. In fact it has a wonderful feel, organic, like growth. It would seem that personal and sensory aspects of the pyramid or even earlier mountain religion come from being high up, and closer to God, having a godlike view, as well as the spiritualism and different feeling one gets from being up on the mountain itself.

Nigel Pennick points out in *The Ancient Science of Geomancy*, that the physical act of climbing a hill, such as Glastonbury Tor, causes physiological and psychological changes in the state of the climber. More oxygen is brought to the brain, producing euphoria comparable perhaps to meditative breathing exercises. Furthermore, he suggests that the view from the top with its change in scale, coupled with more awareness brought on by exercise, produces fresh insights. Mountain climbers know of this. How much greater would this effect be if the hill is also a sacred one!

Underneath the strange upper room was a bizarre lower chamber with round central fireplace with a large swastika in the middle of it. It is an echo chamber, and any sound will bounce off the walls. Very curious, but also exciting for the explorer.

My friend and I went to another tower, but this one belonged to the youth hostel. There was no one at the front desk, and being the intrepid explorers we were, we dashed upstairs to look for somebody, or some medieval treasure to examine.

In fact there was not very much that was very medieval except for the odd decorative suit of armour. On the second floor, there was a large man who looked a little panic-stricken when he saw us. He gave us the German equivalent of 'Vot are you doing up hier?' He adamantly denied that there was anything of historical value to see up there anyway, so back down we went.

The castle itself is unique in Germany for being in the shape of a triangle, with three towers. The main round tower is the good one as it has the 'sacred' rooms, but the whole make-up, including the hill and associated town, also called Wewelsburg, are beautiful wonders.

I think there can be little doubt that Wewelsburg itself is a sacred hill and has been for a rather long time. Archaeology reveals that it has been inhabited from the beginning. Religion there goes deep. Neanderthal skulls were found buried there. There are also Stone- and Bronze-Age burial pits, containing jewellery.

The Nazis may also have noticed that Wewelsburg is part of an ancient prehistoric landscape of mythological significance. It is not too far from the strange rock formations of Externsteine, of ancient religious significance. The *Deutsche Ahnenerbe*, a Nazi-ideology archaeological authority, conducted various excavations also to prove an ancient religious significance at Wewelsburg but the results were a little disappointing.

After the hostel we went back to the main attraction, the north tower, and the Black Sun. Now however the room was full. There was a museum tour guide giving a talk in German, to guests sitting on beanbags around the Sun. He was saying that there is no mystical symbolism here, no magic, no pagan ideas associated with the place. It was all merely Himmler's idea of mysticism.

Then something remarkable happened, which made my mouth want to drop open, and had me reeling a little. I do not understand German very well, but the museum guide seemed to have said something like, 'Let us now send a message and show that we reject the mythology of the Sun, and the evil it represents.'

I watched as the people obediently began to pick up their beanbags. They then hauled them all over to the centre of the room and dropped them all on top of the Black Sun, to utterly cover all aspects of it. It was a little annoying as I wanted to photograph it, so I had to shift the bags back when everyone had left.

I asked my friend what it was that we had just witnessed.

'They were covering up the magic which was not supposed to be there.'

We left Wewelsburg hill at sunset. It is truly a spiritual place, an ancient site of mystery and magnetism, which the infamy of its occupier has clearly not erased.

Figure 3.1: This is an old relief of Wewelsburg, Germany. When we look at the names, Wawel and Wewelsburg (Wawel hill), in two different countries, one must wonder. They could be a similar sacred-hill or tribe name from an ancient forgotten tribe whose ideas spanned the region. The one in Germany was to have been a spiritual capital for Germany, in Himmler's strange attempt at a Nazi religion, which sought out old pagan roots. For the SS, it was essentially *the* sacred grail castle, the end of the quest, perhaps the gate to the underworld itself. The other hill, in Poland, we know, has been holy for millennia, and was the Polish capital for six centuries.

Hohensyburg

The next day was another big one. There was a lot of driving around south of Dortmund, in order to see two different castles. Most importantly, the aim of the trip was to visit Hohensyburg, known as 'High Victory Castle'. Unknown to the English-speaking world which concentrates on Stonehenge and British neolithic sites, this huge hill fort has enjoyed an extraordinary pre-history as capital, or main fortress and religious centre, of many great and forgotten kingdoms. It is a lost omphalos, of potentially huge importance.

We were driving on some winding country roads for a long way. They are quite similar to roads in Australia. Germany, in some areas, seems to have a surprising lack of petrol stations. The fuel tank on the affordable *Smart Fortwo*, is only 37 liters, so it is cheap to fill up. It was rainy and very green everywhere with a grey German sky, but when the wind blows a lot of brown leaves fill the air.

As mentioned, the area called the Ruhrgebiet is one with lots of concentrated cities, power stations, wind turbines, and all sorts of industry. There are about ten million people living in it. One drives along the autobahn and suddenly a huge wind turbine emerges behind the trees which line the arterial road.

Traffic can jam up on the Ruhrgebiet autobahns, among the busiest such roads in Germany, with everyone struggling to get home from work in whichever of the local cities they live. The area of the Ruhrgebiet is almost the same as the famous Ruhr valley, often spoken of in Western sources as being the heart of German industry. When Hitler lost the Ruhrgebiet, the war was finished.

Sylvia, my German antiquarian friend was telling me that Dortmund is the main crossing of two incredibly ancient roads. These are the 'Hellweg' (literally the 'Hell way' or 'Road to hell') and 'North/South-route'. Hohensyburg controls the southern entrance of this North-South route. A hellweg was in fact a common name for a road throughout the medieval landscape of Germany.

Ley line enthusiasts would love to learn about the Hellweg (to my knowledge they know little about it), because it seems to be a road from from one 'hell' or 'hill' to another! The words seem to have a common origin, which is interesting in terms of the context of this book. Is English 'hell' really from Hebrew 'sheol' as the popular myth goes, or is it more from the Germanic 'Hel', which is the underworld, or goddess of the underworld?

Another explanation for the etymology is 'salzweg', or salt way.

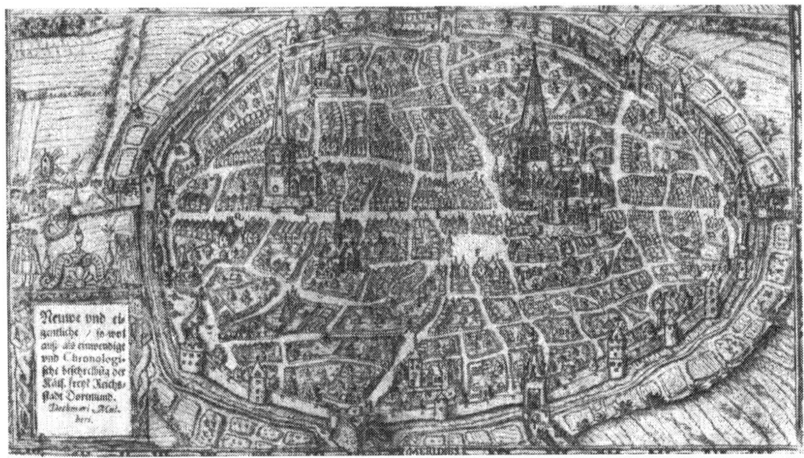

Figure 3.2: The (central horizontal) road to *Hel* passed through Dortmund. I am assuming this refers to some huge 'hill', that is, an underworld representation, which may have been on the route. Hel is one of the three children of *Loki*. She is a savage guardian of the underworld, placed there by the gods, as it was the best place to contain her. The other children are a wolf and the Midgard serpent. The road goes off towards Russia to the East. There is a place in Poland on the Baltic sea actually called 'Hel.' Like a kind of St Michael's mount, it is on the end of a peninsula. Since amber literally washes up on Baltic beaches, ancients may have seen this place as some type of 'end of the world.'

For me, this is less satisfying, but not unreasonable. In other words the landscape is being used as a road to draw presumably straight-ish lines, as that is the shortest path between one hill and another!

Towns possibly formed along the Hellwegs, taking advantage of trade. Voila, one has a 'ley line'. Sylvia explained that the Hellweg route went up on top of the mountain ridges and then it was a station for the E.W. route. Hohensyburg is a crossing of the mountain trail with the N.W. route Additionally, the Sauerland, Siegerland route is the north-south route, which are both Loki territory. In Hagen, a industrial town, there is the 'Balve cave', used since the Stone Age, and also the place where legendary Siegfried's sword *Balmung* was made (a Germanic Excalibur). It was the place where a legendary smith was taught his skills by dwarfs.

Loki is the Germanic Lucifer, or equivalent to Greek Prometheus.

Like Yahweh, he is a helper of mankind, against the will of the 'gods', who are more disinterested or ambivalent towards mankind, and with whom he does not really get along, or share a special relationship. (In fact, does not monotheism often seem to be the worship of some kind of heat or fire-god, like the Sun? This sometimes seems to be coupled with a rejecting of the 'other gods'. That is, the old ambivalent gods who could not have given a hoot whether or not mankind was raised from the jungle, into the city.)

Baldr is a pagan Christ-like figure or shining Apollo-type god. In an old legend, Loki has Baldr killed by his brother in a cruel trick. The gods send Loki to his new underground prison. Meanwhile they attempt to re-incarnate Baldr, who is also the bleeding man-god, who must bleed anew every year. To be re-incarnated in the god world, they must follow the road to *Hel*, towards Asgard, home of the gods. Hel tells the gods that Loki will be brought back if every living thing weeps for him.

What we have in the Ruhrgebiet region, and perhaps elsewhere, is a kind of meeting of mythology and geography, for one reason or another. The Hellweg and Hohensyburg, a great hill near Dortmund, might require an understanding of mythology to explain why they were so significant in the past.

I was quite interested in Loki as he seems to be the father of the Midgard serpent, or something related, and the serpent and the pyramid do seem to be very much associated. As for Hohensyburg, it is not a pyramid. (though it is an omphalos) So why then are we discussing it? One reason is the next-door mountain, which we will get to in a moment, and which looks like a huge barrow. Even without this however, the whole place is one where something rather similar to the religion worshipped at mounds, seems to have been practiced. All the elements of what I would hope to identify as being part of the 'pyramid religion' are found here.

'But Sylvia, I still don't see the significance of this place! Sylvia was convinced that the original World Tree or Tree of Eden, as it was remembered in the Bible, written in later times, was located precisely here.

'Why does it need to be here. Why does the World Tree need to be *here* of all places? Here, in the Germanic cold and wilderness, when this is a Biblical story?' At the time I did not really know that the Bible stories are really based upon much older proto-Indo-Germanic legends. Their relation to Norse mythology, for instance, has been pointed out, in many books about mythology, as being eerily close, even taking early Christian contacts into consideration.

We studied the map. Sylvia was pointing to the nearby hill, next to sacred windy and rainy Hohensyburg.

'Look at this!' I was looking at the map. 'The hill next door is called Asenberg,' she said. The name was familiar, but I could not quite work out why.

Then it hit me. 'The Mountain of the Gods!' It was like a bolt of lightning.

'Asenberg.' Anyone who is familiar with Germanic mythology will at once see the significance. 'Asgard'. Of course! It was the name of the very home of the Norse Gods, a place which lay beyond Midgard (the only world visible to mankind). I did not know it at the time, but now see that it is a perfect name for a type of pyramid with Gods supposedly living inside it, or upon it. Asenberg, literally the 'Mountain of the Gods' is big. It is too big to be man made, but it does look 'artificial'. It is not, of course. But it did not need to be, to be significant.

'It's too big to have been built by man', I said. 'It would be many Silbury Hills in size!' 'Yet, it looks quite strange. It certainly may have been partly shaped by man, with topsoil, subsequently eroded. Why not? It is a very regular type of shape for a hill and looks very much like Silbury Hill, yet there are many natural hills which look regular so it is perhaps one of the latter.' The ordinance survey maps reveal Asenberg as a quite interesting regular-shaped round hill which looks like an incredibly large and regular round barrow. It is perfectly fitting as a tomb of gods, since it is far larger than any human barrow. We may note that large mounds, bigger than human barrows, seem not to have been built as tombs with humans in mind.

Is this the original Asgard? If original Yggdrasil was here, then it could be. Why would Yggdrasil be here then? Hohensyburg is a place of huge ancestral significance, for the most part unrecognised. Not only do we have neighbouring Asenberg, but we have a hill of Hohensyburg itself, that the Saxon nation fought their final battle upon, unwilling to abandon, it would seem, a very sacred shrine. This is likely the place where Charlemagne attacked and defeated the Saxons under their king Widukind in 774. This is a huge hill. But really it is a hill fort. In terms of the extent of its fortifications, it is Germany's answer to Britain's Maiden castle. Maiden castle comes in at about eighteen hectares, and is bare. This German 'version' is fourteen hectares in size and covered with trees. The shrine was so important that Charlemagne had a stone church built in its place. Underneath this stone church, St Peter's, they found a square foundation. This is not the original foundation however. There was some other temple underneath. Who knows how many millennia it might go back!

I found out that Loki is connected to the idea of the dragon in the mountain who is guarding the treasures. I think the mounds, these sacred places connected to mines and fountains, are the gems of the *Brísingamen*, the precious necklace of our lady of natural fertility. England is famous for fertility mounds. There is a book by Michael Dames called *The Silbury Treasure: The Great Goddess rediscovered*, from 1976. It is one of the few books one can actually obtain on the subject of a European pyramid! It convinced me that Silbury Hill was a representation of the pregnant womb of the Earth mother, (as it is sticking out of the Earth) some kind of mother deity who was worshipped in the 'silly' or sexual/fertility season of May.

The ancient hellweg goes through Dortmund. Sylvia explained to me that the Dortmund area is an ancient crossroads from Norway to Rome and Spain to Russia. This crossroads is in the centre of Dortmund flanked by two churches. This basically means the 'road to hell', or to the 'hill', as I would imagine. You go to 'hell', you are buried under the 'hill'. I cannot imagine that the 'Hell Way' goes by actual Hell, but it could go by old cemeteries, which would be mounds. Meanwhile hills are good ancient landmarks, and religious sites. The female Hel, in Germany, might also have been called Holle or Hulda.

Maiden castle in Britain is in Dor-chester and this particular hill is near Dor-tmund so there may be some tribal connection. Sylvia says that Germans in general do not even know that this hill fort exists. They just go and have a look at the small medieval knight's castle which is built on top, a frightfully windy place.

We saw the church of St Peter's, which was very old and also went into the medieval castle ruins. There is a small gatehouse with arrow slits inside and then you go to the next building, which is where the knight would have lived. The ground floor appears to be what is known as a great hall or dining room, but it is smaller than a decent lounge room. There is smoke on the walls in the chimney areas. The whole thing is a ruin. The personal rooms of the knight would have been above this.

In his work *Teutonic Mythology*, J. Grimm stated that in Northern Europe, it was common to erect churches on the sites of former sacred trees or temples. This is where I would place the original world tree, but Sylvia had other ideas.

The whole of Hohensyburg abounds in the remnants of ancient walls. Much of the area feels like there are ancient structures covered with other ancient structures, covered with topsoil. We walked over to the forested part of the hill and looked down off a 'wall' which is a dirt embankment which is typical of hill forts, and I saw about four lower concentric walls below!

Other attractions include a tower with which you pay a Euro to climb to the top. We went to a nearby monument called the Kaiser Wilhelm Denkmal which is a huge cenotaph, with a massive statue of the Kaiser on a horse, and built in 1871. It is near this high position that Sylvia thinks the Yggdrasil once stood. Overall, I think the possible Yggdrasil may have been at the church of St Peters. According to Sylvia, the confluence of rivers below, apparently match the legends of its location, where the Ruhr river meets the river Lenne.

There is another legend, but from Sumeria. In this, the primal mound or world hill is where salt water was first separated from fresh water. I wondered if this is why there was a divergence of rivers, where the Lenne flows into the river Ruhr, a symbolic separation point, or why Irish pyramids on mountains often overlook the coast, where sea turns into the freshwater rivers of land. To the ancients these were important ideas. Salt water cannot be drunk, but freshwater can. Not knowing about mineral salts, the question 'why?' may often have been upon their lips, as well as the horrid and strange taste of seawater.

As mentioned, there is also a medieval knights' castle on top of Hohensyburg which has a sad feeling to it. I felt like there was a voice there which wanted to speak. Sylvia said it felt like something was repressed and covered up. She said it was a voice searching for a channel and also, it was sad because the sacred tree was cut down there. At least that is part of the spin the mind throws upon the eerie feelings that one gets in a strange place.

After all that it became dark and we began to exploring the town. We went to a restaurant and ordered some *steckrübe*. This is German food, the same as Polish *bigos* but without sauerkraut apparently (even though it was very sour). One is supposed to break the bread in half and then use it to eat the cabbage.

Since Hohensyburg seems to be where an Yggdrasil or Irminsul of great importance may have once stood, it would seem that there may have once been a mound up there associated with the tree, unless it was sufficient to simply put the tree on high Hohensyburg itself, or nearby

Figure 3.3: The Church of St Peter at Hohensyburg. There was some pagan shrine underneath that the Saxons were unwilling to relinquish. So many hill forts seem to have their own shrine, or pyramid, or so forth.

Figure 3.4: Below, the river Lenne flows into the river Ruhr. It seems to be essential to have water associated with the mountain/close-to-sky-god religion. If there were any sacred tombs up here, they seem to be long gone. Germany has a much higher population and disruptive invasions (such as Attila) would have removed the existence of the old religion much sooner than in Ireland. We can observe how the tree religion has been disrupted in Germany. In Ireland it seems to be more original, hanging wishes on trees. In Germany it is done at Christmas, the winter solstice, for decorative purposes. No-one knows 'why' anymore, but they still know why in Ireland, unless it is a newer invention.

Asenberg which resembles a very large burial mound.

In figure 3.5 we see a romantic representation of the fall of Yggdrasil. It was said to have been a trunk erected in the open air, and situated not far from Heresburg, now Obermarsberg. This was a centre of Widukind's resistance, with a cave network where people are said to have hidden whenever Charlemagne's forces came near. The Irminsul is something rather similar to a May Pole. We do not know what it looked like, but there may well have been more than one. An old drawing shows Charlemagne's men destroying the Irminsul, while downcast defeated Germans look on.

In figure 3.6 we have the so-called Shigir Idol. Totem poles may have been set up, like certain obelisks in New Kingdom Egypt, for astronomical significance. (It must be added that obelisks are on the East bank of the Nile, for unknown reasons, with the pyramids on the west bank) In Egypt there was always a problem. Any migrants from the north would have been unable to set up a totem pole due to lack of trees. The obelisk was most popular in the New Kingdom, a time when pyramids were largely done away with as a tomb for the dead. In this particular respect, they 'replace' the pyramids, except that they are definitely not tomb markers, or not thought to be. Assuming the Irminsul was sacred for a long time, it is conceivable, to my mind, that pyramids themselves replaced the Irminsul, in the deserts of the Middle East. They were a pillar, or tower, to the heavens. The pyramids in Egypt seem to have been positioned as sundials, with a shadow from Khafra's pyramid falling on Khufu's as part of winter solstice (we will get to that later). They may have acted like large sundials. In the absence of a large tall tree, they may have been the next best thing. The Shigir idol is almost contemporary with a post-hole found in the Stonehenge carpark.

The Irminsul, a possible replacement for the Yggdrasil, was seen as a 'pole' in the earliest tradition, but later even as a pillar or altar. It is written, for instance, in the twelfth-century *Kaiserchronik*, or 'Emperor Chronicle':

> *ûf ainer irmensiule, stuont ain abgot ungehiure, daz hiezen si ir choufman.*
>
> On the Irminsul, an enormous idol is standing, which is called their merchant (literally 'headman')

This idol was supposedly, according to the chronicle, the origin of Wednesday.

Figure 3.5: Irminsul was a Germanic centre of the world. According to legend, the Irminsul which was destroyed by Charlemagne was, like Hohensyburg, in the *Westfalen* region. This is *The destruction of Irminsul by Charlemagne*, by Heinrich Leutemann, 1882.

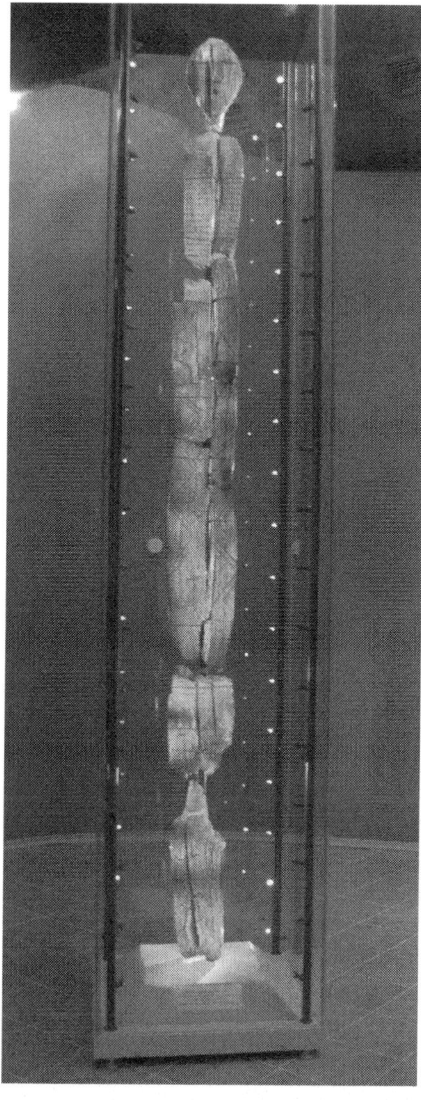

Figure 3.6: This is an image of the Shigir Idol, found in Siberia. It is
the oldest wooden statue in the world. It seems to have some of the
properties one would associate with an Irminsul, or even May pole. It
is incredibly long at eight feet. It is also incredibly old, dating from the
eight millennium BC.

I had my own theory about Hohensyburg. It may have once had cairns on top, possibly stone ones replaced in later times with the Celtic or proto-Celtic grass ones. Why not? The megalithic culture was a sea-faring one which stretched from Sicily and Malta. In the far north, it reached Denmark, Germany, Scandinavia, even the Baltic. This is possibly when the runes arrived. Later Phoenicians are sometimes thought to have brought the runes but they may well have been a branch of an earlier Libyan naval empire, little discussed.

In the first millennium BC, Greeks, Phoenicians and a third people, the Etruscans, who are also very little discussed regarding maritime affairs, controlled great naval empires. The Minoan naval empire gets all the attention, but perhaps the Etruscans, and perhaps in league with Sardinia, held sway over the West Mediterranean until their power waned by about 500 BC. (In talks with a colleague, we more or less came to the conclusion that the Sherden or Sardinians of the 1200s BC, were, as a Sea People-naval empire, responsible in a major way for inspiring the Atlantis stories which Solon supposedly found in Egypt. Their culture was highly advanced relative to their neighbours, and is highly unknown to a wider public: certainly a topic for books by a whole host of future authors!) The Sardinians may have been influenced by an early seafaring culture: the megalithic builders, who perhaps brought aspects of the proto-runes to the Germanics far earlier in time than is allowed. Some information on this is found in Robert Temple's *Egyptian Dawn*, and it will be discussed further a little later. Even the Scythians of Russia and Kazakhstan had their own 'runes.' The more one looks, the more lost alphabets are found. I wonder if the alphabet was not an invention of the pyramid builders in the third or fourth millennia BC, possibly somewhere in Central Asia. We only have good evidence, however, from the Phoenicians, so they tend to get the credit.

Germany has always had perhaps a much higher population than Ireland. More people implies more people to destroy older ruins. Looking down at the waterways, where the Lenne flows into the Ruhr, I tried to imagine the area free of industry and pollution. I tried to imagine it as it once was, with shepherds, farms, fields, and a small town perhaps. It reminded me so much of Ireland. The mound or Irminsul or whatever temple was on top would have been illuminated by fires, so that people could gaze up and know that there was law and order, in heaven and also on Earth.

Chapter 4

In England
(*or the hills of 'Merlin'*)

England is the home of the Saxons. These are a magnificent, beautiful, apologetic, and graceful people, originally from about Denmark, through south to the Rhineland. It was such a pleasure to have been among them. The Saxon invasions of the Dark Ages are merely a latest instalment in Germanic migration. The ancient long-house culture, from Central Europe, was brought to Britain in ancient times, implying a string of invasions from the Germany area, over the millennia.

These 'proto-Saxons' used their long-house burial practice, for making the long barrows of 3000-2000 BC. One could enter these after completion, and for several generations. Perhaps these were *their* versions of pyramids. Eventually they were totally covered up.

When they reached Britain, however, the central Europeans mixed with other peoples. Those known today as the Welsh, but previously as Britons, are in part seemingly derived from Mediterranean stock, as any cursory examination of their features will reveal. Theirs was a cave culture. Their dead were often buried in tombs in the walls of cliffs. The Irish religious culture of 3000-2000 BC was also based upon a cave culture, rather than a turf mound culture, which manifested as mounds of stones.

In Britain we have elements of all these cultures.

Windsor

One can take a short train trip out of London to a very interesting mound. It is actually directly underneath the central tower of Windsor Castle! For this reason it is referred to as a *Norman Motte*. Oblivious to the fact the countryside was already littered with artificial hills, the Normans allegedly raised their own ones everywhere and put a wooden palisade structure on top, known as a *bailey*. We assume the Normans built them all (now found not to have been the case) because we have very few accurate records of England before the Normans.

Windsor Motte appears, to my eye, to be a very ancient mound. It is strikingly similar to Silbury Hill in many respects. Of course, since the Queen lives there, there is little prospect of an archaeological excavation!

I had been looking over the excellent Tudor building in the court-yard. I had also been watching people posing with the redcoat guards. The more people posed with the guards, the more others wanted pictures with them. Tourism is often simply a mad dash to take pictures. I have found it to be. People went up to them and the guards did not move. They are not allowed to interact with the people. They have an iron discipline which would have made the Kaiser's officers jealous with fury.

The guards are young soldiers. They seem like an elite corps. Their costume is all traditional redcoat but the rifle is modern. They stand around for ages like statues. Then they abruptly shout and begin marching in one particular direction, which seems random, to an outsider, and then go stand around some place else. In addition there is a patrol of soldiers going about the castle grounds, keeping watch. They are responsible for the safety of the Queen and royal family.

Suddenly one guard began shouting. A woman posing with him for a photo started tip-toeing out of the way, and was then bowled over as he kept walking in her direction as if she was not there. Then there was none of that ubiquitous English apology. He did not turn his head or seem to notice. He simply kept marching like he was an alien on another planet who did not respond to pesky humans. He was only doing his job. Then there was someone who may have been a tour operator explaining to the bowled over woman that that was just the way it was, and that there was nothing that could be done. One got the extreme impression that if the soldier had stopped to talk or pick her up, it would have been an extreme breach of discipline and he would have been shouted at for several hours, and then booted off his job.

Figure 4.1: This is a large motte. It is much bigger than the so-called *motte* at Antrim. An old harvest hill is perfect for placing a motte, with a nice defensible location. Why on Earth bother to dig a new one when the countryside contained possibly hundreds of such mounds? It was the easiest way for the Normans to build new castles. Build it on something which has been stable for a very long period of time. Many, but not all mottes obviously, may turn out to be of the Stone Age.

One can see the fear in their faces.

I became fascinated by the motte in the middle of the Windsor complex. Was I just dreaming or is it incredibly similar to Silbury hill? If I were a Norman, building motte-and-bailey castles, I would just throw up a palisade on top of any of those old harvest mounds. Plenty of them would have been near enough to cities. It is the easiest way to do it.

An overhead view of Windsor also indicates the proximity of the motte to the river. It is a scenario reminiscent of ancient ritual. I was reminded of the Krakus Mound and its proximity to the river, also.

So, is this an ancient harvest hill as well? Since the Queen lives nearby, I do not think anyone is in any rush to dig it up and find out!

Figure 4.2: The garden of the Windsor motte, which you look down on, reminded me of the 'moat' around Silbury hill. A mound or pyramid needs water. At times, is was almost essential to the pyramid tradition, but not always. Water is a key component of rebirth.

Into Bath

Built on seven hills, like ancient Rome, Bath, or *Aqua Sulis* as it was known to the Romans, is a truly beautiful city. It is a perfect base for a foray into Western England. The bath-stone beige buildings have the feel of strange ancient ruins, like a ghostly semblance of Pompeii, in the cold, morning autumn mist.

The mounds of Britain seem somewhat different to those of Ireland. Firstly, Ireland does not seem to have any step pyramids. England has several. Even the Isle of Man has one at Tynwald (fig. 4.23). Irish 'pyramids' are either deeply ancient stone mounds, or alternately they are like Site B at Navan fort. They are filled with stone, in the old style, but then covered over with dirt, as in the newer Celtic style found elsewhere.

In Egypt there was definitely some relation between the mother goddess and the Pharaoh's pyramid. In his *The Gods of the Egyptians*, Wallis Budge points out (p. 215, second volume) that in the *Book of the Dead* (one of the most ancient religious documents in our possession), there is a chapter in which there is written a chant which would bestow some of goddess Isis' magical power upon the dead Pharaoh. Budge goes on with an amazing discussion to talk about this goddess in Western Europe. There is a temple of Isis in Pompeii, visited once by Mozart. He mentions (p. 218) that Isis was called the 'queen of heaven,' *regina coeli*, during the Roman Empire. Since she was the goddess of wheat and harvest she seems synonymous with the goddess that Michael Dames applies to Silbury Hill in his book *The Great Goddess*. We will later see that the Great Pyramid has something to do with Isis and Osiris.

Whiteness is the colour of the supreme goddess. White linen was perhaps drawn to let the rising Sun into her temple for morning worship. Geologist, Robert Schoch points out the whiteness of Newgrange, in relation to the whiteness of the Great pyramid, back in the day when it was covered in limestone casing stones. Now only the tip of the Khafra pyramid has these stones. In the *Mabinogion* (tales of deeply ancient Britain) there is a fascinating passage which has passed over the attention of most who study it. It regards the White Goddess associated with mounds. She seems to be summoned by standing on top of a mound.

The Mabinogion is an artificial creation of incredible mixed up tales from ancient Britain. In the tale *Pwyll Prince of Dyfed*, Pwyll goes for a walk to the top of the mound. Now there is a faint memory of some bleeding man fertility ritual for he is warned that a high-born man may not be on top without suffering some blows, wounds or seeing some wonder. There we have the possible hint at drug use, or at least being in a spiritually-fulfilling environment. Pwyll brushes off the warning, saying he would love to see the wonder. While on top he sees a woman wearing gold-brocaded silk on a horse dashing past the mound on the highway adjacent to it. He confers with others and they agree she is some messenger. Try as they might, it is impossible to keep up with her. She is like a ghost, or even the solar disc.

The fact she passes a mound on her mythological journey implies this is some sort of resurrection ritual of the dead. It seems similar to the Germanic story of Hermod racing down to 'Hel' on his eight-footed steed to secure the release of the shining god, so that fertility can restart for another year. It could be mixed in with the idea of Sol racing away from the wolf-son of Loki, who will eat her at Ragnarök.

The mounds are also to keep evil away, protect the land and its fertility. In the tale *Branwen Daughter of Llyr*, within the Mabinogion, there is a plague on the continent. A sacred head must be taken and buried on the 'White Mount' in London. Once the head is buried facing the continent, the plague cannot cross the channel as it presumably will be blocked by the divine goodness radiating out of the mount on the London-side of the Channel.

Presumably this blocking power is enough to protect the south-eastern part of England, and beyond. It is kind of like 'activating' the mount by placing a watchful head there, a god inside it. It is like giving the fertility god a sense of vision and direction. This White Mount presumably no longer exists, but the White Tower, possibly in its place, may have been made by the Romans, and then rebuilt by the Normans, who used a strange Roman-like style, for the palace at the centre of the Tower of London. There may have been a white chalk-like mound there, presumably destroyed by ancient Londoners as the city spread.

It may all have something to do with the 'pearly gates'. The Norse god Heimdall was the 'white god'. He kept watch over the entrance to Asgard. Therefore one might suppose that this is why the entrance to the tomb is white. Since one gets to Hel or Asgard by ascending the mound, the tomb on top is presumably his colour.

Norse mythology is very similar to Biblical mythology. Instead of a trumpet of revelation, Heimdall carries a horn to warn the gods when Ragnarök is at hand.

The fact she is also a queen of heaven implies she is a sky goddess (fertility associated with good weather) and therefore can be readily associated with the pyramids, designed to talk to the Gods of heaven.

A tour-bus driver, on a tour I was on, was expressing his indignation at the builders of Silbury Hill, the biggest artificial mound in Europe. He showed us an ancient photocopy from a newspaper article. It showed a seven-layer step pyramid carved out of chalk. 'What I can't understand is why they would build this amazing chalk step pyramid, and then cover it up again!' 'It boggles the mind!'

Silbury Hill

One may imagine living in say, 2500 BC. It has a been a long journey. One has already been walking for two hours after sunrise, and is approaching one of the capitals of what will one day be known as Britain.

Walking up a hill, one looks down into a valley. In the distance, through the morning mist, and past the trees, one can see a white orb, shimmering in the distance. It is the holy of holies! Silbury Hill! This is Europe's biggest man-made mound. Under the turf lies something which resembles a conical spiralling or step pyramid, made of chalk and clay, packed together. Like many religious structures of the past, the ancients decided to bury it.

There is something interesting about the root 'sil'. This might be compared with St Patrick's Irish Cathedral in Armagh, which is on 'Sally' hill. The Germanic root implies something like the word 'selig' which means 'blessed' or even in a state of bliss.

An antiquarian friend told me something interesting about Silbury hill.

'It *is* the Isle of Avalon!' That is, the place King Arthur was taken to, after his demise. Like an Egyptian king, Arthur never really died. He lives forever and will one day return.

'Ave'-bury' is nearby (Avalon-bury?). This could be part of an ancient kingdom subsequently associated with King Arthur. Silbury and Avebury are essentially part of one very large complex which has lost its former splendour due to vandalism, especially in the last several centuries. In a way it is just too big to protect, unlike Stonehenge. (See fig. 4.8)

There are suggestions in the literature that Silbury seems to have had water around it in the early times. It is like a white goddess in the

Figure 4.3: Silbury Hill.

middle of the lake, so it was like an island. An 'Osiris island' is what the Egyptians *may* have called it, had they ever set eyes on it.

The tour bus for Stonehenge and Avebury drove us past Silbury hill, stopping for photos. I saw it from the tour bus.

'Can we go there?' I asked.

'No.'

'Why not?'

'It's protected and under restoration. You're not allowed to climb it.'

'That's a shame!' The thing used to be climbable.

Silbury hill is ridiculously large. It is Europe's largest completely artificial mound. It is 40 metres high and 167 metres wide. It is truly a mammoth-sized pyramid-type structure. It is four times taller and three times wider than Medb's pyramid near Sligo, yet it is only comparable in size to one of the small Queens' pyramids next to the Khufu pyramid, but certainly wider. Its true beauty is hidden. It was traditionally thought to have been built like a wedding cake, in layers of packed or carved chalk, subsequently covered over. Newer information however suggests it was built in a sort of spiral configuration. After it was complete, it was covered over with dirt.

A good question is why have no burials ever been found there, in over two centuries of exploration? It is therefore a kind of ceremonial hill. It looks a bit like a volcano rising out of the ocean. It is like a crater in a valley. The hill itself is like the spike in the middle of a lunar crater.

It needed a lot of manpower to build something like Silbury Hill. Several hundred men would have worked for several decades in building it. Perhaps it was built to a less than specific plan, and therefore not finished for generations. The latest idea is that it found its shape by accident because it was indeed built over several generations. Then again they may have once had a unified plan, subsequently altering it.

We may observe that the massive Cologne Cathedral was itself left unfinished for over five centuries before a united Germany could muster the economic capacity to realise the plan of the medieval dreamers who came up with the idea. That is one reason why projects slow down; money. Archaeologists in 2002 have suggested that there was no extended period of abandonment in the construction of Silbury Hill, and that the pyramid was 31 metres high when it was finished, so it is a little higher now. It is fascinating that archaeologists always write that the death of a king prevented the completion of a pyramid. It happened quite often. Yet since projects invariably run over budget, the disappointment of this may have also triggered abandonment.

Michael Damas suggests in *The Silbury Treasure* that Sil relates to the 'Silly Season'. 'Silbury' is broken down into Sil-Bury. This might mean that it is the symbolic burial of Sil. I would suggest it is the symbolic burial of Loki, the king of the silly gods, along with the Green Man. If there was an Yggdrasil on top of a hill, that may relate to the presence of Loki, or the Green Man (Osiris/Bleeding Man/Fertility God/Sacrificial King) as well. He is another kind of silly.

Damas points out that Sil is a Basque word meaning granary. This is interesting considering many people came over from Spain in ancient times to populate Ireland, and perhaps part of Britain as well. He also says that it may have been for celebrating Lammas, or loaf mass. This was the time for thanking the goddess for the annual food bounty. King 'Sil,' possibly a god, was buried in the mountain. If Sil is a granary, this might explain a little confusion surrounding the origins of the Joseph legends of the Bible, which will be discussed a little later on, though this particular link is highly tenuous. I fortunately do not however need to place any weight of evidence upon the association of Sil with 'granary,' in offering a partial solution to that enigma. It is merely a curiosity.

King Sil (Silly?), the food man, or whatever he was, was according to legend a fascinating character. He was a king who was buried on horseback in golden armour. Actually, this of course makes him similar to the golden knight in the Arthurian lore. In the *Mabinogion*, a storehouse of ancient British lore, told in convoluted tales which have lost their original meanings, we read of a foolish red knight who enters Arthur's court, laughing. He grabs Arthur's goblet and races away.

This red knight is killed by Perceval, later one of the best of the knights. Here, he is a peasant boy, accidentally in Arthur's court, and with a noble lineage, who chases after the red knight. Red is the colour of the setting Sun, but also possibly Loki/Lucifer. It is like killing the shining god or Sun god every year so everything can be renewed and fertility can begin once again the following year. Observing the seasons must have been one of the primordial drivers of fairy tales.

We do not necessarily have to be specific about gods when discussing mythological ideas. There is a lot of overlap. Multiple gods seem to share associated ideas. There is overlap in ideas, and gods. But gods are based on ideas and stories associated with them. The Red Knight may be the setting Sun, racing away but about to be slain. Red is also however the colour of blood, so here we have overlap with another deity. He is also the bleeding god, described in *The Lost Gods of England.* The bleeding god is always fertilising the ground, always being sacrificed for the good of the kingdom.

We can interpret from the story, that the Bleeding God drinks perhaps some hallucinogenic or painkiller substance from a cup provided by the shaman/priest king ('steals the king's cup'). This is accompanied by mad laughter associated with being drugged, so he laughs in the story, and then he is sacrificed. It would simply not do for an assembled audience or even people in the village to have to put up with tormented screams. That's a good bunch of speculation but it could be related to a past reality.

If the reader is interested there are two other huge pyramid structures in Britain which are related to Silbury. These are Gib Hill and the Hatfield Barrow. There are also some mottes with castles on them which formerly may have been harvest hills like Silbury, for celebrating harvest festivals of fertility. Damas talks of the possibility that Silbury was once covered in plants. One might wonder if the hanging gardens of Babylon were not a sort of Ziggurat (they were built to honor the moon goddess), which also venerated the Earth mother, like Silbury.

(Ziggurats were for the moon mother, which is possibly related to Earth Mother)

The great eighteenth-century antiquary, priest, and self-described 'druid', William Stukeley was one of the forerunners of modern archaeology. His passion for ancient Britain was such that he had a miniature Stonehenge built in his garden. He wrote that a skeleton and horse's bridle were actually discovered in 1723, during a tree planting on Silbury Hill, but that these were a secondary (intrusive) burial. I wish we knew why trees were being planted on top. It would have made it more picturesque, but it might also have been based upon ancient precedent. There is no tree up there today.

Fascinatingly there is some recent speculation, based upon the letters of an early excavator, Edward Drax of Bath, who sunk a shaft right down the middle of Silbury, that the structure was seemingly built around a 40-foot totem pole. This makes the structure similar indeed to the mound at Navan fort, which was also thought to be built around a totem pole. It also makes the structure quite similar to the Krakus Mound in Poland, also suggested as built around a pole. All three may be based around a very similar religion. Dare we call it 'Celtic', if it dates, in the case of Silbury Hill, to well before 2000 BC? The other two mounds seem to be far more recent.

So far as 'pyramids' go in England, there is also Merlin's Mount, which is to be encountered in Marlborough. There are a couple of structures by this name. The best one is a sort of circular step pyramid. It is covered in trees. Unfortunately it is in the middle of a school and I did not go there.

In figure 4.4 we have a picture of Merlin's Mount, as it was before a school was built around it. It seems to have been involved in an early geometric pleasure garden. Exit the garden at one gate and walk up the mound, with its little garden house on top, perhaps for playing chess or cards. I have a feeling that the terracing on this and other hills, is supposed to represent the equivalent of Jörmungandr, Loki's snake child, coiled up inside.

The Midgard serpent is supposed to be wrapped around the Earth, itself, but its body lies at the bottom of every ocean, invisible to us. It is to be noted, in this early depiction, that there is some kind of earthwork around the mound, which recedes into the background. I wonder if this was once part of a moat system. This is landscape mythology! Nearby is the river Kennet. This name, shared by various rivers, deriving from the c-word is an embodiment of the sacred female. (See Michael

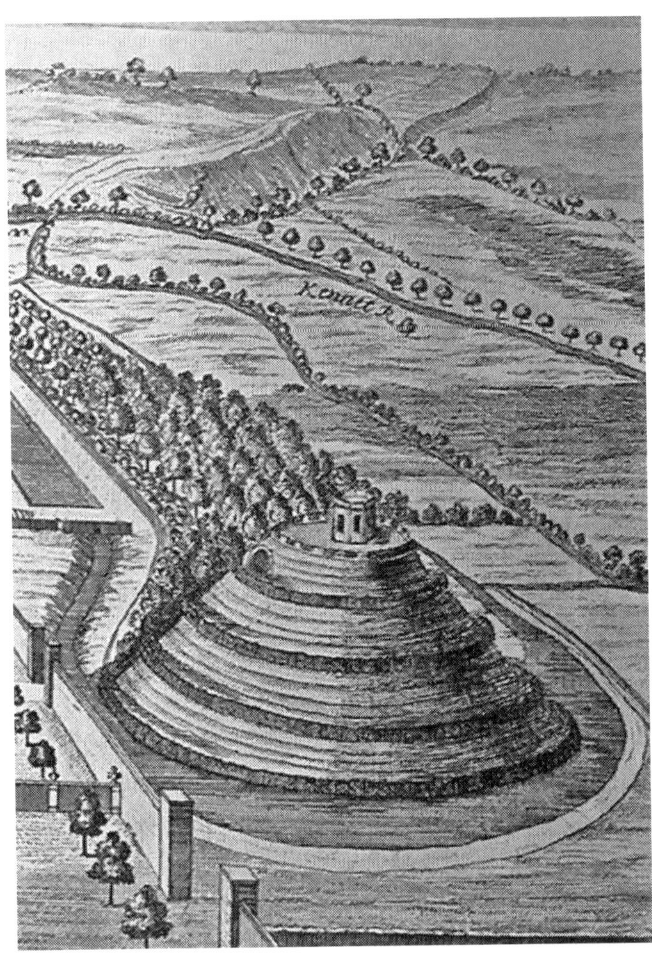

Figure 4.4: Stukeley's 1723 picture of Merlin's Mount.

Figure 4.5: Merlin's Mount. Merlin derives from Welsh Myrddin, pronounced something like 'Marvin'. To me, he seems to possibly be the male form of Irish Medb. By the 19th century, the more formal gardens are no-longer apparent. The style is out of fashion, and the garden is rather overgrown. Yet what is that in front? It appears to be water, or the nearby river. The mount was deliberately built near it. It seems this structure was built, not for man, but for a god, for what we now know as 'Merlin.'

Damas' works on Silbury). It has been brought to my attention by a colleague that there remains a goddess in India called Kunti. The widespread meander from India to Southern England tells of a very ancient deity, certainly Paleolithic, and pre-agriculture, embodying the magic of animal reproduction, rather than food reproduction.

As for the earthworks around the Mount, which recently has been found to derive from the third millennium BC, investigation is difficult. It occupies a central courtyard surrounded by a girls' school. The mount is also covered in large trees. Merlin is still, it seems, imprisoned by the female.

Does Silbury Hill present us with a similar picture to the pyramid of Khufu, and Medb's cairn? King Khufu's pyramid is surrounded by smaller pyramids, like the mound of Medb, and Silbury Hill, and possibly the Krakus Mound, which has some very uneven ground in a nearby grove. The Khufu pyramid, like these structures, seems to have been left in peace by the Egyptians (Copts) for thousands of years. It was opened by Caliph Al Ma'mun in AD 820, and he supposedly found little. That is to say, it was opened by a foreign culture to the earlier builders, perhaps unaware that the pyramid would not contain the type of treasure he was looking for. The same went for heaps of mounds around Europe. Antiquarian gold-diggers threw away their shovels in disgust whenever they came upon the pre-metal era remains of the old Stone-Age religion.

I find it fascinating that the nearby tombs around Silbury and Medb were all plundered, yet the larger structures were left alone. The subsidiary tombs are mere satellites around the central larger untouched tomb. Why? One might fathom that the tombs were obviously built as cenotaphs rather than tombs, mere symbols, like a shrine. Aware of this, earlier generations did not bother to plunder the larger structures, even with the pressing subconscious thought that possible bigger burial ('surely must... please... in the name of God!') spell a bigger treasure, as that tomb would obviously, have belonged to the supreme ruler.

Perhaps it is the satellite pyramids, around so many pyramids in Egypt, that are the *actual* burials. Perhaps a king built himself a pyramid for his god, then put himself in the satellite pyramid next door, so he could be close to his house of god? Obviously one cannot generalise but I would suspect, based on my very limited field-work (tourism) in Europe, regarding what the mound-builders were up to, that this is the case.

It must have been hard to overcome the temptation to try and have a look inside these huge central mounds. But how does one overcome the knowledge from one's ancestors as to what it was really all about: that it is just a sacred hill and perhaps *not* an actual burial? Better still, how to overcome the superstition over what would happen to one if one did try? No amount of gold is worth that, thank you very much! Who in their right mind would risk the wrath of the ancestor gods? Just stick to looking after the sheep!

The stories of early explorers in Egypt right up to and including the 20th century, are filled with Arab guides refusing to go one step further, into the sacred sanctuary, fearing the spirits of the dead, especially after dark. It certainly fit in with Gothic horror novels of the day. Their often-English employers would laugh at this superstition, and usually spend a thoroughly pleasant night sleeping with the Pharaohs.

'Our farming was good enough for our father and our father's father who lived well without chasing foolish unreal ideas of treasure in them

Figure 4.6: Silbury Hill seems to have a huge 'moat' around it. The connotation is water or symbolic water. The third dynasty Djoser pyramid of Egypt, built at a similar time, is also surrounded by something called 'the great trench,' carved out of the bedrock of the Saqqara plateau.

sacred hills! We don't need no curse in this family! Just leave the little people well enough alone! Do you really want them up here and at our throats night and day? What would your poor mother think?' Egypt had the curse of the Pharaohs. Ireland had the curse of the fairies. England also had its sprites.

In Egypt we have Khnum as Khufu's god. Khnum is either a green water crocodile or a green ram, a Loki-like figure. Fascinatingly, Sil would also appear to be a type of water god or goddess. She may not have been green, that is usually the male's prerogative. Bath itself was called *Aquae Sulis* in Roman times. Sul or Sulis was the British water goddess. This means that Bath town was called the 'Waters of Sulis'. Sulis herself would presumably be buried at 'Sul-Bury', which is really not too far off. I wonder if Khufu, in building the pyramid was not really building a burial place for his personal god Khnum, a fertility deity? André Pochan, who called himself a 'highly independent pyramid scholar' of the 1970s, wrote that the Khufu pyramid appeared to be both a tomb to Khufu as well as a temple to Khnum.

Figure 4.7: A closer view of Silbury Hill, revealing a little of the underlying terraced structure.

As mentioned, William Stukeley was a great antiquarian of the eighteenth century. He was a re-discoverer of some of Britain's ancient sites. He had a strange vision of Avebury which is not really apparent today, perhaps as many stones have been removed. In examining his picture of the whole complex near Avebury, fig. 4.8, no longer seen as this, one may come to certain conclusions. To my mind, and in the context of Indo-Germanic or Indo-European mythology (to go by another name) this is a huge serpent. It has a head, and in its belly it has swallowed the world, with two smaller circles inside.

Alternately, the 'world' which seems to be the Avebury circle, is riding on the snake's back. Furthermore, it is 'wrapped' around Silbury itself, guarding it. What does the serpent guard in the Bible? The 'tree of Eden'! He does the same thing in Egyptian reliefs, where there is sometimes a huge serpent in front of a tree, in New Kingdom tombs.

Naturally, this world tree may have been planted on top of the hill. I could be wrong, but I suspect that this could be a massive representation of the snake and tree from Indo-European mythology! There was one type of Jew, the Samaritan, who worshipped on the mountain. These Jews remained in the Holy Land. The Old Testament itself was written by Jews in Babylon during the captivity, a land which has no-doubt been invaded by the Indo-Europeans many times down the millennia. This is perhaps the link, or one of them, to the Bible.

Below is the plan made by Stukeley of the Silbury complex. It seems to be part original design, part imagination. The overall complex has considerably deteriorated since Stukeley's day. This complex has been compared to the Serpent Mound of Ohio. Like Egyptian pyramids, Silbury Hill is on the *west* side, of Kennet river. The beautiful natural hills of the landscape around Avebury, for many miles are truly spectacular and catch the sunlight remarkably, creating such a pretty effect, that I could scarcely believe it. They are no doubt a major reason for the placement of this complex here. The ancients may have considered that 'here is a place of the gods.'

This whole complex, and the Avebury region, may be the original inspiration (or one of many), upon which mythical memories of 'Avalon' became based, in later times. As a representation of the underworld, it is where the dead, especially kings like Arthur, would go when they were finished with this Earthly toil.

Glastonbury

Imagine a public bus squeezing itself through little medieval laneways in South-Western England, for hours on end. Cars continually had to back up on roads made for a horse and cart, in order to let the bus squeeze through with no margin for error. The shiver of the body and yellow autumn leaves complemented the crystal blue sky and the still cold frost of the earth, on an early morning in late autumn, as I went to see this highly impressive and magical place.

In the morning I had gone to the bus station at Bath and thence took the bus to Wells. There, one can change to another bus to Glastonbury, asking the driver to let one off at the town centre. Early morning is a good enough time to visit, as mists can sometimes surround the Tor, creating a spectacular effect of a mystery mountain in the distance.

There are sacred sites, and then there is Glastonbury. Glastonbury was, and is a *very* sacred place, mainly newer than Stonehenge and its ritual landscape of earthworks, so we actually know something about what went on here. It is the site of what is claimed to be the first Christian church in Europe, founded by Joseph of Arimathea, mythical relative of Jesus. He had fled the Holy Land, towards a distant place on the opposite side of the Roman Empire. Like the Dortmund-

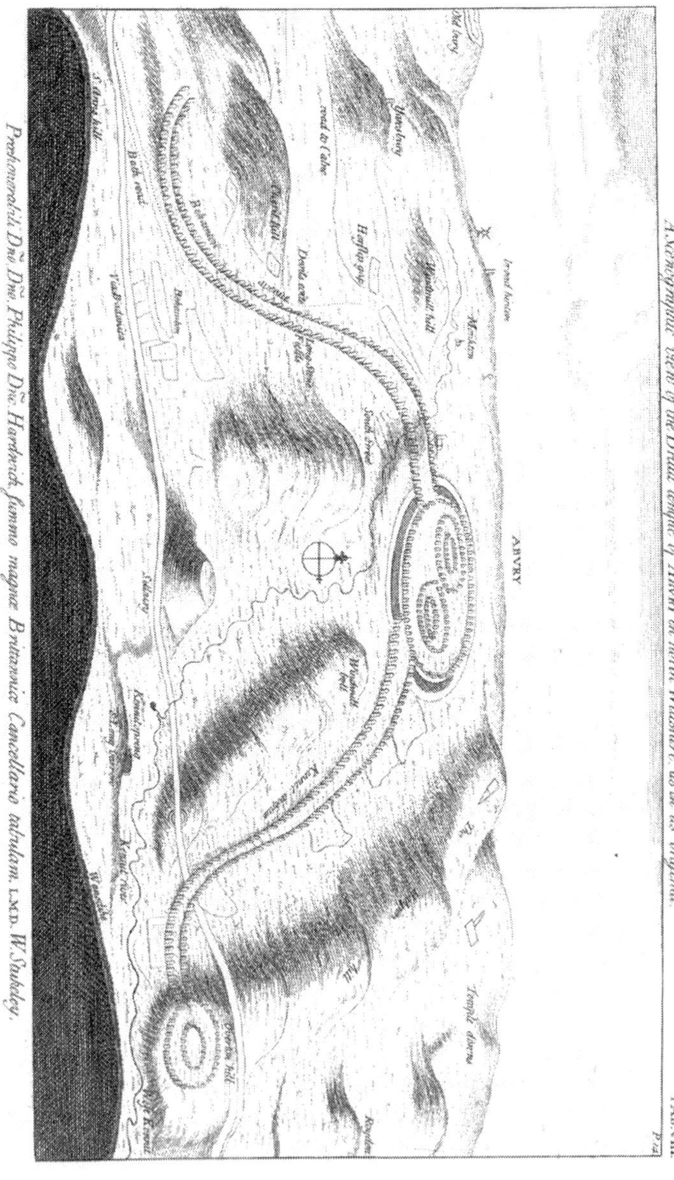

Figure 4.8: William Stukeley's picture of Silbury Hill, made in the eighteenth century.

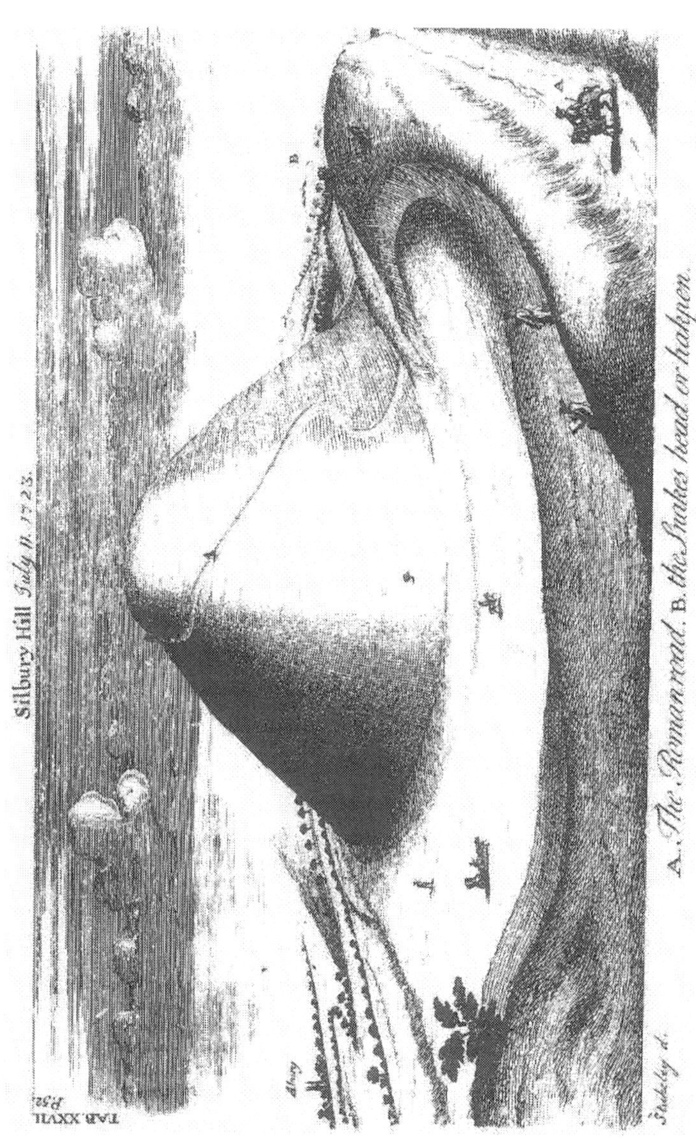

Figure 4.9: This is another Stukeley view of Silbury Hill.

Wewelsburg region, or the mounds in Cracow, or Avebury, Glastonbury is a huge sacred complex. It is a place where landscape meets mythology.

So much has gone on here that it is hard to see where to start. In *The Isle of Avalon*, a book about Glastonbury, I noticed that its author Nicholas Mann, makes comments about the Tor which, as I read them, began to tick all the boxes regarding what is found at other elevated landscape complexes found at other deeply ancient sites.

Essentially, we see all the characteristics of a home for the creator gods, within the sacred mound. Glastonbury was actually a huge island surrounded by water, which once included four hills and the current town. It was joined to the rest of the mainland by a peninsula so it was like a type of enormous St Michael's mount. The surrounding landscape was drained over thousands of years.

The plain is now several feet above sea level, but still rather moist. Mann points to a difference between the two major hills. One, Chalice hill, is rather rounded. The other, the Tor, is rather pronounced. This reminds me of the link between barrow-like Asenberg and Hohensyburg, two major hills right next to each other. In between the two mounds are two sacred springs. One, the White Spring is full of limestone and its water leaves a white residue: perhaps once thought of as the waters of the white goddess. These *Axis Mundi* sites always seem to have secret tunnels or chambers, or rumours of them, regardless of the country in which they are found. These were perhaps ritual centres, chambers of the underworld gods.

Before the end of the 19th century, one could walk into a tunnel in the Tor, which had been carved out by this spring. It was an interesting grotto. It was capped and diverted into a local reservoir. There is an 'eggstone' next to this spring. It is a big egg-shaped rock which looks like it popped out of the limestone hill. For another cosmic egg, see fig. 5.14.

Another well, in between the mounds is the chalice well. The Holy Grail is associated with this area. Joseph of Arimathea supposedly interred it in Glastonbury. Then again, there is a Celtic legend of a 'cauldron of creation' which is a similar concept. Of course recipes need different substances to create things. The water in the Chalice Well, also called the Blood Spring, is iron-red, perhaps once associated with the Earth Mother's menstrual blood. It also may have been associated with the red underworld of Loki. In between the springs is a sacred grove of Yew trees, the centre-point of creation, and counterpoint between two mixing forces?

The Tor looks like a vulva from the air. From the ground it could well look like a step pyramid from along the longitudinal axis. (Mann says it looks like a step pyramid from some angles, and a long ridge from others.) Then again, on the bus over from Bath, I was actually looking almost downwards upon the Tor, from many miles away. The Tor is a limestone plateau, with many tunnels under it, hollowed out by the springs, and therefore undergoing slow collapse. In fact the church on top seems to be lacking extra components, it seems like only the tower is left.

What does mythology have to say? In Celtic mythology, it is the home of the prehistoric Earth Mother, or creation goddess. In *Isle of Avalon*, Mann goes into the mythological situation regarding red and white. For instance, in Celtic tradition, Modron is the mother goddess of Glastonbury. I see a similarity to 'Medb'. He writes that in the *Mabinogion*, which is the most famous collection of Ancient British (Welsh) tales, cobbled together, that in Pwyll's descent into the underworld, all the creatures and animals, and even furniture and clothes are red and white. These are the colours of the underworld. The red and white symbolism will have consequences in the final chapter. The horses of the Wild Hunt are red and white.

Glastonbury was the supposed place where King Arthur was taken after his death. It is the alleged Isle of Avalon, or apples. Mann also writes that Arthur's body was picked up by the Wild Hunt. This is part of a Germanic tradition based upon a much older tradition. At certain times the horned one will hunt people to take to the underworld. He has hounds of hell with him. In the Celtic tradition, the gateway to the underworld was always a mound or magic castle (castles in the old days are hill forts on huge mounds or hills). These sacred places, Mann says, are located somewhere in the west, and surrounded by water. I had fanciful ideas, when I first read this, of the relation with Egypt.

Egyptian pyramids for some reason are all located on the west side of the Nile. At the time, I dismissed this foolish notion. A better explanation would be vague links via a proto-religion from which both ideas descended. This reasoning did not occur to many who in the past suggested strange direct links between the British and Phoenicians, or Israelites. Men had been fascinated by the idea that the British goddess Britannia, on a chariot, was similar to the Phoenician goddess. Whilst links are there, there are too many differences. There are also possible ancestral ties between both cultures, no-longer in contact and developing independently, mother links. These could be examined. In this respect I would highlight the independent development of Ireland, Iran and the Aryans in India. They were not really aware of each other, but developed with related gods, as if they somehow were in more direct contact. It is due perhaps to the spread of tribes in earlier tribes in different directions.

In Europe there is a strange tradition of hills with secret cave systems and impossibly long caves which cannot logically exist. I think some of this is based upon the mythology of what lies underneath. We have it in Poland, especially I found, near places with former Iron-Age hilltop cities, and throughout England. Apparently at Glastonbury Tor, there once was a tunnel leading between the Tor and the Abbey in town. Thirty monks are said to have entered the tunnel. Only three emerged. Two of these survivors had gone insane and the other was struck dumb, by what they had seen or experienced, creatures or visions of the underworld presumably.

Glastonbury town is an amazing and magical place. There are plenty of shops in town catering to neopagans, selling all sorts of magical stuff, trinkets, purple crystals, meditation tools and crystal-skull busts of grey aliens. There were lots of shaman-hippies walking around as well. Glastonbury Tor is a centre for various mystics, in their pursuit of Earth Energy, whatever that is. There was even a strange hippy playing guitar up on top of the Tor, inside the ruin of St Michael's. In sensational Glendalough, Ireland, the ruin of a monastic community, which I think will one day turn out to be recognised as a lost settlement of at least several thousand inhabitants (current population is the staff of the hotel and hostel), I did not have a chance to see a particular odd stone due to a woman sitting in front of it every day. This was until the Sunday when she was not there. She was always sitting there and playing a mixture of what sounded like old Celtic music mixed in with songs from *The Lord of the Rings*.

Glastonbury Tor is like a small mountain really. Along with Stonehenge and Giza, it is one of the capital cities of the 'New Age' mystical movement, and perhaps always has been, since its inception. Once it was an informal place for Neolithic villagers to go, and still is. From the air it looks like a vulva so it is pretty much a huge Earth Mother, or has been thought to be for a long time. One can climb to the top and have a look around at an incredible view. That is typical of what I call a 'pyramid' location on the British isles. It just needs to have an incredible view, or it is a deal breaker.

One of the things I like to do whenever I have the lucky chance to be in Europe is to go into different churches to look for pagan survivals that ninety nine percent of people do not associate with the earlier religion. There were three churches in town and they all have modern refurbishment. By 'modern' I mean post *c.*1550s, and not medieval. This makes every church look basically the same... whitewashed and uninteresting. The medieval decorations in such churches have largely been scrubbed. Between the 1500s and 19th century, Britain radically changed in terms of religion and population, and so they continually updated all of the churches. Henry VIII, not to mention the actions of many desecrators in the English Civil War, destroyed many churches. Once, people would go on a pilgrimage to a medieval church to see the tremendous display. Now, one cannot really see anything truly old except for sections of the structure itself, notably pillars, as well as perhaps a tombstone, once on the old floor, and now stuck in the wall as if it were a huge brick. That at least prevents shoe erosion. The once-fabulous medieval art is about ninety nine percent gone.

I went to the smaller tiny little chapel in town, dedicated to St Mary and formerly a hospital.

'Hello there!'

'Hi!'

'So... this is a church, right?'

'It is indeed.' The speaker was a mystical Merlin-type figure. Altogether, they were a scholarly quiet people sitting around in a meditative circle, with their eyes closed. It might have been a druid's convention.

'You are very welcome to just sit here and meditate with us for as long as you desire.' English people are so friendly and warm! I liked the emphasis on meditation as opposed to prayer. This is the 21st century after all and we are all a mix of religions really! Apparently the place used to be a hospital back in the Middle Ages. It has been run by nuns for a long time after that, as a small chapel for them.

'It's a nice quiet place for meditation actually,' Merlin continued. Many churches in the western world are now often simply quiet places for personal spirituality with no-one forcing anyone to believe in anything they do not want or cannot accept or grasp.

'Thank you. I wish I could spare the time but I have to get up the Tor'. The cute tiny window near the door with its twisted gnarled oak frame looked like it was out of a fairy tale, Bilbo Baggins' house maybe.

Walking down the street, I 'bumped' into Glastonbury Abbey. I had been so determined to see the *Tor* that I had utterly forgotten that this magnificent place was even here in this town. Unlike ruined abbeys in Ireland which either charge a pittance or are free and abandoned, this one is uncomfortably expensive to get in. (England has a lot of tourists) It was demolished by Henry the Eighth as well, but one can walk among the ruins. I did not really see anything 'pagan' at all, which related to the earlier Glastonbury religion, except for some decorations and one little clue in particular! When I was leaving the abbey, on the driveway after the exit there were some old stone blocks to the side. One of them had something like the World Tree or Yggdrasil carved into the side, in rune-like scratches! That was quite interesting, to say the least. It is a fun 'trick' of investigating early-Christian religious sites to pay close attention to these ruined blocks. Curators do not know what to do with them! (they are in fact often the ruins of the previous church, left over from archaeology digs!) Curators often hide away these blocks in weird places like crypts, or along roads for decoration, or under stairwells. I have found that in several different countries, they often have strange pagan faces resembling Apollo, the proto-Christ. Churches indeed must have been very different places in the first thousand years of Christianity, relative to the second!

There was the tomb of King Arthur in the middle of the abbey, which is where the remains of Arthur and his queen are said to have been found in 1191. I stood on top and felt a warm glowing energy which must have been my exuberance. It is outdoors now, but once this 'outside' was the 'inside' of an enormous Abbey cathedral. This obviously may not be the real tomb of King Arthur: just a bunch of medieval propaganda, allegedly designed to bring tourists with money to the abbey. It is really hard to say whether it has anything to do with any of the Arthurian legends.

Let us recap, that I noticed three large 'pyramids' atop Knocknarea in Ireland. There is no other word for them. Two were almost utterly ruined but one could see the foundations. The third, Medb's was still intact and complete. There was a smaller one in between Medb's and another, the two larger ones. One could hardly see it. The setup at Glastonbury Abbey seems to have been much the same, with Arthur's supposed grave discovered in the middle of two 'pyramids' (the chronicler's word, not mine for a welcome change!). (I noticed no pyramids at the site, and imagine they are long gone, along with the medieval graves. The current huge abbey ruins were mainly built after the Arthurian discovery, perhaps with money generated by the discovery). I note the word *pyramide* has been used a long time ago, in the

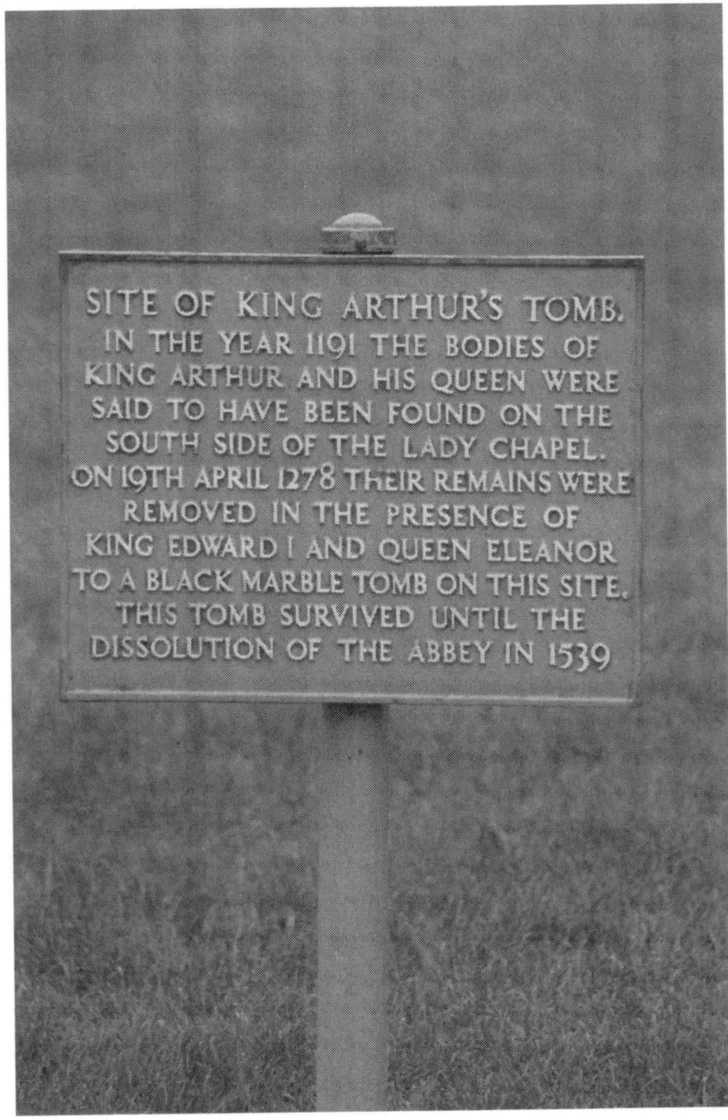

Figure 4.10: The sign at King Arthur's tomb at Glastonbury. Arthur means 'bear' in Welsh. I feel the people who partly forged the discovery of Arthur's tomb here, back in the Middle Ages may have been confusing the king with mythology or pagan gods. The so-called *pyramides* have long gone.

Middle Ages. It may not actually mean pyramid, as we understand it. The translator to William of Malmesbury's medieval 'On the Antiquity of Glastonbury,' calls the pyramids 'crosses.' The word may very well be an antique substitute for 'cairn.'

One clue is that Welsh Prince, Llewellyn, allegedly claimed the so-called bones of Arthur were ox bones (Gilbert, *The Holy Kingdom*). He had been invited to Glastonbury by Edward Longshanks, and invited to see the bones, but burst out laughing and said they were an ox, rather than a tall giant, as had been supposed. That, would perhaps indicate a Neolithic sacrifice just as much as it could point to a forgery. Cow bones, after all, were found at Stonehenge. I think the whole so-called discovery of Arthur's bones was a mixture of discovery and wishful thinking, with even some genuine relics from Roman times perhaps lying around. They apparently mentioned 'Arthur', but the name was also active as 'Artorius' in earlier Roman times, the second century.

After examining the missing pyramids, I walked the wrong direction for a while, looking for the Tor and actually thinking the hill next to me, the very elongated Wearyall Hill, was *it*, since I saw benches up there, but no way to get up from the road. In fact I was walking out of town, in the wrong direction. Then I happened to spin around and look behind me and there was the little thing in the distance, two miles away on the other side of town, with the Tor church tower sticking out of the sculpted jelly-mould mound like the Lady of the Lake reaching Excalibur out to present it to King Arthur, all rather dramatic.

Finally I got back to town and in the right direction. A 'public footpath' in Britain can go anywhere, up a private driveway, open or closed gates on farmers' fields and sometimes through deep mud. One finally makes it to the Tor. The view on top is amazing, however it is a little steep, perhaps to those fearful of heights. It was already getting dark at 3:30 p.m., so I had to get back.

The other thing was that a storm was coming and I was convinced the lightning was about to start. It made for a very mysterious atmosphere, with the deep green of the picturesque fields all around, and the barren dark grey coldness above. In fact it turned out to be merely a cold front moving in without any rain and then it mysteriously blew itself out. By then I was at the gates of the place. I changed my mind and I walked back up again. I then encountered some people on the way down who I had been talking to at the top, previously asking them where the Chalice Well was, and receiving directions which were both lengthy and convoluted, to where Joseph of Arimathea supposedly

Figure 4.11: Glastonbury Tor. In *The Isle of Avalon*, Nicholas Mann writes that the terracing is not typical of the post-2000 BC era but is consistent with the mighty earthworks created *c.* 3300-2000 BC, such as Silbury Hill. Lack of Iron-Age remains would tend to reinforce a view for an earlier date. In addition to the terracing, the greater former-island of Avalon, of which the Tor was only one of four hills, was cut off by a ditch across a linking peninsula, known as Pointer's Ball. It represents a possible sacred limit.

deposited the Holy Grail.

'Going back eh?'

'Yes I'm on my way back up... I need to go get up top and meditate. I forgot to.'

'You know... feel the energies', I added.

The woman accompanying the man looked surprised, fascinated as well as confused and flabbergasted, all at once. She looked at her husband with wide eyes to check his reaction, which was quite pleasantly one of complete brotherly understanding. Obviously some are not strangers to the ideas of these 'New-Agers'.

'Well anyway, see you and thanks for the directions!'

I had a suspicion that the tower on top, the sole remnant of St Michaels, was built on the 'energy spot' formerly occupied by an Yggdrasil. Subconsciously, the energy felt weak but present, detectable to the sixth sense, or subconscious, or however one might put it. I do not really know. How did it feel? The brain, which is a marvellous thing, tried to put the message or feeling into English words and for me, it was this. (Something must have induced the Stone-Age folk to carve out the mountain like this!) The psychological impression was that the feeling of power felt like it was 'going somewhere else' but that something else was 'blocking' it. (At the time I assumed this must have been caused simply by my knowledge of Henry having forced the last, octogenarian Abbot of Glastonbury to build his own scaffold and noose up there, upon which he was promptly hanged.) It was not a strong energy of organic growth, like at Wewelsburg in Germany. To my surprise I would much later (just before publication) read a 'confirmation' of these personal spiritual perceptions. Mann writes in his book that water diviners generally find that the Tor exhibits a complex variety of subtle energy patterns and so is quite difficult to dowse.

Glastonbury needs more than a day, because one needs to find the egg, the well, as well as the ruins and the Tor itself. It is a pity for me that I did not have time to look in the shops. They display amazing objects in the windows, like crystal skulls and books about Earth mysteries, which must be very rare as I had never seen them before. The town, when I got back, had many elderly hippies going home for the day. They were dressed in funny colours, walking around everywhere and carrying bundles of sticks and bags full of gnarled wood and totems and things. I wondered if they were not really Irish 'travellers' or people left over from the potato famine, who had emulated gypsies back then, in order to survive. It was amazing to go to Glastonbury. The website I consulted had said it was hard to get to with public transport from Bath, but Bath actually seems to be an excellent base for day trips in the ancient land of Somerset.

At Glastonbury Tor, we have a 'Church of St Michael'. The tower which is still standing there dates from the 1360s. There are several of these St Michael's mounds in Western Europe. This implies that he may have been confused with a pagan mound god of earlier times. What is he famous for? As mentioned earlier, he basically defeats Satan/Lucifer during a war in heaven. This would be Lucifer or Loki, who is the wicked joker god imprisoned with his wife, like Merlin and Nimue, in the mound. A St Michael's Mound would therefore be a kind of place where St Michael (a Christian sky god or Thor) imprisoned the devil. Actually there are St Michael's mounds located on various

Figure 4.12: The Church of St Michael's on top of the Tor. What temple once stood here? Indelibly it was one dedicated to the destruction of the serpent or forgotten dragon, now lying under the hill. The pyramid or mountain is, in a sense, an embodiment of his creative or destructive energy.

hills around the old Glastonbury island. These are or were atop four great hills which form a rhomboidal shape on the map. From Cadbury castle, for instance, a large mound, one can see the northern major lunar standstill over a 19.6 year cycle, over Glastonbury Tor. There are several of these alignments, which fit lunar standstills, in which the moon stops over a long period of time and proceeds in another direction, as well as solar alignments with the Beltane. I believe these ideas 'centred' Glastonbury with the mathematics of creation.

Bel is a Celtic goddess, perhaps, I would suggest, of the Atlantic megalith builder civilisation of the third millennium BC. Stonehenge was built by these people, not categorically by local 'neolithic farmers', for Stonehenge-type architecture is now proven (almost) as not exceptional to Britain, as in fig. 5.1.

By their spread, these were evidently a seafaring people, and their memory was one of the possible inspirations behind later dreams about 'Atlantis.' Glastonbury Tor is longitudinally aligned towards the rising of the Sun in May, the time of the fires of Bel, when they are lit on various hill tops. This would have possible origins in terms of Bel possibly being an old megalithic-builder god, related to Baal. Mann in *The Isle of Avalon*, identified Bel with later Belial, the snake, whom St Michael perhaps destroys (evidently mixed up with ideas of St George, also patron of England).

Glastonbury was a 'St Michael's mount', an idea of an offshore island found on Atlantic coastlines, home to some creator god of the underworld, and therefore whose Christian patron is the dragon destroyer, to nullify the paganism! (In Poland, which the Atlantic builders did not really reach, and where we have more Asian ideas of the central mound, there is a place on the Baltic, a peninsula into the sea, not called after St Michael, but known as 'Hel' the Germanic underworld. The idea of destroying the snake at the centre of creation would is also perhaps related to the Egyptian cat/hare slaying the serpent at the location of the World tree, as in fig. 6.20) A common origin of Bel in the Celtic world and Baal in Phoenicia and elsewhere might be as some earlier Libyan trading-civilisation god, or even as Carthaginian colonies in the Celtic world.

Bel may also have been a solar god, for lighting a fire at the 'center of creation', exemplified by the mound, would be representing the Sun, which *we* know as the centre of the solar system. Temple covers this topic well in *The Crystal Sun*. Aristotle slightly derided the Pythagoreans of Sicily for their silly idea of a 'central fire'. Temple explains this

Figure 4.13: The view from Glastonbury Tor is amazing. If one looks carefully, in conjunction with a map, one can almost see how a huge area around the Tor was once part of the island of Glastonbury, sticking into the sea.

as saying this is evidently Aristotle's reference to their conception of the 'Sun.'

The Pythagoreans thought the Sun could only be explained by a crystal lens in the centre of the solar system, which concentrated light from a source behind it, focusing this upon Earth and Moon. To me this heliocentrism is an aspect of ideas from the west. Temple visited many British museums and uncovered hidden caches of what generations of curators have referred to by inert labels such as 'mineralogical samples.' These are, he has shown, lenses and small crystal balls, also with magnifying properties. He shows that these were evidently dug out of many mounds and tombs by antiquarians over the past several hundred years, in Britain. My spin on this is that since a mound was seen, perhaps wherever it was built (including Egypt!) as a centre of creation, or replica of an origin point point of creation, designed for fertility and thence recreation, it would be fitting for a replica of a crystal 'Sun' to also be included, the centre of the creation and maintenance of the Solar System!

There are other parallel ideas with Egypt. On the surviving tower of the 1360 church, there is a scene of weighing of the soul, which strikes me as rather odd. I have investigated nearly a hundred medieval churches in former Celtic countries of Europe, for earlier pagan artistry, but this scene is rather uncommon. It evokes images of Egypt, and Anubis and Thoth helping to weigh the soul, which must be as light as a feather. Since there is Atlantic/Mediterranean influence here (especially historically in the Glastonbury region), then perhaps these Atlantic builders, who may have also had a homeland in Libya, also had some basis in Early Egypt, as suggested by certain early Egyptologists, as well as by author Robert Temple. We will talk more of this later.

Also, on the 1360 church is a relief of Brigit and her cow! In Egypt this would be Hathor. This would be a relic from the 'great goddess,' an ancestral triple deity. It is therefore a hill of the triple goddess, and the snake, and the afterlife. I believe these earlier Christian vestiges stem from the pyramid religion. It is also to be pointed out that Carthaginian Baal, or 'Lord', was often represented by a pillar 'sitting' on a throne. He is therefore a kind of omphalos, or marker at the centre of creation.

The succession of churches on the summit may have replaced an earlier non-Christian shrine. Nigel Pennick says in *The Ancient Science of Geomancy*, that Glastonbury Tor fits the profile of something which would have been seen as a World Hill. Allegedly, Glastonbury was once dedicated to the Celtic god *Gwyn ap Nudd*. The old tale goes that there was a supernatural castle up there. It was ruled over by the underworld god with all his courtiers, finery and ceremony around him. One day St Collen went up there and dispersed the lot with a sprinkling of holy water. In other words the legend seems to suggest a kind of pantheon up there, subservient gods to an underworld god.

In Glastonbury we have another sacred tree. Joseph of Arimathea supposedly planted the 'Holy Thorn' which instantly took root and blossomed. The original is lost but we have a huge old thorn based upon a cutting from it, now surrounded by a makeshift staffed glasshouse. That is how special the damn thing is. It also looks like it could do with a good hard pruning, but they are taking care of that and do not want to prune too much. This ridiculous plant could be based upon a memory of Yggdrasil. I have a feeling that an Yggdrasil may once have dominated the Tor. In mythology, the Tor perhaps represented the sacred world mountain at the centre of creation. The tree dominated artificial structures as well, such as the Krakus Mound in Poland. The Tor meanwhile is natural, yet partly sculpted by man into a pleasing shape.

Why does the tradition exist that Arthur was buried here? I wondered if Glastonbury Tor was a place like Silbury Hill, with knowledge that a great king was once buried there, and then they decided to apply the name Arthur to it, in the Middle Ages. What if the original name was similar to 'Arthur', so they thought 'blast it, close enough!' and decided to place his 'tomb' there? Arthur has pagan as well as legendary connotations. The name means 'bear' which implies a god rather than a man. The Ainu in Japan, seemingly part ancient Dravidian and part Indo-European, worship the bear and they buried their dead in houses which they set fire to, pretty much as the pre-Stonehenge long-barrow builders of Europe did, subsequently covering charred remains with soil. Those long barrows were really the ancestor to pyramids. Their ancestors became their gods, whom they worshipped. After a few generations the long barrows therefore possibly were the burial places of gods.

Glastonbury in England, Glasgow in Scotland, Kłodzko in Poland. Are these ancient Celtic god names? If Marl or Merlin were buried at Marlborough, and Sul or Sil was buried at Silbury, whole regions in England seem to be named after pyramids and tombs! (Perhaps this is because they would have been good directional indicators as well as places of worship) Kłodzko (Glatz is the German name) is a city in Poland near the Czech border. It is incredible. If I had a romantic view of what Camelot looked like it would be Kłodzko! Why? Just like an Iron-Age town, it is on a monster-sized hill! The streets go up and down. It is quite ludicrous, but beautiful! I have a German ancestor from there so I was quite determined to explore. There is no pyramid up there, merely a huge pyramid-shaped underground fortress from the Napoleonic Era, which replaced an earlier castle. The tour was essentially an hour of walking and crawling through dark never-ending tunnels in the fortress. It too, as a hill, may have been a very sacred site in ancient times.

Just as the Celtic proto-Dortmunders may have spread to the West to form the Dorset region, the Aryan or Scythian 'Celts' of Kłodzko may have likewise peregrinated west to form cities and areas with quite similar names on the British isles. These were possible ancient journeys of the tomb and even pyramid builders, as they spread their extinct religion from one region to another.

The Tor might have had a cairn, like in Ireland, and in addition a tree on top, (an apple tree it would seem, since it is the literal 'Isle of

Apples') and this has been replaced by the church.

This epic and beautiful monument is something of a beacon in a huge valley. It can be seen from fifty miles away, standing strong in the distance, like a pillar in a huge cup. It is glorious, and there is something else about Glastonbury I really should mention. One can read about it in the mentioned book by Mann. Nevertheless here is the gist of it. The builders of Glastonbury were geomantic maniacs, which remind me of the excessive mathematics shown by Robert Temple to have been used in the orientations of the pyramids of Giza.

Incredibly, the *three* hills associated with Glastonbury town, Chalice, Wearyall and the Tor, form a rhombus with the location of the Abbey and the sacred oak grove, the Gog and Magog trees. The rhombus, which extends over several miles, might have dictated the placement of some ancient religious predecessor to the abbey, in order to provide the site with some kind of symmetry. One cannot place the naturally occurring mounds, but one could place the grove as well as the abbey's ancestor. It is allowing geomancy to generate a sacred landscape.

I was anxious to see Stonehenge. It reminds one of Avebury, in the Silbury Hill complex, but it is additionally also possibly associated with Arthurian tradition, for Merlin supposedly built it. It is also part of the whole nearby sacred landscape of south England. If Avebury encapsulates the Midgard Serpent, wrapped around its hill, perhaps Stonehenge too would exhibit some symbolic mythological structure. But first it was off to Bath to find out about the local gods and effigies of the region!

The Bath Temple

'I had a magical amazing day!', is what I wrote in my daily report. Bath is a city built on seven hills, like Rome. It is one of the reasons the Romans liked the area. There may have been pre-existing hilltop temples here anyway, as well as other monuments.

I was not sure what to do first. I caught the bus from the hostel to the town. They put the darn Bath Hostel right on top of Bath hill, which is ridiculous if you want to walk back. I walked around town and then booked a tour bus to see Stonehenge. It is a lot cheaper than hiring a car and the associated hassle. Usually the hostel gives discounts for attractions but not in this town. I went to see the Roman bath. This is really what the town is all about!

There is a Temple of Minerva Sulis, which seems to have once incorporated the bath. Sulis or Solis or Sol was the water goddess of the region. That is a fascinating thought to hold, when it comes to the 'pyramid', that is Sil-bury hill. The name implies that Sil or Sol was buried there, whoever he was. If he was a god, then a god was buried there, and it was a symbolic burial. He may have been the spring god of the Stonehenge area. It is all in the name, really! Bath itself was the town of *Aquae Sulis*, or the 'Waters of Sul'. Sul is the goddess of Silbury Hill. In Silbury tradition, Sil was a bit like Lady Godiva, since she or he was on a horse, except for the fact she/he was actually clothed in golden armour. Rather than shining with naked beauty, Sulis may have been shining with golden radiance from her armour. (The golden-armour tradition may come from the kurgans of Russia, where a warrior in golden armour with a silver cup was actually dug out of a mound, at the Issyk kurgan. The story subsequently spread, but in ancient times, and perhaps became associated with Silbury Hill) It is also apparent she was an underground goddess. The waters of Sulis are the waters from below. Sulis is yet another form arising from the primal Earth Mother.

Silbury hill is like an enormous round barrow. The fact it is large implies to me that it is built for a deity rather than a man. One problem. It dates to about 2400 BC which is usually seen as before they even started building round barrows, which are really more of a Bronze-Age thing. (The problem is compounded by the fact that there *are* Stone-Age round barrows.) Silbury hill, like Stonehenge and Avebury, are Stone Age and communal long barrows for Neolithic farmers, which were the vogue. Round barrows seem to reflect singular burial, selfishness, property and status, and an expanded population a with social hierarchy. If we are talking about a possible multicultural Britain back then, that also complicates the situation as we would have different burial cultures mixing.

The Bath bath seems to have been dedicated to a variation of the god Sol as it existed nearly three thousand years after the building of Silbury Hill. The bath is right next to the medieval Bath Abbey. I was comparing the Roman layout and it appears that they built the Abbey right next door to where the Temple of Minerva once stood. This was all about the old philosophy of updating the old religion with newer ideas. This temple had something called the *tholos* which looked like a Greek 'temple of the winds' but with much bigger pillars! There was a replica of this in the museum.

Figure 4.14: An unknown protector god of the baths. This face once loomed over the entrance. He seems to be the 'other' god at Bath. He looks related to the green man, or one of several possible deities. Perhaps he is based on the sky or Sun god, with a bit of earth shaker = Poseidon, mixed in, since he looks a little like Oceanus, on the Mildenhall treasure, another possible 'green man'. We do not really know who he is. If he is the Sun, he could even be the Golden Man of Silbury Hill!

Previously, in Germany, near Dortmund, in the village of Soest we saw an old pagan church called Old St Mary's. Inside, Sylvia noticed an effigy of three women looking over the crucifixion, the original 'godmother'! All were of equal height with heads bent just the same way. It is known as the triple goddess but the medieval Christians came up with ideas of them being Mary's relations in various paintings. Some medieval artists painted the triple goddess as Mary's relatives. Others made it rather obvious they were thinking about an ancient deity. I saw this effigy again in the Roman carvings. The associated information stated that the 'triple goddess' was a Celtic deity! It was amazing that Dortmund shared a goddess with Bath but then again Somerset is not too far from *Dor*-set so there might be some tribal connection with Dortmund.

The triple goddess was also in the bathhouse itself, implying waters sacred to the Earth Mother. Was Sul the triple goddess? It is a possibility. The huge 'moat' around Silbury Hill implies sacred waters as well. This may have been carried through into the development of the round barrow, or Stonehenge itself which also has this 'moat', or 'henge'.

The Green Man seems to be a Roman deity as well as being definitely pre-Roman. His effigy or something they might have called 'Oceanus' (a suggestion) was formerly on an arch over the entrance to the bath. I saw the incomplete bath entrance in the museum, and lots of other pillars and statues as well! I also saw the main outdoor bath, with steam coming out. There were also lesser baths and sacred pools around the place! In the 1600s and 1700s English kings came here and they put up lots of statues of Roman emperors. It is really a fine place. There are so many old Roman blocks in the museum that it is simply amazing. Due to the rebuilding over the centuries, Bath seems to be Britain's best 'Roman' site.

Stonehenge

I had to wait for one o'clock to hop on the bus tour. It was a really good experience and it was a very good tour. We passed some villages with thatched houses. I began to get emotional when we finally got onto the long and majestic Salisbury plain, where Stonehenge is located. Along with the Sphinx and pyramids, Stonehenge is *the* premiere location for New Agers, and any tourist really, who is interested in misty ancient things. While I am not of that loose New Age religion, I have been studying Stonehenge since I was a baby, and it all felt very magical. It felt like a true spiritual home, in a way beyond which any words can express.

It was clear that the site for Stonehenge was chosen after a great amount of deliberation between various proto-druids and kings. The monument somehow goes with the surrounding landscape, for fifty miles in each direction.

Salisbury plain, (or the plain of Sulis!) as it turns out, is not flat, but slightly hilly. You can see very far into the distance. It has a very timeless feel to it. The old eroded hills speak to you of the the countless eons which represent the past, and the generations who traversed them. We are of the soil, 'biocrystals' as I like to call them, and will one day return to our home there.

Figure 4.15: Photo of the Triple Goddess, from Bath. These could be the three aspects of the Earth Mother. Maybe a goddess with many heads is required to interact with a sky god who also has many heads, such as Taranis, or Svetovid? They may have been the male consorts. Is that you, Sulis? Incidentally, according to legend, the Germanic triple goddess, the Norns, are goddesses who weave fate. They also live under the world tree, presumably in a mound, which makes them rather relevant to ideas of pyramids.

Figure 4.16: The excellent Roman bath with statues of emperors. It has all been rebuilt in the last few centuries.

We passed some earthworks and hill forts as well. The guide told us that this is actually the UFO capital of Britain! He said that this is also where most crop circles are found. I guess many of them could come from camping hippies on ayahuasca or something they wish was that. The 'UFO' idea however, one might associate with the feeling that there is 'something more' to the place, or at least the hope that there is something more, for Stonehenge is an enigma without explanation. It all has something to do with the spiritual feel of the region.

We were driving too fast to get really good photos, but we stopped at Stonehenge and had one hour with it. A thought came upon first seeing the strange structure: 'What is that fake Stonehenge-look-alike grey gnarly bunch of rocks on top of that hill? Is *that* it... ah yes well I suppose it is!' It was the real thing alright. It is right along the highway. Aircraft circle around it to have a look at it as well.

There were not as many people as I had expected. One reason was that it was a weekday. The other reason was the late autumn season. One can walk around it, but one is not allowed too close. English Heritage security guards with uniforms and walkie talkies watch over the mass of ancient rocky ridiculousness that gypsies used to camp under. There is also a symbolic rope barrier around the primal edifice. 'Thus far, and no further. Look all you want, but don't you dare touch.'

I looked on all the other prominent stones around it. These were perhaps older unshaped stones, the 'heel' and also the 'slaughter stones'. One theory I had formerly nursed was that there was writing on top of one of the trilithon stones. Up close I saw that that was actually an attempt at merely splitting the stone in a different place. I saw the same splitting patterns on stones on Knocknarea in Ireland. I also saw a few faces on the stones that I had noticed on photographs once before.

It later occurred to me that Stonehenge is almost like an English cathedral. In an English or European cathedral one often gets to walk around behind the altar area, the ambulatory. This is often a kind of gallery of saints, which is also horseshoe shaped! Treating the circles as passageways, one can do the same at Stonehenge. Anatomy professor John Young, in his *Sacred Sites of the Knights Templar*, thinks there is a connection between Stonehenge and the round Templar Churches of Britain. That is a long shot, but hardly impossible. The common ancestor would go very far back indeed, and is perhaps found in stone circles of the Middle East.

Stonehenge is on top of a flat hill. That itself is interesting with regards to investigations into the pyramid religion. The stones are *enormous*! The trilithons in the middle are between three to four times my height (6'2") or a little more. It is hard to be sure because you cannot actually walk up to them, unless you are part of a very special tour. Whoever built it definitely knew what they were doing. This is true cyclopean architecture (supposedly built by huge giant cyclopses) in action.

I was so busy taking photos that I forgot to do a bit of meditation at Stonehenge, on my first visit, to see what it felt like. On my second visit a few days later on another tour, I remembered, and it felt something like this. 'Something is sleeping here under the earth'. There was a further message. 'Something will happen'. (If the reader does not like the idea of a spiritual impression, and I can understand that, please treat it as 'architectural licence.' Each building creates its own imagery and associations.) That is what the left brain made out of the right brain's signals, anyway! The stones themselves look like trees. In this respect Stonehenge is a kind of sacred grove. Groves are sacred to everybody, not just the druids. A spectacular 3D, abstract-tree artwork from 2000 BC? Cave art is almost abstract art, why not this?

Figure 4.17: Stonehenge is on a small flat hill, overlooking the surrounding countryside. If we were to cover over Stonehenge and turn it into a hill, the way Göbekli Tepe in Turkey was covered after 8000 BC, we would have, perhaps, a mound with a moat. Such is the design of Silbury Hill.

The stones are densely packed and it feels like they have somehow integrated themselves into the landscape. The 'henge' word in Stonehenge comes from the large circular ditch surrounding the stones. There is actually a *much* bigger natural henge around the whole thing which goes for a mile or less on each side. Is this 'the moat?' All around we have the monuments on nearby hilltops: barrows or grave mounds from different eras. If it is Sul's plain, I do not see why it possibly is not Sul's temple, among a number of other things. A Greek traveller, Pytheas, visited a 'spherical temple' back in the 320s BC, in Hyperborea. He said it was for the Sun. Obviously Roman 'Sun' is written as 'Sol'. (Sul, Salisbury?)

The whole feeling was slightly hypnotic but I did not feel like staying. Maybe if I was walking among the stones it would have been different. I felt there was some gloomy energy or something *deep* underneath Stonehenge. The energy is a sleeping energy, like a coiled snake. It is not an uneasy feeling that I got, but not really that positive a feeling either. It has a brooding malevolence, like a Jack in the Box waiting to spring, like it is going to do something, like it is *supposed* to do something. This might sound creepy but it is almost *pretending*. There are of course many ancient tales about stones which may reflect such subconscious energies. They supposedly used to dance around as men and were turned to stone for dancing on the wrong day. Alternately they wake up at midnight and go down to the water to drink.

A more modern way of expressing possible subconscious energies and subtle feelings of inspiration on the site lie in the lengths some people have gone to prove possible archaeoastronomical associations on the site, as if the site was truly an ancient computer. Without arguing the case of whether it may or may not be, and the highest and most formidable authorities say 'yes' that it is, the reality is that Stonehenge as a structure, represents almost the limit of what was achievable by a Stone-Age culture.

Subconscious thoughts aside, where is the sacred tree on the Stonehenge hill? Apparently there used to be a pillar in the 8th millennium BC. This was the earlier use. Did that venerate the tree? I have the idea that Stonehenge is a flat version of the tree. In this respect it resembles a poplar tree on a stalk. In Ireland the tombs from 5000 BC appear to have no spirals. In about 3000 BC the spiral is established. The cross is the sacred pagan symbol which replaced the spiral. A Celtic cross looks like it has a spiral lurking behind it. The cross, superimposed, almost inspires replacement of an earlier idea.

Callanish, Outer Hebrides, Scotland, a huge cross-like structure, when viewed from *above*, is known as the 'Stonehenge of the North'. Built in 2900-2600 BC, it is sort of like a proto-Celtic cross. The cross shape is found inside hill tombs. It is the structure of the tomb itself. Either it is trying to represent the tree of life, or that happens to be a convenient way of making rooms. There needs to be some kind of symmetry if you are going to do something of that order. It would not do for the dead to have an unsymmetrical tomb. Stonehenge is younger still. It might be speculated that in the time of Callanish, the tree had already been abstracted into the cross.

Why do we not have more evidence? The answer is that everything would have been carved from wood in those days, one of the reasons that Britain is denuded of timber, with the Romans as another early possibility. All the houses and items especially were simply made from wood. It was rare indeed that something was made from stone. Thus it is all gone really, except for the gold, and the rich mythology.

We also passed the Westbury White Horse which was a very long way away. This is a white horse carved in the chalk of the hill, with overgrowing grass and topsoil regularly scraped out. Not so here, for it was turning brown. The tour-bus driver was adamant that these horses were tribes marking territory, rather than religious symbols.

Both bus tours back from Stonehenge played the song: ' *Climbing up on Salisbury Hill... I could see the city lights!*' just when the city lights on Box Hill, and Bath in general were coming into view. Apparently the singer lived on Box Hill and the song was written nearby. The city lights around the valley were indeed a magical experience with the setting Sun, and after a magnificent day touring forgotten glories. I got back to the hostel, so conveniently perched on top of one of the seven steep Roman hills of Bath and collapsed into bed. Bath is a delightful city.

Stonehenge is far older than it seems. As mentioned, Castleden writes in *The Stonehenge People* that it seems to have had some sacred tree stump or possibly even a huge totem pole at the site, which dates to around 8000 BC! This may have been the centre of an earlier cult, possibly related to even a predecessor of the pyramid religion. It was brought to England from elsewhere, after the ice sheets melted.

Stonehenge is built like a tomb, but uncovered. It has a very similar layout of passages, or doorways, to the tombs you find on one end of a long barrow. A friend pointed out to me that although Stonehenge is built as if it were a tomb, the reason they possibly failed to cover it up, is that they had a larger population than they might have expected. Religion moved from the Lascaux caves, designed to be seen by very few, to an area on a shallow hilltop where a great many could stand around and observe whatever spectacles went on there, as people do today, now that the Stonehenge religion in a sense has been reborn. I wonder if there has even been a time in its entire history when people have failed to attend Stonehenge on the morning of the summer solstice?

Krakus Mound, Navan fort, Silbury hill are all built around a solid wooden core. Was this the burial of the world tree or Yggdrasil? I feel the proto-Stonehenge may have been something like one of the above. The cross-like chambers in a tomb also resemble this, the branches of Yggdrasil. Perhaps Stonehenge with its abstracted Celtic Cross-like shape, is an abstracted tree on a mound.

Leon Stover mentions in his *Stonehenge City*, that Stonehenge is really a symbolic chambered tomb. It is 'big brother view' of the after-

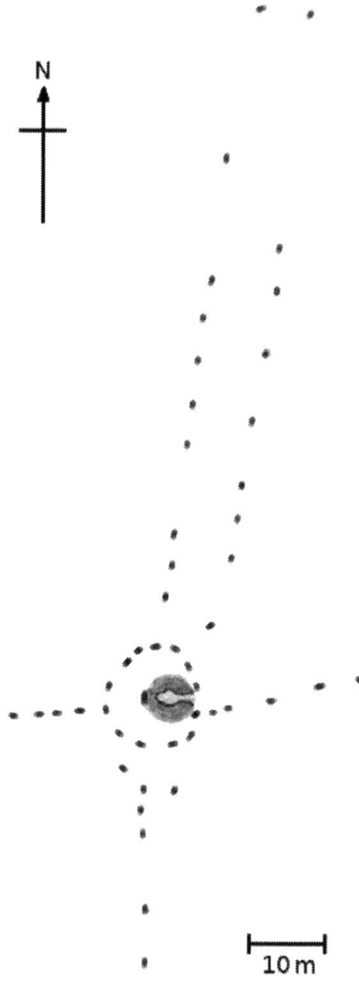

Figure 4.18: Callanish, a huge proto-Celtic cross. Or is it an abstracted tree? There is a chambered tomb in the middle. The off-centre axis may be due to astronomical or unknown reasons.

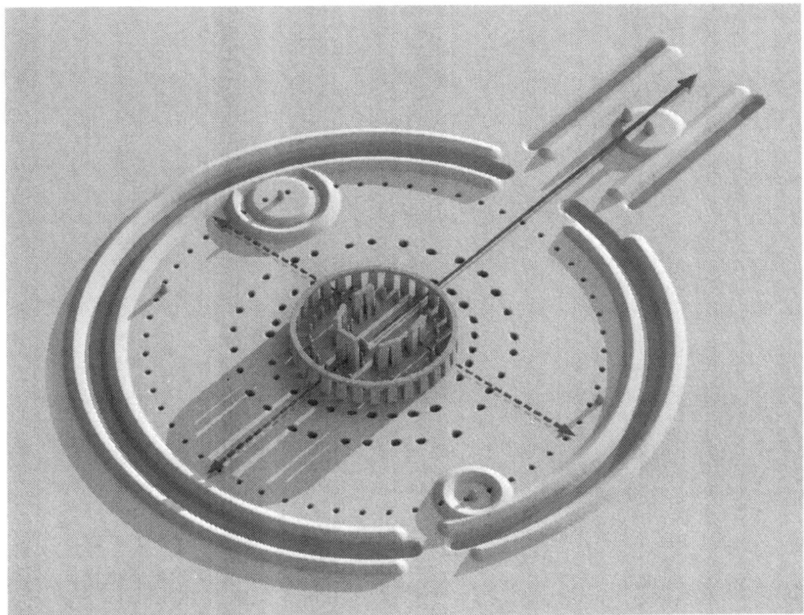

Figure 4.19: An aerial view of Stonehenge showing a cross-like configuration. It also looks like a poplar 'tree' with the 'stem' to the north west, which is a formerly-henged 'avenue.' The Altar Stone can be seen standing up inside the Trilithon circle, towards the rear of the centre of the monument. By Joseph Lertola.

life, as if the tomb walls were transparent. That is the great mystery, but perhaps it should not be. Perhaps there was an idealist philosophy at the time, of matter not really existing, or being that important.

An earlier neolithic long barrow or chambered tomb was built by farmers for their dead. It was a place one could enter. As population expanded, more people needed to see the spectacle, so it became 'outdoor.' There was now no need to cover up the tomb. It occurs to me that Stonehenge was built at the end of the great pyramid-building age of the third millennium BC. It was made just as the temple was replacing the pyramid, in Middle Kingdom Egypt. The temple allows spirits to reside more in the open, instead of being covered. It allows a human interaction with each stone.

Stonehenge was 'solved' by George Terence Meaden, in the 1980s. His solution should probably be endorsed. The Stonehenge rocks are

Figure 4.20: In this old artist impression of Stonehenge, courtesy of William Stukeley, the Altar Stone is shown to have had pride of place in what he calls the Sanctum Sanctorum ('holy of holies'), in the middle of Stonehenge, as an actual altar. In fact we now know that the Altar Stone was probably upright. Unlike the other stones it is a different colour. It is described as light coloured, or a white sandstone, but also as a 'purplish green micaceous sandstone'. (There is a collapsed trilithon on top of it). It is of the era 2600 BC. Inigo Jones, an early explorer of Stonehenge, wrote: '...whether it might be an Altar or no I leave to the judgement of others.' According to Terence Meaden, it was a receptacle for a shadow-phallus arching across from the Heel stone on the solstice. This cosmic coitus re-fertilised the land.

essentially three colours. There are the Sarsen stones. There are the bluestones, brought over from Wales. Finally there is a collapsed 'Altar Stone' which once had a central position in front of the foremost Trilithon. This is a type of sandstone, which is obviously going to have been lighter than the other stones. Meaden says that people looking away from Stonehenge at the Sun above the heel stone are perhaps looking the 'wrong way'. In fact they should be looking into the monument, at the light or shadow striking the Altar Stone (which it obviously no longer does, hence the confusion).

The male penis which is the heel stone allows the morning midsummer light to strike the altar stone for a limited time in the morning. It reminds one of Newgrange, and also that mound's white facade. This is a marriage of the male and female, or the sky god, represented by the Sun, with the Earth Mother, a white goddess at the centre. She is the Earth Mother in a huge uncovered or invisible mound. Compared to the famous slaughter stone, heel stone and altar stone, the famous Sarsen Circle is actually a later addition, from 2000 BC, after the great period of pyramid building was long complete; a fancy touch?

Other sites in England, with a synthesis

England has many pyramids and mounds. A good introduction is provided in the works of Rodney Castleden and also Michael Damas' *The Silbury Treasure*. Chapter nine includes a discussion of Gib Hill, a flat-top hill (excavation revealed no tomb), the enormous Hatfield Barrow (excavated extensively until its destruction by proto-archaeologists in the early 1800s, no fabulous burial was found), the Marlborough Mount, also known as Merlin's Mount (it dates to 2400 BC), as well as Dragon's Hill, Berkshire, another flat-topped mound. The flat-topped mound does seem to be the European way of making these structures.

There are another set of mounds which were partly destroyed by treasure hunters, in about 1815, to provide employment to local people, if not earlier. These are the Bartlow Burial Mounds, Cambridgeshire. Some very rich Roman objects were excavated here, including some chests, with no account given as to what they really were. They are classified as 'Romano-British' but mounds of this order are not really a late-Roman thing to do. Then again, there are seven of them. Romans loved their seven hills, in Rome, Bath, and elsewhere. The largest is mound IV, at about 13.7 metres tall and 43 metres in diameter. One of the mounds is totally destroyed and two are only partly, still in

Figure 4.21: The former appearance of the Bartlow burial mounds. This diagram certainly cannot be construed in any way as evidence, but there appear to have been three prominent hills with possibly sacred groves on top, presumably maintained by superstitious locals.

existence.

The old picture of them seems to present three major mounds, and then lesser barrows surrounding. The three major mounds have some vegetation on top. Today they look quite hemispherical and are still there, surrounded by trees, though some are slightly ruined. The scene in fig. 4.21 reminds one considerably of the mounds at Uppsala.

The Priory Mount in Lewes Castle, in Sussex is an interesting structure, covered by Rodney Castleden in *The Wilmington Giant*. I have a nice authoritative reference called *Castles of Britain and Ireland*, by a British historian with the curious name of Plantagenet Somerset Fry. A prolific author, he called himself after his areas of interest. It states that Lewes castle is one of the few unusual ones with two mottes. Lincoln is another. I think what really happened is that two mounds were found in a suitable location, and a castle was formed around them, incorporating them as towers. Interestingly, the author writes that the south motte (the Priory Mount) was composed mainly of chalk blocks quarried nearby. Castleden says this makes it rather similar to Silbury Hill. Examining a photo of this motte we see a unique processional pathway going up to the top. This indicates it was some kind of religious site in former times, before a certain Guliemus de Warenne decided to change it into a castle a thousand years ago. It has some other similarities with Silbury Hill, pointed out by Castleden. For instance it is exactly

Figure 4.22: The Priory Mount at Lewes, Sussex. It is like a spiral cone, carved or constructed out of chalk which was excavated from a nearby place, then covered over. Little else is known. Rodney Castleden proposes it as a neolithic harvest hill. Apparently crosses are taken up to the top on Good Friday. That would suggest Easter fertility. Crosses were also formerly found on the mounds near Cracow in Poland.

one third the size. It has a slope of thirty one degrees, which compares to Silbury's slope of twenty nine degrees.

Ox bones were also found a foot or so below the surface. Apparently it is often the case that it used to be considered that the bones of the old giants were dug up at old sites, with dissenters always claiming they were ox bones. It should probably be pointed out that the cow or bull might have something to do with the pyramid religion, but perhaps not specifically as the pyramid perhaps represented another world, rather than this one. The bull or cow is also more a religion of the east. In Germany for instance the word for God is Gott, i.e. '(the) Good'. In Poland, or Russia, the word for God is Bog. Bull meanwhile is 'Byk' in Polish. Just one vowel shift is all it takes. By the time we get to India, cows are so sacred they interfere with traffic.

Ox bones do turn up quite a lot, including in sacred sites in Britain. In the *Iliad*, the Achaean people built something very similar to what we know as pyramids, as in fig. 5.2. We have warriors in the Iliad who wrap fat around cow bones, burning it for their sky gods. This is supposedly a memory of Mycenaean times.

The cow or bull was worshipped in Sumeria as well as early Egypt as a kind of chief god. Its face graces the famous pre-dynastic Narmer tablet, surveying the scene of the smiting of the enemies of the Egyptian king.

It is a little known possible fact, that when the pioneering archaeologist Giovanni Belzoni entered below the second, or Khafra Pyramid in 1818, cattle bones, debris and dirt were found in the otherwise empty black granite sarcophagus. It is not known if the pyramid had previously been entered but the conventional explanation is that the pyramids were robbed in antiquity. In *Egyptian Dawn*, Robert Temple, however points out that an empty tomb is a symbol of Christianity. Jesus had to first spend time in his underworld tomb, perhaps like the bleeding god Baldr, before being resurrected. It shows that resurrection has occurred. It is interesting to note that the Bible makes a point that Jesus' cave tomb was sealed, and he could not have escaped, yet there was nothing found inside save for his wrappings. This section might have been written by anyone who had explored an Egyptian pyramid, sealed, yet empty. A magnificently comprehensive book is *Giza: The Truth*, by the authors Ian Lawton and Chris Ogilvie-Herald. They point out, as do others, that the Giza pyramid was a tomb, for Khufu, due to the various evidence such as the security measures, the interior portcullis, the sarcophagus, etc. Or was it? The portcullis in the antechamber, some stone doors which were intended to slide down, shutting off the King's Chamber, may simply have been to prevent anyone entering the King's Chamber, as it was, to vandalise it, even in the absence of burial or royal treasure! There is still plenty in there, even today, which is possible to destroy.

Stonehenge itself, and even pyramids, are perhaps tombs for a god. The lack of burial, as in the pyramids, even around the world, indicates the following. 'This, oh underworld bleeding god, is your home, but the sarcophagus is empty, and always will be, for you have been resurrected to give us a bountiful harvest.' It is a form of forcing the gods around, sympathetic magic in a monument too big for even them to ignore. 'You, have been resurrected. We insist!' The portcullis may even have been to ensure that the god could only be resurrected, rather than leave through the door to return again to Egypt as a ghost, *sans* resurrection. The shafts, which point to stars may point the way for him. There is only one exit from the pyramid, the true magic of resurrection. I also have another explanation for the shafts, discussed later, associated with the counterpart to resurrection, rebirth.

Although the Khufu sarcophagus has been badly vandalised, we can examine it. The inside is perfectly smooth, but the outside has been left rough. This is fascinating. Furthermore it is a red granite. The rough exterior reminds me of a geode. This is a type of rock. On the outside it is rough, but if you cut it open there is a crystal jewel to be found within. It may symbolise underworld entombment, for a period of time. Robert Schoch thinks the Khufu pyramid was built in the Old Kingdom as an observatory platform, perhaps a millennium before Khufu, subsequently turned into a pyramid by that king. He says later on that it was broken into and used for ritual purposes for a rather long time, and during this time, various pyramid texts were modified to incorporate aspects of the pyramid's interior. Tyldesley in *Pyramids*, writes the pyramid mathematics are to help the king get to heaven, though she does not explain how or why. I think it does this because the Earth measurements possibly inherent in the structure can be explained not with the pyramid as an observatory but as a 'centring.' Part of this involves an alignment in different ancient theoretical dimensions. The alleged later 'ritual' purpose may simply be a reflection of old mythology ideas, though Schoch's idea is not impossible. Who would not want to hold a ritual within the Great Pyramid?

I would also like to point out that mound tombs in Britain and elsewhere have an internal cross-like configuration of chambers, so there is one origin of the cross in relation to the resurrecting shining young man god. All this might have made incoming Christian ideas more amenable to the 'pagans.'

A very fascinating pyramid-like structure exists on the Isle of Man, known as Tynwald Hill. Tyn or perhaps 'dun' is a word meaning fort. 'Wald' means wilds, forest or even jungle.

Let us bear in mind once again that some of the best of the ancient world is preserved on outlying islands, free from raids by horsed invaders of the plains. We have here the remnants of a primordial ritual. We actually have, at Tynwald hill, a pyramid-like hill which was used as a parliament or place of assembly until modern times! Nearby, with a pathway leading to it, is a church. This would originally have been

Figure 4.23: Tynwald Hill, Isle of Man, in the eighteenth century. It is one of the earliest drawings.

a pagan temple. A world tree or Irminsul-like totem pole was once placed on top. The Irminsul, a Saxon favourite, was essentially a tree trunk set up in the open air. It could be quite similar in purpose to the tree trunks which seem to be found in Silbury, Navan Site B, and the Krakus Mound. There is a mast there today, in the centre. We do not know how old the structure is.

Is this stepped platform really a pyramid, derived from the old pyramid-builder religion, or merely another kind of entity? The answer to all the questions is possibly 'yes'. A fascinating fact is that the hill is composed of soil taken from all seventeen parishes of the isle. Nigel Pennick says that this is therefore a microcosm of the government, and this is why it has been the Manx parliament, for an immemorial time. I would think that the soil placed here would have had the sympathetic-magic effect of using the interaction of creative gods, associated with the world mountain, to fertilise all the soil of the island, by fertilising just samples of it. This then, is a pyramid, the same as everywhere else that this practice has been encountered.

Of all the pyramids of England, Silbury Hill, however, is the best. You cannot walk on it, so the partially sculpted Glastonbury Tor is the

Figure 4.24: An early 19th-century drawing of Tynwald hill. There is actually something quite like this in China, an effective pyramid complex still functioning. The religion died on Man, but in China it lives on, and we will examine that later on.

next best thing. I thought back to the great day I had had on the Tor. The Sun was setting and I needed the bus back, but as I said, I had forgotten to check the 'energies', or more scientifically, the reaction of the emotive brain to the environment; call it 'architectural licence' if you want, or 'psychological effect.'

The brain tried to decipher the feeling, the energy pattern I got, to put it into words, to the tune of the setting Sun, and shivering cold.

'I had strong energy once but it is fading.'

Chapter 5

Old Europe, Kurgans and beyond

Wherever one looks, one simply finds more and more. We have a religion, with very similar ideas, spread over a very vast area in deeply ancient times. Trading links and migration seem to have kept old ideas alive and thriving for a very long period of time.

There are two sources of stone chamber mounds/pyramids which are rather early. One is the megalithic culture, including Malta to the West, and the Libyans. I believe this group built step pyramids, as well as smooth-sided earth barrows. Another is the eastern one. These people built the smooth-sided earth Kurgans, with internal chambers, and Kurgan-inspired tombs in various places.

It seems these Kurgan people are commonly thought of as the truer, more recent 'Indo-Europeans' who migrated into Europe from the East. That is partly true and partly an exaggeration. It would take a statistician with a full DNA catalogue and supercomputer to sort out the mess.

In the 1960s, the ethnologist Marija Gimbutas came up with the Kurgan hypothesis of Indo-European spread from the east. The idea is controversial because there seem to have been various earlier migrations of Indo-Europeans. Some theorists speculate that rather than migrating from a central source, Indo-Europeans developed by contact, over a wide area. The mounds towards the south and east in Europe correspond to what Gimbutas called 'Old Europe', a civilisation which precedes Egypt. This is essentially Italy to Crimea, the Balkans really.

Gimbutas said that they were neither matriarchal nor patriarchal, but they may have been swamped by a patriarchal religion. There may be something to this, but it is still a controversy, so let us skip the details, because personally I can see instances of matriarchy and patriarchy everywhere. Tribes moved about a lot. They also mixed, while they moved.

One thing that I will insist upon is that in the south east we see a different style of tomb which was more refined and with a larger internal burial chamber, than what was built in the west, which was essentially a few enormous stones up against each other. This style of tomb stretched from Etruria to Bulgaria, to Crimea, to Asia. I would suggest there was even an instance in Ireland, as we have nice facades, for instance at the Tara tomb of the hostages, which remind one of the east, in fig. 1.53.

The tombs of Malta are more like Stonehenge, Cyclopean and sombre, and exceedingly ancient. They could have been based upon a prototype of a North African culture of the Libyans, whom we will discuss again, and who may or may not have contributed to Stonehenge. This style of the East... dare I say it, with its elegant corbelled roofing, really does remind one of what is going on in the Great pyramid of Giza itself!

There are simply too many pyramids in Europe, and around the world to cover even just the major ones. Here is a selection, together with a rationale of the major elements involved in their design. I have not yet had the honour of visiting these ones. They are included in this book for the sake of comprehensiveness, as well as to illustrate the point that there are strange similarities between these and pyramids elsewhere. The similarities are explicable when one considers that Stone Age people were semi-nomadic, or fully nomadic on the Asiatic desert-like steppe. They might settle in one area, or they might cover vast distances should the food run low in a particular locale.

As we go further south in Europe, mounds become less soil and clay, and more stone. Eventually we see bits of Egypt thrown in with the mix.

A secondary consideration to the widespread nature of similar tombs, for both god and man, was that ancient man had to cross a vast sea or ocean. This is not a simple case of Stone-Age migration, but a Stone-Age trading empire. One of the earliest, which preceded both the Minoans and Phoenicians, has not even been officially rediscovered, but information about it is to be found in Temple's *Egyptian Dawn*,

2010. It seems to be *the* lost civilisation people have been looking for, which can help explain various ancient enigmas, for instance the early distribution of the alphabet. This is the civilisation of the Libyans.

Flinders Petrie, forerunner and founder of modern Egyptology, stated that they were in part originators of Egyptian civilisation. Furthermore, he noted that there are similar alphabetic sounds, from the runes of Scandinavia, to the letters of Spain, to Libya, to South Arabia, which all contained more sounds than Phoenician. Egypt clearly has a far earlier alphabet, mixed in their their cumbersome hieroglyphic system! Hieroglyphics are not pure syllables. In fact they have consonants, vowels, as well as syllables, and determinative signs, (a picture sign) to help one capture the context of what is being said.

These people were perhaps, in part, the Atlantic megalith builder civilisation. If we look at a map of megalith distribution, they are invariably all located in coastal areas, Spain, France and Britain, as well as Ireland, and Sardinia, Malta. This implies some connection with an early seafaring civilisation.

They may have been related to the 'Giants' from Africa, according to Geoffrey of Monmouth who may have helped construct Stonehenge. One will not find any monument closer in resemblance to Stonehenge's Sarsen circle than Plate 60 in Temple's book, *Egyptian Dawn*. He found this photo in a very old book, and it is reproduced in fig. 5.1.

Firstly, it would seem that Stonehenge is something like a Mediterranean temple which is built upon a henge, or circular ditch, which is really a central-north European type of thing. It is a mixing of two cultures. So much for the ditch culture. Where did the stone culture come from? What would Stonehenge look like if the builders made another version elsewhere, where the sacred circle was not in fashion? With a single photo, the Libyans become the major culprits.

This culture appears to have constructed trilithons and even something like a 'Sarsen circle' (except that it is rectangular or linear) in North Africa. I cannot say anything about the builders of the Stonehenge bluestones as they are not seen in the photo from North Africa. It is a lost temple in a now forgotten location.

In the black and white photo, the camera appears to be resting on the ground. The photographer obviously did not have a stand with him because there is long grass obscuring part of the picture. Looming in the distance is something which utterly defies belief. The photo, which seems to be genuine (in that it was hopefully not somehow forged when it was taken), may cause a sensation when a few more Stonehenge researchers find out about it.

Whoever I show it to seems to think it *is* Stonehenge, until I inform them it is indeed not! A major difference between it and Stonehenge, is that it is possibly in the shape of a rectangle. Meanwhile Stonehenge is in the shape of a circle. I would rationalise it like this. The builders were partly a sea people who built an outdoor temple to possibly resemble a tomb. There are no burials at Stonehenge other than intrusive ones, so this would be a temple for the gods, or a tomb for the gods, as it is shaped like a tomb. Meanwhile, when this culture reached Britain, they sought to build something in the style of the circle monuments of Britain. Stonehenge is thus a circle, whilst managing to look unlike anything else in Britain, except perhaps the skeleton of a tomb, something rather like Newgrange.

Temple thinks the closest analogue to the megalithic language, if such a thing ever existed, may have been Basque. I would suggest it may also have been close to currently North-European Sami. This is not a load of hot air, for there are strong genetic links between them and the Berbers of North Africa, who are the pre-Arab inhabitants.

The book by H. S. Cowper, *The Hill of Graces*, 1879 is a fascinating one. Basically the book is all about artefacts from the old and neglected Libyan civilisation, and later times. There have been so many Stonehenge books (hundreds, I have not read them all, but am trying!) produced by authors who have totally racked their brains, yet all going in the wrong direction, and who would probably have given anything for this one clue.

Firstly, this was due to the oversight of the author of Hill of Graces with his travel-bookish but beautiful title choice, (it is in fact a travel book, but he might at least have called it something like *African Stonehenge*, in order to be merciful to Stonehenge researchers) which may have put people off. Then there has been an over-cautious assumption by later researchers who mainly limited the Stonehenge domain to the geography of Southern Britain, with certain exceptions, as lintels are not found elsewhere in the Atlantic megalithic civilisation.

In the 1960s there were many books written claiming that Mycenaeans built Stonehenge, partly due to a similarity with the Lion Gate lintel of Mycenae, similar swords, and the then-uncalibrated and incorrect radio-carbon datings of Stonehenge. (It is now officially a thousand years older than previously thought.) Over eight hundred years ago, however Geoffrey of Monmouth wrote that Merlin once informed King Arthur that Stonehenge was erected in Ireland by giants from Africa,

Figure 5.1: I challenge anyone to show this to their friends and ask them what they think it is, and *where* they think it is! That long savannah grass makes me think a lion is going to sneak up from somewhere. This is from a book from 1897 entitled *Hill of Graces: A record of Investigation among the Trilithons and Megalithic Sites of Tripoli*, which contains many photographs of Stonehenge-like trilithons scattered in Libya. Because 'Stonehenge' was not in the title, (why were not 'megalithic', 'Neolithic' or 'trilithon' a sufficient enough clue? Then again there were no library computer catalogues until the last thirty years) no one who has written any Stonehenge book for over a hundred years seemingly knew about this, until very recently, when Robert Temple looked in this old book and brought its existence to the world, or at least those few who have read his book.

who settled there. (I wonder if 'they' brought the 'Babel' religion there as well?) The monument was supposedly subsequently transported to Britain. According to Monmouth, these people also once lived in Britain, before a migratory expedition coming out of the Mediterranean under legendary Brutus, overthrew them, supposedly in the Sea People's era. Naturally this discovery has implications for mound-building or pyramid research, if we compare Silbury Hill, near Stonehenge and Avebury with other monuments and pyramids, built at the same time as Old-Kingdom mastabas and pyramids. An additional implication is that of a shared mythology between Northern Europe, especially Ireland, and Africa. This, as a rectangular temple, could also be a missing link between Stonehenge and Egyptian temples of the Old Kingdom, such as the Khafra valley temple.

The existence of some forgotten trading civilisation would partly explain the major idea being pushed in this book, that Europe does in fact have things quite similar to pyramids, by both religion, which is being elucidated as we go along, and form. The counter-punch of this argument is that various pyramids elsewhere might well have been subservient to variations upon a similar religion, including in Egypt!

These Libyans were not *the* pyramid builders, but they may have been but one later and widespread branch of that much earlier culture. There were different wings of the pyramid-builders. One branch was in the East, from Asia towards Europe. Another branch was in West Europe and in the Mediterranean. There was also an Egypto-Sumerian branch. These branches interacted and there were cross-migrations of different pyramid- or mound-building techniques.

The interaction is too complicated to fully describe, or perhaps to fathom. The independent existence of various wings of these migrations point to pyramid building having started before the third millennium, perhaps in the fourth, or much, much earlier. (see later pyramid-ritual evidence, provided here about Göbekli Tepe) In the next chapter we will once again discuss them briefly. The Egyptologist James Breasted considered in his *Archaic Egypt* that earliest Egypt was a fusion of part Libyan, part peoples from the east related to Sumerians, as well as pre-existing inhabitants.

Greece

Greece has several pyramids. I would suggest they seem to reflect imported traditions from both the north, as well as the south.

'Mycenaean' is a modern term, based on a supposed capital city in Mycenae, a former feudal empire of city states, in the Bronze Age, prior to the Dark Ages which began in perhaps the 1160s BC.

Memories of the Trojan war, which probably occurred several decades prior, could be based upon memories of the lack of stability in the final years of the old order, before pirates started rampaging around, burning down citadels. *'Achaeans'* are the name they go by in the *Iliad*, but it has been suggested this name should be associated with their final, dark days. They built themselves several spectacular tombs. Later Greeks said these were built by giants.

In fig. 5.4, we have the little pyramid of Hellinikon. This is a most fascinating structure. It was known to Greek geographer Pausanias, AD 110–*c*.180, who described it as a tomb. Dating revealed a surprise! It is just as old as the Egyptian pyramids, clocking in at at least prior to 2000 BC. How far back before this is in question, but several hundred years seems about right. The datings are a little controversial, but that date seems reasonable as the third millennium was the great pyramid building age.

Reflecting Egyptian practice, the whole monument is built from limestone, but of a grey type. Also reflecting Egyptian practice, there is a rectangular building surrounding the pyramid. Rectangular buildings are typical of the mastaba of the first dynasty, which contained a small mound in the middle, the prototype of the pyramid. The Khafra pyramid also has a prominent rectangular structure around it, as does the Djoser pyramid of the third dynasty. This is what became of the mastaba outline when the central mound, or pyramid, became much more important! (Don't worry about the Egypt details, we will cover this again) In this instance the remains of this building are about 7.03 metres by 9.07 metres.

Fascinatingly there is no burial. It is a conundrum which stumps one researcher after another when it comes to looking at pyramids and mounds. They are often unaware that so many other pyramids or mounds share the 'no-burial enigma.' Being specialists, they never mention the fact that other mounds seem to exhibit the same phenomena, as these are treated as entirely separate instances. Pausanias mentioned two tombs in the area, but twelve miles to the south west of Hellinikon. One was a regular tomb, another was a common tomb for fallen soldiers. We do not really know for sure what he was referring to, but if this is a tomb, then is it a 'common tomb' as well, or perhaps a tomb for a god?

Figure 5.2: The Treasury of Atreus is a Mycenaean tomb from about 1250 BC. It is basically from the age of the events of the Iliad, or a generation or so before. I am not quite sure what to make of this. It is undoubtedly a type of tumulus, and it has a similar corbel arch structure the Kurgan of Mithridates, in Crimea, fig. 5.6. It is basically a stone structure, which has been covered up with soil. This is not quite the same as a typical pyramid for rebirth. The reason is that the doorway is too large. Pyramids, even the Great Pyramid seem to have often had narrow passages, even if the builders possessed the technology to make large passages, like the Grand Gallery. The reason was the pyramid often symbolised rebirth. Spirits needed to be literally born out of it. This, on the other hand, is more like an actual room, for use! Nonetheless, this is considered a tomb!

Figure 5.3: Inside the Atreus tomb. According to the classical Greeks it was built by gigantic 'Cyclopeans'. The photo contains today's regular humans, for size comparison.

The proud little pyramid of Hellinikon remains an enigma. It essentially looks like someone in the third millennium BC, was excessively fascinated by what was going on in Egypt, or they themselves being Egyptian, decided to build their own pyramid.

The structure has stirred up a great deal of controversy for many years. In 1995, results were announced based upon a then-new dating technique of 'optical thermo-photo illumination', used for measuring ceramics, but in this case the limestone of the pyramid. The result was 2720 BC plus or minus 580 years.

The dates prompted speculation that the pyramid builders of Giza had originated in Greece, and moved to Egypt! It should be pointed out here that in *Egyptian Dawn* by Robert Temple, he and a colleague, Professor Ioannis Liritzis, conducting stone-date testing of the Giza area, registered a date of 3000 BC for the pyramid of Menkaure. This is almost five centuries older than Menkaure himself! (Fragments of a coffin bearing Menkaure's name *were* found in the burial chamber in his pyramid) For this and other reasons, people may well disregard the datings on the basis that older materials might have been used. That

Figure 5.4: Here we have the pyramid of Hellinikon.

is a decent reason but it requires further explanation.

Regular carbon datings of the pyramids, also, have long puzzled people, and almost consistently point to a greater age than is believed. These date the pyramid to a millennium to several centuries older than the chronological dates of the kings responsible for actually building them.

Rather than suggesting the chronologies are mixed up, (they are pretty firmly established) as some have done, I would simply suggest the puzzling datings would indicate the presence of an older, underlying structure, or materials, or a longer ritual use prior to the building of these various structures; in essence, Stone-Age ritual continuing in the same spot, into the Copper and Bronze Ages. That is certainly not impossible. That would of course carry the implication of a Stone-Age religion in one area for a very long time, till the time of the pyramids.

We have other Old-Kingdom era architecture in Greece as well. It would seem that city state of Thebes, and various other Greek cities went through their own 'intermediate periods', that is to say, periods of anarchy, during which all information was lost.

Contemporary with the Egyptian Old Kingdom, we have information that there was another civilisation in Greece, possibly preceding the Mycenaeans, who may have been northern invaders who made their tombs similar to tombs found in Russia and the east in general.

For there is another place in Greece called Amphion hill. It is perhaps like Glastonbury Tor, a natural hill which has been moulded. This is a conical step pyramid associated with the founding father of Thebes, though it is not known who he was. Some say Cadmus. Others say Amphion. Information accessible to the public is to be found on this in the book *Black Spark, White Fire*, by Richard Poe.

Excavations were done here by Theodorus Spiropoulos between 1971 and 1973, who called the site a 'pyramid', despite the fact it was not square-based. It was dated to 2500-2000 BC. He called the people responsible the Minyan Civilisation, and claimed it endured from 2800 to 1700 BC.

A burial chamber was found with no bodies, but signs of ancient grave robbery, even of gold fragments, were found. In his book, Poe thinks old Thebes was possibly composed in part of darker-skinned immigrants from Egypt.

One of the things which fascinates me about this is that there was an enduring legend regarding the site. In this tradition, people from central Greece would come to Thebes and would remove earth from the Amphion when the Sun crossed the constellation of Taurus, (sacred bull presumably) and then put it on the 'Antiope' grave. This would allegedly make their own farms back home more fruitful than Thebes. This is rather like what happened at Navan fort in Ireland!

Soil was being moved about, brought to a fertility hill, an old festival 'hall' of the ancestors, to bless it! As such, guards were allegedly once placed at the burial complex to prevent this. It is as if the pyramid was thought to increase the fertility of the land, by increasing the fertility of the soil around it. Spread the soil around, put it on another grave/mound and 'pow,' instant fertility power somewhere else! This seems to be one purpose associated with the harvest hills.

In his book *The New Pyramid Age*, Philip Coppens writes that he does not like it when conical structures like Silbury Hill are referred to as a pyramid, and that this detracts from what they really are, mounds, and their real beauty and significance. I would have to disagree, for if both mounds and pyramids are based on the same Stone-Age set of fertility ideas, then their difference could be accounted for as regional variation on a common theme.

One cannot really build a mound out of the fine Egyptian dust-like sand of the desert, which approaches the banks of the Nile. It would blow away. Coppens classifies pyramids according to geometric shape, but perhaps not function, or according to mythology, though he does discuss these aspects. There is no geometric-shaped pyramid in any mythology, but there is the world mountain, found all over.

I would say that what is called a pyramid, should be classified according to function, and that shape is partly based upon availability of materials and environment. People may have simply used what 'worked' in different places. (If one builds a pyramid in the desert, one uses stone or brick blocks which have a square shape, translating into a square-based pyramid when they are stacked!)

Nevertheless here Coppens makes an exception. He states that since Spiropoulos is a qualified archaeologist, and the profile of the Amphion pyramid, despite being conical, actually resembles a step pyramid, he is prepared to call it a pyramid also, for that may have been the intended visual effect. (This may be what is critically important, *profile*!)

As for the relation between Silbury and Giza, which were built about the same time, the answer is probably obvious. It was not the Egyptians who travelled to Britain or British who travelled to Egypt. Silbury and 3rd/4th dynasty pyramids are too different for that. Yet they are also too similar! Rather it was a common culture, emerging from Central Asia, or another location. One migratory tentacle peregrinated to Britain. Another reached the shores of the Nile in the time of the third Egyptian dynasty, and began to modify an existing structure, the mastaba, tinkering until it became a pyramid. Both cultures began with the intention of building a huge mound to heaven.

It is hard to find very much information about this structure or other related structures. We just do not know much about this. It just goes to show that we still live in an age of pioneers. There is so much we do not know about the lost and forgotten history of mankind, surviving only now in scraps of mythology, lives of saints based on earlier stories, and old wives' tales.

'Mithridates' in Crimea

'Kurgan' is the Russian word for barrow. It has a Tatar (Turkic) origin. These things are found all over Europe, and Asia as well, with a similar name. Due to geographical proximity, mounds in Sweden might also be called kurgans, despite the lack of Russian lingo in that nation.

In Poland, I encountered the word 'kopiec' more often than not being applied to 'barrow', but 'kurhan' is used as well. Poland has many thousands of kurhans. In the east, the first kurgans allegedly appear in the Caucasus in the fourth millennium BC. I point out that some of the Irish mounds photographed earlier in this book might have been found to date to about 5000 BC. The word seems to be applied to the eastern-culture burials, which can quite often have a chambered tomb which is rather elaborate compared to what is found in Britain and in the west.

There are many mounds across Eastern Europe. There used to be a mound complex at Perepyat, Ukraine.

One of the best kurgans is that of '*Mithridates*', a rather romantic name. It reminds one of Mithridates the Great, a Pontic king whose armies defied Rome's conquest of northern Asia Minor, for a time. The name perhaps would also have been used in Crimea.

In Crimea, we have a tomb, quite impressive and built by a mixture of ancient Greek colonists of the Iron Age, and local inhabitants. This is known as the Royal Kurgan. The similarity of this with the Treasury of Atreus, from 1250 BC, is quite interesting. It would seem to imply that the possible Achaeans from this period who would go on to inspire the *Iliad*, that is Achilles and all the associated late-Mycenaean Greeks, once had a related civilisation living up in Crimea and perhaps elsewhere in Southern Russia. It would perhaps make the Achaeans possibly related to the Scythians.

Alternately that could be nonsense and Crimea could simply have been a Greek colony in the Bronze Age, as it was in the Iron Age. It is known that the Mycenaeans had a colony in Cyprus, but I have not searched the literature for a possible one in Crimea.

I am suggesting that there are similarities between the Giza necropolis and a Kurgan necropolis. How can I possibly say this? For starters we need to deal with various pieces of evidence.

The mounds in Russia seem to be just as old as what is in Egypt. The mound in question however, the Royal Kurgan, only dates from several centuries before Christ. There are similarities between the corbelling in this structure and that in the Grand Gallery of the Great Pyramid of Khufu. Clearly the cultures did not communicate at different times. So, I would like to suggest a common ancestor.

Some proof for this is that the Treasury of Atreus, built in 1250 BC, more than five centuries before the Royal Kurgan, contains a similar entrance. There is no long passageway in the Atreus tomb, but there is tapering off in a triangular fashion at the ceiling of the entrance,

Figure 5.5: Mound complex at Perepyat, Vasylkiv Raion, Ukraine. This is what it looked like before excavation. This was and is unknown in the west. Based upon the definition for 'pyramid' which I pursue in this book, the central mound is the pyramid. The lesser mounds, then, would be the burials. The central mound would serve as an *Axis Mundi* (centre of creation and yearly re-creation) around which other burials are placed. The diagram makes a good illustration for perhaps what a pyramid really is. A king wished to create an area for the re-creation of the gods. Once complete, he himself would participate in re-creation and possibly even resurrection or re-incarnation. The fact that resurrection was preferred to re-incarnation in Hinduism, however (seen as inevitable) shows that the pyramid was built possibly, in some areas, to assist into carrying the royal body, buried nearby, into the higher plane. It would be impossible, for instance, for a royal to be re-incarnated, even accidentally into a peasant body. Perhaps the pyramid was built, in some respects, to circumvent this, to ensure only one route into the afterlife.

Figure 5.6: In this 19th-century lithograph, from the 'Royal Kurgan' overlooking Kerch, we seem to have a chamber which reminds one of the Grand Gallery of the Giza complex. The burial chamber of the Red or Dashur pyramid is also corbel vaulted, as in this painting. This tomb was likely robbed in antiquity, but like other pyramids, there is some debate whether or not it is really a burial. The following is a very untechnical statement, but how else to express oneself? The blocks look rather Egypt-size as well. As in Egypt, there is no writing any-where. This was drawn by Carlo Bossoli. (DeGolyer Library, Southern Methodist University)

Figure 5.7: The view from the tomb of Mithridates is exceptional. Like pyramids in Ireland, and elsewhere, it is built on a high area, over looking an ancient town and the sea. (DeGolyer Library, Southern Methodist University)

as in the Royal Kurgan, fig. 5.6. As well as the temporal separation period of about six hundred years, there is also the geographical separation between Mycenae, on the southern coast of Greece, and Crimea. Meanwhile it is only another further sea trip to the Egyptian Delta. Another cultural similarity would be making a tomb/pyramid which has a smooth exterior, not a step pyramid.

One might like to compare the image below of the Grand Gallery with the Kurgan of Mithridates, fig. 5.6. I would suggest the answer to the conundrum was a migration into Egypt at some time. Robert Schoch points out in *Voyages of the Pyramid Builders* that trade alone cannot really change a burial practice. To get all the details right, one more or less requires the migration of an elite, peaceful or otherwise. An alternate explanation is that priest-architects were hired out to different regions. That is not impossible either. In the Giza pyramid, not only do we suddenly have large internal chambers, as in a kurgan,

Figure 5.8: The Grand Gallery in the Great Pyramid in Egypt is separated from some of the corbelled roof tombs of the east by a thousand
years. Despite the obvious differences, there are some striking and as
yet unexplained architectural similarities.

but also smooth sides. It is as if the step pyramid, which had hitherto
dominated Egypt, was being almost done away with.

There is one problem with the argument. A quick glance in Lord
William Taylour's *The Mycenaeans*, reveals that the Mycenaean Tholos
tomb evolved from something with a lintel, a lot like Stonehenge, with
more rounded blocks, into the more regular sharp-cornered and attractive blocks seen in the tomb of 1250 BC. In other words the similarity
with the Giza pyramid only entered Greece just before the Dark Ages
which began around the 1160s BC and not earlier. This was one and a
half millennia after the Giza pyramids were built. The Royal Kurgan
in Crimea is even younger! In this way, I can rip part of my own argu-

Figure 5.9: The Red pyramid in Egypt, built or renovated by Sneferu, also has this fascinating corbelling. In a book called, *How it was in Reality*, Russian mathematician Anatoly Fomenko and his co-author G. V. Nosowsky, claim that the Egyptian pyramids are kurgans. It assists in his unusual contention that historical periods are completely mixed up (and both sets of structures were supposedly built within the last millennium). I think that either ancient Greeks, who had explored the interior of various pyramids, simply assisted in the building of kurgans, (about the right time for it) or there is another unknown explanation for the similarities, perhaps an even earlier tradition with shared links.

ment apart, but I cannot rip all the way because the two seams seem to snag. The snag is still the geography. Pyramids/mounds/tombs in the east seem to look a certain way which differs to how they look in the west.

Etruscans, Lars Porsena, and Sardinia

The Etruscans, like everyone else, are a mix of various peoples. They had great trading links with Egypt and in their early days controlled a naval empire possibly controlling the Western Mediterranean. This gave them access to money and power, which they used to oppress, and in the days of Porsena, almost conquer the Roman city state. In later years they lost their naval empire to the Carthaginians and so became a poorer land empire. This became a famous fusion of city states, sometimes hostile to Rome, and based upon a loosely common heritage and language.

In the early days, the Etruscans were the bureaucracy and the Romans were the populace. The city state of Rome overcame her Etruscan ruler in the sixth century before Christ. She then went on to absorb all the other Etruscan cities, as well as her culture. Italy has always been made up of many different tribes. Italy too has its 'tumuli', see below. Not all Etruscan tombs are like this, however. Some are caves, holes in the rock with corridors. The Etruscans are a fusion of different burial practices.

The Montefortini tumulus is a famous tomb, measuring 80 metres in diameter and 11 high, about the size of Medb's tomb.

Porsena

The greatest Etruscan king was perhaps Lars Porsena (*fl.* 7th-6th century BC). He ruled over Etruscan Clusium. Rome at that time was not really an Etruscan city, existing on the border of the Etruscan confederation.

It did have an unpopular and 'proud' Etruscan king, Tarquinus Superbus. After his overthrow he went to powerful Porsena for help to regain his throne. The story goes that a brave Roman assassin, Mucius Scaevola, finally managed to infiltrate the Etruscan camp but killed a secretary instead. He nevertheless scared Porsena into submission. By thrusting his own hand into the fire to prove how tough he was, he showed the Etruscans that one should never mess with a Roman, and

Figure 5.10: As we go towards the south of Europe, mounds become more like the cairns of Ireland. More stone is used. They do contain what appear to be former burials and unlike their northern cousins, have very well built burial chambers, with a sarcophagus. They may be more for godlike kings than purely for possible gods, as certain of their northern counterparts. Here we have an Etruscan mound. Despite using rocks, they are still mound-shaped, like those of the north. They are both tombs as well as perhaps representations of the Earth Mother, tombs for man and god. This is the *Tomba dei carri*, near the town of Populonia, Tuscany. By Roberto Zanasi.

Figure 5.11: Porsena's tomb. This is a possible reconstruction based upon the Varro description. By Quatremère de Quincy.

try to take away his freedom. Mucius then told Porsena that there were 300 more assassins, just as tough as he was, waiting to follow. Porsena then made peace, so the story goes.

Porsena's greatest glory appears to have been his tomb. This was built at Clusium and may have been destroyed after the sacking of that city by Roman general Cornelius Sulla, in 89 BC. There are two descriptions of its splendour surviving in Roman sources.

I include a discussion of it here because it was one of Europe's greatest possible pyramids, before its apparent destruction by the Romans. It was not simply one pyramid, however. There seem to have been fourteen 'pyramids' stacked in three layers. It was a collection of pyramids, with smaller pyramids on top. If we take and stack everything described, on top of one another literally, perhaps as in fig. 5.12, the final structure should have been about six hundred feet tall. Fig. 5.11 is a more realistic stacking arrangement. This structure sounds so ridiculous that an uncomprehending Roman author, Pliny, (who died A.D.

79) was hesitant to include it in his book. Nevertheless, he did so, quoting Varro (116-27 BC):

> It is but right that I should mention it, in order to show that the vanity displayed by foreign princes, great though it is, has been surpassed. But in view of the exceedingly fabulous nature of the story I shall use the words given by M. Varro himself in his account of it: 'Porsena was buried below the city of Clusium in the place where he had built a square monument of dressed stones. Each side was three hundred feet in length and fifty in height, and beneath the base there was an inextricable labyrinth, into which, if any-body entered without a clue of thread, he could never discover his way out. Above this square building there stand five pyramids, one at each corner and one in the centre, seventy-five feet broad at the base and one hundred and fifty feet high. These pyramids so taper in shape that upon the top of all of them together there is supported a brazen globe, and upon that again a petasus from which bells are suspended by chains. These make a tinkling sound when blown about by the wind, as was done in bygone times at Dodona. Upon this globe there are four more pyramids, each a hundred feet in height, and above them is a platform on which are five more pyramids.' The height of the latter, Varro is ashamed to add, but, according to the Etruscan stories, it was equal to that of the rest of the building. What utter madness is this, to attempt to seek glory at a great cost which can never be of use to anyone; not to mention the drain upon the resources of the country. And all to the end that the artist may receive the greater share of the praise!

He may as well have been talking about King Khufu.

I see something significant in the description of Porsena's tomb. I think it is a lot closer to what we know of the stupas of Asia, especially with the idea of pyramids on pyramids, rather than the fanciful pictures which have been constructed of Porsena's tomb, over the centuries. The description may thus have come from a lost book of Asian travels. Asian stupas had lots of little pyramids on top of the steps, of much larger step pyramids, as in fig. 6.1. Such an arrangement might fulfil the 'on top of' arrangement of platforms on tops of pyramids on tops of a hemisphere on top of pyramids in the description.

The complex at fig. 6.1 may have been somehow similar. Then again a model-building from the nearby but slightly older Nuragitic culture in Sardinia, in fig. 5.13, seems vaguely similar to the description of the Porsena tomb.

The ruins in Sardinia are quite interesting and among the finest in Europe. A lot of it is Sumerian-looking, and surely bears a certain eastern influence. The Sardinians had a great civilisation, including what are perhaps Europe's oldest life-like statues.

Their culture is unexplored and basically untaught in archaeology courses, relative to Greece and Rome. This is probably due to a lack of written record. The importance of written record cannot be overemphasised in terms of our perception of what went on back when. An example is the Bible. Here we have a case of archaeologists being inspired and driven by a historical record of Solomon's wonders. They then seek to find out what went on in the relevant archaeological layers and come up with a somewhat different story. A Dark-Age chasm is located between the Bronze- and Iron-Age levels, where very little building work went on. Like King Arthur or Robin Hood, texts often represent a fusion of ideas from various traditions. Several Solomons or related characters may simply have become glued together in the storyteller's mind. Sardinia has no written record so no-one knows what particular temple or structure or palace to look for. It is however, keenly interesting.

In many respects Sardinian archaeology is representative of the lost civilisation of the Sherden, one of the many 'Sea Peoples' so-called by the Egyptians, who invaded the Near East, and were defeated in Egypt by various kings. This was just before the collapse of civilisation into a Dark Age in about the 1160s BC. They had the architects, the statues, and the architecture. What we really seem to lack is the written record. Caught between the Greeks, the Carthaginian and Roman empires, the Sherden, who may be related in part to the Etruscans, lost their indigenous civilisation to imperial conquest.

Fig. 5.14 is fascinating. It is an image of a step pyramid in Sardinia, apparently unique there. It is sometimes described as a Ziggurat and comes from the Sumerian era. In front of it lies an egg-shaped rock. This feature is almost Asian. In Asian lore, the stone monkey broke out of the cosmic egg. After causing trouble in heaven he was expelled to Earth. He is a Loki-like figure of wisdom. (Thoth, Egyptian god of knowledge is represented as a baboon or an Ibis). These troublemakers in heaven may be thought to have been associated with the rise of

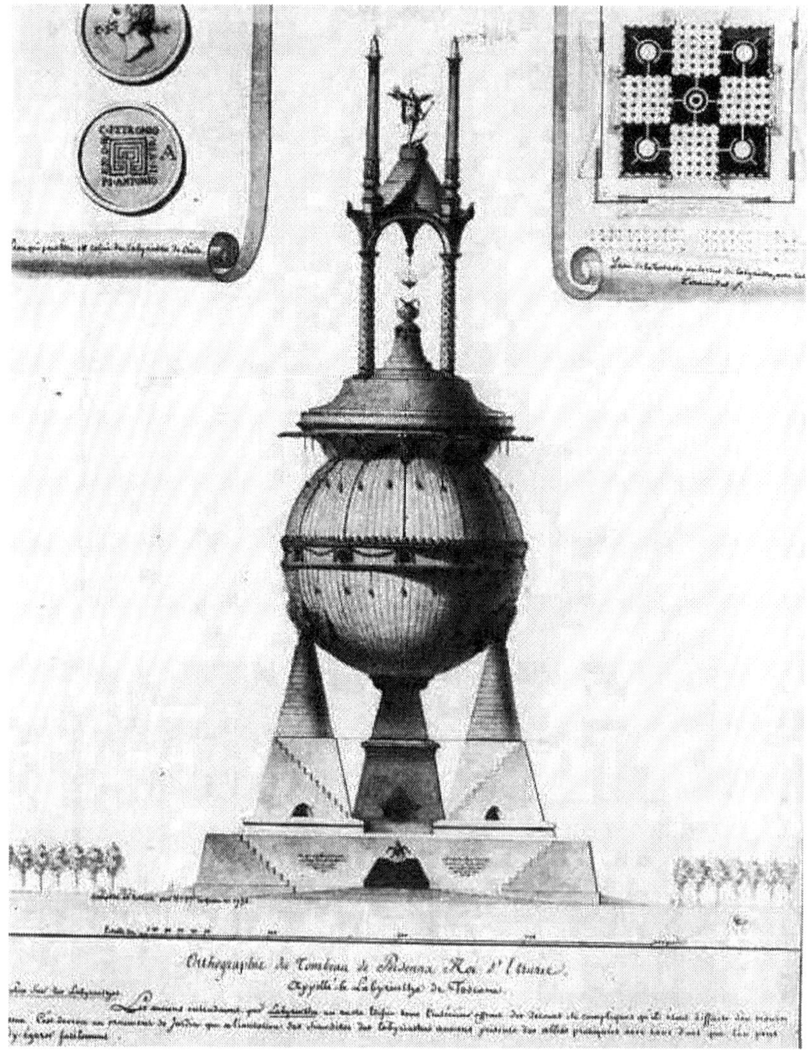

Figure 5.12: The descriptions of Porsena's tomb have been interpreted in a number of different ways.

Figure 5.13: Here we have something from the Nugaric culture, of the 7th-6th centuries BC. This culture was in Sardinia, not too far off from what would become the Etruscan naval empire. I believe it to be the closest equivalent we have to what Porsena's tomb was once like. It is from the Museo Nazionale and is said to be a bronze model of a nuraghe. That is, it is supposed to be a representation of one of Sardinia's many strange stone towers. Be that as it may, it seems to fit, in many respects, the description of Porsena's lost tomb. One may note the 'hemispheres' on top of 'pyramids', i.e. pillars in this case.

Figure 5.14: The strange step pyramid of Monte d'Accoddi, Sardinia.

mankind. *Someone* had to have been helping mankind, looking out for him, in the face of the brutal indifference of mother nature. There seems to be a large 'ramp' in front of this pyramid. Herodotus mentions that there used to be ramps around the Giza pyramids. Certainly in the image, one can envisage that it may have been used for building the structure, as well as possibly hauling up a large animal sacrifice. Behind the egg there seems to be a sacrificial altar, akin to what I saw in Ireland. What is that in front of the pyramid? I wonder if this is a proto-Easter egg? Easter itself is a fertility ritual for springtime and pyramids seem to be fertility mounds. It is amusing to think that they once may have gone together. That is certainly not the case now.

In Egypt there is a national celebration known as the *Sham el-Nessim*. It is not based on today's Egyptian religions and seems to be based on the old practice of spring fertility ritual; it is celebrated on the first day of spring. On this day people go out to a park or somewhere with some sort of greenery for a picnic and paint Easter eggs.

An alternate egg legend from Egypt is based on the cosmic egg legend. There is one version, associated with the Ogdoad, eight deities, worshipped in the pyramid-building era of the third millennium BC at Hermopolis. That is the third to sixth dynasties. These deities are four couples of male and female. A cosmic goose or celestial bird lays the egg on or in a cosmic mound surrounded by water. (Echoes here of Silbury Hill). The egg gives birth to Ra, the Sun. In many world traditions the cosmic egg is wrapped in a snake. It would seem the egg is also associated with pyramids, but to a lesser extent than other deities and ideas which have been mentioned in this book.

There are also some step pyramids/terraces in the Canaries which the ethnographer Thor Heyerdahl was convinced were built by the Guanches, an apparently indigenous, tall, red-headed people who once lived there. In the late 1990s, however the pyramids were dated to the 19th century.

Stone spheres have been found on the Canaries, as in South America. These could be cosmic eggs of creation. Heyerdahl had had a great deal of experience with archaeology and its methods in his lifetime, and was convinced the pyramids were genuine, until his death in 2002. He had even convinced a Norwegian friend and entrepreneur to purchase the site in the 90s. It is now an ethnological park.

For Heyerdahl's scenario to have happened, the stones might have been moved from some place else and dumped on a 19th-century layer, now underneath the pyramids. This may have been done by anonymous

conservators of the 19th century, in the spirit of antiquarianism. I am
not ruling out that the pyramids were not totally rebuilt from early
building materials in the 19th century, as they resemble other step
pyramids on similar latitudes, and what does a farmer need a weird-
looking possibly impractical terrace for anyway, which was probably
very time consuming to build?

Pyramid author Philip Coppens in his 2007 work *The New Pyramid
Age*, thought they were partly genuine and quite old, as the area was
once a Guanche capital. However the archaeological dating is reason
enough to exclude these structures from any consideration in this book.
There has been little archaeological work done on other similar-looking
step-pyramid structures recently found from the Azores to Sicily, which
do tend to make one wonder. There are plenty of photos, but little
discussion regarding these structures. It is really better not to discuss
them in any length in this book, because they are a little too recently
discovered and could really turn out to simply be follies built or rebuilt
by country squires over the last few centuries, possibly like those in the
Canaries.

The Berbers

Heading south of Silbury now, and south west of Old Europe, west of
Egypt, we have a curious tomb which architecturally reminds one a bit
of Egypt, Silbury (European burial mound) and even a little of Old
Europe (Italy to Crimea) all in one.

This could well be an emulation of the kurgan burials, but it also
looks like a European flat-topped burial mound. I think the reason this
is surely a tomb, is that it was built long after the pyramid-building era
of the third millennium, in which pyramids need not have been tombs,
but were either built directly above them, or were closely associated
with them.

The Berbers are a fascinating tribe, the pre-Arab inhabitants of
North Africa. Of course, there are repeating patterns in migration
history, so there may have been Arab invasions in deeply ancient times
also, as well as in the previous millennium. We have something known
as the tomb of King Juba, who was a highly educated man of the time
of Christ. I am not convinced we know enough about the origin of
this building, but by its appearance, it has all the hallmarks of having
been built in the first millennium BC, and is actually thought to have
been built in 3 BC. Pomponius Mela of the first century AD said it

Figure 5.15: In this, the tomb of King Juba, Algeria, we have something quite interesting. Firstly it is a lot like Newgrange in layout, though the appearance is different. In fact Newgrange is one of the closest analogues I can see, along with certain Etruscan tombs, as well as kurgans and the Egyptian pyramids. We see pillars here, around the edge.

was *monumentum commune regiae gentis*, or a communal monument/ mausoleum for the royal dynasty.

I think it may well have been rebuilt from something else, just as various Normans rebuilt Roman-type structures or their own structures from Roman bricks in Britain, for instance. The lore of the site is that it is called 'The tomb of the Christian woman', or 'The tomb of the Roman woman.' I believe this is some kind of link with the sacred female, though it could well have simply been a tomb with no real history of this, in terms of a religious purpose.

Like various old pyramids or mounds, it is more than just a tomb. For instance, there are legends that in 1555, Salah Rais, who was the Pasha at Algiers, ordered the destruction of the mausoleum. It echoes other orders given in the last two millennia or so, to destroy the pyramids of Giza, which ultimately failed. Like a scene from *The Mummy*, the legend goes that huge black wasps flew out and stung some workers to death, causing the effort to be abandoned. In the late 1700s, another man, Baba Mahommed attempted to destroy the monument with artillery, as allegedly did the later French.

All efforts to defeat the ancient structure were in vain. I do not know who perpetuated such legends but I would imagine it would have been locals who were aware of some ancient magic protecting the site, and with a healthy respect for their ancestors, knew it should have been built to endure forever.

The structure is very interesting. It is similar to Newgrange in that we also have also have stones lined up around the base, as if they were Stonehenge-style lintels, or the tops of pillars. See fig. 1.43. The rest of the Juba tomb resembles a European/Early Asian mound for some reason, or even a stupa in India, as if it were also possible to simply build it out of earth. The existence of this structure partly defeats my argument, later in the book, that square blocks build square mounds, but not utterly. If one wants a smooth and even finish, one will use square or rectangular blocks to build a square-shaped mound. The Juba mound may represent a fusion of European/Asian/North African ideas, but also of peoples, coming from the North, but also from the East, along with earlier indigenous inhabitants, as burial customs are often inherited rather than emulated. This is certainly a product of a mixing of ancestries, as pretty much everywhere else!

There are also other structures on nearby islands. The ruins on the island of Sardinia, and perhaps several smaller Mediterranean spec-like islands, seem incredibly old, but are of a rather different, earlier tradition. I have not attempted much of a mythological explanation of these as I have not done any field research. Lacking a diagram of these pyramid complexes, and their overall layout, this would be a foolhardy thing to do. Pyramid complexes seem to be maps of the underworld, but I am not sure of the area surrounding the Juba pyramid.

Based upon all this experience in looking at various structures, we are now ready, perhaps, to begin to piece it all together. But first let us look a little further afield, towards...

China

What if we could make it all easier? What if we could literally step into the world of the pyramid priests and ask them what is going on, and what it is all about? In China, we can do just that. For China is one of the world's few surviving ancient civilisations!

One of the most famous mounds of China is the *Temple of Heaven*, in Beijing. In a bookstore I stumbled across an obscure publication from China which goes by the same name. It occurred late in the research of this work, when the writing was done. I was stunned, as usual, but not surprised. It had all the hallmarks of what I had grown accustomed to finding, but in much greater detail, since it is a living religion. (I have discussed this with Chinese people, asking them what their stupas are for. 'For good luck,' or 'for worship,' are usual answers.)

Firstly, there is the name. It implies a representation of heaven, upon Earth. This is a typical hallmark associated with the Egyptian ritual landscape, particularly alluded to in recent publications. The Egyptian pyramid, after all, is acknowledged by all to be based upon the primordial world mound. So let us look over the mounds, here then, in the Chinese equivalent.

In examining this book, I looked over a ground plan. I was on the lookout for two major 'pyramids', and possibly a third (according to my pyramid definition that is, provided after the introduction, implying function over form. If you want geometry look elsewhere), possibly of the Sun and the Moon, as is often the case, (and as shall be seen later on as well). There are in fact two major 'pyramids' on the site. Both are circular, round, stepped affairs. They are called the *Altar of Prayer for Good Harvests*, and the *Circular Mound Altar*. I suspect that the former is of the Earth and Moon. It is where the emperor prayed for a good harvest. It also has a circular temple on top. The latter has no such temple and is open to the sky. The latter is for sacrifice to heaven. Such a sacrifice is made on the winter solstice, and also to pray for rain in early summer. It is white and green in colour.

It is amazing that we can actually name structures such as this, unlike mounds everywhere which have no name other than the ruler responsible for building them. For the former, there are strange crocodiles or dragons sticking out of it, very much as in the case of the Teotihuacan Citadel pyramid. The Egyptian equivalent may be the Khufu pyramid, since Khnum, Khufu's god, is a crocodile. Both mounds are also white, like the Egyptian pyramids were supposed to have been, with their former limestone casings, or like Newgrange. In this respect they are likely to be representative of Moon/Earth on the one hand, and Sun on the other.

Temples near the Egyptian pyramids were re-discovered after many thousands of years. It is fascinating that Chinese pyramids and mounds have adjoining temples. This points to the idea that large mounds

Figure 5.16: The *Circular Mound Altar* inside the greater *Temple of Heaven* religious complex. There is a slight resemblance to Tynwald hill on the Isle of Man, fig. 4.24. That hill conferred legitimacy to the Man kings. This temple did the same for Chinese emperors. There are strong similarities between this complex and Angkor Wat, Cambodia, as well as Borobudur, Indonesia. Similar temples were built by both Buddhists and Hindus. Angkor Wat was both Buddhist and later Hindu, but I believe there is also a far earlier influence as well, underlying the religions. It was the Emperor's sacred duty in China to offer sacrifice at the winter solstice, and also in early summer, for rains.

such as Silbury Hill, or even the so-called Indian Burial Mounds of the United States also may have had adjoining temples, once made of wood, subsequently destroyed by time.

Like the Giza complex, surrounded by a Cyclopean wall, this complex too is surrounded by a wall.

I think the 'third' pyramid might be the *Imperial vault of Heaven*, which is a circular complex, the third major one of the larger complex, which lacks a pyramid inside it. It is an enclosure with a temple. That sounds awfully familiar and is comparable to what is found on the Saqqara plateau in Egypt. (Patience please, we will get to this!)

Stonehenge researchers, get out your notebooks! When I started to read the measurements, I was amazed. The *Hall of Prayer for Good Harvests*, stands atop a three tiered mound. The dimension of the circle of the temple is 32.72 metres. (Stonehenge Sarsen circle, meanwhile is 33 metres in diameter). It is 32 metres high. With the platforms it gets to 38 metres. There are 28 pillars in the circular structure. (At Stonehenge there were 30 Sarsen uprights. Unlike Stonehenge however, this arrangement looks more like Woodhenge. They are not all spaced on the outside but in concentric rings.) As at Stonehenge, sarsens are topped by mortice and tenon joints! It is written in the book that only palaces, temples and very important buildings were allowed to have mortice and tenon joints! The book also tells us that 28 pillars suggests 28 constellations in heaven.

It is all rather curious but there is a revelation on each page, which could help us to better understand the old religion of *Axis Mundi*, of the third millennium BC. The ground of the hall is covered in dark green feldspar. I am reminded of the green floor of the Black Sun at Wewelsburg, and wonder what aspects of the old religion the Germans were trying to emulate.

We are also told that in the middle of the *hall* is a marble stone, with a carving of a dragon and another of a phoenix. This would be the omphalos, the Greek word which means 'naval' or centre of the world. The two creatures, if fused, would be a feathered serpent. The phoenix itself is a bird of the underworld, because it is born from the ashes. The book tells us that in the olden days in China there was an overriding belief that everything which is under heaven, owes its origin to heaven. Furthermore, all humans can be traced back to their ancestors, another point of origin.

We are told the predecessor to the described hall was the *Grand Hall of Sacrifice*, which was built in 1420. This was built soon after Emperor Yongle shifted his capital from Nanjing to Beijing, and perhaps according to a similar idea to that governing the later temple, because it was based on the *Grand Hall to Sacrifice to Heaven and Earth* in Nanjing. This was something of an aberration. We are told that it was customary to offer sacrifices separately to heaven and Earth. Overwhelmed by news of his empire's calamities, however, an emperor of the Ming dynasty called Zhu Yuanzhang began to do the sacrifices together. Previously he had followed the practice of the Han dynasty, of eighteen hundred years ago. Insofar as this, he built an altar for sacrifice to heaven on the sunny side of Zhongshan mountain, southeast of Nanjing. He also built an altar for sacrifice to the Earth on the shady side of the mountain outside Taiping gate, Nanjing. (Is there one altar on each side of Knocknarea?) This effectively splits the mountain into two spiritual halves. We are also told that *Forbidden City*, however was the later favourite place for sacrifice to heaven for harvests.

We are also told that sacrifice to heaven was not the same as sacrifice to the celestial god. The former had to be done on an open-air altar. The latter was conducted in a bright spacious hall.

It is all rather curious and there is a good deal of historical information on mounds in the far east. Mounds in the Pacific and Tonga, for instance, are also still in use. In the west however, the pyramid or associated mound religion has long been ancient history, usurped by strict monotheisms.

Conclusion remarks

Already we are reaching towards a synthesis, a uniting religion, deep in the fourth millennium BC which can have inspired all of these similar offshoots. The task is a difficult one because some ideas were never meant to have been combined. Then again we know there was a great spread of peoples in ancient times and we know also that a religion which is spread across the world, as this one is, can only have deeply ancient roots, perhaps of the fourth millennium BC or earlier. Therefore there is basis for investigation here. In the following final chapter, I hope to unite quite a lot of what has been discussed, but also discuss what differentiates various sites.

This chapter has been a continuation of the pyramid topic in the context of the spirit of the title of the book. What is happening in Giza, however is perhaps just a little different to the pyramids of this chapter, save for the kurgans of Russia. The pyramids in this chapter, save for the kurgans, seem to relate more to the first three dynasties of Egypt. In particular I draw the reader's attention to a re-discovery made by Robert Temple, of what could be one of Egypt's first pyramids. (*Egyptian Dawn*, 2010). This is the pyramid of King Enezib (Adjib). It is a rectangular step pyramid-like structure from the first Egyptian dynasty, around 3000 BC. The following chapter therefore really is a continuation of the ideas presented in the first four chapters and the information that I collected on travels and later on.

Egypt exists on a land bridge between Africa and Asia. Throughout its history it has never been able to develop uninterrupted, without some form of invasion. It was excellent and well-sought after real estate for ancient peoples who once sought a tropical home for themselves. Like all the peoples of Earth, the Egyptians find themselves a product of mixing with many different tribes in the past. The Egyptians themselves, genetically, as well as in terms of their religion, and phenotype, or appearance, seem to represent a fusion of proto-Indo-European (possibly 'Caucasian'), from different places, as well as African ideas from the south, and Arab/Mesopotamian ideas from the East, with an underlying Berber Hamito-Semitic language base. Based upon this knowledge we are able to tentatively embark upon a study of various extremely old mythological ideas which may be universal to pyramid builders.

The Sami, are an aboriginal tribe of Northern Scandinavia with quite a proto-Indo-European background, in terms of their mythology. They worshiped weather gods similar to Thor and other deities, but with subtle differences. They are now known to have genetic links stretching into Asia as well as Libya and the Mediterranean. These links stretch to before the beginning of the pyramid age. They may represent one surviving branch of the Tocharians of Asia (among the proto-Chinese), as well as other possible pyramid-building races, such as the former Guanche people of the Canaries. There are also relics of this people in Iraq, who are today known as the Marsh Arabs. They were popularised by Thor Heyerdahl as possible pyramid builders in various books, in particular *The Tigris Expedition.*

Heyerdahl sought out cultural similarities, as well as burial practices, between pyramid builders across the world, but he never really seems to have gotten down deeply enough into the essential study of mythology. Nowadays of course, we have the internet and it becomes very easy to search things out.

It is a very strange old Stone-Age mythology one requires if one wants to analyse pyramid building, and it seems alien to us. In a later book I will have an opportunity to perform a more thorough synthesis, partly using the very old mythology of the Sami and of other peoples, into the type of underworld that seems to be represented by the Giza pyramid complex, and its surroundings. This is a religion (of *Axis Mundi*) which is well over six thousand years old and may pre-date much of what we know about the Egyptian religion.

In the final chapter, we will be able however, to sufficiently analyse Giza, and elsewhere, to demonstrate part of what was perhaps going on in the minds of the pyramid builders. It is not perfect, but one would not expect that. I think it seems a rather good 'fit.'

Chapter 6

Synthesis

We now come to the final chapter, which is really a sort of 'part two' of this book, or even a kind of 'book two.' The 'introduction' is out of the way. Armed and equipped, with a little travel knowledge of the hill and mound religion in Eurasia and North Africa, we are ready for a fully-fledged and also unprecedented 'assault' on the mystery of the Giza complex, from the mythological perspective of the pyramid-building religion in general, and with a more general and practical 'pyramid' knowledge, than I hope, is displayed in any other pyramid publication.

I would like to re-iterate the contention that the three main Giza pyramids are representative of what Rodney Castleden calls in his books about Britain, a 'Harvest Hill'. This was a hill typically built for good luck and fertility rituals, primarily revolving around the idea of a good harvest.

In particular one must have provided that the hill was a sufficiently large home for the shining fertility god who must have risen from the pregnant belly of the underworld (pyramid) every year. The bigger it seems that this structure was, the better. There are of course small possible harvest hills such as the Antrim Motte, detailed earlier in this book, which may or many not be ancient.

This harvest religion would have dealt with issues as old as agriculture. Essentially, there were perhaps first prayers and rituals for a good harvest. After the harvest, in autumn, there would have been a form of 'thanksgiving.' There were astronomical considerations, incorporated both at Giza and at European sites such as Cracow. This would have been an additional link between the pyramids as representation of the fertility cycle, and the mathematics of the fertility cycle, the cosmos. It was perhaps a form of sympathetic magic, to ensure that nature could not ignore the will of the people. Stone circles also as a form of uncovered tomb, or underworld representation with a view to the cosmos, may also have been partly based upon this conception.

The pyramid-building culture is older than we know and was spread out towards many different points well before the beginning of Egyptian history in about 3100 BC. There may have been one type of infusion of pyramid-building culture into Egypt from an unknown point, between the first and third dynasties which was more 'Sumerian'. That is perhaps based upon the bull or other sacrifice, and is represented by sacrificial altars around pyramids. Thus we seem to have an altar at the third dynasty Djoser complex but none at Giza. The European turf mounds or 'pyramids' as I call them perhaps needed no altar. Any sacrifice, disgusting as it seems, is absorbed directly into the ground. In Egypt one cannot really build a mound of turf, especially in the desert. One needs stone. By fourth dynasty Egypt, the step pyramid is somewhat out of vogue. A new fashion intruded involving building smooth-sided pyramids. Why is this? I would suggest that in part they were trying to build something known to their ancestors, something resembling the smooth-sided mounds of Eurasia. With that controversial statement out of the way, let us begin.

Stupas and Buddha

Stupas and other pyramids follow a similar structure to the European mound-pyramid with the tree on top of it, or wishing tree nearby. They may have been built in Asia by the Tocharians. These were a partly-Asiatic, Indo-European people of ancient times. They are associated with the Scythians and Sarmatians.

We then come to Buddha. I am not talking about the famous prince, Gautama but the earlier 'previous incarnations' of Buddha, who happened to have the same name, and with great irony. For Buddha's namesake appears to be Odin, a wise war god. I would like to quote the late Sikh professor, poet and mystic, Sher Singh, who stated his belief that the Jats in India are related to the Jutes by common ancestor, which I paraphrase from a travel book, *Chasing the Mountain of Light*, by Kevin Rushby. Furthermore, he claimed that Odin and Buddha are manifestations of quite a similar religion, over a wide area.

According to the story, the historical Buddha, despairing with regular ascetic Hinduism, fasting and other forms of self restraint, finally

Figure 6.1: Here we have a drawing of a Shwemawdaw Stupa, Pegu, Myanmar. This engraving is of the late 18th century. It is all rather fascinating. Here we have something which is not too far from Porsena's tomb, for as can be seen, it has many little 'pyramids' on different levels. The hemisphere is lacking in this drawing, but is seen in other stupas. On the top of many stupas is something resembling the world tree. The aim was to make something extremely large, for very good luck.

sits under a sacred tree, fasting almost to death and finally acquires 'wisdom.' What does this ancient tale mean? The tale may very well have a pre-Buddhist origin. How about, 'Buddha is the god in the mound underneath the tree of wisdom', therefore 'hanging' under it just like Odin did. In so doing, and like Odin, he may have been said to have acquired the mysteries of the universe. In other words, we are not talking about a biography of Gautama in the recent B.C. era, but older mythology.

There is a definite overlap between Odin (and similar Woden?), who replaced the sky god 'Tiwaz' (or 'day' presumably) and Loki. Odin may be partly a product of a simple confounding of the sky god with Loki, and other bits and pieces. For instance, like Loki, Odin is said a trickster and a liar. There is a lot of war god in Woden as well, and this makes for confusion with Loki, also a rather nasty character.

Odin, like Loki, is a god of wisdom. He is also, like Loki, almost a god of fire, as is his Latin equivalent Mercury, closest to the Sun. Like Loki, Odin was also 'punished', but by being placed on a tree or gallows, rather than under a mountain with a snake dribbling acid or lava on him. Branston in *The Lost Gods of England* tells us that it is Woden out of all gods who has the most place names associated with him. It is to Odin that sacrificees were dragged up mountains and slain.

The proto-Odin cult of wisdom seems to have extended to Asia. It was altered with each incarnation of 'Buddha'. The Buddhist way of life itself, an introspective one preoccupied with finding silence in one's own mind, seems to be deeply connected to the Yggdrasil religion. Every stupa in Asia seems to have a 'tree' on top. In addition, stupas often contain a tree trunk sometimes down the middle, just like the Krakus Mound, and one of the sites at Navan Fort. These latter sites seem to actually be European stupas, (In particular the Krakus Mound which is quite hemispherical) spread westwards presumably by the spread of the Aryan or 'Scyth' tribe, perhaps these days known as the 'Celts', being a later European manifestation of something following after their culture. Stupas are built for any number of reasons, often for some kind of good luck.

I could be very wrong, but I think Gautama's personal Buddhism went a little more in another direction, due to the emphasis he placed on the word 'desire.' This simple word shift, from the word 'want', is a major part of what separated his teachings from what had come before. It may have been something like 'how can I stop thinking about *her*'. The answer: remove 'desire.' It is something very close to the heart, closer than mere material wants.

Love is the greatest of all desires. We come to the idea of the Asian Stupa. This is built for good luck in one's lifetime. It is a hemisphere with a parasol on top which resembles a tree. It has a 'Tree of Life' in the form of a tree trunk going down the middle. Ultimately the stupa became associated with Gautama, and his relics, even though it may have been also used for ideas about Odin getting wise on the world tree, back in Europe!

This may well be the proto-Buddhist religion, brought to Europe by the Aryans of India, or another tribe. These certainly seem like the European equivalent of stupas. They contain no burial because they are not tombs, but were possibly built for wealth, fertility or good luck! These were not plundered because to destroy a stupa is to murder it and incur severe bad luck. Older 'pyramids' such as Newgrange or Listoghil are more like actual tombs, seemingly not stupas, but they may well be proto-stupas. Newgrange is still more like a cathedral containing tombs, than a mere tomb. In Ireland, I was puzzled by why every other minor tomb around Medb's ancient cairn was plundered, yet her tomb, which should by any definition contain a much larger treasure, was untouched. Was there too much bad luck involved?

This brings us to another point. Much of Europe is highly fertile. Egypt is very fertile. (There were famines however.) Why go to such an extent to build such great structures in fertile lands, in effective breadbaskets? One answer may be plague.

For some reason in 90 BC it was decided at Navan Fort, to throw up a mound around what had been the site of a feasting hall for centuries. Samples of all the land in the kingdom needed this blessing for some reason. Ireland suffered from many plagues, written of by monks in her chronicles which are reported to have decimated the population.

What if the pyramid was built to bring the fertility goddess to a new region, in order to bless the land and wipe out disease? The great pyramids have been described by certain dreamers as being the barns of Joseph. Naturally they are not big enough to save a significant quantity of Egyptian produce from the feared seven year El Nino/La Nina pattern seemingly described in the Old Testament. But what if they are harvest mounds designed to prevent this, via magical effect?

If so, why is this information not found in the Bible? For starters, the Old Testament writers were utterly opposed to the religion of the tree, which seems to go with the religion of the hill or mound. Secondly, the Old Testament was largely put together during the forced Babylonian Exile, in the sixth century BC. Nebuchadnezzar either needed to break the power of the Temple priesthood, or wished to populate Babylon. I am wondering if the story of Joseph, is not really mixed up with a story regarding the building of the Djoser pyramid, which was rebuilt twice, successively larger, from a mastaba.

Some commentators have said that Joseph *was* Djoser. We certainly do not need to go that far. Jews who remained in Israel during the exile became known as the Samaritans. These claimed to be the practitioners of the original Jewish religion. They were mountain and perhaps mound worshippers, subsequently repressed. I would suggest that not only old Israel but old, Old Egypt had been suffering from conflict between many different religions for quite some time, millennia in fact. The Egyptian religion probably represents a fusion which became a cohesion.

In the New Testament Jesus actually ascends a holy mountain and begins changing colours in an event known as the Transfiguration. I was shocked to find a similar tale in a Tibetan text (in *The Way to Shambhala*) discussing Buddhism and what happens during enlightenment. In the Tibetan text, one becomes like a rainbow on the holy mountain. It implies a common origin, a proto-Indo-European background to the biblical tale.

Natural Pyramids, for worship

What about natural pyramids? While travelling by train through Silesia, I noticed some remarkable hill-shaped peaks which reminded me very much of the ones in Bosnia at Visoko, northwest of Sarajevo. These are simply natural volcanic-type formations covered over with topsoil and grass, but I am guessing they were nonetheless of great ritual significance, due to their shape.

In Victoria, Australia, there is a town called Pyramid Hill, which contains a huge basalt natural pyramid. It was named this by its discoverer in honour of the Egyptian pyramids. I went there in 2006 hoping to find some archaeology but as far as I could see it was an entirely natural, enormous structure.

Basalt is a funny thing. It can form crystals of various highly geometric repeating shapes. The crystals can only be stacked together in a certain way. While cooling from lava, they crack at regular intervals, and so they eventually resemble bricks stacked together, of various shapes; hexagons, parallelograms, etc.

The cracks then fill with mud over time which hardens and even fossilises, so it can even look like mortar was used to hold the old walls together. I noticed such a formation: a natural 'pier' on a beach at Phillip Island, Victoria. It looked like it had been cobbled together with bricks, which in some places were remarkably regular. Yet in other places the pattern unfortunately broke down. One saw the same pattern, the 'mortared' up 'bricks' in other places, where bricks had no business being, like sticking out of a nearby cliff, so one could conclude the formation was natural. In light of all this, although we wanted it to be real, having been built by man, we had to conclude it was not.

This brings us to the sensation regarding the pyramid-shaped hills found popularised in Bosnia in 2006 by sociologist Dr. Semir Osmanagić. In particular, there is Visocica hill, a towering formation which interestingly resembles a pyramid from the vantage point of the town

Figure 6.2: Silesian pyramid mountains, purely natural, yet of possible former religious use, due to their appealing appearance. I saw these while on the train, while traveling between Jelenia Góra (Deer Hill) and Wrocław, Poland, and snapped this photo.

of Visoko. This is a place which has been of interest to all pyramid researchers. I cannot do better than point to the geological descriptions of the site by Dr Robert Schoch, who concluded it is a natural hill. That however is not the end of the story. Firstly, the hill puzzles those who set eyes upon it, including Bosnian geologists working with Osmanagić who claimed that some aspects of the geology were artificial. The hills are really something which is rarely encountered, even for a geologist. This in a way makes them rather special.

It is fortunate that we do not need to see everything in black and white. The arguments of both Semir Osmanagić, as well as those criticising his interpretations have some merit and I feel that somewhere something was 'lost in translation,' as well as in the excitement of discovering unusual, almost unique, yet probably natural geology underlying the pyramid's shape, which has only served to confuse everybody, as everyone is talking about something different, and perhaps the issue itself, which is relatively straightforward to define, but by no means simple. (The simple fact is that the word 'pyramid' does not have a suitable definition. This I feel, has helped to confuse everybody. In addition, the question of the level of artificiality of the pyramid has left few seemingly willing to meet half-way and say that the pyramids are part archaeology, part natural, which is what they may be. Most commentators seem to be content to say they are totally one or the other, which leaves little room for compromise on what a pyramid actually represents.)

The geological conclusion of Schoch and others does not mean that the hills in Bosnia were not *seen* and even *used* as pyramids by primitive cultures, merely that we in *our* day do not accept them as man-made pyramids! Mountains have been worshipped upon, everywhere, since the beginning of time, because they bring one closer to heaven.

It is also a test of physical endurance, (worthiness) as well as a personal spiritual pilgrimage, to climb any decent-sized hill, and especially elegant ones. I would humbly suggest that with a bit more nuance, the argument of those working on the site in Bosnia might be successfully reworked into something reflecting this.

I would point out that the name of the place, *Visoko*, seems to be related to a Slavic word which in English would mean something like 'heights.' In Polish, for instance, the word for height is 'wysokość.' In Ireland we have *Ardmore*, with a picturesque round tower on top of a hill on the coast. The Irish words 'Ard' and 'more' translate roughly as 'height' and 'great' and refer to a place which in the Middle Ages was occupied by a monastic settlement, upon which was built the most elegant round tower in Irish history. One may surmise that before the monastery, it would have been a temple or wishing trees. Great heights were for ritual and worship, and would especially have ancestral connotations if they were thought to have been built not by men, but giants, as at innumerable megalithic sites. The resemblance of the hill to an actual pyramid would facilitate this.

The fact that Visoko was a capital city in the Middle Ages, as well as a place probably for the crowning of kings, or some other religious festivals, furthers this argument of probably ancient significance. The fact there was a medieval city on top of the pyramid-shaped mountain suggests it replaced an earlier settlement from the time of the savage Iron Age, when hill forts were very much resorted to. The deeply ancient tradition of the written record in the Balkans, that is the Vinca writing from the fifth millennium before the common era, also suggests a past stretching back to the pyramid age, where the pyramid-shaped hills were possibly venerated, in Old Europe.

There are too many pivotal things going for the Visoko hills, to ignore. One fact is that the hills, based upon reported information, seem to have flattened tops. This is rather characteristic of such places of worship. Another fact which ties into the research in this book is that the pyramid religion and the mountain religion were similar. One of the most interesting facts is that the hills are three in number! Osmanagić has romantically termed them the pyramids of the Sun, Moon and Earth. He may not be too far off the truth in ascribing them these names. The extent of what the site means for archaeology really depends on what one is looking for. If one is looking for a place where the pyramid or fertility religion may have been practised, one is certainly on the right track. If one however is looking for huge and exclusively man-built structures such as Silbury Hill or the Giza pyramids, one may have to look elsewhere.

One thing which is interesting is an old legend associated with Visoko town. Local lore has it that in the time of the Turkish invasion, an old woman maintained that no-one was allowed to live on top of the hill unless they were prepared to guard the secret of it with their life. She said that the town hid a secret 'that wears two layers.' She said that one layer had been brought there but was always being washed off by rain. This might refer to the layer on the mound, the earth which Osmanagić has been excavating, which appears to cover natural terracing, which would have been of religious significance leading ancients to believe the hill was sculpted by former men or gods, as possibly at Glastonbury. It is also a similar situation to the Teotihuacan pyramids in that they were deliberately covered by earth. The old woman held that the layer underneath was a fragile shell, which protected whatever contents were underneath. Damaging the shell would cause the contents to be washed away, resulting in bad luck for the town. It is a fascinating legend. The most significant part would seem to be the fact soil was brought to the place. It suggests fertility.

To conclude, there would seem to be a high likelihood that people once associated pyramid-shaped hills, possibly everywhere, with religion. It is also likely that pyramid-shaped peaks may have been considered to have been constructed by giants, or were seen as the tombs of giants, such as Loki, or even Arthur! That is mere speculation.

Are the Bosnian pyramids 'real' pyramids? Absolutely, because a pyramid does not have to be completely man-made to have been treated as a pyramid by ancient peoples! For all they knew, it was the work of giants in the past, just like every other pyramid they encountered. What is in Bosnia certainly meets the tentative criteria I have provided after the *Introduction* of what seems to constitute a 'pyramid' in terms of the lost pyramid religion of 'World Axis'. I wrote that a pyramid 'may be natural or partly shaped, or entirely built by man.' Firstly, the Bosnian hills resemble pyramids. The pyramid of the Sun might well have been partly shaped by man, with an addition of topsoil as at Silbury, having already been a naturally-shaped pyramid-like hill from the beginning. Secondly, since the Medieval town was on top, these were used for ancient worship. Thirdly they were seemingly covered over by soil, which was protected, to bring good luck to the town below, so they were used for fertility. The main 'pyramid of the Sun' in Bosnia greatly resembles a pyramid from the perspective of the town underneath it, so the effect of power projection was also achieved on the population below, even if the other sides are merely the sides of the rest of the hill behind it.

It has been pointed out that only a few sides of each Bosnian pyramid actually look like pyramid faces. The rest is clearly *not* pyramid. That is quite OK! In his book *The New Pyramid Age*, Philip Coppens raised the existence of a very shallow mound at Ollantaytambo, Peru, which is actually little more than a field of crops, at first glance. At second glance, one realises that the subconscious is starting to play tricks. Remarkably, it is a field of crops designed to look like a four-sided three-dimensional step pyramid from a distance, even if it is just a field which is for the most part, almost two dimensions, or at least quite a flat mound! Furthermore, the soil is known to have been perhaps ritually brought from elsewhere, echoing pyramid tradition of a sample of soil of a home region needing to be blessed by the fertility gods. Coppens, as well as a couple other authors are aware that pyramids seem to be something that soil is brought to, or taken away from. Like some of the so-called Bosnian pyramids, this Ollantaytambo pyramid only has two faces. That is all that is required to convey the impression that it is a pyramid, and thus to use it as one! The Bosnian pyramids are ritual pyramids even if they are not fully man made. I rest my case.

The reason the pyramids would partly be an Indo-European tradition would be that the tree of life is itself part of that tradition. Odin or Merlin/Maeve may be represented by the mound in question. Nikolai Tolstoy describes this religion in his *The Quest for Merlin*, (in the Epilogue). According to the shaman view, there is the soul residing on top of the apex of the hill, with the world tree presumably being nourished through it. The tree somehow communicates the soul of the hill into the heavens. Tolstoy sees Merlin as a historical sixth-century figure residing in the lowlands of Scotland in a pagan enclave, as a prophet. Tolstoy sees a correspondence between Odin, Varuna, Hermes and Mercurius, of the Norse, Indians, Greeks and Romans. These are not direct equivalents, but all are associated with being lord over beasts, for omen and divination reasons. The links go further. They seem to stretch wherever the pyramid builders landed their ships. For instance, why is a Mayan pyramid associated with a feathered serpent, and the Wawel hill associated with a dragon? The answer would seem to be that there was some contact at some stage, some ingression of the proto-Indo-Europeans or a related people into the Americas.

Whether or not this is the case, it is clear that as a trickster and enchanter, Merlin or the related above gods are muddled up in terms of mythology. This means that they may be more recent names mixed up with far older Stone-Age gods.

So is this pyramid god a male or female? Is it Medb/Maeve, or is it Merlin? What is going on? It would seem that the pyramid is but a 'horizon' as in Khufu's case, or a meeting of the two gods. (Not all Egyptian pyramids are called horizon. Many are simply named for the endurance or beauty of the king who built them.) In other words it is possibly the interface where spiritual communication can occur. In many respects it is the pyramid or mound which is female and the sky which is male. Then we have the moon idea. Looking at Newgrange it is quite clear that some things are apparent. The ritual takes place at dawn, when Father sky would take over from mother moon. From our vantage point, the night and day meet, copulate, and give 'birth' to a new day, and a magical young morning. It is apparent that Newgrange has a facade of white quartz taking up a semicircle of outer circumference of the mound. In other words, Newgrange is a shiny crescent moon, with the crescent facing the Sun, and with the darker 'spherical' remainder behind the crescent. This would imply there has been some conflation or even confusion between ideas of the Earth mother and Moon mother, even back when Newgrange was built. Which exactly were they venerating? To go into Newgrange, is to go into the moon! (See fig. 6.3.)

Knocknarea is an enormous natural version of Newgrange, a crescent moon represented by its white sea-facing cliffs. In fact in Sumer, the Great Pyramid of Ur, built about 2000 BC, seems to be female. It is built for the Moon goddess Nanna. (Or is the pyramid male, in order to interact with the moon goddess?) The Earth Mother meets father sky at the temple on top. On Buddhist Stupas, we have umbrella-like objects on top which look like trees. On an Indonesian pyramid we have a tree-like temple on top. The tree is also a kind of 'horizon', the first pyramid! It is half above ground and half underground. So it is half Sky Father and half Earth Mother! The horizon is the ground level, where the two worlds meet.

In fig. 6.3, we have the Snow Madonna, a goddess from Poland. The blackness of the typical Black Madonna, from Poland, comes not seemingly from the idea of Mediterranean skin, for the skin is much darker than it needs to be. It is not olive, it is literally often quite black as the name would suggest. Her clothes are silver like the moon, which she sits upon. By mixing Luna with Earth Mother they really try to show she is an all-encompassing female. This association or fusion was possibly in place as early as the Stone Age. See fig. 1.42. Is Newgrange a shiny crescent of whiteness, or the pregnant Earth Mother? Lunar pyramids, or mounds, which also represent the pregnant Earth mother appear to be found from a moon mound in Poland, to Newgrange in Ireland, to the American Pyramid of the Moon, to the Sumerian Ziggurat, built for the moon goddess. She no longer looks like this. The silver clothing, contributed by locals has been taken off to an ecclesiastic museum.

By all accounts Khufu had a long life, but he may have merely completed the pyramid. It is the 'horizon of Khufu'. It is the border of two realities, or two worlds.

Merlin is 'Myrddin' ('Myrthin'), in an earlier form. Allegedly, the Latin form Merlin may have been invented for chronicle writing to avoid writing something like *merde*, 'shit'. Names in chronicles usually had to be written in Latin. The way I managed to explain it to myself is that Merlin is partly another version of Odin. Therefore Merlin might be related to he who hangs on the world tree, which is the bridge to heaven, learning sacred knowledge. The world tree is placed on these hills. Therefore we have Medb's cairns in Ireland and Merlin's (Myrddin's) mounts in Britain. In the case of Ireland, it could be a female version of Merlin as it is somehow mixed up with either the snake goddess associated with the tree, or the female mound itself.

Merlin is associated with a mound. His possible counterpart with a

Figure 6.3: This photograph of the 'Snow Madonna', is from a four-hundred year old church in my mother's former village of Żegocin, in Poland. It illustrates the confusion between moon goddess and Earth mother. The Black Madonna (a dark skinned lady with dark skinned child) is popular in Poland.

Figure 6.4: Gamla Uppsala, Sweden, and its three major mounds.

similar name, Odin, was said to reside around the strange three mounds at Gamla Uppsala, (Old Uppsala), Sweden. This strange monument, once surrounded by thousands of burials, was a place of parliament and ritual for generations. It featured a temple with a strange triple god. That is, three statues were worshipped, Odin (Wotan, representing war), Thor (representing fertility) and Fricco, (representing fun) a kind of Norse Priapus. Many sacrifices were brought to this temple. I would argue that the triple mound was instrumental to the belief of these three gods. The mounds are dated to the European dark ages, however one might argue that these datings are possibly based on intrusive burials and the structures could be of a much earlier date. This may be an especially prudent hypothesis considering the great importance of Uppsala, which must be based upon ancient precedent, as well as re-datings of structures such as Merlin's Mount, which turns out to be Bronze Age, and not Norman.

We can summarise some of the things learned. Mounds may very well be associated with wishing trees. The wishing tree may be one and the same, or related to the famous Germanic Christmas tree or the Germanic World tree. For the reason why people needed a mountain for a world tree, we can look to the myth of Shambhala. The pre-Indo-European culture spread its tentacles as far as even Indonesia, Thailand, and the Pacific in ancient times, so looking for relations in Tibet, where we know that related myths are found, is not a stretch, if we are looking at similar information, which would have been based on a parallel source. For instance, these eastern ideas tell us that there is a world mountain at the centre of the world. Around this is the axis of the world. There needs to be a tree in the middle of this.

We then have the idea of the snake. The idea of the snake is huge in Ireland. For a nation with no snakes, they occupy a disproportionately huge part of the mythology! St Patrick banished the snakes, presumably because he banished the tree of the snake, the world wishing tree. There could be the idea that the snake is the dragon, the fire which is the word 'pyra' in Greek, in the larger 'pyramid'. As mentioned, in Ireland, I was even shocked to discover that in Ireland the snake is associated with Christ. Just as Christ resurrects, so the snake sheds its skin.

The Yggdrasil religion is a form of proto-Christianity! It is really the origin of the cross religion in Europe, which precedes Christianity, and which superseded the spiral religion. Thus Stonehenge is possibly a symbol of a round tree on a hill. The Stonehenge of the North is also in the shape of a cross, but Stonehenge is more a Celtic cross.

Synopsis

There is an old Anglo-Saxon rhyme which talks about Woden smiting a snake after it bites a man. The snake flies into nine parts, smitten with the 'glory-twigs.' The tale represents parallel tales to very old ideas, the cutting up of Osiris, a fertility god, Eden and other ideas. The story of the snake and the tree are well proto-Indo-Germanic. The idea of the Rainbow Serpent even in Australia, as a creator deity tells of the extreme antiquity of the snake as a force for creation. The story may be as old as mankind as we know him.

> A snake came crawling, it bit a man.
> Then Woden took nine glory-twigs,
> Smote the serpent so that it flew into nine parts.
> There apple brought this pass against poison,
> That she nevermore would enter her house.

The rhyme contains many of the elements of the tree of Eden legend, but it's really garbled and thus perhaps not worth interpreting in any great detail. Nevertheless, we have the snake, the twigs of the tree, Wotan or the sky father intervening to smite the snake, and even an apple which is presumably the fruit of the tree which is poison against evil. We also have an element which relates to the mistletoe smiting Baldr, just to show how confused things can get in mythology. Baldr, shining god, is being associated with the more insidious joker fire god. Nevertheless, both of these gods were imprisoned in the underworld.

In summary of what we have learned, there is some genius creator residing inside the world mound, sometimes represented by a pyramid. The pyramid itself is female. The sky is Wotan, or the male god. We could get into names but various male and female goddesses merely have aspects of the earth mother and sky father. I suspect most names may originally be simply geo-cultural interpretations all referring to much the same thing.

The old gods are stronger than the newer Eastern/Roman gods in Ireland. They have asserted themselves again. Men do not fear the consequences of hell from no church attendance, and yet they fear the old gods to a surprising degree. A guide on a ghost walking tour in Belfast told us not to interfere with the fairy rings. He was a young man, university educated, intellectual, tall and skinny, with glasses, and very skeptical. Yet he feared the old stories, because irrespective of the lack of ritual, they somehow reached forward through the centuries, to interfere in the lives of men today. It is the power of the unknown which makes things scary. The old gods do not know that newer Gods have replaced them! They do not care! They reach out through the darkness, sweeping aside newer deities, unheeding whether or not the powerless new religions might seek to get in the way. Like the curse of the Pharaohs, they strike irrevocably and mercilessly!

'I'm a grown man but you wouldn't catch me going to one of those fairy rings. I stay well clear of em, never been to one.'

Tree, snake, and mound, or pyramid seem to be highly synonymous. They form a pattern. We seem to see this pattern in many cultures. This pattern is even seen in America. I will not touch that too strongly in this book, but will point out that their 'world tree' seems to be a cactus. Mexico City was built where the Aztec tribe saw an eagle perched on a cactus... *eating* the snake! It is sort of like the sky god overcoming Loki's son, the serpent, where the tree of life is.

So who were the pyramid builders? The short answer is they were pretty much one of the ancestors of the people we know of today as the Indo-Europeans, as well as the Native Americans, as well as various North Africans and Middle Easterners, and Africans presumably also, but due to higher civic populations in the south, and more time for civilised life, the older traditions seem to survive more among Germanic, Chinese and Asian mythologies. It is all extinct in Egypt. 'Indo-European' is the loose name for a hypothetical tribe, based upon language, which existed in many places simultaneously, spread over a huge area, Ireland to possibly Japan and China. Indo-European refers to 'Aryan' in some contexts, and means farmer ('arya'). In other words, a civilised society driven by agricultural produce, and the wealth this would produce.

Let us not ask where Indo-Europeans come from. That is difficult to answer! It seems there were many migrations, conquests and battles. In the end the Indo-European culture spread from India to China to Japan and Iceland, and I would argue, Egypt, which at several times absorbed aspects of Indo-European mythology, along with other mythologies. Let us ask another question. Where do pyramids come from?

I suspect trade routes into the Pacific resulted in similar pyramids being built there. The heavily built Pacific Islanders and Maoris seem to have some kind of tattooing tradition which may be related to that of the Celts (The word Celt is an unfortunate term, which derives from 'Gaul', the Roman word for any one of the tribes living in that region.), through to the Scythians (who are partly Sarmatians/Tocharians, another Indo-European tribe).

If we look at the pre-Roman Etruscans, (the Romans absorbed perhaps half of the Etruscan institutions as their own) it is clear that they were a strange composite of several cultures. On the one hand they buried their dead in cliff caves, very much like the Persians and Phrygians from the east. On the other hand, one of their greatest rulers, was Lars Porsena (*fl.* 6th century BC). He very nearly destroyed Rome and buried himself in a ridiculous structure whose description defies belief. Destroyed by the Romans, it has had a number of bizarre artist representations associated with it. I think the description would have made it look very much like the Indonesian pyramid of Borobudur, with pyramids built on pyramids. Virgil tells us the Etruscan nation which partly became Rome basically mixed two cultures, invaders from the East, who would have been the cave-buriers, and native Latins, who may have been the mound or pyramid buriers of Europe. Migrations can really mix everything up!

There seem to be two major pyramid traditions. One is the tradition of putting the body in a cave (or leaving the cave empty) and building the pyramid around it. The other is omitting the cave, making a closed mound. Various authors have speculated that the cave burial practice originates in the Mediterranean. (This may correspond to a tradition of joining the Earth Mother, and it seems the Greek region was a home to the Earth Mother. This differs from the North, where some joker god may have been enshrined in mounds). One does not really want to let him out.

Ireland is a mixture of Mediterranean and Viking. Since their famous old queen was called Medb or 'Maeve' with that Spanish 'bh' sound, these may be the shorter 'fairy' people, the descendants of some we possibly see walking around in Dublin these days, though the countryside seems to be more dominated by Viking types. This possibly explains the tradition of the stone cairns, and the much larger Medb Pyramid near Sligo, which is too big to be called a cairn. (There is also the related word 'carnac' for stone complex, which as pointed out by Robert Temple is found from the Caucasus, to Egypt, to Western Europe).

Links between the pyramid builders, and their origins

We have discussed Loki. Loki was led to a cave by Thor and one group of gods. Meanwhile another group of gods went after his sons, killing them. One was a wolf or was turned into a wolf. The other was a snake, possibly the Midgard serpent, hence the association between Loki and the devil. The guts of his son were used to tie down Loki. He was thrown to the ground and bound. Three slabs were erected around him, similar to the case of a dolmen in a hill. A snake was erected somehow to a stalactite above him. This might be the dragon in the mountain, such as at Wawel hill. The snake dripped poison on him, which sounds like some kind of acid, as it always made Loki writhe in pain, creating earthquakes. Covering the whole thing up is a way to immortalise Loki in the mound, since he is a creator god. It also perhaps immortalised Baldr, a shining or Sun god, who needed to be resurrected from Hel every year. Providing an underworld home for the gods, the pyramid possibly, in the eyes of some ancients, helped to facilitate the year itself, and its reincarnation, with all of its changing seasonal magic that they could not understand.

There is a link between pyramids, Stonehenge, and Potbelly Hill, also known as Göbekli Tepe. This is a ridiculously old temple discovered between the 60s and the 1990s in Turkey. Back in the 1960s archaeologists noticed that on top of this large hill there was a lone tree. Locals called it the 'wishing tree.'

The complex dates from the ninth millennium BC. For some reason, the temple (this is what most people think it is) was deliberately covered with a mound. Archaeologists have been scratching their heads wondering why such a nice structure would have been covered over. Yet, the pattern re-emerges. Perhaps Stonehenge too was 'intended' to have been covered, since Stonehenge itself greatly resembles an uncovered tomb, and yet is is five millennia younger than Potbelly Hill! (See fig. 4.17.) Then again Navan Fort was a mound built to house either a god or ancestral spirits from dining halls, also covered up ritually, but in 90 BC. Four thousand years is really not that much if you consider it is only perhaps 120 generations of parents passing similar stories down to their children. The 'covering-up' tradition may be intrinsically part of the pyramid tradition. It began by respecting the temples and dining halls of the ancestors. After a while the mounds possibly became places of worship and sacrifice.

Whatever was going on at Göbekli Tepe, pushes our possible understanding of the origins of the mound or pyramid cult back very deeply in time. It is hard to date any mythology and we seem to have scanty or any mythology from this time, and very little way of knowing what ideas they had about anything. We do not know what of the surviving mythology relates to this time and which does not.

I would suggest, however that Göbekli Tepe is in fact one of the oldest 'pyramids' (see the definition after the introduction). The location could have been at the edge of the borders of 'Old Europe'. The reason for my suggestion is what the backfill contains. It contains quite a lot of weaponry! There are arrowheads and all sorts of flint points. Flint is the main backfill. It reminds one of stones being used as backfill at Site B of Navan Fort in 90BC. Why flint? Flint is a *useful* product for mankind.

Bringing 'back' the flint, to the mound, or Earth Mother from whence rocks come, is a way of honouring the gods. They are buried in their product. It is essentially thanksgiving for helping mankind. The god being thanked is not the fertility god then, (or maybe it is as well)

Figure 6.5: Göbekli Tepe (Potbelly Hill) was filled in. It seems to have been a mound on a large hill, typical of a burial complex on a hill with a view.

but perhaps some proto- Prometheus or Loki, god of the underworld, who assisted the hunter gatherers, a toolmaker.

Whereas a later Neolithic mound might honour agriculture, a Paleolithic or Mesolithic one might honour the pre-agricultural gods! By giving thanks, one completes the circle. It is a bit like carrying dirt to Navan or sacred objects to fill an Asian stupa with, as is done. The mound is an enshrinement of good luck, as are later ones, but in 8000 BC.

In figure 6.5 we see a view over the ruin of what has been excavated at Potbelly Hill. There is probably much more remaining which needs to be excavated. This area had been covered over. Many old villages were also filled in, in ancient times, whether deliberately, or not. A buried settlement is known as a *tel*. They are thought to have been filled in by the winds of time and accumulation of debris. Consider the name 'potbelly'. It implies a kind of hemisphere, much like we see in the Krakus Mound in Poland, and elsewhere. Unlike those mounds however, this one dates to the eighth millennium BC. It is a type of mound, for gods, and ancestors, well before the pyramid age. Archaeologist Dr Klaus Schmidt, who has spent the most time on the site, called it a 'hilltop cathedral.'

If, the Göbekli Tepe mound is one of the earliest 'pyramids', this provides us with a fascinating link to the Black Sea region. One might hazard the idea that the Black Sea would have been one of the earlier cultural points of origin, back in the pre-4-6000 BC days when it was a smaller freshwater lake.

The reason the sea is 'Black' is presumably the same reason that Ukraine is renowned today for having black soil. In essence, it was and is the 'Black Land'. We do not know how long it bore this title, but then again we find names like *Chernobyl*. The 'Cherno-' refers to 'black.' You would have the black land, and then perhaps the adjoining Black Sea. Then we have Egypt, known as the 'black land' or 'Khem' in ancient times. It was perhaps a word for soil which was rich and therefore habitable. One could venture into the desert land where no-one lived, and then return safely to the black land, where one knew food would be abundant. The importance of black obviously refers to agriculture rather than hunter-gathering, and therefore it implies the existence of cities. Herodotus said the Scythians had no cities. Then again, even the Mongols had a capital.

Wherever rich earth existed, there was probably some level of civilisation, because population needed somewhere secure for their agriculture and proto-agriculture. I feel that this area, in addition to being a source of speculation for both Indo-European and later on the Slav peoples, could also be a source area for what seems to be the Aryan/Indo-European pyramid religion. Archaeologists currently dare not call Göbekli Tepe a civilisation, but I feel the definition of civilisation itself may be too exacting. How can a culture capable of elaborate stonework, with its own mythology as well as the no-doubt considerable and wealthy trade links needed, not to mention a dedicated priesthood *not* be called a civilisation? To overcome the paradox the current argument is that hunter gatherers built the structure in their spare time. I would argue that hunter gatherers had no spare time, and if they did then they built from wood, not stone, which requires stone-building skills. Furthermore, they had great artists. But there were no grains! We cannot call them agricultural, even if agriculture came from nearby, a long time later. Does a civilisation *really* need grains? If so, then perhaps we cannot call them a civilisation, so let us at least settle for 'proto-civilisation.'

What of Ukraine? Nearby Kazakhstan itself is an old home of the

Indo-Europeans/Sarmatians and does resemble something of a wild orchard, which might be based upon steppe semi-nomad permaculture. Their 'wild' apples are as large as regular apples found elsewhere. For this reason apples are thought to have originated there. This implies some form of early cultivation.

The Black Land in Egypt was referred to as 'Khem'. Alchemy was thus 'The Black (Magic)', or Black Arts. No-one seems to translate it as this, preferring, 'The Egyptian magic', but the other definition also seems prudent. What else do we have here? We have the 'black' root of 'Khem' used even in 'Camelot', and perhaps as far away as Cambodia, another pyramid-building culture. Camelot was Arthur's land. It was the richest kingdom in the land! Arthur was able to use his wealth or military ability to exert control over all the other nearby kingdoms, achieving immortal fame. The King Arthur legends themselves have Indo-Germanic origins, just as Egypt appears to have come under Indo-European influence at some stage in their history. The Arthurian legends themselves partly come from the East. Kazakhstan maintains Arthurian-type myths to this day.

Potbelly Hill is so old in time that we could be looking at the common origins with native-American religions, and their pyramid-building culture as well. The Potbelly pillars appear to be abstracted phalluses. They are square instead of rounded. It may have been a 'modernism' of the day. Different 'phalluses' have various animals carved in: fox, bull, crane, perhaps various aspects of a totem cult. Each pillar rises out of the ground, like generative force: the 'Earth Father', perhaps a proto-Loki or Hephaestus, and are very unusual! Animals are shown as the energy of the earth. Potbelly hill is a buried tomb-like structure, just as Stonehenge is a tomb-like structure. I would suggest some ancestors were cremated on the Potbelly structure around the 8th millennium and then the complex was covered over to make sure they stay in heaven. It thus becomes their house in the sky. Potbelly hill was just a mound, an idea, not really a true pyramid like we find in Egypt. That idea was far in the future.

In addition to the earliest pyramids in America, which seem to be tomb-like structures near Tiwanaku, we also have others. There are also Brazilian pyramids built entirely out of seashells which date to 3000 BC. For years it was thought they were rubbish heaps. Robert M. Schoch points out in *Voyages of the Pyramid Builders* that the Clovis people seem to disappear in Europe around 14,000 BC in Spain, and re-emerge in America in 9000 BC. These Cro-Magnon children of highly-skilled tool builders were perhaps related to the builders but it is so far back in time that it is almost ridiculous to even begin to think about an association.

I had wished to avoid too much theory in this work because there is much more to the pyramids than we will ever know. In addition, too much speculation will certainly lead us into the wrong direction, however it would also be wrong to be silent and say nothing about the fact that pyramids everywhere seem to share cultural links based upon migration and trade in ancient times.

America and Europe/Asia both share a pyramid-building culture, as well as a mound-building culture. There is also a phallus-worshipping culture in central Asia through to the Caucasus and the Levant, and even into the Mediterranean (in ancient times), just as Europe in the instance of the Zbruch idol (Svetovid), a phallus-like god of thunder, or god of the universe. This culture could have originated out of Central Asia, spreading to the peripheries, along with traditional ideas of migration from this point. There is a strong possibility of a shared culture in ancient times. The sheer number of Amerindian languages suggests many isolations and migrations and a very long cultural history indeed. One branch of the pyramid- or mound-building culture reached America from the Pacific. It encountered another branch, in later times, reaching it from the west. Ideas mixed.

I see the tall Cro Magnons originating out of Europe and Asia, and one branch of the pyramid-building culture out of the Black Sea region, from where it spread to Egypt, Sumeria, China under the Tocharians, and into the Americas through either the pacific or Atlantic. These would encompass the religion's 'true' pyramids, (I am pushing the idea these are pyramids to worship a god or at least more than one ancestor) rather than mere burial mounds for individuals, most of which seem no earlier than about 6000 BC, (except in the case of Turkey). There was another branch possibly originating on the Atlantic coast, the cairn builders. These too may have swept into Egypt. Egypt was a possible meeting point of various styles, especially between the first and fourth dynasties. By the Middle Kingdom and second millennium BC, pyramid-building was no longer a predominant style so we see developments away from the pyramid in Egypt. In this later time, we even see pyramid shafts no-longer aligned to the north. In that later era, *Axis Mundi* may have been less important as a religion.

Robert Schoch sees the early culture as originating in the possible drowned civilisation of former Indonesia known as Sundaland. (*Voyages of the Pyramid Builders*) This people spread to both the east, as well as towards the west, the Americas. Schoch says that these people were not necessarily pyramid builders themselves. Rather, he says, their mythology incorporated that of the comet as well as catastrophe. These helped affect climate change and migration. The pyramid, he says, is associated with the serpent, an allusion to the comet, (or possibly the creature which fell from heaven.) These ideas, he says, are memorialised in the pyramid, and its shape, as a platform for sky worship.

Long after this spreading of mythology, trading links between various traditions, as well as elite migration in particular, made certain pyramids similar to each other, even an ocean apart. This is because they shared a common foundation. Schoch points out that the Mayan pyramids look very much like the S.E. Asian pyramids. Meanwhile the Tiwanaku area seems very much African and Middle-Eastern in style. He also points out that the Teotihuacan pyramids, emphasising the horizontal, are rather close to those found in China.

Schoch also notes that the pyramid seems specifically designed, unlike every other building, to survive a catastrophe, another relation to comets. I would suggest that a possible reason for this is that the builders of pyramids literally wanted a building which would last forever. They did not spend their life in toiling away at the pyramid for nothing. They perhaps did it for their children as well. They wanted to ensure the land would have a good harvest for themselves, but also for their children and children's children. Ancient texts in Egypt and old Irish chronicles talk of various deluges and disasters, so these ideas may always have been on the lips of bards, probably to entertain and scare people. The ancients needed a huge structure which could survive any mythological catastrophe, not so that anyone could survive hiding inside, but rather, I feel so that the land would survive and endure. More importantly, the gods would see that man had given them a home, among them, right next door to their city or settlement! (For instance, in 2007, a Roman town was discovered in the shadow of Silbury hill). It was a home that the gods could always call home, a huge stable one, and so never forsake it. Schoch's research is very meticulous, yet I think there is a lot more to the pyramids as a representation of pregnant Earth mother and underworld, in terms of an interaction between this and the sky.

Schoch's *Voyages* work was a more general view on pyramids. In his 2005 book *Pyramid Quest*, he concentrates on Giza. The Great Pyramid, he suggests, was first an observatory, and in later times a place for ritual. Schoch does not concentrate on the mythology associated with the creating of a world mound or a world centre, however. I feel this is something common to the tradition of the third millennium BC.

Links in terms of the spread of pyramids are interesting. Pyramids are not the only archaeological relics left over by the civilisation of the pyramid builders. I showed the pictures of the Irish royal jewellery of 2000 BC (effectively of the Neolithic) from the Dublin museum, to one of my antiquarian friends. Her reaction was telling. (There is some link between Egypt, America and Ireland here).

'I didn't believe in the Atlantic- contact hypothesis until I saw this. This is so similar to Pre-Colombian American jewellery!'

I also showed the same pictures to a Brazilian photographer and avid tourist of worldwide archaeological sites, whom I met in a hostel in Galway.

'Hey, I found some nice ancient jewellery at the museum in Dublin.' I brought up the pictures on the screen.

'Here, what do you think of it?'

'Yes, looks very Inca.'

I think I swooned and almost fell of my chair at the remark. She had said this spontaneously without me mentioning anything about the point of origin. I find it easier to believe there was some trans-Atlantic seafaring going on four thousand years ago, than that the similarity of the royal jewellery is a hangover from the earlier Clovis migration from Spain to the Americas, almost an eternity earlier. Nor is it acceptable to suggest that the idea of similar jewellery (like pyramids) are fundamental to the human consciousness everywhere, and so there is a subconscious drive to make it a certain similar way. Simply, if the idea was common to human psyche then why are we not making similar jewellery today? Why have we almost (but not quite) stopped building pyramids for ritual?

In the past several decades, numerous pyramid complexes dating to the third millennium BC have been uncovered in the Americas. One significant unfinished pyramid of a more recent date is located near Lake Titicaca and is known as the Akapana.

In *The Tigris Expedition*, Thor Heyerdahl drew parallels between the Titicaca Indians, and the Marsh Arabs of Iraq whom he considers the descendants of Sumerians. Lots of them, he finds, have red hair, just like the surviving Long Ear family he encounters in Easter Island in the 1950s, who claim to be descended from the real statue builders. They were largely exterminated several centuries ago by the other inhabitants. Heyerdahl never really, however gets around to the idea of an ancient migration from Europe. He says that the Long Ear family he met thinks their ancestors might have been Norwegians. I would suggest Ireland as a strong candidate.

There are even old Irish stories, in addition to the more famous Brendan voyage on a leather boat, regarding a journey from Ireland towards the south west. One is called the *Tír na nÓg* which is a journey to the underworld which seems to be mixed up with another tale of an ocean voyage. By sailing south to the Canaries one could hook up, as Columbus did, with the trade winds, as well as trade currents. The combination of both would combine to ensure a rapid passage to the Americas. The trade winds would perhaps have taken the travellers towards Mayan cities. There was no printing press so apart from a few legends, few would ever find out or believe them.

For the 'true' pyramid-building culture, or at least one component of it, I would suggest a point of origin somewhere between west Europe, up to the Black Sea. This is because some of the earliest 'pyramids' we can find, seem to be in Ireland, though various authors have not yet realised it. There may well have been earlier ones and the pyramids could therefore be a Clovis invention which spread from Spain (from whence they emigrated to Ireland and the Americas). If we discount later contacts and concentrate on the Clovis, then the idea could also spread in an easterly direction. The idea would have spread to central Asia, and the Americas (more likely via the Atlantic than Pacific?). Later it would spread to the Pacific and SE Asia with further migration. There is the fact that the Olmec statues of Mesoamerica seem to look like Polynesians or Negroes as well, to contend with. This was one of the earliest true civilisations in the Americas.

Then again pyramids also may be based on the idea found at Göbekli Tepe in Turkey, with its temple which was filled in in 8000 BC, with seeming offerings to the flint god. This was a form of thanksgiving to him. This may be an extension of the Kurgan/Indo-European culture, the 'Old Europe' of Marija Gimbutas. This was an area between Italy and the Black Sea, an old home for the mother goddess.

If we want to find the 'original' pyramid Gods, I would look into the rich mythologies of the out of the way areas of Europe. This would encompass Germanic mythology, but also mythologies in Spain and Ireland (both are also based largely on Germanic). Unfortunately these do not seem to tell us much and it is harder to find information about them.

A Buddha variant in Egypt?

We have Prometheus, who gave knowledge to mankind, trapped on a mountain. We have Merlin the genius, buried in a mound, trapped by an Earth spirit of some kind. We have Loki associated with the mound spirit. We have king Zal, or 'Silly', (or even 'Sally' in Ireland) some kind of cosmic joker or blessed solar deity perhaps, trapped in the Silbury pyramid, and celebrated during the 'silly season'. We have the mounds of Krakus and Wanda with no burials.

We have the *stupa* mounds all over Asia supposedly containing the relics of the genius Gautama Buddha. This idea may be based upon a confounding of that Buddha with the other earlier Buddhas, with 'Buddha' as an earlier mound/pyramid god rather than prophet. Then we have Odin who could be Europe's answer to this more-primordial Buddha character, and who is also Prometheus-like and Christ-like. In Buddhism the Buddhas are reincarnated after several millennia or so. Gautama was not the first and nor are his mounds the first in Asia. Tibetan Buddhists claim their religion is the oldest on Earth.

'Buddha' was one of the monotheistic gods of the early Eurasian peoples. His surviving form in Europe was perhaps Odin. Did he have a form in Egypt? Certainly! I believe he was the Egyptian God par excellence, and creator god of everything. This is *Ptah*. Egyptians did not write all the vowels down and Egyptologists think the name was vocalised as 'Pitar'. He would seem to have the same role as cosmic Buddha which is a rather odd coincidence. Like the Buddha who as a fertility and luck god is placed in pyramid/stupas all over Asia, Ptah is essentially the supreme resurrecting god of nature. People migrating into Egypt from the East and effectively conquering part of it would not suddenly drop their old religion. It would have become incorporated into the Egyptian 'pantheon'.

This book is aimed at highlighting the existence of pyramids in Europe and re-defining the term according to function rather than form, as well as highlighting the worldwide spread of this strange Babel-like religion. The point of including Ptah in this book is to prove that there was migration into Egypt from central Asia.

Buddhism may have been the religion of Gautama Buddha, who adapted and altered it. As mentioned, many Buddhists and others believe one of these alterations was shifting emphasis from nullifying 'ego' to nullifying 'desire', thereby still maintaining the idea of a soul or separate existence. Basham in *The Wonder that was India*, however says there must have been something startlingly original in his teach-

Figure 6.6: Introducing a statuette of Ptah-Sokar-Osiris. What is the link between these three gods? They are essentially all Egyptian variations of the one god, the Green Man, or bleeding man. They are fertility gods, depicted in Egyptian art with green faces. Sokar was a fertility god of the early dynasties, replaced some time in the fourth dynasty by Osiris ('Osir'). Ptah on the other hand, was an Odin-like character of wisdom as well as of fertility. His symbol is the pillar or bull (which makes him very stone age in a universal sense). Ptah is also an artificer god.

Figure 6.7: Introducing 'Buddha', but not as we know him! Rather this is *Ptah*, a supreme Egyptian god. I do wonder if the knowledge of Hermes Trismegistus (Triple Greatest), some form of triple deity, as well as subsequent Neoplatonism, Stoicism in Rome and Buddhism in Asia, as religions of the personal mind, did not have some common inspiration which enabled their foundation. Since Indo-European peoples had a migration from a common source in central Asia, I do think the idea should be taken seriously.

ings, revealed under the sacred tree, to enable the spread of his cult. His name was not originally Gautama Buddha but Prince Siddhārtha Shakya. The 'Buddha' epithet implied he was a reincarnation from an earlier figure. Furthermore, his tribe was the *Shakya*, perhaps derived from the Sakas, or Scyths of central Asia.

Since the 'Scots' of Northern Ireland and Scotland possess a typically East/Central European haplogroup, unlike others in the West, it is not inconceivable that the name, as well as religion spread right to the west of Europe before the onset of recorded history. Since we have some evidence for this Asiatic migration, the idea of mounds being built in Egypt for similar reasons (pyramids), to stupas in Asia, becomes apparent. The Roman and Greek equivalents of Ptah are Vulcan and Hephaestus. That would make his Norse equivalent Loki, or even the 'ring lord', Völundr. Though he is often pictured with red skin and a green face, he is here pictured in mummified form, as he is also a resurrection god, like Osiris.

'Budha' is in fact a planet, Mercury, in ancient Sanskrit India, which would make him similar, perhaps in earlier times, to the fire god (invariably associated with a serpent) that we keep discussing in this book. The Mayan pyramid of the feathered serpent, El Castillo, at the Mayan ceremonial complex of Chichen Itza, built about a thousand years ago, contains several built-in astronomical ideas. Firstly the Sun is supposed to shine on the pyramid, encasing most of the sides away from the Sun in shadow, causing the 'serpent' along a certain stairwell to use a shadow trick to descend from the top, crawling along the edge of the staircase, down the pyramid from heaven to Earth. This happens on the spring and autumn equinoxes, when day and night are of equal length. The only thing missing, it would seem is the tree of knowledge, or life, but Mayans certainly had a world tree.

It is sometimes suggested that the pyramids of Mesoamerica are different from Egypt as they are temples rather than tombs. On the contrary, Mesoamerican pyramids have also been used for kingly burials, but not always. I would suggest both Mesoamerican and Egyptian pyramids are adaptations of a possibly earlier mound worship. Therefore both are perhaps a temple, but also a tomb for gods in the sense of a recreation of underworld, as well as possibly a tomb for men.

Pyramids the world over seem to be synonymous with the Earth Mother. It might be part of the human condition to think of them in this light, for Neopagans as well as certain anthropologists to identify various mounds in this way. The pagan mounds of England are often identified as representing Earth mother. They may well be Earth Mother rising up to meet with Father Sky, in a kind of *Hieros Gamos*, or sacred sex, but without human players.

In various old religions we have gods enshrined together. Lady Godiva cannot be naked unless she is on her horse. Far from being merely a part of Saxon or British tradition, I saw a grotesque on a Catholic church in Cracow appearing to display her. She may well be fundamental to early Germanic tradition.

Concepts are interleaved. For instance in the Mithra religion arising from the Persians or others in the Near East, we have a religion similar to one type of early Christianity, but whose deity is a man riding a bull and slaying it. Both elements are interchangeable, both are inseparable. Without evil good cannot exist. Without the dragon, St George cannot exist, so he is always pictured as slaying it. His spear is forever stuck in it. It is forever flaying around in its death throes, an image frozen in time. That is because the gods and goddesses are for all times. They are there for the eternal reincarnation of the year. By representing a swollen underworld the pyramid provides a home for a collection of deities who oppose one another, but who collectively represent the renewal of the year.

They are also identified by early man in terms of stories which relate to them, in which there are multiple characters. For instance, should the shining aspect be the sun, Sol, or should it be Baldr, the shining one? Relating these spirit characters to gods with names was not easy, but they managed, slipping here and there. Odin sometimes has some characteristics of cheeky Loki. Meanwhile Loki is wise, but not quite as wise as Odin.

It seems we have the serpent, as well as the tree, as deities associated with the pyramid. What is missing here? The Earth Mother, Eve! Eve is associated with the serpent and the tree. They form a kind of pagan trio. They represent all that monotheism purportedly stands against. Analysing the chronological succession in the Old Testament it is clear that first we have Adam. He is thus Uranus, or 'world' or a sky deity living with God in Heaven. Secondly, Eve, or Earth mother is created to keep him company. Perhaps they meet at the 'horizon', or is that the 'horizon of Khufu', the name for the great pyramid? This is a cosmic unity which perhaps reunites and re-fertilizes the world every spring. Thus the pyramid or mountain is a kind of 'renewal' or even eternal-life device if some king chose to be buried inside it, or nearby. That is getting well towards the realm of speculation but not perhaps an unreasonable stretch. Khufu was supposedly a hated king, and yet the Egyptians actively maintained his pyramid until later Islamic times when necessity called for the casing stones to be used to build houses. It was not entirely his, but theirs. It belonged to Egypt. (There was also something of a Khufu cult in later times.)

Eve pulls Adam to 'Earth' with her ambition, and they now must toil in agricultural labour. In the apocryphal *Gospel of Adam and Eve*, of uncertain origin, the Garden of Eden is literally another place floating above the Earth and not really part of it. Now that Adam has taken the form of man, imprisoned in the flesh as it were, by the sin of the pagan festival to Eve, man is trapped in agriculture, trapped by the very gods he feels it necessary to worship, to provide him with a yearly harvest. Gone are the days of lower populations which might be sustained in one area by gathering blackberries and hunting the local mammoth or bison. Adam and Eve have become fully human, and now they must worship the sacred tree that they had later seen to have chosen in preference to God, for the Jews of the Old Testament written-era of the 500s BC, based on who they thought Yahweh was. Yet their ancestors possibly saw things quite differently, worshipping the sacred tree, as well as the mound or mountain.

I feel that to examine the pyramid religion is to really examine the religion associated with the inter-relation between the dragon, a river or body of water, Eve, Adam, a sky god, and probably the tree. The Egyptians themselves have the 'Germanic' or Indo-European idea of the huge world snake and tree in their mythology. The Chinese or Aryans in India were one huge tribe, and therefore their civilisation endured for thousands of years, evolving and changing, never wiped out. Yet Egypt, also with a huge enormous population, the largest in the whole area, considering the size of the pyramids as monuments compared to everything else in the west, had their civilisation destroyed.

They seem to have left us with comparatively fewer written records from ancient times. The Egyptians were certainly a multicultural society. There were natives, men from the south, as well as the north. We have the ancient possibly semi-Negro appearance of the Sphinx and then we have the idea of the snake and tree. The northerners may have found themselves mixing their ideas with those of the more totem or even voodoo-like ideas of the natives. The gods have human bodies and animal heads, based upon African ritual, but also perhaps European shaman ideas from the north, where Vinca shamans wore a mask. Egypt was a real spectacular extravaganza of mixing ideas. Both

Figure 6.8: This scene seems to be related to the widespread pyramid religion. Stories about Adam and Eve, as well as other biblical tales such as the flood, seem to be linked to places in which pyramids are now found. The snake, (sometimes an eagle), tree, are found together in proto-Indo-Germanic mythology. The eagle, snake and cactus was an Aztek symbol, now the national symbol of Mexico. In that instance, the eagle eats the snake. It is comparable to Horus, Egyptian sky god, or Thor, swooping down to put Loki, perhaps represented by the snake or horned one, down into the underworld. The spread of this idea across the world in primordial times, compared to the like spread of pyramids is a fascinating association. By Titian.

Egyptian priests and Asian monks shaved their heads, apparently independently of each other. It may well be a product of an ancient related religion.

There have always been a bunch of enthusiastic amateur authors who have never ceased to knock on the door of the Egyptologists' opinion that the spectacular pyramids of Giza, and in particular the Great Pyramid are 'merely' the tombs of several Pharaohs. The curator of the Armagh museum may have joined their ranks, at least insofar as a European mound is concerned. What on Earth was going on with the mound in Armagh at Navan fort? That mound was a tomb built to enshrine a ritual, creating a type of 'God in a mountain', or even an Earth mother, employing various different types of soil in its construction, after a house was purposely burnt underneath. By bringing the essence of the empire to Site B at Navan fort, different kinds of soil and stones, they sought almost to create a god out of that very essence, a unique fertility spirit based upon the structure of the landscape itself.

Egypt

Having got a lot of stuff out of the way, we are now finally, after discussing aspects of the pyramid/mound religion elsewhere, ready to discuss Egypt. 'Giza' is part of the title of this work and I do not wish to leave the reader disappointed. What is discussed here will be greatly enlarged upon with new information in a future work. Until then I invite the reader to look at some interesting aspects of the prelude to the pyramid religion in Egypt, before discussing that religion in some detail.

First dynasty Egypt

We have an interesting mastaba, or tomb, built for King Anedjib/Adjib/Enezib of the first dynasty. The tomb is surrounded by 64 subsidiary burials. In the monumental *The Complete Pyramids*, by Mark Lehner, it is described as a 'stepped mound' but also a 'pyramid precedent' and 'stepped tumulus.' Although I was taught at school that the pyramid evolves from the Mastaba, a large box-like structure, it would seem that archaeologists are also aware that pyramids may also have evolved from mounds! This is rather apparent when we investigate the archaic mastabas of Abydos.

The so-called pyramid of Anedjib/Adjib/Enezib was inside Mastaba

3038. It is rather striking. Flinders Petrie had the belief that Libyans, that is people west of the Nile made a significant contribution to the beginnings of Egyptian civilisation. Its existence suggests that pyramids did not originate from the mastaba, as per the 3rd-dynasty step-pyramid of Djoser, which was transformed from one and is thought to be one of Egypt's first pyramids. That explanation localises the step-pyramid, seen as initially a series of mastabas, to Egypt. That is a problem when the step-pyramid is clearly a world-wide phenomenon.

In fact pyramid building, by layer upon layer, was common in the Americas. Rather than being 'either-or', I would like to say that both explanations are permissible. Egypt was obviously composed of many people and many different minds. They had their own evolving pyramid tradition, but they may have also imported various aspects of other traditions.

Walter Emery uncovered the strange structure of Anedjib's pyramid, when he realised that Anedjib's tomb was built on top of, and around a smaller step pyramid! (it is called tomb X and clocks in at a rather small 15.1 by 7.2 by 2.5 metres). Meanwhile there is another Mastaba called 3507 which is built around what Lehner calls 'a low rounded tumulus', which is directly above the burial chamber. The tumulus is thus a spiritual component of the burial which does not even need to be seen from the exterior! Nor does it need to physically contain a burial! It is merely *associated* with the burial. This seems to be a rather clear link between the mound religion and the pyramid religion, though it occurs several dynasties before the Giza pyramids. It reflects an evolution into the third dynasty complexes which were a huge rectangular arena around a central step pyramid. The implication is clear. One cannot make an earthen mound in Egypt or the powder-like sand will blow away and the jackals will get at what is left! It is something of an import. The pyramid/mound needs to be protected and enclosed, or made of bricks or stone.

Emery liked to talk about the Mesopotamian influence in the first two dynasties, such as in his *Archaic Egypt*, 1961. People possibly swept in peacefully from Mesopotamia with their step pyramids. The structures of Mesopotamia and Egypt are partly divergent from a similar origin. The direction of the migration is unknown. We also do not know how far they went.

In third dynasty Egypt we have a mastaba, a kind of flat tomb with various chambers like an afterlife-mansion, being turned into a pyramid. In first dynasty Egypt, we have a tumulus/pyramid being

Figure 6.9: Anedjib's first dynasty mastaba was is built around an internal stepped structure. Pictured here is something different, the exterior of the mastaba of Ptahshepses, Abydos. He was a vizier of the fifth dynasty. In fact, in addition to possibly containing an interior mound or pyramid, the typical exterior of a mastaba looks like this, a very steep rectangular step-pyramidal platform. I do not know if anybody has developed the idea of the pyramid-like aspect of mastabas. Mastabas similar to this surround the Khufu pyramid. Something like this, perhaps, is what a burial looks like, in Khufu's Egypt.

turned into a mastaba! It is almost like a clash of cultures having gone on, since the other mastabas do not seem to have a pyramid hidden inside. Then again one can read too much into this.

Primeval mound

We have mentioned earlier that at Hermopolis, there was an egg laid in the primeval mound, a place of myth rather than geography. There is more information about the primeval mound. We know a lot about the fire god *Ptah* from the Palermo Stone. This is a controversial artefact, which was probably made in the fifth dynasty. We also know about him from the Shabaka Stone. This is a relic from the Nubian Twenty-fifth Dynasty of Egypt. This is inscribed with a religious text known as the Memphite Theology. The Shabaka stone is a slab which measures 66 cm high and 137 wide. Memphis is the buried city of the fourth-dynasty kings. It is about 20km south of Cairo. Manetho, an Egyptian historian of the Ptolemaic era referred to Memphis as 'Hut-ka-Ptah'. This means 'enclosure of the god Ptah', who is essentially the fire god, as well, it seems, as a god related to Buddha, presumably intruded into Egypt by Asiatic migrants. (See fig. 6.6 and 6.7.)

The text claims that it is the surviving content of an old papyrus which had been eaten by worms. It was allegedly found by King Shabaka who was in Memphis, inspecting the temple of Ptah. Worried about the loss of content of the papyrus, Shabaka kindly decided to have the surviving content written on stone. Later on the stone was used as a millstone, defeating some of Shabaka's purpose, but enough survives to give us a sound insight into the mythos of Ptah. Ptah is placed as the creator god at the centre of the universe. This is essentially not only the position of Loki, but also of the pyramid, or mound complex, as well as Germanic Yggdrasil. Some confirmation of this idea results from the fact that at Memphis, priests of Ptah had identified their god with the primeval mound. This is the place where Atum (a later Adam?) first arose. The primeval mound story here would be related to another one, the cosmic egg being hatched at the primeval mound at Hermopolis.

Linking Ptah to the mound is essentially like linking Loki or other figures to it. Does this tell us that the pyramid is a home for the fire god? Maybe it at least tells us that the pyramid was thought, at Memphis, near Giza to have been the representation of creation. Other cities did not have Ptah as their chief god. This is merely the deity at

Memphis, a capital of the kings of the fourth dynasty.

Djoser

Robert Temple describes the technological difference between the second-dynasty Egyptians and third-dynasty Egyptians as a huge leap. 'Asiatics', or peoples coming in from the north east may have entered Egypt causing the mound aspect of the earlier burials to assume a more significant function.

This could simply be ascribed to a changing fashion, or it could be ascribed to changing religion as well. Djoser's step pyramid of the third dynasty was a unique structure, rather new and unprecedented in Egypt, reflecting step-pyramid ideas from Sumeria. I have noticed that various controversial authors have stated that Djoser seems to parallel the biblical Joseph. They argue that therefore he *was* Joseph. Nothing could be further from the truth, and that argument requires more nuance and modification. Djoser or Djozer could well have inspired much later ideas about Joseph and the 'Jews' entering Egypt in a deep primordial time. Firstly it needs to be pointed out that Djoser was king in about the 2700s BC. The Old Testament meanwhile was written down in the 500s BC. There was plenty of time for a game of 'Chinese Whispers' to have gone on, two millennias' worth of mixing the story around.

I had learned something in my academic work which I was fortunate to have been able to do, in researching the Robin Hood legends. I would look at medieval romances written in the 1100s AD, for aristocrats, and see how aspects of them were told by jesters and balladeers in the 1400s. One could literally see how the more boring aspects of earlier legends and stories had disappeared, and names would sometime vanish, but exciting plot aspects and leading rolls associated with earlier characters were often retained.

I also noticed that similar stories and ballads would easily combine into new stories. Essentially the ballad-teller was a kind of jester who told jests, or 'gestes.' These were humorous and engaging tales. He was not a historian and he did not care whether his stories were 'accurate' because they were designed for entertainment. He was also not necessarily the dwarf who sat next to the king dressed like a clown, seen in popular media, but a travelling storyteller, who picked up scraps of stories and combined them. The more talented jesters made new stories which others imitated. Eventually the development of the early legends of Robin Hood froze solid in about the 1500s, when the printing press was invented. By then however, a lot of modification had gone on, in only say two or three hundred years of development from earlier tales about forest outlaws.

Now let us consider the modification which might have been encountered, over the span of two millennia! Although in the Old Testament, Joseph is not the king of Egypt, merely a kind of overseer and advisor, myth is not history and does not need to be treated as such. A spark of inspiration is enough to set stories going in various directions.

In the Joseph story, barns are built in Egypt after the king has dreams which are interpreted as what would seem like a kind of *El-Nino/La Nina* pattern of seven good, and seven bad years. It seems that medieval people thought that the actual pyramids of Egypt were barns or granaries which the Pharaoh of the story built to protect against the bad years. Why should they think that? It might have been based on an indigenous tradition which travellers picked up in Egypt, that pyramids were objects of fertility veneration, 'for the harvest' or 'for the famine.'

Later Jews, who wrote the Bible, in Babylon, were not the earlier 'Samaritans' of Israel who remained there during the exile, and who claim to be the original Jews with their original mountain religion which the other Jews abandoned. These were the temple-worshipping Jews. (The change in Jewish worship in fact reflects changes in Egypt, from pyramid, or mountain representation, to a concentration upon temple, in the New Kingdom) Assuming the earlier legend was about suddenly starting to build ridiculously large pyramids, under someone thought to have been called 'Joseph' to increase good luck in harvest, this would not fit well with the lack of pyramid-building going on in Israel at that time. They would not understand how huge pyramids possibly could trigger fertility, and nor would the audience they were trying to win over. Hence 'barns.'

There are a few very interesting things regarding the Djoser pyramid. Firstly, architect Imhotep was celebrated as a genius, but he is more of a god in later tradition, as if he had had some role in somehow saving or founding Egypt. I would suggest that Imhotep has some of the role of biblical Joseph, interpreter of dreams and Vizier of Egypt. Joseph was a man who told pharaoh to 'build'. Meanwhile the biblical story is associated with 'Joseph' and possibly remembered under that name because that was basically the name of the Pharaoh of the day.

Then again there are certain similarities between hypothetical 'I-O-

SEPH and IM-HO-TEP, as well as 'Djoser' which would blur them all for later generations who did not care for names, only good stories. 'His name was Imhotep'... 'really, old man, who cares? Tell us a good story and skip the names and honorifics! We don't want a history lesson, especially not about Egyptians!'

I am not Jewish, but to me, Imhotep is a rather Egyptian name, one that later Jews, with different names, would perhaps not really care to remember in their stories. Then again Imhotep was the greatest of the great of Pharaoh's servants. Who else was there in such a position? The Egyptian culture was wiped out by later conquests but the Jews seemingly remembered a man who *did* have a Jewish-sounding name, 'Joseph,' a man who was not the king, but very close to him. Was Imhotep Joseph then? Certainly not! Rather, I think the memory of this time at least played a part in inspiring later stories which inspired some of what was written down in the Bible.

There is something of great desperation behind the building of the pyramid of Djoser. I do not say this lightly. I read a fascinating bit of information quite late in the stage of the writing of this book, which was very exciting to me indeed, and which I will presently discuss. Many know that the pyramid was converted out of a mastaba. Few however, know of the bizarre treasure which is held underneath. For starters, there are a great many chambers underneath the mastaba around which the Djoser pyramid was built, in about 2700 BC. These chambers are as big as a cave complex. In several, 40,000 pots have been stacked. These are not pots made in the time of Djoser, and even necessarily for him. Where are they from? They are pots made in the previous several centuries.

The Mystery of the Pots

I would like to hypothetically reconstruct what was perhaps going on in the minds of the builders, if we take a pyramid as being that described in my definition (provided after the introduction), as a place for fertility, then the meaning of these pots might become clearer. What are pots used for? Pots generally carry agricultural produce and water. They are there for fertility bounty, as the pyramid is a fertility mound. These pots need to be filled. They evidently contained nothing of use to the dead Pharaoh. 'Thank you, and please fill them up again!?' The pots were essentially ransacked from various graves across Egypt. Many of them contain the names of previous, sometimes unknown kings.

Robert Temple, for whom I have a great deal of respect as a researcher, but do not agree with in all of his claims, said that Imhotep may have been a historian. As such, he says the pots are down there for two reasons. Firstly, Imhotep was interested in reconstructing an early history of Egypt, hence the bowls are a historical archive. Secondly, says Temple, the bowls are cast stone, superior cement, seen as magical to the Egyptians, citing a theory of chemist Dr Joseph Davidovits. Temple states the reason that the famous razor-blade cannot be inserted between certain limestone casing stones on the Giza pyramids is that they were simply cast in an overlapping pattern. Imhotep was fascinated by the technology they represented. In supposedly applying this technology to the pyramid, he was later seen as a god. In *The Complete Pyramids*, which is much closer to conventional and traditional archaeology, Lehner is of the opinion that the the pots are an archive.

I do not think either possibility is a satisfying enough reason why so many bowls should have been placed in the chambers of the mastaba beneath the pyramid, in the time the pyramid was built out of that mastaba. A massive and incomprehensible amount of evidence is often required to trigger a paradigm shift in thinking, and perhaps rightly so. Otherwise a theory will always resort to the status quo. The archive explanation passes academic tests because it removes the need to explain away a case of possible ancestor worship in ancient Egypt, and the need to frame it within a religious context. It also states reality. The pots, with their inscribed king names, *do* in fact constitute an archive of sorts.

This archive was inaccessible to later Egyptian historians, but it was an archive nonetheless. The fact that we cannot really explain why the objects of the ancestors were placed underneath an enormous religious structure, the greatest glory of Imhotep, and alleged tomb of Djoser, when they could have been deposited in any cave in Egypt, or anywhere else in the Saqqara burial complex, is interesting. As far as a religious explanation, in *Pyramid Quest*, Robert Schoch suggests that Djoser may have been re-interring materials ransacked from earlier tombs by his predecessors. Alternately, he suggests that pots accumulated in warehouses and storerooms were now being put into use for the dead king. An alternate explanation would simply be that there was no reason and they were just acting randomly and it seemed like a good idea at the time.

As far as we know, it would seem that the pots were placed there by the same generation which built and enlarged the pyramid, rather than others. The real reason was perhaps symbolic, and religious. Firstly, well-made pots are the celebratory vessels of the ancestors who reside in the afterlife. Placing them all in one place concentrates their magical potential. It turns the area into a kind of Valhalla on Earth. The ancestors too are gods.

Site B, which is the second mound in Navan Fort, a literal round possible feasting hall, representing the ancestors, was burnt down and filled with stones and soil brought from all over the old polity, as part of what seems to have been a sympathetic fertilisation ritual. This was turned into a circular hill. At Newgrange, remains of the ancestors were placed into a large tomb which was also associated with the moon goddess and Earth Mother, as well as the Sun, an earth giant and shining young fertility man. It is as if putting everything in one place would ensure that re-creation takes place and the weather cycle and yearly cycle could continue.

Is Djoser's tomb supposed to be a tomb for Djoser, or for everybody in Egypt who had ever lived up till that point? Why would there be so much pottery in there, from previous generations? Perhaps it is both. Perhaps the answer is rather elementary. This is thanksgiving. 'We have feasted from your bounty, oh creator gods. We place these bowls and vessels here, under the fertility mound, as a remembrance, and a sacrifice, and ask that they be refilled by your creative potential.' There may have been a famine, or some kind of desperation, for what could have forced the possible desecration of so many graves, or the apparent waste of so much antique pottery, within it seems, a generation. Then we have the fact the pyramid was enlarged. 'It is too small. The gods will not notice. Make the magic stronger, so that it is sure to work.' Is this 'Joseph's Granary,' or maybe just the spiritual component? I think both, but possibly more of the latter.

The proto-Jews were said to have been brought to Egypt, seeking a new home, by Abraham, and out of the North, perhaps from someone in the fertile crescent, such as Assyria. The religion in Egypt in the third dynasty, likewise seems to be something of a record of an invasion. I think the legends are possibly based upon pyramid builders from the east, building a different type of pyramid, subsequently enslaved when a rival Egyptian kingdom took over. They may even have encouraged Djoser to build the pyramid in the form of a Ziggurat from the east. Those were temples for fertility, not even tombs. We do not need to work out all the murky details, but there are some parallels to archae-

Figure 6.10: Djoser's Pyramid, 3rd dynasty.

ology, even if the time periods are all mixed up. Myth making tends to ignore historical intricacies and focus on what wants telling.

In fig. 6.10, we have Djoser's pyramid. We do not really know where most of the tombs of the second dynasty kings are even found. Here, it is different. The third dynasty was something new in Egypt. Stories of Joseph may have been inspired by Djoser's actual glorious reign, which actually was a time of economic prosperity.

Djoser's pyramid seems to be based upon the mastaba, but with a huge variation. What was formerly an internalised mound or step pyramid/platform within a mastaba, now became incredibly large. In fact the Djoser pyramid was transformed out of a mastaba. It was turned into a step pyramid, and then into a much larger step pyramid in several steps. It was as if someone had decided to, in my opinion, turn a mere tomb, into a mountain, a central point of worship reflecting older ideas of the world mountain.

There are stories of Jews entering Egypt, often (or always!) ascribed to the Hyksos of a later period, and maintaining their culture for four hundred years, (lengths of this captivity differ, archaeologists say their rule was a century). Why the difference? Four hundred years sounds like the record of a dynastic stretch. Enslavement may have occurred with a conquest by the south, or Upper Egypt, over the pyramid-builders of Lower Egypt in the delta. This perhaps enslaved the pyramid-builders, or mountain worshippers, as the earlier proto-Jews possibly also were, at the end of the Old Kingdom. People who are not aware of the incredible flexibility of the development of legends, (they do not record history, merely entertaining stories) ideas contaminating various later stories, over time, often seek to relate everything Hyksos to everything Biblical. On the contrary, we may be dealing with notions of an earlier invasion from the East as well. 'Abraham,' for instance travelled to Egypt, apparently long before the Hyksos.

In the Middle Kingdom era, the pyramid returned to being subservient to the temple encompassing it, as in older times, and similar to the mastaba. The possibly much earlier invasion (the people of the third dynasty) which may have led to the building of very large pyramids (presumably peoples coming from the East) may quite easily have become entangled with later Exodus legends of another event, or even set of events. When later Egyptians tried to build pyramids, they later crumbled, and were not necessarily given priority in terms of mortuary architecture, over the temple around them, which was becoming more important. It implies the later dynasties were, obviously, a slightly different civilisation, who still built the pyramid for reasons of cultural conservatism, seeing the great pyramids of their ancestors. There became two varying Jewish traditions, both seen in pyramid architecture, worshippers at the temple, and worshippers at the mountain.

Colour

Whilst on the theme of immigrants from somewhere to the east, in Asia, or elsewhere to the north, I point out that the colour red is sacred in China, based upon ancient precedent. It represents energy, life and happiness. I mention this because red seems to have featured in the colouring in of aspects of monumental architecture of the Fourth Dynasty. We have the Sneferu 'red pyramid' of Dashur with its red granite exterior, as well as a burial chamber whose corbelled roof reminds one of the entrance to the burial chamber of the much later Royal Kurgan in Crimea. (In *Pyramid Quest*, Robert Schoch expounds his reasoning that the Red Pyramid of Dashur is built to encapsulate an earlier megalithic core, representing a different type of building style)

The pyramids of Khufu and Khafra were both almost totally white. Khafra has a platform of two layers of granite red blocks, (which Kurt

Mendelssohn suggests has a structural purpose to prevent slippage of casing stones) but the Menkaure pyramid has a very prominent entire lower section of red blocks. In addition, the Sphinx was once painted red, exemplified by flecks of red paint, possibly a New Kingdom trend. The Khufu pyramid also has these flecks of red paint, but unlike the other pyramids, no red granite was used on the exterior.

Here I make a fundamental point. One can provide a little more evidence that might show that the Giza complex seems to have been built according to a pattern, as various authors have suggested. Aspects of the three goddesses are not quite equal or the same.

See fig. 6.23. The central Khafra pyramid would have been designed to be 'lesser' than the Khufu pyramid (upper right) when complete. His pyramid already occupied the far-less prominent position, further away from the cliff edge, more away from the Nile, so it was already harder to spot from proto-Cairo. The answer might be prior planning. Either the Khufu pyramid had to remain the best, even when Khufu was no longer around, or the lesser locations on the plateau meant that his demoralised successors did not bother to try as hard. In fact, why should they even have bothered? The Menkaure complex (lower left) is only 80-90% complete. Two Queens' pyramids are unfinished, as is the Menkaure pyramid itself. Yet, they did bother. They bothered quite a lot. I would like to provide something of an answer before this book is over.

Sneferu was the founder of the fourth dynasty, as well as of the Old Kingdom. He was the greatest builder of all, and people wonder why he built three pyramids for 'himself.' Can he really have been that indecisive? Ideas of the Egyptian king come from the image of absolute power. He can do what he wants, so he does, a view perpetuated by Hollywood myth-making, as well as images of Egyptian kings holding a crook and whip. Then again, other Stone-Age cultures also featured a figure in some absolute command.

I do not know instances more prevalent than in Egypt, where mind-changing is a dominant explanation for unknown intricacies in strange architecture, within one generation of builders. A traditional argument, for instance, is that Khufu simply changed his mind about where his tomb was going to be, resulting in three possible burial sites within the Great Pyramid. That explanation might work well in terms of the unfinished chamber below the pyramid. It does not work so well for explaining the effectively completed King's and Queen's chambers. Khufu then changed his mind again, having possibly bankrupted Egypt to build an enormous structure, and was buried elsewhere, yet at Giza, and strangely enough, near the pyramid in which he perhaps did not want to be buried.

The chambers in the pyramid may simply have been dummies, or there was a *coup* and his successor Khafra did not care for Khufu's correct burial, (a pattern later possibly repeated with almost every other pyramid). But then we come back to the indecision explanation and its unsatisfying inadequacies. Whilst it is possible, it is also odd behaviour contingent on the fact that Khufu was an indecisive man in command of a very resolute and obedient workforce. So was his father Sneferu. Both fit the Hollywood pattern of a control freak taking pleasure in working his people to death and then altering his plans at every instant, to make them even more miserable.

Several authors have argued that Sneferu may have really just renovated structures which were begun and left uncompleted by others. That might explain why he seems to have built more than one pyramid 'for himself.' There is controversy, for instance in whether the collapsed Meidum pyramid was originally his, with some archaeologists suggesting he took it over from Huni, and then proceeded to build two more pyramids.

The answer may be that he was building multiple harvest mounds, leaving the option open of whether he may or may not have intended to use them as chambers for burial as well. They were built perhaps for the good of the harvest. It was an investment in Egypt's future, and therefore easier to sell to the people, than if the pyramids were mere tyrannical projects. The pyramids needed to be as big as possible to make them as magical as possible. In Egyptian magical spells, the gods tend to be bullied around quite considerably. Make the hill huge and the gods just cannot look anywhere else.

Khufu—fourth dynasty

We can now get onto the tricky stuff, which is truly exciting. For now we trace a pattern from religious burial mound, which needed to be integrated into a mastaba, for the burial magic to work, to pyramids themselves. Based upon the plateau-worship religion in Egypt, the stone circles in the Western Desert (Libya), so similar to Europe, (and even American stone circles), I think we can safely presume the former existence of a Eurasian-influenced Stone-Age mythology, which seeped into Egypt. This is a possible 'ticket' into the minds of the Giza builders, a puzzle which continues to stump mankind.

We see at Giza a reproduction of the underworld, around which burials were placed. There have been a number of popular books about the Egyptians building 'heaven on Earth' at Giza, but these discuss astronomy, without really mentioning the early and widespread Stone-Age gods whose memory was perhaps venerated. Some authors treat Egypt as segregated from the world, when it is a bridge between two continents. In fact each new dynasty, of which there are over thirty, has the potential to have represented a possible invasion and conquest by another people or religion, as well as a civil war, later absorbed by the population.

As I researched, I became considerably more excited, noticing various parallels between Giza and other Stone-Age sites. I would love to say there was a time when it suddenly hit me that the Giza religion was widespread. The realisation was gradual, but one point of impact would have been mainly on the days around my little Knocknarea expedition, when I realised that I was on a hill which was the proto-Irish version of the worship of the widespread Babel religion. 'What on Earth was the Babel religion doing in Ireland?' was what I asked myself.

If the parallels I mention seem a little far-fetched, that is mainly due to geography and distance. However it is to be borne in mind that Stone-Agers were nomads who spread their religion far and wide. We can ignore national borders and even nations as these are modern ideas. The fact that Stone-Agers were not as soil-bound as we, is reflected in their fascination with agriculture, as though it were something odd and magical, which they could control with early spells and ritual. To this extent, the mound was produced as a form of magic to control it, perhaps lest harvests fail, as in the Babel legend in *Genesis*. That story implies that if their ancestors could not control something unspecified (agriculture?), they would resort to a nomadic existence, a migration to other cities, or perish. The tower to heaven was a necessity for them.

From the first to third dynasty we see a similar culture which gradually evolved its burial practice from a rectangular enclosure, sometimes with a mound or pyramid in the middle. In the third dynasty this took on terrific proportion in the Djoser complex. Between the Djoser complex and the Khufu Giza complex however, the burial practice changed and the influence of earlier Egypt became markedly less, what we might call reflecting Mesopotamian influence. That is sometimes seen as quite a controversial statement nowadays in Egyptological publications, because nothing is exclusively diffusion, but I was nevertheless taught it in university archaeology class because it is a good way to summarise the issue at hand, to the students. It is also a rather traditional view which probably will not change, though from the earliest days of Egyptian study, it was also preferred to treat Egypt as evolving in isolation, another pattern which seems to be ongoing concurrently with the desire to discuss foreign influences. The two methodologies tend to cancel each other out with authors generally agreeing to an influence from the east, but not an invasion. It is hard to see however, why Egypt would have adopted Mesopotamian-like burial practices early on, if there was not some shared culture or large influx of foreigners.

Compared to the third dynasty, fourth dynasty burials are essentially telling us 'mound too small. Make mound bigger, much bigger, and reduce ratio of rectangular enclosure.' What do we see here? This is really a return to roots, because it reflects the huge mound as predominant, as it is in Eurasia, with a reduced emphasis upon the subsidiary temple. (There may have been subsidiary temples at every hill mound, but these rotted and were recycled. For an example, see the rectangle on the hill in fig. 1.46 a later Roman temple). Despite these changes, there was less of a change in burial methods, for even royal figures, at Giza, *continue to have been buried in mastabas.* For instance, Khufu's son Khufukaf, is buried in one, at Giza, which is not that different from mastabas of the previous dynasties.

Other than that, they now demanded a huge mound. I think they wanted something like what had just been built elsewhere at Silbury hill and other places. This speaks of migration, a new tribe in command. It is after all, a new dynasty. (To be balanced, the counter-argument would be that there is already a clear development of the pyramid becoming increasingly larger inside the huge mastaba complex, in the case of both Djoser and Sekhemkhet at Saqqara in third dynasty burials, without having to argue the migration idea.) These are not hidden pyramids like those found in the first dynasty burials.

To counter the counter argument, which is the orthodox idea, one might say that the infusion into Egypt may not have been based upon a single migration, but a complex sway of competing influxes and influences. Rulers wanted to be seen as credible Egyptians. They also however wanted to retain certain burial practices of their ancestors. The influx may simply have been ongoing since the first dynasty, with competing influences from Libya, as well as from the west, as well as the alternate Egyptian civilisation, probably under control of the pyramid builders, to the south, (even if they did not really build pyramids at this time, in Upper Egypt). One of the great puzzles has been that first dynasty kings built cenotaphs in the north, at Abydos, with no burial, and placed their actual burials in smaller parallel, less grand tombs in the south, upper Egypt. This strange behaviour was probably to reflect their ancestor's seat of power.

We can look at the tombs around Giza, in figs. 6.11, 6.23 and 6.24. Khufu's pyramid is surrounded by mastabas. In this book I present the idea that a 'pyramid' should be defined as something which may or may not contain a human burial, but is often representative of buried gods, essentially being a derivative of the mound religion. It is a home of the gods, a symbolic burial of them. Building a pyramid or mound, centres the Stone-Age religion in a particular locality, making sure that the gods of the underworld do not forget about actual burials nearby.

In fig. 6.11, we see mastaba burials close to the Khufu pyramid. Herodotus was the famous 'father of history', or 'lies', depending on one's point of view. He was informed by priests of Sais, five centuries before Christ, that Khufu was not buried in the pyramid. Rather he was buried elsewhere on site, in some pit which seems to resemble the shaft of Osiris, also found on site. The physicist, Dr Kurt Mendelssohn (*The Riddle of the Pyramids*) presented the view that since we find burials in no pyramid, it appears that something other than a human body may have been ritually entombed. (Presumably an Osiris burial) He furthermore stated that the pyramid requires fewer workers as it approaches the top. This means that a highly specialised and professional workforce goes to waste unless it is put to work building the next pyramid while another is under construction. In other words the Giza pyramid complex may not correspond to the lifetime of the kings associated with it.

While Khafra's pyramid has some burials and buildings to one side. Menkaure's pyramid is rather destitute of nearby burials. The fact mastabas were used makes it clear that the earlier burial practice was not abandoned. So why does Khufu need a different burial? Firstly, from the first dynasty onwards, it is apparent that the mound is only one component of the burial. There is a wider mastaba complex around it. Nevertheless it is the heart of the burial. The mastabas of court officials found clustered around the Khufu pyramid, perhaps as elsewhere, did not need a mound in their own tombs. They relied upon the proximity to the Khufu mound, as representation of the afterlife, and primordial Earth Mother, which contained a set of fertility gods.

There is also the fact the pyramid of Khufu is not what it seems.

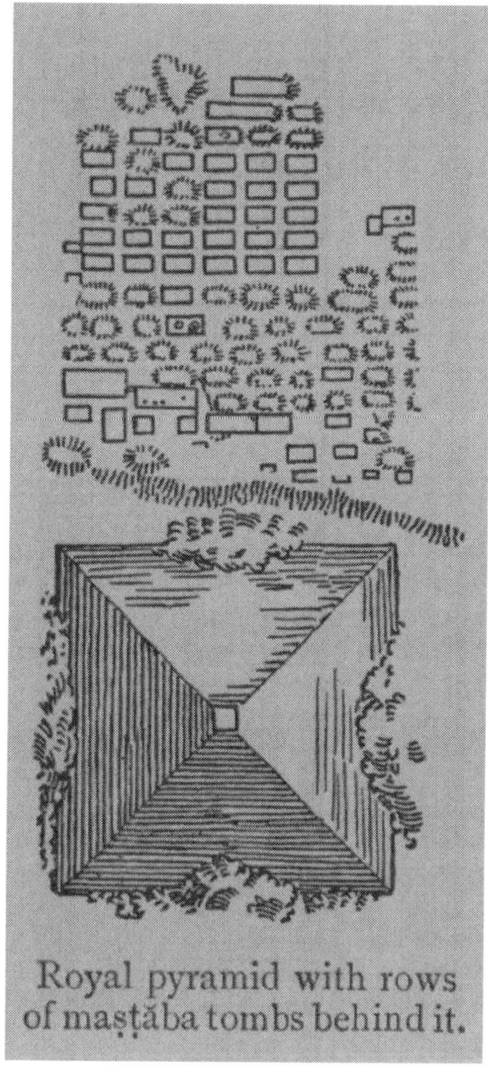

Figure 6.11: Despite building the pyramids, Egyptians kept building the smaller mastaba for royal and high-official burial, at the same time, a relic of the Predynastic period. The central mound which was once contained in the mastaba may have simply been increased in size.

The interior is filled up with wood, reeds, mud, ashes and other organic matter which was dated by radiocarbon between the 1960s and quite recently, to about a hundred, or several hundred to a thousand years before the reign of Khufu. One would imagine that these would be aspects of the agriculture of Egypt, requiring eternal blessing. Blessing representations of this flora would perhaps bless it everywhere in Egypt.

The dates also seem to indicate that some other earlier structure, perhaps on the same site of the pyramid, was employed to build up the pyramid. Robert Schoch considers it may have been from an earlier possibly pyramid-like structure dating from around 4000-3000 BC. This could be why Khufu's name is not plastered all over it. It might have been seen back then, as a possible case of blasphemy, or at least very bad taste. (As a counter-argument, there is no writing in the Valley temples either, and there is no evidence these are based upon earlier structures. Schoch thinks there was a proto-pyramid in the place of Khufu, and certain valley temples date to this earlier time).

The only relic of his name seems to be in builders' marks in red paint, which seem to be genuine, but designed not to be easily seen. It is almost as if the builders were following a religion which was un-accustomed to any form of writing. The earlier carbon dating puts the proto-Khufu pyramid, or whatever may have come before in that place (speculation) at about the same age as the first pyramids in the Americas.

Herodotus tells us that Cheops (Khufu) and Chefren (Khafra) are not buried in their pyramids, but nearby. If the pyramid was solely a tomb for man, then why would Khafra go to the trouble of building another pyramid for himself and then following in Cheops' footsteps of probably not being buried there? (We don't know for sure.)

In addition to the body of the young king, the tomb of Tutankhamun contained a very weird *additional* burial, which is never really mentioned, as it is not really a treasure. It was a tomb to Osiris. Inside a roughly man-shaped coffin was found nothing but Nile-river soil. Seeds had been pressed into this which had sprouted: the resurrection. Here we have a direct instance of the burial of a god, as the burial of soil. It echoes Navan Fort. Instead of burying a king next to a burial mound (pyramids were no longer built in the New Kingdom), they put the god of resurrection in there himself.

The resurrection of Osiris was celebrated at Abydos in about March/April, paralleling the later Christian Easter. In fact the word Easter seems quite similar to Osiris. The Egyptian version of Greek 'Osiris' was really 'Wsjr', pronounced something like 'Ausar'. I would here hazard a speculation that the 'Esterka' mound in Poland, which we have mentioned, is really some sort of Easter mound.

So far as it was institutionalised into ritual hierarchy, by the Egyptian as opposed to in earlier Stone-Age nomad times, the pyramid is no longer really just an Earth Mother, a representation of Hel and a pregnancy of the Earth (early on it may well have been) but, I would speculate, the product of more a patriarchal and highly regimented civilisation, or empire. It is something more complex than a mere mound. The pyramid is fundamentally designed with geometry to display order and power. It demonstrates the power to order nature on a large scale and the economic power of the rulers. This imperial idea of a pyramid dominating the local town may be an idea associated with the Aryan tribe, who spread their tentacles from Ireland to Iran, and to India and perhaps elsewhere.

In Sumer, we are taught, the pyramid or ziggurat was built to remind men of a higher God, as well as of the power of local authority. The same is obviously true at Giza/Cairo. It towered above everybody. I noticed precisely the same guiding idea in Ireland, in particular in the west (being less developed, the obliteration of early archaeology is slower). We have huge tombs towering above both Sligo and Galway (somewhat smaller and more distant), to remind people just where the real power lay.

On a walking tour in Galway I asked about the huge tombs on the mountains nearby, clearly seen from the city centre, but the guide did not have any knowledge about what they represented. These were built at the same time, or prior to the Ziggurats of Iraq. Egyptologists are not necessarily aware of the background to the huge European mounds, equivalent perhaps in time and perhaps also similar in religious terms to the Egyptian Old-Kingdom pyramids.

The way I am trying to define European 'pyramids', is that they are a burial for a god. They are a symbolic burial. Who is symbolically buried underground? Loki, the fire god, or any fire god! The Greek word 'Pyramid' is tricky to deal with. Either the Greeks were merely putting together something which sounded the same as an Egyptian word for 'house', or they were being *really* clever and putting a little translation into it as well. Unfortunately we do know that the Greeks actually were incredibly clever and devious with their language so this tends to complicate things. So either it is *'Per-a'* (one way of writing 'house', in Egyptian) 'in the middle' or literally, Greek *pyro*, or fire 'in the middle', if we follow the translation sense. Does this mean Loki is the fire god in the middle? The 'central fire?' It seems reasonable enough to accept the museum explanation of the pyramid at Navan Fort. This stated that the Irish there wanted to bury a genius god in the middle of a mound, about a century before Christ. Loki the fire/trickster god seems to be the one they buried, as he belongs in there according to Germanic mythology, from Scandinavia. The name 'Merlin's mount' suggests a name of a prophet-like figure, being entombed for worship, or in fact a physical temple or pulpit for sermons and sacrifice. (or both). The association with Merlin suggests some kind of intellect associated with the pyramid.

The antiquary Stephen S. Mehler puts an interesting spin on this in *The Land of Osiris*. He was told by a certain Egyptian, Abd'el Hakim, self-professed guardian of an alleged indigenous (pre-Arab) tradition regarding the pyramids. We can grant that the Egyptian understanding of words must have changed considerably over millennia.

Hieroglyphs were still being used to represent the same words over a great expanse of time, which the spoken language may have modified. This allows for some deviation in definition. Personally I cannot really agree with what most of Hakim says. Any indigenous teaching, if still surviving, would now be inaccurate, just as Herodotus' advice from learned priests in Egypt so long ago, was not quite correct. However, Hakim considered that *per-ka* are mere tombs, the *per-ba* are the temples, and the *per-neter* are the pyramids. He says the Greek *pyramis* comes from this. He claims that the word 'nature' is what the Greeks derived from *neter*. This is an old and still controversial idea of scholars. (It involves an association of the 'Hamito-Semitic' Egyptian language with the 'Indo-European' language, which are usually treated as separate entities) Therefore he translates *per-neter* as 'House of Nature', or even 'House of energy', presumably the divine force of nature, or I would argue, 'potency' to create a rebirth of the seasons. That is an attractive idea. The hypothesis is conceptually attractive, if utterly unproven, (perhaps it cannot ever be proven or disproven) because it bears the hallmarks of influence from a tradition of the mound builders.

Since nature is usually the mother, the *per-neter* would be the house of the nature goddess, the Earth Mother, presumably as elsewhere. Perhaps there is really nothing intrinsically wrong with the *Per-Neter* suggestion, even if Egyptian language specialists place less emphasis upon it. It would accord very well as a correct definition for what a pyramid actually is, according to pyramid structures found elsewhere.

We have to have some caution however, before we finally believe one thing or the other. It could be the case that Pharaohs each built a pyramid as they each wanted their own link between Earth Goddess and father sky.

Gods are discreet entities but ideas are continuous and overlap. I have found that gods behave a lot like mythological heroes. The underlying story is also more important than the names of the gods involved. In fact it would seem, at least in my experience, that a story plot is what is passed down. As people migrate around, new gods are brought into an area and they are made to fit existing stories. Old names are dropped and new ones inserted. In this way, it has been suggested, and just about proven, that many 'lives of saints' actually might contain stories about pagan gods.

Where is Loki in the Egyptian tradition? He may be related to the God Khnum, protector of Khufu, but it is hard to really make that case! Khnum is similar, in that Prometheus/Loki in some traditions created man and taught him fire. He is a bit Ptah as well. (a knowledge god and Green Man, father of Imhotep) Khnum was man's special friend, to help get mankind out of the golden-age carefree wilderness, and into the age of brass and iron, the later debased times, of the first book of Ovid. In this respect he is a kind of serpent of Eden. Khnum was possibly Khufu's protector. There is definitely a lot of nature god in him and he seems a kind of water god. He is depicted as a green goat, among various guises. Funnily enough, he could be related to Svetovid, or the Zbruch idol, as he is depicted as being one of the heads of a four-headed deity. Whilst he is water, the other heads are Shu (fire), Geb (air), and Osiris (death). It is all very complicated. Khnum is also a kind of crocodile in other traditions.

We could be on *very* shakey ground but there is something very special about Khnum which relates him to Indo-Germanic tradition, at least in idea, even if he is a different god (remembering that gods are just 'individuals' or names really with basic properties, somehow attempting, thanks to humans, to each encapsulate ideas regarding a more ancient or more recent mythological tradition).

According to the *Mabinogion*, the red knight steals Arthur's cup from him and flees in great haste, laughing. Only innocent Percival can stop him, becoming the next red knight by taking his armour once the red knight (or is he the setting Sun?) is destroyed. This links the setting Sun to the grail, and to rebirth, which is what the harvest hill is all about. (Remembering that soma could have been administered

Figure 6.12: Khnum, shaper of man. He is one of Egypt's earliest gods. From *Egyptian Magic*, by Wallis Budge.

in any old shaman tradition from a holy cup on a hill). Red is blood and therefore this links it all to the bleeding king-god of ancient British grail lore, another rebirth figure. Being a green water god also links him back to the tradition of the holy grail, or a story related somehow to it. In Egyptian lore, Khnum is known to be a green water god, but he is also a red god of the evening sun. (This unfortunately will have to be a teaser for another book, but basically, a remarkable fresco at Ravenna shows Jesus being baptised with a dish, in the river by the Baptist but also a green water god standing near, It makes Khnum similar to this European green water god.) They did not really have rain in Egypt so instead of having a rain god for fertility they had a river god instead.

What or who is Khnum? Khnum, as Khufu's god may be the god of Khufu's pyramid. That the pyramid is a 'horizon' means it is, perhaps a sacred meeting place between Earth and sky. (Hawass alternately says horizon means the place where Sun rises and sets, i.e. Khufu as Sun god, 1990) With his goat's horns and crocodile (serpent?) aspects, Khnum seems to have a great deal of overlap with Loki, possibly god of the 'pyramid' at Navan fort! Khnum seems to be part green man, part Loki (he makes children on a potters wheel, out of clay and implants them into mothers' wombs.) He is a genius, friend and benefactor of humanity. (Old Testament Yahweh also forms man from soil. Silbury hill is filled with all sorts of junk, but its structure is mainly clay and packed chalk. As well as structural value, this is perhaps also the clay the god works with, to create life.)

The Giza Great Pyramid may well be partly dedicated to the god who forms man from soil. Khnum is a kind of 'serpent' in a way, being a crocodile, a bit of a devil. This relates a little to the serpent which fell from heaven. A fascinating feature of Loki (Lucifer) in legend, is that when he was trapped underground, he was tied to three stones. If the Giza hill is symbolic of the burial of Loki, the three pyramids may be the stones, sufficiently large for the purpose, which hold him in place, guaranteeing fertility in the region. In addition, two of the pyramids have three subsidiary pyramids. 'Three' is enshrined at Giza, though the details are complex for us to resolve.

Since Khnum is a green water god, or crocodile, and since water seems to be always associated with pyramids, this links the pyramid religion with the grail tradition, dealing with baptism. I wish to try and show in another book that they could have a common origin, after which ideas assisted in a bit of a divergence. To summarise, all this could point to a much older *common* tradition between the various cultures, but it is hard to say. All this merely proves is that everything is so confused that it is hard to get anywhere and we can but try.

Regarding the water idea, water is common to the pyramid tradition. A journey through the water towards the afterlife is part of Germanic and Indo-European traditions. Next to Khufu's pyramid we have five ancient boat pits. Presumably all once contained boats. This was perhaps his entourage for a journey to the afterlife. Herodotus told us that Khufu was actually buried underground, in the middle of a lake. Around Silbury hill we have a 'moat'. Around Stonehenge we have a 'moat' which is the henge or ditch itself. The tor at Glastonbury used to perhaps be an 'island' amidst marshes, traditionally identified with the Isle of Avalon. These mystical places are surrounded by water. Perhaps the pyramid gives birth to the new waters of life, the green man, the water goddess, the earth mother, all conspiring to renew the land.

Why are there sarcophagi for humans in pyramids if they are intended for gods? The answer could be a complicated rather than simple one. Perhaps the pyramid was intended as a place for burial in *spirit* as well as in *fact*, (at least occasionally), and subsequently plundered. All this, in addition to being a huge tomb for a nature deity. Perhaps these pyramids, as harvest hills, were transformed into tombs, by individual kings, according to a later tradition, yet the people never forgot the symbolic value, and continued to worship at the pyramids, due to the presence of a later Temple of Isis.

Looking at the great Giza constructions, they also strike one as something one would build, only if the site had already been sacred for many thousands of years. Was the Menkaure pyramid built off centre? Either the site was better, as has been suggested, or there may have been, as I would suggest, a pre-existing sacred shrine on that spot.

Nancy Jenkins writes in *The Boat Beneath the Pyramid*, that there were two possible ideas behind the pyramid itself. In the archaic period, boats were buried at the north of the mastaba, reflecting a possible archaic 'stellar cult.' That is the phrase Egyptologists seem to use in referring to the very primitive Axis Mundi religion, prevalent before the rise of the cult of Re-Atum, later transformed into that of Amon-Ra. This was a competing or complementary cult to that of Osiris. According to this stellar cult idea, the boat faces the north star. The buried king takes the boat to join the imperishable stars which rotate about the north pole. In later times this idea may have been transformed into a solar idea. The discoverer of the boat pits, next to the Khufu pyramid, Kamal el-Mallakh, continually referred to the boat as a 'solar barque.' Jenkins points out that the Sun, however, already had a boat, in Egyptian mythology. The fact that 4th dynasty boat burials are not planned around the north of the pyramid, suggests for Jenkins, an *independent* boat burial tradition in this era. In other words, boat burial may have been around in Egypt since the earliest times, but the one prevalent in the 4th dynasty at Giza, may have had a different origin.

The pyramid or mound is for communication, also, with the solar deity. One goes up there, to be closer to the Sun. It may also be a marriage between Earth mother and Sun, but if shining white, it surely represents a kind of Sun, like the golden man Sil trapped in Silbury Hill. It is a kind of solar deity, a genius, a mind. It was a former king so old that no-one knew who he was anymore, other than that he was some deity, to be venerated, and who was associated with the regeneration of life. From the outside at least, the pyramid is a light which is the 'spark' of inspiration, not the dark underworld within. It has an aspect of permanence and endurance about it. The outside of the pyramids were designed to be white, at Newgrange, Silbury, and Giza, all vague contemporaries, reflecting the idea of the Sun or the Moon or other astronomical objects.

The Triple Goddess lived at Giza

Now we are truly getting somewhere. Robert Temple writes in *Egyptian Dawn*, that the Giza plateau building layout, a large square, can be divided into a sort of grid with nine equal size squares, possibly representing the Egyptian sacred group of nine gods, or Ennead, over which the Sun presides. There are indeed nine major pyramids at Giza (and a few smaller satellite pyramids.) It is a little coincidental that both the Menkaure and Khufu pyramids have three little pyramids next to them, but the Khafre pyramid does not require them.

In addition to ideas regarding Khnum, it would seem that other mythologies interplay in the 'pyramid' complexes we have seen in this book. The Avebury complex is simply remarkable. It seems to show a proto-Germanic World Serpent, which would be known in Egypt as Apep, which may have been guarding the tree, perhaps once on top of Silbury Hill.

I have seen the triple mound several times in various mound complexes, but not always. There could be a pattern. The building time of the Egyptian pyramids is rather unclear. They may have been rebuilt over a period of some centuries, or even longer, as Stonehenge or Silbury Hill or other mounds and pyramids were. It may not have been built all in one go. I would suggest, as others have, that Giza was built to one design. In fact Arab legends tend to point to this, even if Herodotus wrote that each of the three was built by a separate king. For instance, Muhammad al-Maqrizi (1364-1442), wrote a work, *Hitat*, containing various different traditions. He says the Copts (Egyptians) called *Saurid* the builder of the Great Pyramid. This accords roughly with what Egyptian historian Manetho (*c.* 3rd century BC) wrote, saying that *Suphis* built the pyramid. Manetho quotes Herodotus' ascribing of the pyramid to Cheops, implying that he disagrees. He writes that Khufu had nightmares about stars falling from heaven and an impending deluge, and decided to built the three pyramids to protect his knowledge and treasures.

Then we have Diodorus Siculus, who wrote a very grand and much neglected work, *Bibliotheca historica*, in about the time of Julius Caesar. I believe that many elements of the lost historical books of the Library of Alexandria have found their way, to a large extent, into his voluminous historical writings. He actually thought that the pyramids were built only half a millennium before himself, by the Saite kings who were obsessed with the site. In this respect, he wrote that the Khafre and Menkaure pyramids were built respectively by Amasis II (570-526 BC) and Inaros I (*c.* 665 BC). However, he thought that the Khufu pyramid was quite different in being built for Harmais, (Hermes, presumably, the Roman Mercury, Norse Odin and English Woden), who would seem to be a god or very early Egyptian king. In other words, the tradition is that it is built for a god. He suggests another name for Khufu as 'Chemis.' That would possibly be 'the black (man?)' It also sounds like Khnum, Khufu's god. He also wrote that the Khufu pyramid was a beautiful white, but missing its top.

So much for the historians. Perhaps surprisingly, we might apply the lessons learned to the Giza complex in Egypt. I would suggest that the three pyramids of Giza, as many pyramids elsewhere, seem to be in part based upon an Earthly reproduction of the triple goddess, even if they are also tombs to the kings of Egypt. The triple goddess was found throughout Eurasia, including in the Middle East, and was perhaps an integrated sacred aspect of mounds almost everywhere.

The triple goddess at Giza may be guarded by Anubis, protector dog of the underworld, or the original '*Hel* hound'. In *The Sphinx Mystery*, Robert Temple makes a reasonably convincing case that the Sphinx was originally something like Anubis, more dog than lion; its head having been re-carved into that of a person, in the Middle Kingdom. (It must be pointed out that other gods are drawn in the likeness of the Sphinx. In particular, there is an Egyptian image of the Sphinx with Seth's head, so we may never really know for sure. Seth, like Anubis however is something of an afterlife god. He guides the boat of Ra and spears a cosmic serpent, Apep, getting in the way. We are likely, however to be dealing with a god of the underworld, since this is a necropolis, so it might be a choice of Seth or Anubis.

New Kingdom Egyptians, it must be pointed out, may have thought the Sphinx was once a lion. There was a small open-air chapel in front of the Sphinx with the Dream Stela at the back. Around there were found some lion statues. Greek inscriptions found on the paws of the Sphinx say it was the 'guardian of the tomb of Osiris.' These would have been inscribed around two millennia after the building of the Sphinx, or its re-carving, in the Old Kingdom.

In the earlier tradition, Osiris' dead body gets tangled up with some tree, a reflection of the Odin myth. There is no carving up of the body.

In later myth, from the New Kingdom, it is stated that after Seth carved up the body, bits of Osiris were hidden all over Egypt. Robert Schoch astutely suggests (in *Voyages of the Pyramid Builders*) that this mirrors the Buddhist idea of Buddha's relics being placed in various places all over the countryside, inside stupas. That is, there were relics of Osiris placed around Egypt, perhaps in earlier times, and this was reflected in New Kingdom mythology, about earlier times!

In fact, there were possibly Osiris tombs all over Egypt. I do wonder if the mounds or pyramids were not seen as Osiris or pre-Osiris tombs, by the New Kingdom, as well as tombs for kings. There is an Osiris tomb shaft at Giza, and even one inside Tut's famous tomb, as already mentioned. Osiris and the king may have been buried close together in certain instances, for means of assisting in resurrection.

The Sphinx, as it currently is, is especially strange considering that usually Egyptian god statues have an animal head and human body, instead of the other way around. It is a radical conclusion, and seems also to be based upon ideas from mythology.

In Germanic mythology we have a gigantic blood-stained wolf called *Fenrir*, son of Loki, who ultimately swallows Odin. (This may be a relic from a much older common mythology.) This makes Fenrir more powerful than Odin! Africa did not have a wolf, so with a similar story, Caucasians entering Egypt perhaps chose a jackal and called him *INPW*, or Anubis in Greek. In Greek mythology we have the guardian of the underworld in Cerberus, a triple-headed dog. A similar god to Fenrir is *Gamr*, Hel's personal hound, pretty much the same god. Fenrir lies in the underworld bound to a rock. Fenrir and Hel go together. Greek Hecate is similar to Hel. She is a triple goddess accompanied by a hound. At Giza, we see that the Sphinx is centred relative to the three pyramids, being in front of Khafra's, the middle one. The Sphinx is therefore perhaps associated with all three of them.

In Germanic, the word Hel means 'bright'. Thanksgiving, one of the most primordial of ideas, celebrates the autumnal harvest. In the north, in Europe, the snowfall starts. It gets dark in the Arctic circle and the northern lights appear. It is a bright time, so it is Hel's time. We also have Halloween, a time in which the barrier between the worlds is lessened, perhaps to celebrate the thanksgiving. 'Witches' and 'ghouls' appear, to demand food from people's houses.

In analysing what the triple goddess represents, we have a comparison of many different mythologies. Firstly, there is a relation between Hermes Trismegistus, a wise Egyptian mystagogue, seemingly once a human, and the Sphinx. A name quite close to Hermes Trismegistus seems to have been written nearby the Sphinx on the Dream Stela, a much later monument lauding the statue. This inscription is of supreme importance in analysing the gods of Giza, because it is written in 1401 BC, 'only' perhaps 1200 years after the building of the Great Pyramid.

What happens is that one day, the king Thutmose of the 18th dynasty sleeps under the Sphinx and has a dream in which it talks to him. He thinks the Sphinx was built by Khafra. Here is a translation of part of the text:

> Look at me and observe me, oh my son Thutmose. I am your father Horemakhet-Khepri-Ra-Atum. shall give to you the kingship... all... The desert sand, upon which I used to reside, [now] is against me; and it is to cause you to do what is in my heart, that I have waited.

Horemakhet-Khepri-Ra-Atum is a rather interesting collection of God names, glued together as if it were the one god, and certainly reflecting worship at Giza in the second and perhaps first millennia BC, perhaps two thousand years after the building of the Giza pyramid. Atum is a creator god of Heliopolis who created himself out of the primal mound. In this case the mound would refer, little doubt, to the pyramids. Ra is the Sun god. Khepri is interesting. He gives us a clue to what the Khafre pyramid is all about, as Herodotus tells us that the Khafre pyramid was for a king called *Chefren*. Khepri, like other Egyptian gods, is a human in terms of body, but with a beetle for a head. The dung beetle was called Cheperi. Actually it is known that all three are aspects of the Sun at different times of day. Khepri-Ra-Atum translates as: 'Morning Sun, Midday Sun, Evening Sun.'

In other words, past, present, future, youth, middle age, old age. The triple deity, and the question behind the the Riddle of the Sphinx, written down right under the Sphinx's nose! This here is the 'proof positive' that the triple deity, a god or goddess shared by the Old Europeans, seems to have been worshipped at Egypt, at Giza, in the *second millennium BC*, even if she is a goddess of far earlier times, and was on the way out by this time.

'Horem' is a mystery, but seems to be the name of the Sphinx, and this later became known as 'Hermes', to the Arabs, builder of the Khufu pyramid. We have already seen the 'riddle' attached to the name. The riddle, an old Greek myth, may well have been the question faced by those Greek travellers who went to Egypt and attended the Isis shrine.

According to the inscription, Thutmose would have cleaned up the Sphinx and erected the stela in honour of the event, in 1401 BC. Horemakhet is essentially, but not quite, 'Horus' Horizon' (Tyldesley writes this is 'Horus in the Horizon'.) The Egyptians, writes Tyldesley, had no trouble with seemingly combining Horus with various ideas, in different words. Ra-Horakhty for instance, is a powerful Sun god.

In Egyptian parlance, horizon is perhaps associated with a concept like 'rebirth' or fertility, or perhaps even creation. Firstly Horus is the god of the sky and the Sun, and war. In this respect he is almost an Egyptian Odin. (except for the bit about being a Sun god) But *Akhet* is also the name of the inundation season. Khufu's pyramid is Horizon of Khufu, 'Akhet Khufu.' The hieroglyph is written in the form of the horizon, a Sun between hills, rather than the form of the inundation season. Then again, we know that in Europe and elsewhere, huge mounds seem to have been erected for fertility and good luck. It could even be a case of both possibilities rather than one or the other. There were three Egyptian seasons of four months each, but as months were not used in the Old Kingdom, there is confusion about when they began and ended. The *Akhet* season went from about September to December. It was merely inundation. The next season was *Peret*, 'season of the emergence' which was January to early May. The next season was *Shemu*, or 'low water' (summer). This was harvest time. Harvest in Egypt was May to August. Winter in other words. *Akhet* is therefore the fertilizing with the river during inundation.

Another meaning of *akhet* is 'Bright mountain'. The pyramids literally were *bright* mountains! I would suggest that the Khufu pyramid, on the edge of the 100 metre plateau may have been intended to have been reflected in the waters of the Nile from a significant point on the opposite bank. The Red Pyramid of Dashur still retains most of its formerly-shiny limestone casing. Silbury hill and Newgrange were also bright with shining white chalk. We do not really know which meaning to ascribe to Akhet. It remains a mystery, but all three sound quite reasonable.

There is a triple god in the Sphinx, of New Kingdom date. *Horemakhet* is also written in Greek as 'Harmachis'. Egyptologist Herbert Ricke calls the associated temple the 'Harmachis Temple' in his book on the excavation of the Sphinx. In *The Sphinx Mystery* Robert Temple says it is an unfortunate name as this Greek-named deity was not around in Egypt in the 2000s BC. Be that as it may, there is a link to 'Hermes'. Ancient Greeks or Egyptians reading the dream Stela would have possibly thought that the Sphinx, reading 'Horemakhet-Khepri-Ra-Atum' was a quadruple god. Possibly he was like Brahma, or Svetovid, with four faces. One might suppose that this can also be read as 'Hermes (Khepri-Ra-Atum)', which can be reduced to possibly 'Horemakhet triple god', or even more speculatively to 'Hermes Trismegistus'. (See fig. 6.15.) We also have the case of the existence of statues to a strange Romano-Egyptian god called *Hermanubis*. This combines the messenger god Hermes, or Mercury, with the dog god. It is represented by Anubis' head on a man. This could be either based on earlier memories, or invented by the Romans. It does seem, however, that the Sphinx is associated with or is, one of these multiple-head gods.

Let us now go deeper into the name *Horem*. It actually does not seem to be the same god as 'Horus,' though some claim it is, as in *Hor-em*. I do not want to say whether it is or it is not, but it is possibly related or derived from Horus. However, the strange name would suggest that this is *not strictly originally an Egyptian god* and may not have been venerated anywhere else in Egypt! King Tut, seems, in 1400 BC, to be calling the Sphinx something like 'Hermes' even if this is an Indo-European god, and the Greeks would not conquer Egypt for another thousand years. To the Greeks, the Sphinx was *Harmachis*. To old Wallis Budge, it was *Heru Khuti* (Horus of the two horizons). He chooses to write it without the 'm'.

In Norse mythology, we have a messenger god similar to 'Hermes' who is called *Hermodr*. (Hermod in English) He is a messenger god. He is also a 'hero', because he rides down to hell on an eight-legged steed and begs Hel to release Baldr so that fertility can begin again. (Obviously the 'Sphinx' is a little different but a dog is also a messenger of sorts.)

As Robert Temple points out in *Egyptian Dawn*, the Old Kingdom Egyptian designers of the Giza area were obsessive compulsives. They just went on and on with their geometrical intricacies and representations. The more one looks, the more one finds. One of the little-discussed features of the Giza plateau until recent times is the 'Tomb of Osiris'. This is a essentially a very deep shaft, eighty three feet below ground level. At the base is a sarcophagus on an island surrounded by water. According to the former chief of antiquities, Zahi Hawass, this is an 'Osiris Island.' (It is striking that an Osiris island is similar in conception to Silbury Hill, a place of the afterlife surrounded by a moat).

According to Robert Temple, the deepest part of the shaft is Middle Kingdom, so let us discount that island idea for now. Nonetheless, the shaft is a sort of 'underworld'. Let us say it is a symbolic place for Osiris. Osiris is the Egyptian Green Man, or bleeding god, sometimes he is painted green or blue. That idea works better in the north than it does in Egypt, which is at an evergreen latitude. Every year he naturally must die when winter takes over, but he is resurrected again the following year. This is a fundamental proto-Indo-Germanic motif. He must presumably be resurrected, and resurrected well or there will be a bad harvest. (The idea of Osiris being chopped up and the pieces joined back together is a later New Kingdom idea. This perhaps relates to the idea that bits of Osiris were buried in 'Osiris tombs' such as in Tutankhamun's tomb, as well as possibly in pyramids, whose empty tombs may actually have been dedicated to either proto-Osiris, a form of Baldr or shining Sun god, or Egyptian kings.) He is a fertility deity. 'Osiris' himself is unheard of in Egypt before the fifth dynasty, yet he is the equivalent of the Indo-European bleeding god.

The bleeding god is essentially a sacrificial victim killed to appease the gods and create a good harvest. The story is similar to that of Norse Baldr. By placing 'Osiris' so far in the ground, the Egyptians literally place him in their version of 'Hel'. I was interested in the location of the 'tomb of Osiris', known to be at Giza. If it was located close enough, this would possibly imply that it is part of the same mythological idea as the Sphinx-dog. To my satisfaction, it turned out to be located behind the Sphinx, to one side, approximately half-way between it and Khafra's pyramid. This Osiris location is essentially part of the Sphinx complex! It is as if the Sphinx has popped out and left it behind in its wake, though that is an 'artistic' statement! It must be pointed out that a new dating technique possibly shows that the lower Osiris tomb may be Middle Kingdom, or post 2000 BC in terms of date. (Temple's *Egyptian Dawn.*)

Naturally, one cannot claim to have all the answers. This is all speculation and merely one possibility. Since, however the Giza site seems to be a fertility complex, we can look for the dog in mythology in this regard. Tocharians were an old partly red-headed tribe once living in China, but originating somewhere towards the west. They were part of the milieu which may have helped to found early aspects of Chinese civilisation.

Today, the dog features in Chinese mythology as a fertility deity, but also to protect the dead. According to legend, the dog brought the first grain from heaven, possibly by communion with deities of the underworld or sky. In this regard it is a kind a agricultural messenger, or dare we say 'Hermes' or 'Mercury' between that place, and here, for these gods are messengers. The Chinese also make 'foo dogs' which are a dog with an ugly face, resting, but also poised and ready to protect the dead. They also make paper dogs which are to float on the water, also to protect the dead or drive away evil spirits. Two competing theories for the Sphinx erosion are the ancient rains, (See Robert Schoch's work for an accessible explanation), or Robert Temple's, *The Sphinx Mystery*, for information on the idea that the erosion may have been caused by the Sphinx sitting in its own artificial pond.

We now come to the pyramids themselves. As mentioned, we have the famous 'riddle of the sphinx'. It is an old Greek story. In the riddle, the Sphinx (which may not be the same as the Egyptian one) asks what walks on four legs in the morning, two legs in the afternoon and three legs in the evening. The answer is a child on all fours in the morning, a man at midday, and an old man with a stick in the evening of his existence. In this respect the idea was brought to ancient Greece that the Sphinx 'guards' this riddle and its sacred meaning.

On the Giza plateau, the Sphinx guards none other than three pyramids. These are perhaps past, present, and future. Why? Firstly, the pyramids were once white, like Newgrange, capped in white limestone, representing femininity, or the White Goddess. Secondly, if we analyse the triple goddess in various mythologies, wherever they may occur, we find that she represents, in general, the unquenchable and unstoppable forces of time. That is, birth, life and fate, wisdom and decay.

Let us go through some of these. In Norse mythology we have the three Norns. These three women represent Urth (past), Verdandi (present) and Skuld (future). The Norns rule the destinies of gods and men and live under the world oak, Yggdrasil, presumably within the mound or mountain it is sometimes situated upon.

In Greek mythology we have a whole host of different triple goddesses, all deriving from similar ideas, but under different names in different places. For instance there is Selene (the Moon in heaven), Artemis (the Huntress on Earth), Persephone (the destroyer in the underworld). We have the *Moirai* sisters, who spin man's fate. These are Clotho (the spinner), Lachesis (the allotter), Atropos (the unturnable). We have the *Hesperides*, representing the past, present and future. These are Aegle (the dazzling-light), Erytheia (red), Hesperethusa (the red sunset glow). We have the Muse, Aoidē (song) Meletē (practice)

Figure 6.13: The triple deity need not be exclusively female. In the case of Giza, and if they do represent the triple deity, the three pyramids may not be all 'female' representations, though it would be hard to tell. We just do not know. Here we have a triple deity with possible Odin with one eye. He is the god of creation, war and wisdom. Thor is possibly in the middle, god of thunder and weather. Finally there is Freya, holding onto an ear of corn. They combine their creative skills to make a harvest for mankind.

Mnēmē (memory). We even have the *Graeae*. These consist of Deino (dread), Enyo (horror) and Pemphredo (alarm). It just goes on and on.

In Roman mythology we have the Moon goddess, represented in triplicate by: Luna (heaven), Diana (Earth), and Proserpina (the underworld). Uni, the Etruscan supreme goddess is represented by Luna (heaven), Diana (Earth), Proserpina (the underworld).

In *The Lost Gods of England*, Branston points out that even Shakespeare uses whatever he knew about the triple goddess at the start of *Macbeth*. These are the three witches on the heath. They bubble bubble their toil and trouble, causing confusion on heaven and Earth. As they have created, so they bond the fates of man to their destruction.

But surely these are all European mythologies, unlinked to Egypt. On the contrary! Egyptians and Arabs are ultimately, Caucasians, mixed with darker people from the south, and so their mythology must in part originate in some lost point in Caucasian Eurasia. Examining Arabic mythology we have *al-Lat, al-Uzza, Manat*. These are supposedly three daughters of God once worshipped in pre-Islamic Arabia. Respectively they are the mother goddess, the mighty one (the youngest) and fate.

We finally come to Egyptian mythology! Here we have the trio of Hathor (Birth), Nephthys (Death) and Isis (Rebirth).

Whenever we have the trio of what I call pyramids in Europe, they are never the same size. One is always bigger than the other two. One is often small. In the Giza complex, I would hazard the speculation that the pyramids of Khufu and Khafra represent past and present, adulthood and old age, in uncertain order, since those pyramids are mature and large. The Menkaure pyramid is just a baby, perhaps representing the future. That is a stretch, but I feel it at least reflects mythological ideas possibly present in Egypt at the time. The kings would have built them, perhaps intending them or an area next to them, as tombs, or as symbolic tombs, as well as a representation of mythology. The pyramids may have also been thought to bring them good luck, which is a major reason for building a stupa in Asia, to this day.

This idea ties into existing ideas regarding Egypt, making it all less of a stretch than it seems. It is presumed widely that the pyramids were built so that the king would watch over Egypt forever, protecting it, and ensuring rebirth every year. By building an epic representation of the triple goddess, the cycle of birth and death would go on forever

Figure 6.14: Hecate (or Artemis) with her faithful hound, from an Ancient Greek dish. In this way, Hecate, is a Greek version of Germanic Hel, with some differences. It has been suggested that the Giza Sphinx has a dog's body, even if it has a man's (or woman's) head. From a cursory investigation of that structure, it is apparent that the carving of the Sphinx's face lacks the erosion found on its body and may therefore be younger.

and Egypt would always have food. We need to be careful however. We do not know it is a triple goddess at all, which was being venerated. Perhaps it was even a triple deity which incorporated both males and females, as in fig. 6.13.

In addition the pyramid is like Germanic Hel itself, as a place. Goddess Hel herself lived under the roots of Yggdrasil. Since she is a little demonic, as are the three goddesses, they may be somehow related.

All three of Loki's children seem to reside in the underworld. These are the serpent, the wolf, and the lady Hel. The pyramid or mound is a huge underworld, built above the surface, built perhaps in order to have the underworld gods in one place, to venerate them. These were Merlin and Nimue, Loki and his wife, Hel, the three sisters or triple goddess. Whatever names they went by in various nations, the ideas seem to have been related.

The Sphinx seems to be originally based on the wolf, later perhaps related to 'Hermes Trismegistus', during the New Kingdom period, due to some memory of a triple god residing in the area. This is Hel's brother, Fenrir. Now, what about Hel's other brother, the serpent Jörmungandr? These are the three children of Loki. At Silbury Hill we have once had some serpent made of standing stones, which seems to have vaguely coiled around the hill, protecting it. At Giza, as at other places where harvest mounds are found, we have the river to perhaps represent this creature. We have none other than the serpent of the Nile itself.

We therefore have the serpent, the dog, the triple goddess. We are missing a tree, which we are about to get to! The Egyptians could hardly make a huge Irminsul, or totem pole from a tree they did not have. There are differences as well as similarities. It does not have to be all the same, and it is not. Then again since the pyramids were packed with organic matter, maybe *they* were the old ritual objects, especially considering they carbon-date to centuries before the time of Khufu!

Just as the temple in front of the Sphinx had the Dream Stela, there is also an Isis Temple at Giza, which housed the 'Inventory Stela'. This was built by the 26th or last native dynasty, or the 21st Dynasty, according to an older school of thought. They were the ones who came up with the fable of Atlantis for Solon, passed to Plato, and they were fascinated by Giza, digging various shafts there.

It is very interesting that the Isis Temple is built alongside one of the three 'Queen's' pyramids, to worship a goddess, Isis, which the In-

Figure 6.15: The Sphinx of Giza faces the rising sun. If it is a dog, this is clearly his object of interest. Meanwhile Fenrir, son of Loki, the huge fearsome wolf, who will one day kill Odin, chases the Sun, Sol, and her daughter (Venus?). This is what drives them along, powering the fertility cycle. This could link the dog with Mercury, closest planet to the Sun, and the Roman 'Hermes', or messenger. Mercury is the wolf chasing Sol and Venus across the sky. As the author points out, the Sphinx has a name which the Greeks may have translated as 'Hermes.' By Karl Gjellerup, 1895.

Figure 6.16: This is one triple deity in India. There are so many triple deities, together with their consorts. Here we have four-headed Brahma on the left with his consort Saraswati. In the middle is Vishnu with his consort Lakshmi. On the right is Shiva with Paravati. They are seated on lotuses. *c.* 1770.

ventory Stela refers to as 'Mistress of the Pyramid.' (Though the same inscription also says the pyramid beside the temple is built for Henutsen, the king's daughter) This may be a piece of evidence indicating that the Queen's pyramids are in fact for female goddesses, the triple goddess perhaps, or that the Great Pyramid itself represents Isis. If we look into Isis, she is a kind of Earth Mother, but a name given in later times. The Egyptian form was *Aset*. She nurses a baby Horus, a sky god. The stela also claims that Khufu renovated the Sphinx. While this suggestion is not impossible, it is not kindly looked upon these days.

There are other bizarre things at Giza that we see elsewhere. There are boats accompanying the structure. This is a burial-like aspect which typically belongs to a seafaring people, who spent their life on the waves. It is perhaps based upon a memory of a heroic pirate ancestry.

Vikings 'buried' themselves on boats because they spent their lives on one. Superficially at least, this would imply that one origin of the Egyptian Kings would be from across the Mediterranean, a sea voyage being necessary to establish such a burial tradition. Reality is more

Figure 6.17: The 'Mistress of the Pyramid.' Here Isis nurses Horus, the sky god. Osiris, Isis, Set and Nephthys are children of an earlier union of Earth Mother Nut and Sky Father Geb. Since the Isis cult was not really firmly established in the time of the Great Pyramid, if there is a link, it is through Isis as representative of the Earth Mother. From *The Gods of the Egyptians*, by Wallis Budge, 1904.

complex. For all of the history that we know about however, except for the later abortive Sea Peoples' invasion, Egypt was ruled by landlubbers. An alternate view is that the funerary boat, which is not fit for sea voyages, is essentially a means of river transport. The presence of boats which accompany Egyptian burials for the first several dynasties, imply that even if the king was not buried inside the Great Pyramid, at least he was placed nearby, perhaps near one of the river boats.

Egyptian World Tree

Something I noticed which related Giza to Europe also, was the enigmatic place, 'Giza Plateau.' This is essentially a large hill overlooking what is now Cairo, the capital of Egypt. Like in Ireland and elsewhere, people were supposed to look upwards and see these huge things on the horizon, and recall the power of the ancestors. The Khufu and Khafra pyramids are built on their own outcrops of rock. In other words they incorporate possible earlier structures built on the very highest parts of the Giza hill. This was part of a religion which needed to be close to heaven.

In this work I emphasise an understanding of the neolithic to understand Giza. Andrew Collins takes a similar line in *The Cygnus Mystery*, 1999. He noticed that ancient sites around the world seem to be based upon a religion which is determined to point religious structures to the north (possibly in relation to the *Axis Mundi*). He dates this religion to about 15,000 BC, based upon the alignment of a constellation and other ideas. I would favour a more recent set of ideas, but there is perhaps something in what he says.

One thing I have not really mentioned is that in some cases Yggdrasil is supposed to reach up to the north star, in a true axis of the universe. Around this all of creation spins. If the Giza complex reflects the Yggdrasil religion, it too would be a kind of world centre. The other, more conventional explanation for the pyramid entrance pointing towards the north star, is that the king's soul could reach the circumpolar 'never dying' stars, of the north, and join them. The Giza complex is located in the centre of the Delta axis. Furthermore, the Great pyramid has its entrance shaft aligned to the meridian. This is a north-south axis. We are only just scratching the surface.

Herodotus mentioned that Khufu was cruel for closing down the temples and making everyone slave away. This suggests that like Akhenaten, he was interested in his own religion, rather than the existing one. I wish to show that Giza reflects aspects of the mound-builder religion, as seen elsewhere, just as it reflects aspects of the Egyptian religion. The aspects seen are obviously not identical, but they are similar. Giza appears to represent a cool fusion of Indo-Germanic mythology with the then-native Egyptian/Berber religions. This helped shape a new Egyptian religion, forming the basis for a glorious future.

The sacred place at Hohensyburg in Germany, next to the 'mountain of the gods' would seem to have been chosen because of a natural hill which looked like a huge artificially-made underworld home of the gods. Furthermore it was located at the intersection of two rivers. Here, fig. 6.18, we see that the pyramids at Giza have been placed at the intersection of the the greater Nile with the Delta. (Nearby Saqqara could also match this in terms of location significance.) In other words it centres the pyramids in Egypt.

This was done for political, aesthetic, or religious reasons. The

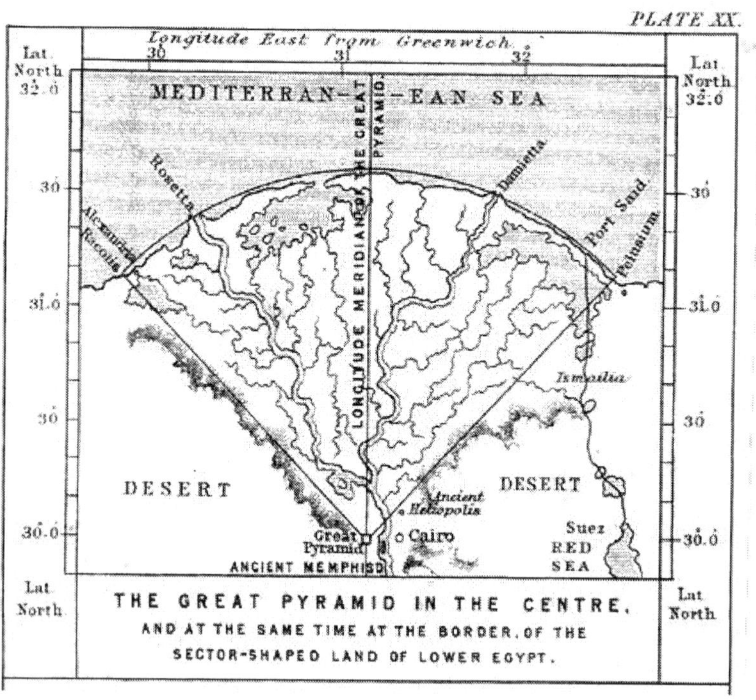

Figure 6.18: Pyramidologists in the 19th century (and today) are known for their remarkable and ridiculous over-exertions. Some geographical ideas however, are fascinating. Picture by Charles Piazzi Smyth.

religious rationale would be they are following old ideas of creating a world mountain at the centre of the world. They perhaps were not trying to divide up the world, having first surveyed the world, as the Pyramidologists ambitiously claimed. The answer to the centrality of Giza is simpler, but it perhaps requires some mythological as well as mathematical perspective.

It should be pointed out that that Giza even seems to have had its own Yggdrasil at one time. This was a huge Sycamore tree which was apparently located in front of the Sphinx temple and destroyed by lightning. (I have seen 19th-C photos which show a huge tree near the Sphinx.) The source for this revelation is on what goes by the popular name of the 'Inventory Stela.' This document dates from the Saite 26th dynasty, whose folk built an additional chapel at Giza, the tiny 'Isis Temple', built against the south face of one of Khufu's Queens' pyramids. They were so enthusiastic for the Old Kingdom that they even broke into Menkaure's pyramid and placed their own wooden sarcophagus or coffin in the burial chamber, now missing). Tree worship at a central location is quite similar to Yggdrasil worship. It seems related to the old Indo-European or worldwide mythology, but inside Egypt. The reason for the Earth ratios inherent in the Giza pyramid may be that it is an *Axis Mundi*, or representation of the World Mound itself, from whence creation ensues.

Figures 6.19, and 6.20, are fascinating. Egypt does not really have many trees, (it had far more in the Old Kingdom) yet it preserved a tree religion. Here, in a odd twist, a cat god with rabbit ears slays the snake, which is guarding the tree. It seems in Egypt we have all the elements necessary to suggest that ideas shared with the proto-Indo-European mythology once held sway in Egypt. We have the woman with fountain and tree. We have the snake around the tree. By legend the sacred tree was on the world mountain, perhaps represented in Egypt by the hills of Saqqara or Giza, or mythical primordial mounds found elsewhere. We even have the world mountain which would be the Giza pyramid, or any pyramid really. Then again the pyramids could also be representations of the world tree mixed with world mountain. They almost all align north. The entrance shafts point to the north, almost towards the pole star. For astronomical use, I think it would have been more useful if they pointed south. This would indicate more of an interest in astronomy, in general, rather than specifics, as it would relate to a great many more stars including southern stars, due to the greater sky rotation and hence variety away from the pole. The entrance shafts are

Figure 6.19: The Egyptian goddess of the Sycamore tree. Compare to the Norns, fig. 1.20. This is fascinating because the Inventory Stela found in the Temple of Isis and dating from the 26th dynasty preserves some memory of ritual at Giza. A Sycamore tree once existed on the Giza plateau. This could be a home for the goddess. The tree itself could be seen as a world centre. Each Norn in Germanic myth has their own fountain under world mount. It is to be noted that the old Egyptian hieroglyph for 'n' is three wiggly lines. This also means 'waters.' These may in some respects have referred to the three fountains of heavenly water from the world mound. From Budge, *Gods of the Egyptians*, 1904.

Figure 6.20: We find the same old religion in Egypt as well as Eurasia, and even America: essentially where pyramids are to be found. (Thebes, tomb of Inher-kha, reign of Ramses IV, New Kingdom.)

perhaps not for astronomical practical use, but designed for symbolic meaning. Anchoring them to the pole anchors them to the centre of the world, and of creation.

Egyptian statues excavated at the Menkaure valley temple in 1908 by George Reisner, refer to Hathor as 'Mistress of the Sycamore'. (There is a name in Britain similar to Hathor. It is the girl's name Heather, given to girls in the 19th-20th century. It refers to a shrub with a white flower. It could have a common origin with Hathor as it is an ancient word based on Middle English *hather*.)

It has been mentioned in various publications that there was once a grove of sycamore trees to the south of the Sphinx. Pioneering Egyptian archaeologist Selim Hassim has also mentioned the grove of sycamores that once stood south of the Sphinx in relation to a home of Hathor. There once seems to have been an adequate possibly underground water supply at Giza, and even perhaps waters around the Sphinx, responsible for erosion around it, though Schoch disagrees. See *The Sphinx Mystery*. At Hohensyburg, as well as at Knocknarea and Belfast's Cave Hill, I have noticed that water flowing out of a mountain was an indication of a sacred site of great ancestral significance, for people as well as for their gods.

The 26th-dynasty Inventory Stela found in the Isis temple at Giza, refers to Isis herself as the 'Mistress of the pyramid'. In other words, by the seventh or sixth century BC, the worshippers at this little temple saw the pyramid as the home of a female deity. This of course does not tell us anything about what the pyramid was in the 4th dynasty, when it was built.

We do not need to get into the murky details for we can reach a general conclusion without them. This would be, in essence, that Giza, like so many mounds and mound complexes, was seen as the home of a female deity. It was an Earth-mother temple. The Giza plateau itself with its water supply may have been seen as an extension of the pregnant and fertile Earth, swelling up in its fertility, towards the sky. It was a perfect place to build a tower to heaven.

An Innocent Question

Tower to heaven? While in Ireland, I more or less convinced myself that I was dealing with something rather like the tower of Babel religion, except for some reason I was finding it in a place which was not Babylon!

I noticed that the ancient Irish had been utterly obsessed with building a large mound on the highest possible point, the summit of any small mountain. The centre was placed on the highest point. This presumably made the magic stronger. The burial complex at Knocknarea, certainly contained no Ziggurat, often portrayed as something similar to the tower of Babel.

I would suggest that the Babel story in the Bible effectively evolved as a suitable response to an innocent question. 'Why are huge burial mounds to be found all over the world, in whichever country we visit, wherever we sail? Why are there pyramids in Egypt as well as Iraq, and elsewhere?' A convenient and impressionable answer, which may even have been taught in Babylonian or Israeli or Phoenician schools in ancient times may have been: 'A great tower was first built in our country. God did not like the arrogance of it, so mixed up the languages and scattered the people, so now towers are built everywhere, even if people in each of these distant various kingdoms cannot understand the other. Of course we worship God differently now, in a more modest temple, so we do not get punished like they were, having had to migrate everywhere.'

Eventually this possible 'old wisdom' told by old men found its way into the Bible. All the world 'was once one language' but that was merely the wide spread of a Stone-Age tribe, and a Stone-Age religion. That 'one language' would only really have been an earlier form of proto-Indo-European, with their vast spread over the Berber regions as well as into Sumeria, but this is a controversial topic and various experts disagree upon it.

All the Old Kingdom work at Giza seems to be largely towards creating a representation of the afterlife. This centres the mythology of Egypt, there, at the rough centre of Egypt, near Cairo. Since it recreates mythology, the Giza plateau is in a sense equivalent to the former religious complex at Hohensyburg, possibly Tara, (with its tomb of the hostages where Loki may have been trapped), as well as the huge Avebury/Silbury complex.

Each seems to be an attempt to create a 'centre of the universe' or new home for a group of fertility gods who have helped to create mankind and ensure his survival, against the overall oppressions of the universe. Hel was an evil woman. The snake was evil. The wolf/jackal was perhaps relatively evil, aside from ideas of domestication. Yet without them, there would never have been an inundation or harvest, for the bleeding man as Osiris would never have been slain. There would be no possibility for the resurrection of him, were it not for Hel's mercy in allowing it, provided everyone should weep.

For Stone-Age people, life was rather short and the world was a harsher one than we are accustomed to in this age. It was all something they felt they needed to do. The old ones knew that the gods, indifferent or evil as they were, had set up the world 'just so', so that man could have his time on it. It wasn't about worshipping 'evil' deities. It was about being humble to reality.

There we have it. The Giza area seems to be a representation of a mythology, of a primordial Stone-Age religion. This mythology is not isolated but is analogous (with certain unique differences) to that shared by the Indo-Germanics or Kurgans or Indo-Europeans who swept across Asia in their conquests. By analysing parallel mythologies we can start to see something relating to what the Old-Kingdom Egyptians may have been inspired by.

Perhaps among the greatest pieces of evidence that the pyramid religion comes out of the mound religion, is that the Great Pyramid was built around a mound sticking up out of the plateau bedrock. Schoch notes it may have been easier for the engineer to simply level the site if he wanted to build a pyramid. Instead the builder wished to memorialise an earlier structure. I cannot make any pretence to knowing all the details, for this subject is rather complex. The Giza complex was built up over many generations and ideas simply changed, so I do not think the Egyptians themselves knew all the details either.

The Clockwork of Fertility

At Stonehenge, we have a system where the Earth mother is represented by the circle, as per the work of Terence Meaden (*The Stonehenge Solution*). We then have light coming in on the solstice which strikes the white lady in the middle, that is the white Altar stone, which once stood up there in the centre. (See fig. 4.19) The light rises above the heel stone, (the phallus) and strikes the white stone in the middle at the solstice, but so does a shadow, possibly the symbolic phallus. It is thus fertilised for another year. At Newgrange also we have an older system, like a closed version of Stonehenge. It too has the 'Sarsen circle' but its huge blocks form a circle around the base, lying on the ground rather than as lintels. Above this is a white facade which receives the light, like a crescent moon. This is symbolic of both the lunar goddess as well as Earth mother. It is really a representation of the heavens on earth for the purpose of fertility. Additionally light enters the huge chamber from a light box, reaching the middle to fertilise whatever object has been placed there.

At Giza, I would propose that we have a similar system. The pyramids were quite light in colour when their casing was freshly attached. In this they are mother deities, but also lunar deities. It would seem that the astronomical system for Giza was partly solved by Robert Temple (*The Crystal Sun*). In he 1990s, he noticed that during sunset of the winter solstice, the shadow from the Khafre pyramid fell on the south face of the Khufu pyramid. Temple points out that this makes a linear angle on the pyramid of 26 degrees which is the same as the angle of the ascending and descending shafts, and also a geometric 'golden angle.'

There is another shadow display at noon of the same day (the day of the longest noon shadow). He thought it was odd that no-one had ever noticed the effect before. Temple writes that this implies that the Khafre pyramid was deliberately positioned, to precision, and of a certain size, to allow this effect. He also writes that the effect may point out the position of the King's chamber, or even other unknown chambers or passages.

The fact the Menkaure pyramid has no part in this shadow play, as pointed out by Temple, might imply that it also was of deliberate size and shape to be excluded from the 'fertilisation'. In way of some corroboration of this, we can look at Saqqara hill, fig. 6.30. This had three main complexes, perhaps in the third dynasty, like the Giza hill. There was the main one, and two others. I am betting that this one, though I do not have the resources, or skill to test this, would have a complementary alignment rather than the same one, perhaps a sunrise, an equinox or a summer solstice? (It is to be noted that Knowth and Dowth have light-show effects at different times or times of year, than Newgrange, and they are rather close, all in the Boyne valley.)

In looking at the map, it appears that the south side of the main Djoser pyramid could be illuminated by the lesser Sekhemkhet pyramid, in the style of Giza, but I do not know this for sure. Furthermore, the third pyramid enclosure of Saqqara, (see figure) out of alignment with the other two, and further from the river, in the place of Menkaure, rather than being a little pyramid, as at Giza, simply has no pyramid! That is another possible way to make sure it does not interfere with the cosmic fertility season, which only requires a male and female! This proposed alignment however, is speculation.

Is the Great Pyramid part of Giza's refurbishment?

There is circumstantial evidence that the Great Pyramid is not the original structure at Giza. Imagine Cologne Cathedral without its litany of smaller predecessors.

If we choose to compare the information of Temple's discovered alignment with Newgrange, built several centuries before the Khufu pyramid, in which light of a certain low angle enters the mound at sunrise, we are aware that that light gradually creeps up the passage, but initially via a light box above the passage, until it lights up a bowl in the back of the chamber. With the Great pyramid, which is closed off, the only thing the light can do is create a symbolic representation of ascending up the passage.

This might imply that the predecessor in the place of the Giza pyramid, which may have been in the same position, may have employed a similar effect to that of Newgrange. Covering the pyramid over with casing stones created a newer 'modern' and futuristic structure, which perhaps retained the symbolic ritual quality of its predecessor, and a representative effect to honour it, which may therefore have had a southern entrance, in the pre-Great Pyramid era.

All Egyptian pyramids, however have a northern entrance, so the Sun is striking the 'wrong' side, performing an older ritual which does not exist anymore, in light of the newer monument, which nonetheless is aligned precisely to allow it. This previous structure may have been built around or before the time of Newgrange, in about 3200 BC, since Newgrange and Giza seem to reflect a similar ideology. Then again, the previous structure might even have been located in another land if we are dealing with Stone-Age migrants to Egypt! Both the formerly-white Khufu pyramid and the white side of Newgrange receive the winter sun on the southern face at solstice.

I do not think this is the full solution. There may have been more monuments at Giza, no longer extant. The obelisk has been associated with a solar ray, since Roman times, but it also reminds one of a maypole, or Irminsul as it was called in parts of Germany.

If there were some of these scattered around Giza, they would have been the clockwork of the mathematical sundial system. I have a problem with one white pyramid fertilising another white pyramid, yet there it is. Then again in the primordial religion of woman with child, exemplified as Mary and Jesus, Mary is fertilised by a monotheistic sky god, presumably once thought by some to be related to the Sun.

It should be pointed out that the Great pyramid, which is being fertilised by the 'shadow' has a 'womb' at its heart, like Newgrange. It has two major chambers internally as well as a crypt underneath. Those pyramid shafts may be abstracted Fallopian tubes, seed falling from the sky god in the heavens, (since they point in that direction, yet are closed off) and into the womb.

As to the chambers themselves, it seems it may have been an original intention simply to build a chamber under the pyramid. This idea was clearly abandoned, as most authors point out, as the chamber was unfinished. Another shaft rises up into the pyramid. The lower Queen's chamber was called as such, not because a queen was found there, but because there is a gable or peaked roof, associated in Arab burials with a female tomb. Meanwhile male burials have flat roofs. Furthermore the colour of the chamber is that of limestone.

We can then go back along the passage whence we came and continue upward and onward, until we reach the King's Chamber. The colour inside this chamber is red granite! I would like to suggest something here, but not knowing anything about the history of burials in this part of the world, it could well be very wrong. (The Khafra and Menkaure sarcophagi were actually black granite, perhaps symbolising the Earth God, or personal taste, if the king was indeed deposited here.)

The male element trapped in the mound, according to old tradition is the fire god, Vulcan, or Loki, or Ptah, if we are talking Egyptian, Buddha if we are in Asia. This is a fire god. This could be his chamber. The male element must always have a consort in Stone-Age traditions. The limestone chamber is white, Luna, the Earth and Moon Mother. She is below the fiery chamber because the Earth is lower than any artificial internment of 'Loki', which was the product of the sky god's rage.

On the other hand the colours could well have been down to personal preference, as they are today. It is to be noted however that Chinese tomb will have lots of red. Colour is not entirely a matter of preference, but religion. It does not matter, for the pyramid theory espoused in this book, whether a king was or was not placed in the chambers. The pyramid as world mound was for all who were buried nearby, including the king.

No human burial

An archaeologist called George Reisner (1867-1942) came across the tomb of Hetepheres, mother of Khufu, in her pyramid. Everything was present. There were canopic jars containing the lady's organs, in embalming fluid. There was a great deal of furniture. When the sealed sarcophagus was opened to the fanfare of world press, it was found to be empty, like all the others. Reisner later stated that perhaps the burial had been moved hastily from elsewhere. Now this is thought not to have been the case. This was the burial. It is a great mystery.

Dr Zahi Hawass thinks that the king himself became the resurrection god, Osiris, so the pyramid was both a tomb for god and man. I am not a great fan of this idea. The resurrection man typically is a type of green man, who also bleeds and dies every year, an idea sometimes associated with ritual sacrifice. (On a related note, Diodorus strangely tells us that Egypt in early times sacrificed 'red' people, of which there are now few (in his time) remaining. This was because of a religion to Seth, a god represented by red, who killed Osiris. These people were apparently sacrificed outside tombs to Osiris. These tombs might well have been pyramids, god-representations of fertility and creation.) For a king this might have been a way into immortality, but I see these as two different types of resurrection. Surely no-one wants to come back as Osiris, and be doomed to die every year? Naturally there was also no widespread Osiris religion in the 4th dynasty, but the equivalent may have been Khufu's god Khnum.

The Khafra pyramid has no 'womb', having no chambers except for one beneath the pyramid, so it is possibly 'male'. (The Sami and other shaman aboriginal peoples often erected two Irminsuls, one male and the other female. An alternate explanation is that the Khafra pyramid has no shafts because it and the Menkaure are also not built to the same perfection as the Khufu pyramid. Less funding was involved so the chambers were done away with as well.) A key argument against my idea that the Khafra pyramid was intended to have no womb based upon an earlier design, is that there was an intervening king in between Khafra and Khufu. This was Djedefre, who ruled about ten years. Tyldesley writes that Khafra's pyramid design with its simpler chamber models that of Djedefre's unfinished pyramid complex, which is not found at Giza, but Abu Rawash, and is the most northerly of the pyramids. Since it models the design of a pyramid built elsewhere, this would argue against Giza as a grand plan. Then again, Djedefre may have utilised earlier plans in his own pyramid.

The Menkaure pyramid, meanwhile is also 'male,' having only an underground chamber, though a tunnel does pass through part of the pyramid on the way down, with another false tunnel also penetrating the pyramid. The red stones at the base might mark it out as being 'Loki', or Ptah. Naturally this conflicts with the idea of the three pyramids as being the three women. Then again why should Giza be an *exclusivist* representation? It is known that in the Stone Age, gods and goddesses of whichever sex, generally had a consort! Even Loki, imprisoned in the mound, is held there with his wife. Merlin is held with his consort Nimue.

Fig. 6.16 shows an Indian version of the consorts *within* the triple deity. If the mound is representative of a whole underworld religion, with many gods, including possibly Egyptian versions of Hel, her brothers the snake, and possibly the wolf, not to mention a cosmic egg and the three women with fountains near the roots of Yggdrasil, then why *not* adopt a physical interpretation, in Giza's format, which is complex? What I would suggest, and the reader can take this with quite a lot of salt, is that there is some 'funny business' going on.

Ancient Greek mythology has quite a few instances of betrayals and affairs between deities. Essentially the male component of the Khafra pyramid, in winter, is fertilising the female component, the womb of the Khufu pyramid, the largest one and mother pyramid. I do not wish to speculate at this stage on which gods or goddesses these may represent. The more one might speculate away from the central theme which is presented, that the Giza pyramids represent the triple deity, the more inaccurate one is going to get. Nevertheless, the triple goddess from a relevant period, is, as mentioned earlier, Hathor (Birth), Nephthys (Death) and Isis (Rebirth). Their male consorts are Ra or Horus, Set and Osiris, respectively.

Another triple deity is Hathor or Mafdet, Bast and Sekhmet. These three females have their subsidiary male consorts as Ra or Horus, Ptah or Anubis and Osiris. If the Giza pyramids were built to a single design, it might explain why the Khufu pyramid was built first. It was the most important. It was the grandest Earth Mother, so needed to be gotten out of the way first. It was the one with the innards, the 'womb'. In fact the Khafra valley temple had two portals dedicated to the goddesses Hathor and Bastet respectively. Each portal was guarded by two colossal sphinxes each.

Geodesy

The old 'pyramidology' idea of the Great pyramid representing Earth geodesy, or measurement, is intriguing. Ideas regarding it stem from the precision of the pyramid, but also astronomical considerations. The Arabs always considered that the pyramids were built to house the mathematics of the world, and lost sciences, so it is not a new idea, but rather one of the original myths about Giza. The Arabs or Copts also said that Khufu had had some very bad dreams, interpreted by the priests as stating that a deluge or invasion would come and wipe out Egypt. The pyramid was built to prevent this. It is a similar story to the Bible story about Joseph and the granaries.

In the late 19th century the pyramidology idea was taken to unseemly and unscientific extremes with some suggesting Biblical representation and forecasts of the future based upon a Bible which had not yet been written in the time when the pyramids were built.

Robert Schoch in *Pyramid Quest*, thinks there is some merit to certain geodesy measurements, however, a view with which one must concur. Delphi in Greece, for instance, itself a kind of centre of creation and world centre, is located on the Giza longitude. It is also apparent that the Egyptians located their pyramids on what they may have thought was thirty degrees north of the equator, (it is close but not quite), and therefore one third of the way from equator to pole (ninety degrees). This was done by stellar measurement with a kind of protractor, but atmospheric refraction may have altered the measurement from exactly thirty. Then again, there may not have been a better-situated plateau to place the pyramids upon, and they may have ignored this consideration utterly since they were merely looking to place a site close to their lost capital city, which has now been taken over by Cairo. (Saqqara is close to Giza, another possible 'thirty degrees north' site.)

I do not really buy into too many of the claims, and never really intended to discuss which ratios found in the pyramid might relate to Earth measurement, but certain points are unavoidable. Many people who have a sound knowledge of astronomy and mathematics, as well as the Giza plateau, have discussed geodesy. Giza is also unavoidably an astronomical observatory of a sort. For instance, Robert Temple writes that when he brought up the fact to Egyptology supremo, Dr Zahi Hawass, former director of the Giza site, that the shadow of the Khufu pyramid falls upon Khafra on the winter solstice, Hawass was rather surprised. He was momentarily lost for words, (perhaps wondering why Egyptian history does not reconcile the link) but concurred that what Temple claimed was in fact true. Archaeologists do not know about this. It is not their fault. They are busy in other areas, or have no interest in it and are really drawn to Egypt for other reasons, such as an exploration of the art, religion, fashion, the writing system, or general culture. Instead of Giza, the now-respectable archaeoastronomers mainly gravitate towards England and Stonehenge, a place which may in fact have little more astronomy associated with it than any other mound or megalithic site they pass along the motorway in getting there. Nevertheless it has had more written about it in this respect than any other megalithic site could well hope for in the next several centuries. I wonder when an expedition will be launched to check up on the astronomy of the Stonehenge-like site of Messa, in Libya and also, if it still exists.

My point in bringing up the geodesy issue is to say that the Khufu pyramid has received too much attention relative to the Khafra and Menkaure pyramids. (They are also not as precise as the Khufu pyramid.) Temple writes that the Menkaure shadow does not reach the other pyramids on the solstice. It has no part in the shadow ritual. It is not therefore part of the sacred fertilisation which may also be shown to occur at Stonehenge and elsewhere.

I wish to bring up a simple speculation here. The Khufu pyramid has ratios which are all associated with the Earth. For some reason, early pyramid mathematicians, or pyramidologists, including Isaac Newton seemed to think the Khufu pyramid was all about the Earth and its circumference. Why? I do not know why, but I would suggest that since the pyramid does have its 'womb' or internal chambers, these need fertilisation, such as at Newgrange, another huge mound with a white facade. Thence the other pyramid, the Khafra pyramid, which casts the phallus shadow, is all about the Sun. Khufu is the de facto pyramid of the Earth and Moon. Khafra is the de facto pyramid of the Sun (though not in Egyptian mythology, merely some vague kind of equivalent). Measures and ratios regarding this would therefore relate, not to the Earth, or moon, but Sun. In fact I would suggest that some of the ratios of the Khufu pyramid which 'don't work' for Earth, might in fact work when applied to the moon. Furthermore the reason for the bend in Sneferu's white Bent Pyramid could well be an interplay between the pyramid reflecting ratios of the Earth, as well as of the moon, but I have not examined this. (The fact the Bent pyramid, thought to be an architectural mistake, is almost the same height as Sneferu's other pyramid, the Red pyramid, not an architectural mistake, implies there may be some hidden ratio common to both.)

That is a very *very* deeply radical speculation, which scholars do not make, but I do not think, based upon the astronomy, representative mythologies and overall situation, that I am out of order. What is merely lacking is knowledge of an Egyptian reference to this, unless we look closely. We do not really have references to much in the Old Kingdom at all. The Khufu cartouche graffiti found by Richard Vyse in the Great Pyramid in the early 19th century refers intriguingly to 'Khnum-Khufwy', not Khufu directly, although the associated cartouche also implies 'king'. The statement apparently means 'Khnum is my protector.'

Khnum is one of the many Egyptian equivalents of the Green Man, fertility God. He is painted in green. He is the creator deity inside the pyramid. His symbolic chamber may be the King's Chamber. The Queen's chamber may belong to his consort. He has several, for instance, Satet, a goddess similar to Artemis but of the river, was one of his later consorts. In Giza times, the best fit might well be *Heqet*. This is essentially, Greek Hecate, an equivalent. This is the Triple Goddess, the primordial Earth Mother and a very old goddess indeed. That is to say, she is the three Norns, in one. Khnum moulds people from clay, earth mixed with water, and the pyramid certainly contains a lot of datable organic material, as well as a former water supply. (According to Herodotus, the Khafre pyramid did not have a water supply. Why would it, if it possibly represents the Sun, or at least does not represent the Earth, or represents it to a lesser extent?)

The Khufu pyramid then, was to symbolically mould people, create and fertilise life throughout Egypt, hence it was placed at the 'centre' of Egypt and had such a ridiculous amount of work put into it. This was therefore a great project of the Egyptian people, to provide eternal fertility for their land. It was as big as possible so it could be as lucky as possible, impossible for the gods to ignore, and also impossible to destroy, so that Egypt, with her tombs, would endure forever, through all of the cataclysms of the future, and yet remain fertile. Archaeologists actually do say that the Pharaoh is there to protect Egypt, from the afterlife perspective, but the fact that the pyramid is so similar to fertility mounds, harvest hills of Europe, as well as pyramids where sacrifice for fertility occurred, in America, (and it seems in Ireland), is overlooked. In this book I do try to look at the overriding Stone-Age culture of the pre-third millennium BC situation, rather than events and ideas entirely specific to Egypt.

I hope that this is a better explanation than Herodotus' convoluted one, which states that Khufu was vainglorious and wanted a large tomb, but that he also despised the gods of Egypt. The research and writing can go on and on, but I would rather save more for a book specifically on the topic of Giza, (where I hope to reveal some juicy morsels about the land of origin of one component of the Giza builders, and their shaman religion, gods, and names, rather than merely their mythology, as in this work).

Below, in fig. 6.21, we have Khnum. He has aspects of the Norns, fig. 1.20, in that he is a source of the waters of creation. The Island of Elephantine in the middle of the Nile, relates to the island where the creator god, the Ring Lord was imprisoned, and also Silbury Hill with its moat. It was a centre for his worship. Khnum makes humans out of clay. He is the creator. He is the Earth father, with aspects of Dagda, or the Green man of the river, or Saint Christopher, who carries the divine child across the waters.

Herodotus stated that the Khufu pyramid had access to the Nile waters. There may or may not have been an underground supply. He also stated that the Khafra pyramid did not have water access. (It also lacks a 'womb'.) With these waters he states, Khufu was buried in a subterranean chamber surrounded by a moat, not actually in the pyramid. Thinking back to Newgrange, which is Earth Mother as well as crescent moon, as well as the composite ancestral Snow-Madonna goddess from Poland, we see that the Khufu pyramid might well be a representation of the Luna-Earth combination. The fertilising shadow which falls across it from the Khafra pyramid represents fertilisation by the solar phallus. The Khafra pyramid being dry, in the heat of the Sun, does not require Nile Waters. Nor is it a womb. The Menkaure pyramid might be associated with Ptah or some underworld fire god, even Khnum possibly. It lies further from the Nile, towards the hot desert, away from life. It is to be pointed out that the pyramids can still be 'female' because each male god had a female consort. Merlin, locked in the mound, had Nimue. Loki, imprisoned in the underworld, had his wife Sigyn to assist him.

The multiple representations raised might make it seem like I am finding non-existent snowflakes in Hades. To counter this criticism, I would suggest that I am not inventing the stories being raised. The stories are representations of earlier primordial stories associated with pyramid and mound-building.

Figure 6.21: This is Khnum, an Old Kingdom god. The Great Pyramid may be his homage, as well as that of his female consort, Heqet. Gods in those days were not singular, but had many aspects, complicating our understanding of older mythology. In this old picture, he has aspects of the bull. (Jean-François Champollion, Brooklyn Museum.)

Figure 6.22: Is this the meaning of the Great Pyramid? A house for this pair? Khnum and his consort Heqet, or 'Hecate' conspire to create man, and fertility. Heqet, the triple goddess, feeds life to Khnum's creation. The King's chamber may be for Khnum, with the Queen's chamber for Heqet. Meanwhile there is also an exterior representation. The Sky father *also* couples with Earth Mother in ancient tradition. A pillar of shadow descends upon the south face of Khufu on the winter solstice, the Egyptian season of growth.

The Giza plateau is endlessly fascinating. In the case of the pyramids here at least, in fig. 6.23, rather than the numerous mastabas of other burials, it is not simply a case of sprouting them spontaneously as they were required. Take for instance the three tombs next to the smaller Menkaure pyramid. Two were never finished. It is as if design were more important than need. Alternately somebody simply changed their mind about where their future tomb/cenotaph would be. The clustering of buildings around the Khufu pyramid on the left, indicates he was perhaps the most enthusiastic of the pyramid builders.

In fig. 6.24, we can see the structure of the Giza Plateau which rises above the Nile Valley. Fascinatingly, one can see numerous tombs clustered around the pyramid of Khufu on the left. The other two pyramids are rather neglected by comparison. Why is this? Quite

Figure 6.23: Here is a map of the Giza complex from above. North is up. It would seem that part of the geometry relates to the mythology of the beliefs of the Stone-Age builders. (A puzzle for future generations!) By Karl Richard Lepsius.

Figure 6.24: Giza, from above.

simply, the pyramid of Khufu might well represent the Earth Mother, out of the three. It is the one with the internal chambers, the 'womb' as well as being the biggest. It is the best one and therefore it is somehow better for the afterlife journey. It gets fertilised by the shadow of the Khafra pyramid.

Of course there are other reasons for the clustering. For instance, if Menkaure lost interest and re-opened the temples, there was less time for tombs to be built around the other two pyramids. One may also note its position, right against the edge of the plateau. It was the first pyramid built, and commands the choicest real estate, as it is to be seen from the Nile, now a suburb of Cairo. The Khufu pyramid is the one which therefore faces civilisation, and the one with the internal chambers. It is probably designed to awe the people living along the Nile. One may compare this arrangement to what is seen at Golub-Dobrzyń, Poland (fig. 2.13), with the castle on the Plateau, as well as at Sligo, (fig. 1.16) where the enormous Medb cairn may be seen for miles all around. Based on the similarities with what is going on, I would suggest the Great Pyramid is rebuilt from an earlier mound or other structure, representing a widespread Stone-Age religion.

Now we look at the mythic idea of why the Great Pyramid is on the 'edge'. The Great pyramid is closest to the 'edge', where desert meets the black earth. Pyramids are often on edges, boundaries, and rivers, sea and coast. This is the edge of desert and land, where substances meet. It is as if two substances flow, in different directions out of this *Axis Mundi*, or centre of creation.

I certainly cannot claim to have all the answers. Then again, neither did the ancients. It is widespread knowledge that what Egyptian priests presented to Herodotus five centuries before Christ, regarding Egyptian history, was rather scanty and not altogether true. We cannot see what went on in the heads of the old builders and dreamers, except by what they have left behind. They presumably all had their own interpretations. For although every pyramid complex, wherever it is to be found, has certain similarities, they are also all so very different! Each area and kingdom had its own variations and ideas regarding the primordial Stone-Age religion.

Above, we have Mithras. He is the shining man on the bull. On the one hand the bull, sometimes associated with god, or perhaps geological or weather forces, might kill Mithras. On the other hand, the shining man, progenitor of Christ in this Mithraic religion, popular in the Roman Empire, possibly represents the old year god and is always ready to return for another year.

A pantheon of inseparable gods may be based upon old stories based upon changing geological and weather forces, at seeming war with each other, causing cyclical changes, and given various human-like names. The supposed war between them was told to children to satisfy them about the origin and development of the world and its wonders. A lot of studies have been done regarding the Mithraic cult, but very little is known about it. In the figure of Mithras, a Roman representation, we see Mithras slaying the bull. Above him are the Sun and Moon. Below is the snake. Mithraic reliefs usually also have a dog, near the bull. There is sometimes a bird as well. It would appear that the religion is based upon some creation story containing all these elements in a syncretic unity. Since it is thought that the Mithraic religion originates in Asia Minor, a possible early home of the mound religion, in terms of Göbekli Tepe being covered up in the eight millennium BC, this may be one descendant of the early pyramid religion, with the bull as a kind of Loki and Mithras taking the role of both the bleeding man, who may become skewered, as well as Thor, who punishes the great horned god, sending him down to the snake of the underworld.

Figure 6.25: Mithras.

The Final Builder of Giza

By Menkaure's time, the religion being expressed at Giza was on the wane. Herodotus mentions that he was the final builder at Giza. He was kinder to the regular Egyptian religion than wicked Khufu and Khafra, who had despised it and shut it down, so everyone could concentrate on the pyramids. He not only built a smaller pyramid, but actually re-opened the Egyptian temples and allowed sacrifice. Furthermore the three satellite pyramids of his pyramid were left uncompleted. It is as if they were built at the same time, but not for bodies. (Then again one or more of the three Khufu satellite pyramids may have been used as burials.) The Khafra pyramid has one satellite pyramid. The Khufu and Khafra pyramids have three major satellite pyramids. Why did both of these kings have three associated people they needed to bury? These could also be representative cenotaphs of the three Norns, the three women of mythology. (Perhaps three select members of Khufu's family get to be buried with one of the Norn representatives, a chilling thought!)

Herodotus mentions that Menkaure's life was shorter than his predecessors. In his lifetime a prophesy had forecast his doom, and he wondered why the gods were punishing him for his compassion in his lesser oppressions. This could be some memory of the end of the Giza-building program and the return to the regular religion in Egypt. In some way, Herodotus' words might convey some old memory of the Giza complex as a great failure of vision. The priests who talked to Herodotus, two millennia after the building of Giza, regarded it as an extravagance, and ultimately as a kind of folly, which resulted in suffering for the people. Their words cannot be trusted, yet we do seem to have evidence of many unfinished aspects, like those satellite tombs of Menkaure's pyramid. There seems to be a memory of disaffection, that they did not quite live up to their goal. Later Egyptians, including the priests mentioned by Herodotus seem not to have known what they were for, nothing about the shadow-play, and and certainly not that similar structures had been built around the world.

Ultimately there were different committees hired to discuss the design and function of the Old Kingdomer's vision of the future of Giza. Rather than being built to an initial plan, there may have been deviations. I think it honours the triple female deity, in a fundamental way, but that may not have been the last word. Once the mathematicians and architects got stuck into it, turning it into a type of sundial, or sighting system for astronomy, it all began to get rather complex. All good things come to an end. Though it was built with great skill, it was ultimately abandoned by successors, including perhaps in spirit, by its final less enthusiastic builder, Menkaure. Redundancy had already been built into the complex, the shadow clockwork was now in place to make it 'work.'

A great many details I have provided and discussed might well be wrong. Others need ironing out, particularly in terms of relations to what we know about the Egyptian religion. As the ultimate proof that this rationalisation is not without merit, I would suggest, as in the introduction, that genetic studies discussing the widespread Indo-European peoples, the links between Sami and Berber in deeply ancient times, suggest the mythological ideas expressed here have a good foundation, as they were quite simply very widespread in the Stone Age. Given the corridor-like geographical location that Egypt has, it was certainly not immune to their invasions, which included people and ideas from various unknown places. I would like to make a much firmer case for the stance in a future book dedicated to Giza and its builders, by which time, hopefully more details will have become clearer and better understood.

So, it seems we can reconcile the pyramids of Giza, and its complex, for a major part, with Indo-Germanic/Kurgan/Indo-European mythology. This, the proto-Berbers may have passed on to the Egyptians. This is certainly quite a radical interpretation! We know that this mythology seems to be an ancestor to that represented today in most nations of the world. The old Egyptians share common elements of mythology, passed from earlier migratory nomads, with Europeans, Eurasians, the North Chinese, Koreans, Japanese, and all those places, including the Americas, where this pyramid religion perhaps spread in ancient times, after 5000-3000 BC.

Wherever this religion went, it retained ideas traceable back to the earlier mythology of Eurasia. Additionally, when the religion entered Egypt it mixed with African religions and peoples, creating a unique cocktail we now call the Ancient Egyptian religion. It mixed the shamanism and animism of Stone-Age Europe with pre-existing Eurasian and Berber ideas from earlier invasions, and also with shaman religions of Africa. This religion, once established and developed was a conservative one, always looking back in awe to the past wonders of the Giza and other ages. Old ideas, a common ancestor between Egypt and Eurasia, branched into different pathways in whichever kingdom the seed fell.

American link

Stone-Age builders truly did migrate far and wide. Antiquary and pyramid enthusiast Ralph Ellis in his book *Thoth* mentions that the pyramids of Teotihuacan are three, as at Giza. I do not agree with all of his theories but this one, specifying some sort of a link, seems interesting.

European explorers asked American natives who it was that built the huge mounds, then covered in dirt. The natives did not have a clue, but pointed out that one was called Pyramid of the Sun, and the other Pyramid of the Moon. Seemingly the most important pyramid is that of the Moon, as a pathway leads up to it. There is a bigger Sun pyramid next door, and next to this the smallest of the three, a step pyramid with lots of serpent gargoyle-like creatures all over it, so I suppose this might be referred to as the pyramid of the serpent. It differs quite remarkably to the other two, which have plain faces. Another pyramid researcher, Dr Semir Osmanagić, notes that based upon his travels, pyramids seem to come in pairs, often with a pyramid of the Sun as well as Moon. These are presumably Stone-Age representations of the male and female, astronomically aligned so that the male casts a shadow on the female, as at Stonehenge and other possible sites.

A fascinating thing going on with the pyramids of Teotihuacan is that they were covered with Earth, a stone layer underneath, and then a clay structure, similar to other pyramids covered over, implying that it is a similar religion at work as at Navan Fort, Ireland, with buried soil layers having strong significance. The Navan fort mound also strongly emphasises the horizontal, as at Teotihuacan. Dr Schoch says that they relate to Chinese pyramids, which also emphasise the horizontal.

The map of the Teotihuacan complex is fascinating. It resembles the Giza complex, in both scale, the amount of work put into it, as well as three main pyramids with, a smaller baby one, as at Giza. The Pyramids of the Sun and Moon are visible. The Temple of Quetzalcoatl to the below right is the third large pyramid. The reader might like to turn back to figure of the Giza complex to compare them, fig. 6.23. Mark Lehner writes that the Egyptian pyramid complex is built to worship a confluence of Sun, Osiris (bleeding man and green god), and Horus (possible sky father). Here by contrast we have feathered serpent (possibly also represented in Old Europe as a snake or bird woman), the Sun, and Moon. The argument of this book is that a pyramid represents a mother goddess with consort.

By sizes and general orientation, the Teotihuacan complex could be 'mapped' onto Giza, at least the main three pyramids. Fascinatingly, this would correlate to Khufu's as Moon pyramid, Khafra's as Sun pyramid, and little Menkaure's as serpent pyramid, with its red bricks on the base representing the underworld. There are other similarities. The Khufu (Moon?) pyramid is surrounded by smaller buildings. The Khafra (Sun?) pyramid, far less so. The same is true here. Khufu's pyramid has lots of associated smaller pyramids, and is the focus of the complex, the most important pyramid.

There is another piece of evidence which is quite intriguing. The Menkaure pyramid has granite bricks at the first sixteen courses of

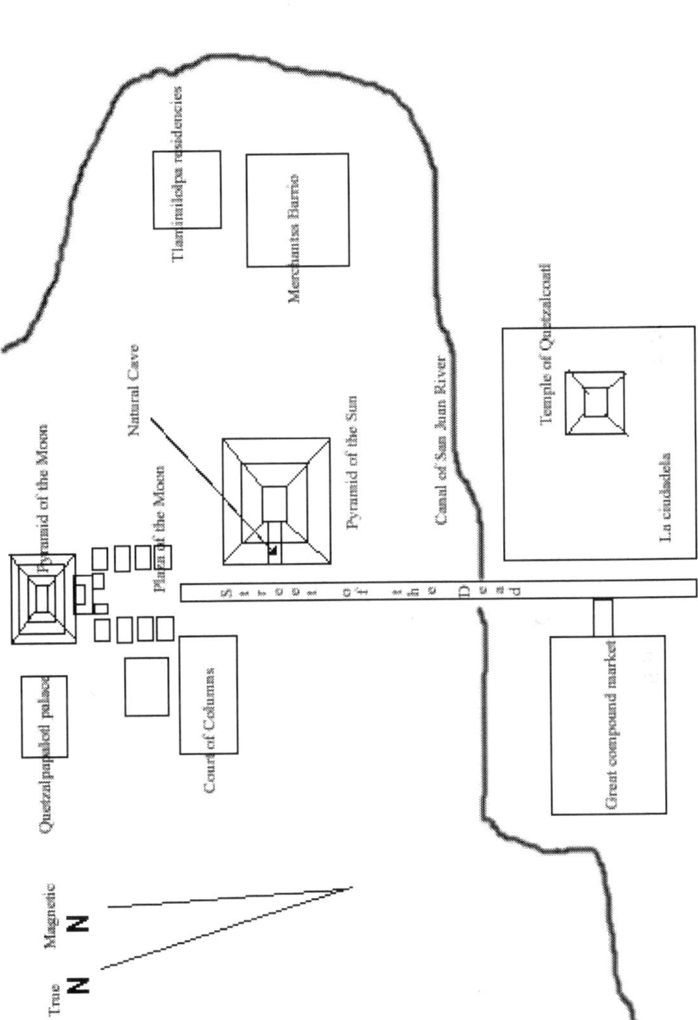

Figure 6.26: Map of the Pyramid complex at Teotihuacan, Valley of Mexico, 30 miles (48km) North East of Mexico City. By Maunus.

the base, the rest being finished in white limestone. In photographs I have seen, some of the granite stones look blue, others quite pink and red. A computer reconstruction of Giza in Mark Lehner's book shows the red intention at the base of the Menkaure pyramid as well as red granite also used on the Mortuary Temple and Sphinx Temple of the Sphinx/Khafra pyramid, with none used on the Khufu pyramid. Fascinatingly in this regard the Menkaure pyramid may have been intended as a red pyramid, built half-heartedly. The Khafra pyramid is also a little red, due to granite here and there. Robert Schoch points out that the Khafra pyramid also has lower red courses of stones. He says that this implies there may have been some rebuilding works from earlier structures. I think the red down the bottom could imply the beginning of the underworld. Alternately they wanted a hard stone for the base, softer limestones above. We see three layers. There is a red underworld of lower courses, white limestone (Midgard?) followed by a hypothetical capstone (Asgard?), once the pyramid reaches a sufficient height. The Khufu pyramid does not have this exterior granite feature, but it may have been painted red, with flecks of red paint described by both Vyse and Pochan. Nevertheless, these may be from the red paint which was used for hieroglyphics, found on the inside of the pyramid.

I always like to provide an alternate explanation. Kurt Mendelssohn wrote in his seminal *The Riddle of the Pyramids*, that Menkaure's pyramid represents the final large pyramid of the fourth dynasty, and may well have simply been built out of leftover building materials from the other two structures. As such there would have been many granite casing stones which people needed to find some use for. The structure represents only one tenth of the volume of each predecessor. It was a final winding up of the great age of pyramid building.

According to conventional ideas, the God Ptah was winning out over the cult of the priests of Ra at Heliopolis. A more orthodox religious idea, to explain the red coating would possibly be that the pyramid is a representation or home for the fire god Ptah, over the other two which are white and therefore have some kind of solar representation.

A religious fusion

We have statues of Menkaure standing next to various gods, Egyptian ones. This may reflect Herodotus' story of him turning back towards Egypt's gods. For instance he stands next to Hathor to his right, and another obscure female goddess to the left. Since we know about Egyp-

Figure 6.27: A drawing of a statue of Khafre, flanked and guided by Horus. By A. Peters.

tian gods, why use these older gods to interpret the pyramids? There are a number of reasons. The main reason, however, are the stone-datings and carbon datings which have been carried out, and which point to the fact that there is very old material at the Giza complex. If the pyramids were rebuilt from this older material, it would imply the complex was designed in an earlier era, for older gods. It would therefore be more intelligible in this manner, especially as no-one has interpreted them based upon what we know about Egyptian gods.

According to Herodotus, writing over two thousand years after these kings' lives, Khufu and Khafra were heretics or atheists who shut down the temples, forbidding worship of Egyptian gods. They enslaved the nation and forced them to work on the pyramids. (Archaeology tells a slightly different story, showing a possible religious revolution at the end of the reign of Khufu. Khufu is not associated with Ra but Khaf-'ra' and subsequent fourth dynasty rulers *are*.)

The explanation for the behaviour remembered by Herodotus may be that the pyramids represented a *different religion* to the then-Egyptian Gods. Khafra is usually depicted in his statues as alone, but he has Horus, a falcon sky god, to protect and direct him. Horus (The Hieroglyphic form is *ḥr.w*, or 'haru') is a sky god. I believe that like Hathor, a supreme cow god, Horus may be based upon a partly-monotheistic sky-god religion, introduced into Egypt.

We need to look at the position of the pyramids on a plateau, close to the sky god. Horus may have a common ancestor with Odin or Thor, or Taranis, or Zeus, (as well as Slavic *Perun*, and possibly British *Merlin*, Hittite *Tarhunt*, possibly Roman *Mars*, Greek *Heracles/Hera*, Indian *Indra*) a patriarchal sky god. Part of the evidence for this is his position as sole director, or protector of Khafra. In addition he encapsulates both the Sun and Moon. Each is but one of his eyeballs: the sacred lunar female is nullified by his existence, and Ra is nothing to this god! His eyeballs are among his most significant features.

Naturally this makes our interpretation of the pyramids rather complex, for where is the triple male/female god of Menkaure? The Norse were able to worship Thor or Odin as a supreme god, but they also had an Earth Mother, as well as having an assortment of underworld gods, who had been sent underground by their deity. Thor, or Perun or perhaps Horus ('haru') were not necessarily a case of 'Thou shalt have no other gods but me.' Inter-relations between gods in terms of their primordial and enduring conflict, which sustained the Earth, meant that one could not subtract one without the whole mythology falling apart and ceasing to exist. Loki needs Thor to send him underground. Thor needs Loki to show he is supreme. New-kingdom Akhenaten gets all the credit for his monotheism, but people forget about earlier Khufu and Khafra, probably because we do not know about their personal gods. By his statue, the gods of Khafra, despite what Herodotus says, are Horus, and dare I say it, Moon and Sun. The Sun and Moon are Thor's parents. Taking the moon as associated with Earth Mother, rising up to Sky, their child is Thor, the weather god of thunder and war.

Giza Trinity

Inescapably, we see a trinity venerated at Giza. In the image of Menkaure, we have a bull/cow on one side, and a bull/cow on the other side. The implication is that Menkaure is the third 'bull' of the triad, perhaps entering the afterlife to live at the foot of the mound of creation, as the Norns do, represented by the pyramid. This is a representation of the

Figure 6.28: This is Menkaure. He has 'Bat' beside him, on his left. Bat is yet another cow goddess. I wonder if we got the word 'bad' from her, as those horns might look rather devilish to members of a more patriarchal religion. Cairo Museum.

triple deity. Giza itself provides us some evidence for veneration of the triple deity.

From Giza temples, unknown and buried beneath the sand until modern times, we have original third millennium BC statues of Menkaure and Khafra, but nothing about Khufu. His temple seems to have been exposed and destroyed utterly in ancient times, save for a black granite floor.

In the image, Menkaure is with two goddesses. They form a triad, three gods in one. The one on the left is Hathor with horns typical of an African bull. The bull is the premiere god in eastern Stone-Age religions. Bat and Hathor are both male and female. They have horns above them, yet are women. Does this statue have any particular *purpose*? Certainly it is a temple statue. These were often found at Giza in deep pits, when the sand of eons was finally uncovered. In the publication *Temple of Heaven*, about an altar complex of cone step-pyramids in Beijing, we are told that sacrifices to heaven for the benefit of the harvest took place in the presence of a statue or tablet to the god, which was in the presence of that of a royal ancestor. This has occurred since the Xia and Shang periods (post 2000 BC). The practice, we are told, is based upon the ancient precedent of paying homage to the god, and respect to the ancestors. One also prayed to clan tablets of the ancestors, reflecting a Moses link to a proto-Egyptian practice, or a practice also employed by the Jews before their possible entrance into Egypt.

As shown in the figures, gods of Giza seem to have certainly included a supreme Cow goddess, represented close by Menkaure, who accepted Egyptian gods, as Hathor and Bat. His ancestor Khafra preferred Horus. I make the suggestion (It has probably all been suggested before, but not altogether noticed or accepted, because it is not archaeology. See for instance, G. A. Wainwright *The Sky Religion in Egypt*, 1938. He suggests that Egypt's gods are based upon much older gods which did not originate in Egypt, but fused with them) that Horus is based on the proto-Indo-European sky goddess. As we get closer to Egypt, the name actually gets closer to 'Haru', in terms of Slavic *Perun*, and then Hittite *Tarhunt*. Then again, the re-constructed form for the primordial god, before it diverged into various languages, 'Perkunas', sounds nothing like Horus! (I partially disagree with the reconstruction as it presumes that the proto Indo-Europeans emerged out of one central, concentrated area, (still unknown) and thence proceeded to populate the Earth. I think it is the more complex case of reinforcement by

Figure 6.29: Hathor is a 'Norn'! She herself may be an equivalent of the Triple Deity, the triple woman who according to old Indo-European fable, lives at the base of the world mountain. There is a fountain of water for each Norn. Compare this to fig. 1.20. (From Wallis Budge, *Egyptian Magic*)

repeated overlapping migrations over many thousands of years, and co-evolution or name reinforcement over a wide area.)

What better place, however, to worship the sky god, than the Giza plateau. This sky god is not really covered by Gimbutas, as this is not part of the slightly more matriarchal 'old Europe'. She was an archaeologist who considered what she called 'Old Europe' to be pre-Indo-European. The problem is that as a plateau with caves, Giza could have had older gods associated with it as well, and these may have been different deities than held by the kings of Giza, as their particular personal gods.

Look at the map of Saqqara. This is but nine miles from Giza, and therefore it would be expected to represent a similar religion, even if it is largely, but not entirely of the previous dynasty. It too is a

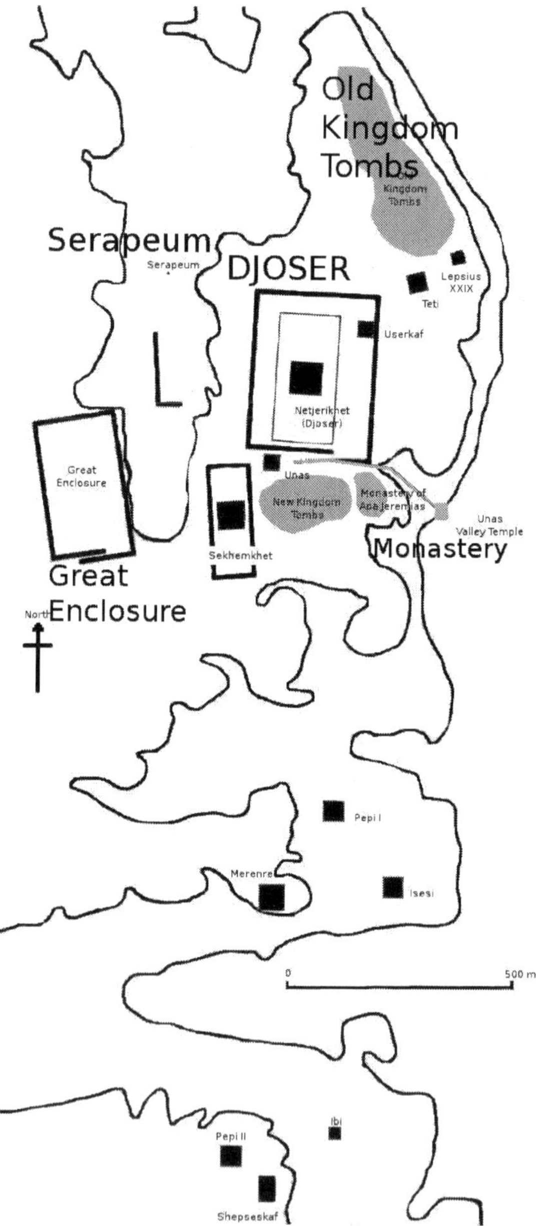

Figure 6.30: A map of the pyramids and tombs of the Saqqara plateau.

plateau and therefore representative, perhaps of the primordial mound of creation, and the plateau-builder religion.

In one later version of the Egyptian mound of creation story, Ra, also known as Atum (Adam?), sat on the mound of creation, sneezing and spitting. Two children, Shu, the dry air and Tefnut, his sister, the moist air, came out of his mouth. These two begat the sky goddess Nut and Earth god, Geb. These two would go on to bear Osiris and Isis, and so on. Thus all of creation of the gods is associated with the mound. The Great Pyramid is placed on the edge of the desert. The Nile cannot really be seen to fertilise the plateau, even if it supposedly had a water supply in ancient times. In fact the Nile would once inundate around the plateau. The pyramid was thus at the border of dry air incoming from the desert and the moisture of the Nile, as if these were in fact being created out of the pyramid.

The Egyptians seemed to like building their pyramids on top of hills. There are certainly a lot of monuments on this hill. The complexity witnessed is representative perhaps of different time periods and ideas which have created this complex cocktail of monuments and tombs. What I see, coming through this, is a reverence for the number three.

I have never been the greatest fan of the Orion Correlation Hypothesis, of Robert Bauval, by which the three Giza pyramids could map to the central stars of Orion, though that idea is very exciting, and will always remain an idea for a possible inspiration for Giza. One major aspect going for it is that Osiris as fertility god was indeed associated with Orion.

I will propose an alternate scheme, with the pyramids representing planets (gods) rather than stars. In *Giza: The Truth*, Ian Lawton and Chris Ogilvie-Herald point out several discrepancies in Bauval's theory. Chief among them seems to be that the three stars of Orion's belt seem to be of almost equal magnitude, not reflected in the Giza pattern. Furthermore the off-centre star, Mintaka, does not line up fully with Menkaure's pyramid. Another problem is that Orion is not really visible on the ground, merely the three pyramids, with some possible other pyramids representing other stars of Orion, but this is not especially convincing to me. I am not fully convinced by my upcoming proposition for pyramids as planets either, but I think it is worth knowing about.

The Giza pyramids do however form a kind of curve. Here, in fig. 6.30, in the upper squares, which represent pyramids, we have an alignment of six pyramids in a kind of curve as well. We also have a Great Enclosure which is out of alignment with this curve, indicating a possible earlier design, out of kilt with the curve. Pyramids were built in Egypt, to the west of the Nile. Therefore civilisation and people are to the right, off the edge of the cliff-face. The curve might imply that Egyptians did not want to create straight lines of pyramids. This might have been seen to create a dis-harmonic effect.

Looking up from their farms, at the Saqqara complex, people would have seen firstly, in earlier times, that pyramid marked as 'Djoser', in a large rectangular enclosure. Of similar era are the two other enclosures, making three. The Great Enclosure has no pyramid. No pyramid was intended, for the wall is complete. Between them is Sekhemkhet's pyramid enclosure. The sequence could replicate the form of Khufu building his pyramid where it could be seen, on the cliff edge, with other structures of his successor away towards the desert, and away from public sight. The three enclosures perhaps replicate a sacred trio, seen at Giza, which is not too far away. The two minor pyramids closer to the cliff relative to Djoser are of Teti (built 400 years after Djoser) and 'Lepsius XXIX', named after an archaeologist. Old Kingdom tombs are the dark shade on the cliff edge to the north. New Kingdom tombs are the shade in the middle.

To the right of this shade is the Monastery of Apa Jeremias, another shade. The implication is that it is there to take worshipers away from paganism, like the church on top of Glastonbury Tor. There is also a Serapeum up there to worship Serapis, a Hellenistic fusion of two Egyptian gods. These earlier gods were Osiris the resurrection god, and Apis the bull god. Why stick them together? I believe this is simply an alternate Mithras, the young man and the bull, attached. Dare I say it, the older equivalent of Baldr, shining young man, and Loki, horned one. These are both imprisoned in the underworld of the cosmic mound. The implication is this is a hill of resurrection, a primordial world mound: with three enclosures for the Earth Mother. One, yet to be filled with a pyramid, possibly represents the future, as the three aspects of the triple goddess often represent past, present and future.

Three pyramids, three gods

Gods of the third millennium BC are at the crossover of Neolithic and Bronze Age. In other words, agriculture. But there are earlier gods, Paleolithic gods, which are a hangover from a time when agriculture was less important as a food source. It is quite possible the Giza pyramids were erected on the basis of an ancestral memory of earlier gods. This would make the pyramids difficult to define, as an underworld representation. Schoch, for instance writes that the Great Pyramid was specifically built around an older mound. Since it would have been easier to level it first, in terms of building a stable structure, it may have had religious value.

Marija Gimbutas wrote a book called *The Goddesses and Gods of Ancient Europe*. It deals with the gods of a culture found from Italy to the Balkans, to Crimea, which she called Old Europe, and peopled by those she considered pre-Indo-European. The gods and goddesses she describes, based upon archaeological materials, date from about 6500-3500 BC. I think the archetypes behind the Giza gods are in there.

In looking at the statues, associated with Menkaure and Khafra, we see that the two main gods of Giza seem to be the bull god, in possibly triple form, as well as the sky god, encapsulating Sun and Moon. But in looking at what is going on at Giza, we really need to look at even *older* gods, as various indications seem to suggest the area was in use before these kings as a religious centre. One goddess figure, to which Gimbutas devotes a chapter, is known as 'The snake and bird goddess.' That would somehow relate to Loki, a kind of snake underworld personality, turning into the bird in order to fly away, as he does in legend. This might also be related to Völundr, the ring lord. He also turned into a bird to escape a secret island, where he was making jewellery as a fire god, a parallel of Roman Vulcan.

The Snake and Bird Goddess might also relate to the story of the Phoenix arising from smoky ashes. This would then relate to the small pyramid at Teotihuacan, the feathered serpent. It more or less implies there is a pyramid in America dedicated to some form of what once was something like this goddess. Quetzalcoatl, and perhaps thence also the small pyramid at Giza, that of Menkaure, may be related to a similar god. Quetzalcoatl is related in Amerindian lore to a migration of people from the west, but could also have entered America as a primal god along the land bridge from Alaska, via the east. Why would an American tomb complex have anything to do with Giza? Simple. Again, this is a Stone-Age religion we are dealing with, of very deep antiquity, and Stone-Age peoples were migratory as their needs dictated.

Three Teotihuacan pyramids. We have the moon, which is the main one. 'Sun', a little bigger, just as in the possibly related case of Khafre, then a small one, a step pyramid called the Citadel, full of Quetzalcoatl imagery. The small pyramid is nevertheless found in a large enclosure.

This has parallels to the large empty enclosure on the Saqqara plateau, facing away from civilisation, as the Menkaure pyramid does. To me, this is a similarity, a relation. It would imply that the Menkaure pyramid could be dedicated to snake deities, the old snake goddess. I am suggesting that pyramids have an interior as well as an exterior representation, which will be seen down the ages. The interior representation is quickly forgotten as soon as the chambers are closed. I have suggested that the King's chamber is for the Green Man, Khnum, and the other is for his consort, an Earth mother, a Paleolithic deity.

The moon goddess or pyramid, might be dedicated to what Gimbutas calls, 'The Great Goddess'. Being the Sun, Khafra's pyramid would perhaps be the year god. The Khufu pyramid is Earth/Moon goddess, like the Snow Madonna in Żegocin or in the structure of Newgrange as both Moon and Earth.

The major goddess, or at least one of the three, is the Triple aspect goddess, the triple deity. This is what Gimbutas calls 'The Great Goddess of Life, Death and Regeneration,' represented by a dog as Moon goddess, or doe, or toad or turtle or hedgehog or bee, butterfly or bear. She says this survived as Hekate (a 'hag'?) and Artemis.

The third major goddess mentioned by Gimbutas is the pregnant vegetation goddess, shown as dot or seed and enthroned pregnant goddess or pig. This is Demeter, Kore, Persephone. One conundrum is this. Since there are three goddesses, are these all actually aspects of one Earth Mother, one triple deity? I would suspect that it was all rather mixed up! It must be pointed out that we already have a triple goddess in the Great Goddess. I think that for sure there was some confusion, even among the ancients, when their proto-Druids tried to sort out who was what.

The Stick God, or gnomon

There is a great male god of Old Europe which is a year god. This is the phallus god, or what Gimbutas calls the Ithyphallic Masked God, or the bull with human mask or divine child or sorrowful god. 'Bull with a human mask' sounds a bit like the Sphinx, (or it could have been a dog, or both!) Fascinatingly this would make the Sphinx a kind of Sun god, and year god. As an example of this stick god, which is more intelligible to us, consider Roman *Janus*. This is January. Imagine a doorway, or a stick with one mask on each side. This is the god looking backwards and forwards in time, from one year to the next.

There is a question of which direction he should be facing. East-west would seem appropriate, like an early Christian church. In this way he faces sunrise and sunset, or backwards and forwards in time. I have seen strange heads on the ceilings at the entrances and exits of various medieval cathedrals and chapels in Europe. It is as if one has the 'head of god' to welcome one as one enters or leaves.

Naturally a stick is also a gnomon, as well as a kind of *omphalos*, a Greek word for symbolic centre, or marker of creation, around which worship could proceed. In fact Mark Lehner points out in *The Complete Pyramids* that the Sphinx was seen as a Sun god in New Kingdom times. If Khafra's pyramid is the stick/Sun god, in a mainly already-deforested ancient Egypt, this might explain why it casts a winter-solstice shadow on the Khufu pyramid, as pointed out by Robert Temple. Another sort of stick god, Svetovid, of Poland/Ukraine to the north, meanwhile, looked to the four corners of the universe. These were spatial rather than time coordinates, unless the east-west faces incorporate a time dimension. Svetovid may have been aligned to the north-south, and east-west, using a line drawn to the pole star.

On the other hand, Nicholas Mann writes that often Neolithic sites are aligned cross-wise to the northeast, northwest, southeast and southwest. This is to create alignments for the rising of the Sun on Beltane, May 1, as well as Lughnased, August 1. The cross-wise pattern reflects points which lie in between the solstices and equinoxes, despite the importance of these other dates. Time dimensions thus become geographical coordinates.

Svetovid is like a compass. There is even an omphalos, called the *compas*, in the Church of the Holy Sepulchre in Jerusalem under a dome in the Catholicon. Jesus was supposedly crucified there. It is a lot like Odin hanging on the world tree, at the centre of the world. Jerusalem is near the bridge of three continents. For this reason, in medieval times it was seen as a centre of creation. (If America was ever drawn into a monk's world map it would have been a kind of island next to a large three petalled flower, one petal for each continent) I would suggest, in jest, that a more appropriate god than Svetovid for this location would be Taranis, who has three faces.

Though a church was more for east-west Sun/Apollo/Shining/Bleeding-God worship, as prototypes of Christ in early Christian times, it was laid down in the shape of the cross, pointing to the four corners of world. The alternative to something which points is of course the mound. It does not need to point. There are of course round 'churches',

(Stonehenge is some kind of prototype which does not point north, or possibly towards, I would suggest what was once magnetic north, but there are many explanations) some of which have a central altar which Nigel Pennick in *The Ancient Science of Geomancy* says represents the world centre or *omphalos*.

In England, archaeologists know that a burial is Christian, when it is found lying east-west. Jesus was supposed to rise again in the east. A pagan burial by contrast will be north-south. Why this direction? What easier way to align oneself to the mound of creation, the centre of the universe? In fact, lodestones were known in ancient Egypt as the 'bones of Osiris,' the resurrection god, presumably because he was supposed to align to north-south, being at the centre of the world. Pyramids are generally always aligned to this coordinate. The axis of the mythical Yggdrasil is said to reach the pole star. It is like being buried at a pyramid, the mound itself, without needing one. One's alignment probably simply becomes the sacred gnomon. Looking at the Khufu sarcophagus, it is north-south facing, which might suggest resurrection god rather than year god, but they are much the same. When the 26th-dynasty enthusiasts broke into the Menkaure pyramid and placed their own sarcophagus there, it was north-south facing.

Lost Gods of Giza?

So much for the stick god. The gods described by Gimbutas are the gods from 6500 BC to 3500 BC. That is just about 500 years before the start of a pyramid building era in around 3100! These gods occupied a wide area in Europe and possibly Egypt as well, though Gimbutas does not associate this civilisation with Egypt.

In the legend told to Herodotus, wicked Khufu enslaved many and closed temples, presumably so everyone could work on his pyramid. Why did Khufu close the temples? The answer could be very simple. He looked down on the people as a bunch of pagans! This was not his religion! Either he invented one of his own, or he was following another. Khafra then followed in Khufu's footsteps, with an allegedly equally long career.

In the Herodotus legend of Menkaure, we have something different happening. There seems to have been an interruption to Menkaure's reign. There might have been some poor health which led to disillusionment and an abandonment of the project. Menkaure's pyramid complex is not only smaller than the other two pyramids, but unfinished! Something made him turn back to the regular Egyptian religion, possibly ill health. He furthermore consulted an oracle which said that he would have a short life. This made him indignant. He raged that his father and uncle had enjoyed long and prosperous lives, even if they 'took no thought for the gods', in shutting the temples and forbidding sacrifice. Condemned by the oracle to live for only a few more years, he endeavoured to double this time by staying up every night. The legend was presumably invented afterwards to explain why there was a smaller pyramid built, or why his pyramid was abandoned. He was remembered as the favourite king of Egyptians, and his legacy is that he may well have abandoned the perfection of the Giza complex, to become closer to the people and native gods.

Gimbutas says that another Paleolithic or Mesolithic deity, the snake and bird goddess (presumably where the feathered serpent comes from) was a predominant image in Old-European traditions and even something of a nursing goddess. Gimbutas refers to these goddesses as Old Europe or Pre-Indo-European, with the European one perhaps a little more patriarchal, but not necessarily. I wonder if this snake goddess, being the third goddess, is the one which is supposed to be represented by Menkaure's pyramid. Then again there is a lack of evidence for this.

Conveniently (and confusingly, for ancients perhaps also) in Gimbutas' book, there are three major goddesses, though each one could in their own right be a triple goddess. These are, firstly, the Mistress of the Waters, who is the Bird and Snake goddess. (Ancestor of the feathered serpent, and maybe a bit of Artemis as well?) Secondly, *The Great Goddess of Life, Death and Regeneration.* (This would be the past, present, and future goddess, or triple goddess.). Thirdly, there is the pregnant vegetation goddess. Gimbutas reckoned that these were the goddesses leading up to 3500 BC.

Which goddess, which pyramid?

I am still very hesitant to say which goddess might refer to which pyramid. I note in the publication, *Stelae of the Giza Necropolis,* that there is a lack of information about gods in the stelae regarding Khufu's dignitaries who were buried at Giza, near his pyramid. There is however a great deal of record of how much linen they were assigned as reward, and so forth.

There is more we do not know than we can know, but the Khufu pyramid does seem to be of the Earth and Moon, with Khafra possibly more representative of the Sun. (This could be in an oblique way, in the way the Heel Stone at Stonehenge is 'solar,' because it casts a shadow on the inner goddess, the toppled altar stone.) Khufu would then come under the category of Gimbutas' 'Life Death and Regeneration' or triple goddess. Khafra would represent 'The Pregnant vegetation goddess', or Hathor, whose consort is Ra, the Sun, and also Horus, another type of sky god. Like the Khufu pyramid, it too is quite large and so is swelled with underworld life force.

Then we have the third small pyramid, like the one at like at Teotihuacan. Here perhaps we have the snake goddess, the third of Gimbutas' holy trio. This is a kind of nurse goddess as well. Then again, who knows! Perhaps all three are the 'Great Goddess' that is the precursor to the 'norns' or three women. This is all speculation, but I like it, and once again, it is based upon Stone-Age mythology, not fancy. If the pyramids were world mounds, as everyone says, then these are among the deities who were once associated with them. The fact the pyramids may well be rebuilt from earlier structures, however, really does complicate the overall issue.

The Great Goddess of the period 6500-3500 BC seems to be the ancestress of the three Norns. If we apply the concept of past, present, and future, which they are supposed to represent in European mythologies, then the pyramids would possibly be 'life' as Khufu, 'death' as Khafra, and 'rebirth' as little Menkaure, the Phoenix, or perhaps winged-snake rising from the ashes! It is probably a lot more complex that that, however. For instance the Khufu pyramid has funeral boats! Hardly 'life' but it is 'regeneration' and therefore eternal life. Then again, the funeral boats are around the pyramid rather than inside and may be part of funeral arrangements of the kings rather than intrinsic to the god or goddess representation of the pyramids themselves. Furthermore, the Khufu complex may not have been all built at the same time, based on wide carbon datings, and a potential earlier structure on site upon which newer ideas were based. Although there is no significant feathered-serpent god among the Egyptians, there is a snake goddess in Old Europe who was of great importance. This is perhaps related to the winged Loki, or ring lord.

Then there is what Gimbutas describes as the year god, which is the phallus or perhaps Irminsul or four-headed god. This was a large stick essentially, like a sundial. As mentioned, this was a precursor to Stonehenge in the 8000s BC. Stonehenge may always have been a temple for worshipping the year, essentially for the past ten thousand years. Later on it became a *lot* more complicated, such that mathematical minds are still racking over the details.

Another piece of evidence relating the Khufu pyramid to the moon goddess is its strange relation to Newgrange. Both the Khufu pyramid and Newgrange were presumably the first (the only, in the case of Newgrange) on site. They were thus the sole and original representative of the Earth Mother, who may have had a triple aspect. There is at least a double aspect at Newgrange as it is part Moon, part Earth. The Sun enters it, fertilising it and perhaps awakening old gods, including the year god, to begin a new year.

In Gimbutas' book, there is also something from the civilisation of Old Europe in Bulgaria, known for its deeply ancient golden treasures: a dog figure wearing a human mask! This might be a form of proto-sphinx. We do not know what the Sphinx was carved from. Although it seems to have been a hound, it may even have been carved from a larger, earlier, human face. It might have been re-carved from an earlier face, when the Sphinx was restored in the Old Kingdom (that's how old it is!) which in turn was re-carved from a hound. Let us imagine, momentarily, that it indeed was a hound. This allows us to explain several details. Gimbutas says that the dog was a principal animal of the *Goddess of Birth, Death and Regeneration* in Old Europe. (Triple Goddess) That is the region where the Kurgan-like mounds are found, which I have shown relate strongly to Old-Kingdom pyramid architecture. *That* is interesting! The Sphinx and the three pyramids... the triple goddess with her hound? This Old Europe-link could be a source of aboriginal-European ideas, shared with an earlier Egypt.

I rest my case on the goddess

Stone-Age man did not care or know of border or nation. He knew of tribe and went with that tribe, or perished. On the one hand, he travelled to West and North Europe, building various mounds and pyramids there, and on the other hand also travelled down into Egypt, (or up from Egypt and into Europe) building different pyramids there. For me, this is the most likely potential explanation for the origin of corbeled vaulting for burial chambers in both Old Kingdom Egyptian, and Kurgan burials. These happen to be found in all the regions of Gimbutas' 'Old Europe' civilisation, from Etruria to Crimea. There is, as pointed out, a similarity with Mycenaean burials. The Kurgan burials which spread on the one hand to Crimea, with corbeled vaulting, and on the other hand to Egypt to the south, taking their gods and possible boat burial with them, even if boat burial does not seem to figure strongly in the extant kurgans.

The other explanation for corbeled vaulting, that it was come up with independently, does not work. For then it would be found in greater profusion elsewhere, with a random distribution, rather than along similar longitudes. Another explanation is that Kurgan architects actually entered the Old-Kingdom pyramids in the second and first millennia BC and examined the burial chambers. This seems unlikely. If they went to Egypt at the time the Kurgan burials were built, they may instead have been inspired by New-Kingdom burials, in caves in a cliff, (though these obviously may have been kept secret), or even by later Saite-dynasty burials underneath temples. Additionally, tourists often do not steal other tribe's or kingdom's burial practices, but have their own, which they hold sacred.

Let us talk of a pyramid religion. If Silbury Hill is made for the Great Goddess, as Damas points out, why would not the Great Pyramid, built at about the same time, not be another offshoot of this culture, and thence also built for the Great Goddess? These would be the idea of nomads, very probably sea travellers who were possibly pirate migrants. Like the Vikings, they went and plundered, setting up settlements in favourable locations as they migrated. Perhaps these in very early times are a precursor and relate to migrations of the Sea Peoples, except two milennia earlier.

I am far more comfortable with the idea of the three pyramids simply representing the three Norns of the Great Goddess, rather than attempting to state which pyramid is which particular god, or form of the Great Mother, and thence ascribing to Giza a further multiplicity of purpose. Nevertheless, I try to make some inroads. The former idea is more simple and elegant. Ascribing goddesses to the pyramids, as I have tried to do, complicates and weakens the argument. Then again I am more or less being forced along this path, by evidence from several sources.

Firstly the Irminsul came in pairs. There was a male and female. Since the Stygir Idol seems to be an Irminsul from ten thousand years ago, this is clearly a very old religion with probably exceedingly widespread descendants, Ireland to the Americas. Secondly, at Stonehenge and seemingly at Newgrange, we have Mother Earth being fertilised by Father Sky. This was part of the fertility cult. The Khafra pyramid might be central Sun/staff/year in this respect.

Thirdly, the Teotihuacan experience suggests division of pyramids by god. In the fourth instance, field work (tourism) I did in Europe seems to reveal that there were often mound/pyramid complexes as part of a wider landscape of the underworld. These would have multiple major central mounds, but not always, and this was surrounded by real burials much smaller than the pyramids in the middle. As to the question of whether the pyramids represent various gods, the answer would be a tentative yes. They might represent Odin in the north, Merlin in England, Buddha in the East, Ptah or Osiris or Khnum in the south, a god of wisdom. Thoth too is the moon god, associating knowledge with Khufu's pyramid. An old Arab legend states that the pyramids were built to protect the old science from future deluge. The problem of which gods however, if any, is an incredibly difficult one, so not too much emphasis should be placed on any particular deity. The speculations I have provided, are, and will remain speculations, but backed up by Stone-Age religious ideas, rather than an imposition of modern pyramid ideas upon the ancients. In the case of the Khnumm-Khufu pyramid, however, they are rather stronger than speculations, backed by inscription, and more particularly in light of the winter solstice fertilisation ritual. It is the hope of any author that his arguments, however should carry some conviction. This hope is the basis of his work, as it is here.

We have heard enough about the Triple Goddess, or the three goddesses and the three pyramids. I rest my case.

A Little Pyramid Mathematics

We have just seen from Gimbutas' book that the three major goddesses of Old Europe are the *Mistress of Waters: Bird and Snake, Great Goddess of Life, Death and Regeneration* (triple deity) and *Pregnant Vegetation Goddess*. These could well be the three pyramids of Giza, but not necessarily in that particular order or arrangement, since I do not think ancient peoples had any bureau of international mythological standards.

People have heard of Robert Bauval's Orion Correlation Theory. I would like to introduce, or re-introduce, if someone has not already covered it, a form of Planet- or God-correlation Theory. In the ancient *Akbar Ezzeman* manuscript, of the Bodleian Library, it is written that the geometry, astronomy and science of the world was preserved in the

Great Pyramid, and would one day be revealed to those who could understand it. The pyramids were, in this old tradition, built by 'wise men' and would carry this science beyond the deluges and cataclysms of the future. In *Pyramid Quest*, Robert Schoch expresses his support for the idea that *pi* and *phi* are incorporated into the Great Pyramid.

We are perhaps now living in this scientific 'future,' envisaged by some ancient people, and perhaps have been for several hundred years. As far as geometry is concerned, several famous pyramid mathematicians, such as Livio Stecchini, or René Schwaller de Lubicz, have stated that the Great Pyramid incorporates the number *Phi*, or 1.6180339. I will not discuss the merits of their case here, but Phi is known to be found often in Egyptian art. What better way to geometrically represent organic growth, than according to a number which reflects the famous Fibonacci sequence? It is the ratio found in the snail shell, or any form of spiralling growth, or even stock-market trends, a number of nature herself. It is a fitting metaphor for the pyramid as a nurturing Earth Mother, of Egypt, probably built for good luck and fertility, that it too should be presented as having grown organically from the ground, by representing this ratio, as if it had, like life, grown of its own accord!

The theory I have espoused in this book, that pyramids are the tombs of gods, as representations of the underworld, has serious consequences for what is represented on the Giza plateau, and this needs to be addressed, though I am reluctant about it. I do not like pyramidology, but as this book was about to be published, I found myself dabbling in something rather similar, but without the religious overtones. As people are usually aware, a mathematics mind and a humanities mind are usually not compatible. This leads to a lack of falsifiability potential from a large section of ancient historians who will not touch the topic. Nevertheless, we have an Egyptologist, in Joyce Tyldesley, who in her *Pyramids*, mentions that the Great Pyramid contains the *pi* ratio, as a proportion of height to base.

We also had a man, Livio Catullo Stecchini, (1913-79) a genius with two doctorates, (Roman Law and Ancient History) who was obsessed with ancient mathematics. He wrote the appendix found in Peter Tompkins' *Secrets of the Great Pyramid*, 1971. He also wrote some more obscure works which are to be found on the web. He wrote that the pyramid builders initially intended the pyramid to be 280 cubits in height and 440 in length. At the last minute before building, they modified the height and base length. The latter was changed to

439.5 cubits, so that 921.453 became the new perimeter, and thence half a degree of latitude at the equator (thence the pyramid is a representation of the Earth). I am unsure if he was the first to make this deduction. Stecchini said his works were often ignored. In examining the mass of numbers he has come up with, I sympathised with the behaviour of other scholars, feeling that it would equally be at home in the mathematics section, as in the humanities.

Though reluctant to enter this topic, the spur in this instance was a book called *Pyramid Odyssey*, by William Fix, written in the 70s. William seems to be a rather careful man, (reading his book shows me that he is rather careful and critical with archaeology theories, including alternate ones, but a little less so with parapsychology, a fad of the 70s) which made me look twice at some of the mathematics, which I would normally simply overlook. Out of all the jargon of the pyramid theorists, he has three discoveries about which he thinks very highly indeed, and which are rather impressive. (He rejects many ideas as based upon earlier inaccurate surveys) Both theories he presents also fit together due to the presence of pyramid quotient, 43200, sourced from Stecchini's work. Let me summarise this impressive work. Stecchini stated that the Great Pyramid itself is a representation of the northern hemisphere of the Earth, (the biggest mound of all, and perfect home for a fire god? A combination of a scale model of his actual home, inside the spherical Earth, as well as the traditional mountain representation!) which is projected on the pyramid's flat surfaces. The apex is the Earth's pole and the perimeter is the equator. In his 1971 work: 'The Great Pyramid represents the northern hemisphere in a scale of 1:43,200; this scale was chosen because there are 86,400 seconds in 24 hours. But then the builders became concerned with the problem of indicating the ratio of polar flattening of the Earth and the length of the degrees of latitude which depends on the ratio of this flattening. [thence they reduced the height of the pyramid] Next they incorporated into the Pyramid the factor *phi* as the key to the structure of the cosmos.' Interesting indeed.

The results of Fix's arithmetic are so impressive that I almost do not wish to mention them, for fear they might be just some coincidence, mistake, or something better left to others, yet there they stand, almost unavoidable, and so here we go!

In *Pyramid Odyssey*, Fix has come up with, or refined, a couple of old pyramid-math ideas. Certain enthusiastic ancient-mystery authors of the past have simply mentioned every calculation they could get their hands on to prove the grandeur of the pyramids, to show that they must be perfect. Not Fix. He really simplifies things and just mentions three conclusive measures. In examining Giza personally, he was looking for a convincing calculation of the pyramid's perimeter (do those words have a relation?). Firstly, he pointed out that the pyramid's perimeter is equal to half a minute of latitude. He also mentions that no-one doing the various pyramid calculations has looked at the fact the Great Pyramid is built on a huge level platform which is 55cm thick. He says that once this platform is taken into consideration, the old calculation of of the Earth Radius/43200 equalling the pyramid height, becomes even more impressive. For it comes to within 119 metres of the polar radius of the Earth (distance from surface to centre).

I can think of one reason why the Egyptians would want to know the radius of Earth, of all things. Firstly, the pyramid is 'centred' at the centre of the world axis. It points to the Pole Star, but it also points directly up as well as down, so it works for ancient flat-Earthers as well. It is the axis between Stone-Age conceptions of the world above, Asgard, Midgard, and the world below, the underworld. I apologise for using Scandinavian terms. I would like to use the words of the nomadic stone builders, whose pyramids are found not just in Egypt, but do not know what they were. (The priests who built the pyramids possibly thought to reconcile this flat Earth mythology and cosmology, with reality, in a unique structure.)

An Egyptian heavenly paradise was *Aaru*, to the east (like Eden). *Duat* was their underworld. If the Egyptians knew the world was round, naturally the radius is the exact distance between Midgard and the heart of the underworld. The radius is the distance to the 'central fire,' if they were aware of such a concept. It is another way of 'anchoring' the pyramid to the gods of re-creation. The pyramid god, being the genius he is, would presumably understand what humans were trying to come up with. Would the humans even try to show him the distance to his 'other' home, as the centre of the Earth?

Fix noticed four holes on each side of the pyramid just outside each corner. These are square shafts in the ground. He uses the outside edge of these as a square measurement. In a second discovery, Fix says that the perimeter from outside the four shafts on each pyramid corner, 921.453 m, is 1/43200 of the equatorial circumference of the world. In other words, precisely 1/2 a minute of equatorial longitude. (Polar longitude asymptotes to zero. Do not despair if the ancients somehow had a similar system to us today, for we too use a system of

360 degrees for our circle!) Multiply the perimeter (circumference of the Mother-Earth representation?) by this pyramid number of 43200 and one has the circumference of the Earth.

Venus, Mars, Mercury?

'Well,' thought I, since the Khufu pyramid seems to have Earth ratios, long talked about, and since I think I know it to actually represent the pregnancy of the Earth Mother, based upon this research, then why would the other pyramids not represent other gods in the form of heavenly spheres? The revelations made me comfortable enough to attempt not a new ratio or invention, but just the *same* formula, merely applied to the other two pyramids, which would be other god/goddess consorts and therefore other heavenly spheres. So we can take the 43,200 multiplier for the other two, based upon the original heights of these pyramids. For Khafra, for instance, with an original height of 143.5 metres, multiplied by 43,200 divided by 1000 gives '6199.2 km' instead of Venus' actual radius of 6052 km. Planet Venus in Egyptian is *Ba'ah* or *Seba-djai*. That may or may not be related to the Old-Kingdom Bat/Bad goddess found in Menkaure's tomb. It is also etymologically related to *Ba* or soul, a great shining light flying about in the heavens that one might associate with Venus. The other Egyptian word for Venus is Seba-djai, which I do not know what to do with. Then of course Egypt has many many fertility goddesses who might have been associated with Venus at one time or another.

One does the same to the Menkaure pyramid, based upon an original height of 65.5 metres, and it gives '2829 km'. (Mars' radius is 3390 km. Mercury's radius is 2440 km. It is very close to the mean, but that means nothing to this inquiry) I do not know which planet this last pyramid could refer to but I suspect it is or was a representation of the feathered-serpent goddess, associated with one of Gimbutas' goddesses, the Snake and Bird Goddess. *Mar*-s and *Mer*-cury have a similar root in Latin, so there was some confusion between their representational god at an early Pre-Roman stage. It is much harder however, to measure the radius of Mercury than Mars, so I would suggest Mercury, to account for the difference, which is quite negligible. One can only really see Mercury when it is very low in the sky near the Sun. In this instance it changes size continually, shimmering as the dense atmosphere refracts its light. Venus is seen much higher, the interfering atmosphere thinner, possibly allowing a more accurate reading.

The Menkaure pyramid could well be Mercury in representation, because Hermes/Mercury has aspects of Loki/Lucifer, the trickster. It is a redder pyramid, with its strange red-granite casing stone base, and hence close to the fiery centre. (Then again it could also be Mars. This is speculation!) Incidentally, if Khafra and Menkaure contain a reference to Venus and Mercury, as I suggest, this might explain why the Sphinx might have been a dog, according to Temple's idea.

In the old Germanic mythology, which I think to be a surviving outpost of Old-European ideas, safe and secure in the Scandinavia redoubt, out of the way of various later Indo-European invasions, the great hound actually chases Venus and the Sun around. I feel that the little dot of planet Mercury may have been seen as this great wolf in the sky, and eagerly pointed out by proto-Vikings to their children.

Why would 'Venus' cast a shadow on Khufu on the winter solstice? That is not too hard, for Venus is a fertility goddess. The male consort of the goddess would be the one doing the shadow casting. Venus is also 'blocking' the Sun, in between it and Earth. In Sanskrit, 'Budha' is actually the name of Mercury and 'Mangala' is the name of Mars. We know that Buddha is supposedly buried in every stupa, which honours him. This is some evidence that a planet or god can actually have a pyramid built in its honour. The Norse Mercury is Odin. He is a traveller who traditionally looks a bit like Gandalf from *The Lord of the Rings*.

A planet's radius might be measured by occultation of a star behind it. Then an hour glass is set up to find out when the star appears again. I do not wish to say any more about this topic, as it is a very speculative one, and it is a weakness therefore in the entire argument, though it is not intrinsic to it, and a mere curiosity that I have chosen to add, to show that the arguments in this topic have certain consequences. I would merely like to say that to attempt all this, the Egyptians would need a conception of parallax, to measure the distance of the planets from Earth, which could allow a radius measurement. This appears to have been first done in Europe by Giovanni Cassini in the seventeenth century, when he measured Mars at opposite times of the year (so Earth was spaced out on two sides of the Sun) to check its changing position of Mars against stars. It is a rather difficult topic! Would someone like to take it up?

Robert Temple makes a convincing case that some of the ancients possessed a telescope in *The Crystal Sun*. He also says that Giza could not have been all laid out with such precision without a theodolite, a surveyor's instrument with several lenses. I have been accused in jest, by an antiquarian colleague of having been 'spoiled by civilisation', in suggesting the Egyptians could have used a telescope to measure the diameters of planets. It is not really very hard to build, however, compared to building the Great Pyramid. (Refractive properties could be discovered by any ancient glassmaker). My friend argued that any hard edge could enable naked-eye measurements, of which there are no shortage at Giza. There could also have been reflections using prisms and glass and so forth, without having to resort to the telescope.

I have been an avid amateur astronomer since Halley's comet in 1986, (and possibly before that) and personally speaking, I think it is all much easier with a telescope. The doors opened up to astronomy by the telescope really do allow considerable knowledge advances, as shown by the growth of astronomy following the development of the telescope, over the past several centuries. Without lenses, the diameters of planets might always have remained a mystery.

The Strange case of the Pyramid of Sekhemkhet

I would like to introduce another factor into the argument, to help develop, as well as finalise it. We have the case of the pyramid of Sekhemkhet, an unfinished ruin, built about 2645 BC. Sekhemkhet was actually the successor to king Djoser of the third dynasty.

The ruin is known as the 'buried pyramid' and was discovered in 1951 when the Egyptian Egyptologist Zakaria Goneim noticed that there was a rectangular hump in the desert sands. Investigating, he found a wall and then an unfinished pyramid. This was of the step pyramid era and only one step had been completed.

Funnily enough, the burial seemed to have been in place. He found stone vessels, a decayed wooden casket, gold bracelets, beads and jars with Sekhemkhet's name.

Goneim himself believed the pyramid was a cenotaph. In other words, a representation of the king's burial. But if that is the case, why lay everything inside as if it were real? Why 'waste' everything? In fact, why build an 'inside' at all? The sarcophagus was apparently sealed or blocked in some way and there was a lot of difficulty in opening it. It was rather unusual in its build. It looked like a solid piece of rock with a simple door on the side for a body to be presumably slid in lengthways. When it finally came time to open it, in 1954, it was found to be empty.

I would say it could well have been a tomb for a god. The sarcophagus itself may be circumstantial proof of this. By looking like a huge perfect cut stone, not designed to be opened, it showed in effect that whatever was supposed to be inside was effectively entombed in stone, forever, as if by magic. The mound of creation, or pyramid, then built on top, shows this was an entombing of a god banished beneath. So why then, the king's goods?

For Cyril Aldred, Egyptologist, the pyramid helped the king transform from a Horus, as he was on Earth, to an Osiris, or resurrected deity, who would in future be responsible for the protection and fertility of Egypt. The reason then for building many pyramids in that case would be that the death of each king was the birth of a new Osiris, recreated, and requiring a new mound of creation. It is an elegant theory, but I would suggest not a complete one which explains everything. For there was no kingly burial, in Sekhemkhet's pyramid. (The empty tomb might at least symbolise his resurrection.) There is none in any other. The burials are symbolic, or they are burials of gods, or temples built for gods, or even kings who have become gods, or kings wishing to be associated with gods.

The strange alabaster sarcophagus of Sekhemkhet has a trap door, and no lid, as if to trap something inside, so that what was within could not escape. It is a perfect prison for the fire god, symbolic of his banishment within the Earth.

The *name* of pyramids

The word 'pyramid' is an enigma carried over from ancient times, which will never be solved. Did pyramids have a name in Europe? In Germanic countries they may have been named after Hel, an underworld deity. The reason is that she is the goddess of the underworld and seems to have some aspects of the Great Mother religion. It is easy to see a link also between *Hel* and 'hill'. There is also 'hole'. In Germany we have the hellweg, which I was introduced to in Dortmund. Pyramids as a home for a female deity, therefore, would not be mere tombs for men, although as the centuries passed, times would change and people could be entombed anyway as ideas changed.

According to another authority, Hel is not a goddess but simply a word for 'death'. Therefore the pyramids would simply be death hills, or hills for the dead. It is just another word for 'tomb'. The association with Loki is that Loki is Hel's father. The trickster kills the tricked.

Perhaps he supplies the victims.

Mounds may have been called *Caer* in Britain. It simply means castle or settlement in the old tongue. There is another name pyramids may have gone by in Britain. How about 'Lady of the Lake'? We have the association of pyramids with water. Mark Lehner suggests that artificial lakes were built near pyramids to facilitate transport of stones to them. However I think there was more of a symbolic purpose.

The mound at least, was perhaps supposed to be in the middle of a lake or moat. We have the idea of a sacred henge or water moat surrounding various holy tombs and structures. We have Silbury hill, originally a white structure in a kind of valley, surrounded by a sort of dry moat (hole/holy) as if it were a motte. Silbury hill is supposed to be a great goddess. We have Glastonbury Tor. It might be a natural structure but it is at least partially shaped, by men. It was used for both pagan and Christian purposes. It is called the 'Isle' of Avalon. It may have been surrounded by swamp waters in earlier times, as is suggested. Alternately it looks like an isle anyway when viewed from a great distance on a cold morning, due to the mists which surround it at a lower level. When king Arthur died, his sword was returned to the 'lady of the lake' by his instruction. He himself went to the Isle of Avalon, which is often associated with Glastonbury Tor. One may ask the question: why would he not have been buried with his trusted weapon?

We come now to the Silbury Hill and Avebury complex, partly sketched and no doubt romantically embellished by Stukeley prior to its widespread destruction. It is to be noted that Avebury is on a different side of the river Kennet to Silbury Hill. Avebury may also represent Arthurian Avalon, the place where the dead go, but Silbury is literally a place of the dead, on the other side of the river to the village of Avebury. Then again, a small Roman town was discovered under the Silbury mound in 2007. An antiquarian friend informed me that a possible alternate name for Silbury Hill in the old days would be 'Blessed Hill.' The ancients may have remembered the water goddess Sul and there is the fact it looks like a fortress. On the other hand there is the Germanic root for 'Sel' or blessed.

A pyramid or huge mound was a place from where a blessing literally stemmed. This is why tombs were placed around it, to receive the eternal blessings. For the sake of those buried nearby, and for the sake of the landscape, the pyramid or mound had to be huge and immovable so no-one could destroy it, for eternity. It had to be able to withstand anything in mythological or even legendary 'memory', any cataclysm which might have been able to destroy it, enduring until the end of time. (I wish to cover this idea further in another book, which I have had great difficulty writing and rewriting, still unfinished, in which I will describe the 'future science' of the pyramid builders, as they conceived it, according to mundane astrological cycles, which allowed them to make forecasts of both weather, as well as of civilisation's, progress or decline, thousands of years in advance). One reason the pyramid had to endure forever, was to protect the burials *around* it, perhaps rather than the burials within, if there ever were any.

We come to another name of the pyramids: 'Devil.' I note that in Britain the 'devil' is invoked by country-folk to explain away almost any prehistoric site. It is as if the early Christians went around brainwashing every farmer's family and destroying folk memory. Might this be so? I doubt it. The devil apparently threw *this* rock, or dropped *these* stones here, or there, or they say the devil threw this rock from another hill and it landed on this particular hill. One can read of such legends in *Mysterious Britain*. What does it mean? 'Deva' is a god in India. Here, it is perhaps simply 'Da-Eva', '(The) God Eve'. This is the earth pregnancy, or perhaps mound. The apple tree above the mound fertilises and nourishes Eve, as a mound.

At the start of the book I presented an enigma. I suggested that the pyramid god is written in the Bible as 'Lord'. By some synchronism, while I was writing this, I had some religious people at my door, showing me instances in the Bible where YHWH had been re-written, everywhere as 'Lord.' In examining this word, we seem to have something rather similar to Medb ('Meave'). We have two vowels here, 'YW'. The consonants appear to merely lengthen what is being said. I am not the first to suggest that YHWH is essentially the same word as Eve. The idea readily turns up on articles on the Internet. A friend also pointed it out to me. Thence we have Eve's association with apple 'tree,' as well as serpent. The issue deserves a more comprehensive discussion, which cannot be provided here.

The sacrifice ritual

The pyramid religion of the north, with the wishing trees, seems different to the religion which sacrificed on the pyramid, but it is hard to say. In one Norse myth, Loki (the trickster) tricks Höder into throwing a mistletoe sprig at the wounded God, Balder. Balder dies and there is retribution. Loki is bound underground with a snake dripping poison on him. The relationship to snakes speaks of his entire character. It is convoluted and twisted, like serpents are, but also like tectonic activities. There are also treasures in the ground, like ores, salt, gems, which are beneficial to mankind. This is Loki's domain also. Loki is a character, whose archetypal inspiration is hard to dissociate from the pyramid religion.

It is really hard to say anything for sure regarding the origins of the strange, bizarre and wonderful pyramid religion. Simply, queens and kings needed sufficiently large tombs for people to worship. Society demanded it, not just for the maintenance of society in a spiritual way, as suggested especially in Egyptian mythology, but also in a practical way. The pyramids towering above truly ancient towns in Ireland suggests this.

In addition to the sacrifice ritual, and the ritual marriage which the pyramid perhaps represents, there is also a fire ritual. This was *Beltane* in Ireland. In India, the fire god on the mountain was Shiva. Then again we have the 'burning bush' in the Bible. Shiva was a creator as well as a destroyer God. Therefore, in other words, Shiva creates and destroys the crops of the new year. In order to create, first you must destroy. I wonder if the sacrificial victim would have been compelled to wear a 'crown' of mistletoe, to show he was about to be killed by Loki's device?

Final remarks

One aim of this book was to present to the public the idea that Europe and Asia too have their unknown pyramids, even if they do not look like Egyptian pyramids.

They were built from whatever building materials the landscape allowed. In Egypt or the Middle East, one really needs stone, as sand is rather dry and blows around. Lacking sufficient clay, topsoil placed in the desert is simply going to blow away and grass will not hold it together, as it might in Europe. Mounds in Europe do not need any stones to hold them together.

It is a different story with them, but do they reflect a similar religion, that of the pyramid builders? At least I thought, I could show that they seemed to reflect a similar set of myths. These are ideas associated with the *Axis Mundi*, and with very old creation stories, quite widespread and carried about everywhere by very early hunter gatherers before they finally settled down.

As this book was written, I began to realise that certain pyramids in Egypt also fit a pattern seen elsewhere. This is possibly the relic pattern of a lost and forgotten pyramid-building religion which may have had some of its origins in Eurasia or the Mediterranean. The myths elucidated in this book are not all original ones known to the pyramid builders. Rather they are all that is left. It is therefore hard and problematic to simply relate them to ideas of five thousand years ago.

Realising the problems, I initially decided to make this into a more informal travel book, hesitating to say too much, yet still desiring not to say too little, when it seemed to be evident and prudent to do so. The result is something between a travel book and a more comprehensive presentation of the argument that pyramids are based upon a widespread Stone-Age religion and did not evolve independently in Egypt. In an otherwise excellent book, Joyce Tyldesley re-iterated a rather conventional view when she wrote that the pyramid evolved from the world mound surrounded by water, an idea spawned by land emerging from the Nile when the waters fell. I cannot agree with this elegant idea, for the world mountain is part of a world-wide prehistoric religion, as are its derivative product, pyramids.

We have facts. We have the fact that pyramids were built at the beginning of civilisation. They mark the transition from the farming or nomadic neolithic, to established civic life. After that they seem to have largely gone out of fashion.

We know that mankind has a series of common mythologies, and also that Stone-Age people moved about a lot. If it began at Göbekli Tepe, by the third millennium the pyramid idea was already very old. In a way, Newgrange and Giza both represent pyramid abstract art! At Newgrange, the crescent moon is cleverly wrapped around half of the world mother, represented by the mound, creating an interesting fusion. It is 3200 BC abstract art, to represent Moon and Earth in one body!

At Giza, we have another case of ancient 'modern art.' With a bit of hyperbole, we have three 'perfect' smooth and inaccessible monoliths sticking out of the desert, possibly a representation of previous structures, upon that sacred hill of Giza, but in a more modern and cohesive format, which would have been visually pleasing, and in a remarkable new fashion, to the Old-Kingdom kings, dreaming of a glorious future.

The Great Pyramid is essentially the Earth Mother which contains two tomb-like chambers, for male and female, god and consort, and possibly a third unfinished chamber below for a possible human burial (typically underneath a pyramid) which never took place.

Dr Robert Schoch has done a fairly noble job with his *Voyages of the Pyramid builders*, but one can still poke holes in the arguments therein, as one can here. Nevertheless, things are always difficult when one introduces a new theory. It is never perfect or right from the outset.

I feel that investigating links between pyramids, a subject perhaps introduced to a world-wide audience by Thor Heyerdahl with his re-constructed sea voyages in the 1950s and 60s, may one day become an emerging and exciting interdisciplinary field: 'pyramid studies'. This will one day hopefully be attached to a university's prehistory or an-thropology department. In the end we can acknowledge the difficulties in comparing things as widespread as pyramids. We can point out the similarities, as well as the differences.

Finally, here are some concluding remarks recapitulating some of what has been learned, and what may also be inferred, about the lost religion of the pyramid builders.

Bringing back the crops

Baldr needed to be weeped 'undead' in order to restore him to the gods, to make him a god again. The only way to do this, was Hel's test. Hel said that if every single person in heaven mourned Baldr, then he would be restored to the gods. Of course this means that the cosmic yearly cycle would come back and he would be reborn again.

This was necessary so he could be killed in the following year (winter time) and again and again. The loose Egyptian version of this god was Osiris, though Osiris also has a lot of Odin in him. Since the Egyptian king was often identified with Osiris, this could be why it was thought prudent to possibly put him in the pyramid, or nearby, to assist in helping Egypt. Students are taught in archaeology class that the king of Egypt would protect Egypt forever, if buried properly.

In order for the Gods to see 'Osiris' or 'Baldr', why not place him on top of the mountain? That is to say, why not make a huge ceremonial tomb (Medb's tomb near Sligo, for instance). Outside it you have the sacrificial altars. There could have been figures imitating Baldr. For instance, who were to be sacrificed. By placing everything in such a prominent location, all of heaven would see what is going on, on Earth, and remember.

Sky Father

Pyramids may well have arisen out of the sacred marriage consummated every year when the Sun hits a certain white pillar or rock, like at Stonehenge, the crushed altar stone representing perhaps the white Earth Mother, even if the civilisation which built them may have been a patriarchy, like the Mycenaeans, who also built mounds. This was part of the silly season games, the time of May, Robin Hood, the Bacchanalia, the Green Man festivals. It was a time of light and life, where the living went to the dead to thank them for being their ancestors. I think the white-light ceremony is part of the *inside-of-the-pyramid* ritual.

By burying the ritual area, or ritual cave, as at Silbury, Newgrange, (Stonehenge is like an unburied tomb with just the walls standing up), and elsewhere, particularly in Malta, with its Stonehenge-like tombs, as well as Potbelly Hill in Turkey, we have the situation of either an abandoning of an earlier religion, or simply an institutionalisation of the old religion. With the Gods established in their mound, it was now fitting to leave them alone, and let them work their magic for the future protection of the polity, kingdom or farming community. Long barrows also were covered up after the space of several generations.

The short answer for who the pyramid builders were is 'we don't know'. It is impossible to be really specific. The more specific we try to get, the more wrong we will be. A possible weakness in the argument presented in this work regarding Giza is that fourth-dynasty Giza seems a different culture to what is going on several centuries earlier at Saqqara, not too far away. That complex is strange, but not completely different from Giza. There are about six pyramids lined up in a curve. (a possible serpent of creation, or merely pyramids following the cliff face)

There even seems to be an altar in front of the large step pyramid of Djoser. We do not really see that at Giza. The style of Djoser's pyramid certainly reflects that of the Ziggurat to the east. Boat burials seem to have figured in Egypt since the first dynasty, however they seem to accelerate in importance with Khufu's several boat burials near his pyramid. At Saqqara there are first-dynasty boat burials in mastabas as well as a large boat burial near the 5th-dynasty pyramid of Unas. There is no (discovered) boat burial at Saqqara from the third dynasty, despite it being mainly a third-dynasty burial complex. (That indicates a possible different pyramid culture which I believe came in from the east (as opposed to west-origin pyramid builders).

It has been speculated before that the 3rd dynasty represented a more Sumerian-style rulership, with clear links to the culture of the east. In his *Voyages of the Pyramid builders*, Schoch considers that trade links are not enough to foster such religious changes in pyramid design, and that the pattern of the pyramid, in general, would be more likely altered by the migration of an elite to a new land. 3rd-dynasty people seem to have been less interested in the boat burial and therefore perhaps the sea voyage also. (The journey from the west is a possible sea voyage over the Mediterranean. The journey from the East is a meander along the fertile Crescent, then down through Palestine to Egypt, like Abraham's journey to Egypt, or via Arabia, which is less reliant upon shipping.). They were however interested in the pyramid.

There are also small 'cultic step pyramids' as they are described in the literature, with no burials or chambers. These were built by Huni of the third dynasty, and others, and are near various royal estates along the Nile. These perhaps were for fertility. Significantly, it is thought that these cultic step pyramids mark the transition between the third and fourth dynasties. Here is some evidence that the Egyptians built a mound for the sake of building a mound, rather than burial, and with small structures, as in Europe. The Giza pyramids, I would argue, are in part, the big versions.

The pyramid idea seems to have been one of the number-one projects of the proto-state. The amount of time and effort into building something like the Giza complex or Newgrange or one of the other mounded complexes shows a determination to have somewhere to pray to the gods. There needed to be a physical place where people could see evidence of the other worlds, above and below. Perhaps the flourishing geometry of the Egyptian mounds shows a great link between state and pyramid religion, which other peoples simply could not afford, though it is clear Newgrange was engineered on a huge scale. If they are harvest hills, as I would suggest, the three large Giza pyramids represent a development of them tied to elite interests of the state, moreso than elsewhere. One can climb the mounds in Europe. The once-smooth walls of the Giza pyramids told the masses, 'this is not for you. It is for Egypt, and for the everlasting glory of our kings.'

We still search for a unifying definition of what a pyramid actually *is*, a dangerous attempt perhaps, for we cross lines of culture and time, but not necessarily, I would argue, mythology. Clearly, a pyramid is more than a burial. Three pyramids of Giza, three mounds on top of Knocknarea, (2 destroyed) three mounds of Gamla Uppsala, Sweden, long argued by archaeologists to be natural formations, too big to be barrows, (yet containing some burial artefacts,) and certain other sites such as Newgrange where the number three figures strongly, with its three chambers, as at the Khufu pyramid.

These may be the triple goddess, the Earth Mother. These are Shakespeare's three witches, the weavers of men's fate. A pyramid in its primordial form seems to be a 'Michael's mount', that is a place where the cosmic serpent was banished, by the sky or weather god, 'Thor', and where he lies unto doomsday, whence he shall be unleashed. He is a consort of buried Loki. The mound itself is a pregnancy of the Earth, riding up to meet Sky Father.

In Germanic mythology the weather god Thor is a product of their union. He is a fertility god. Thor's slaying of the cosmic serpent is a metaphor for the banishing of winter, the unleashing of fertility forces. The pyramid itself is a metaphorical conduit, a place for the channelling of Thor's energy, the power he derives from the Earth, known as *jardarmegin*. The yearly ritual, its sacrifices which occur on the pyramid, or around it on a mountain top, all this, I would propose, is the primordial purpose of the pyramid. Stonehenge has a similar role. Sky Father and Earth Mother meet to presumably give birth to a new fertility god every year. True burials of kings and nobles of subsequent generations then take place around the central area, the pyramid, or perhaps stone circle. These burial-makers perhaps took advantage, spiritually, of the eternal regenerative forces of the central mound, or pyramid. These burials are much less venerated than the central area, less protected and less sacrosanct.

In conclusion, the pyramid, where it is to be found, is designed with several purposes in mind. These may lead us to an awareness of a new definition for what a pyramid actually *is*. It seems a pyramid may enshrine astronomical knowledge, as well as mythological ideas. In this it is a burial for gods. It symbolises the female water god, Sulis. It may contain an altar or have an altar adjacent. Then again, it may not. It may be associated with the triple deity, needing three springs to nourish them, and the world tree. It is associated with the religion of the serpent, the tree. It is also associated with Earth Mother and Sky father. We cannot name him. Zeus/Jupiter are not in the same league as Uranus, or Brahma/Svetovid. They may be different gods. Then again, ideas may not have always been so rigid as to not permit some sort of flexibility. Finally, the pyramid is also associated with the trickster, the horned one who can also fly away.

If one commands the position of the ground gods, one commands the sky god. The male sky god, sometimes female, is a natural consort of the mound. This would allow people to 'control' weather and the elements, at least bringing fertility to their region. It would also possibly demonstrate to the people that the king had control over the weather. In Norse mythology, Thor, the weather god is the product of the union of Earth Mother and Sky Father. This is perhaps why the pyramid needed to often be seen, hovering over a population centre. Unless we delve deeply into the mythological record, perhaps there is little more than we can ever hope to know.

'For good luck and fertility'

Now we come to ideas regarding Egypt. The idea of plundering a pyramid explains some of the 'curse of the pharaohs'. This was a fabulous curse, quite genuine, except for a bit about Anubis killing anyone who entered the tomb, perhaps tacked on to sell papers. The Egyptian pyramids seem to have been both tombs, as well as *something else.* That something else may have been monuments built for good luck, or wealth. We only need note that Khufu is remembered by Herodotus and others as having been an incredibly greedy man who even prostituted out his daughter for the sake of financing the pyramids. Yet, this grasping, greedy and cheap man built the grandest pyramid of the lot, perhaps spending everything he had! Why? To perhaps make more money? Or was it to perhaps leave a monument for Egypt which would endure forever, recreating the mythologies, the swollen womb of the Earth Mother, clothed in white tiles, the home of the imprisoned world serpent perhaps, home of the associated creator god. The perpetual consummation of the weather god, perhaps Khnum for Egypt, from the lineage of sky and Earth? We do not know for sure!

Speaking in general terms however, Giza in essence is built as a world centre, a fertility centre. The main builder, Khufu, would have had his burial there, as an honour, for having possibly conceived the idea, perhaps with his father, the great pyramid builder Sneferu. Giza is a home of the world tree, the Sycamore and Hathor, and various other mother goddesses such as the triple deity. This would be symbolised by the three pyramids representing the past, present and future of Egypt. From the perspective of being a fertility cult, we see it is built in a central location in Lower Egypt. Thus the Delta would effectively be fertilised by water flowing past and being blessed by it, and by the Great Pyramid, the womb of Egypt. In this respect, Giza is built in honour of Lower Egypt, early home of the pyramid builders in Egypt. As a centre of the world, creation flows from the Great Pyramid in all directions. It makes a fitting home, for Khufu's god, Khnum, in whose honour, in part, it may have been built.

Finale

This book has only scratched the surface of the pyramid enigma, but hopefully it may help to encourage further investigation, at least attempting to introduce the topic. Europe seems to have some of the oldest pyramids on Earth, if the reader has not minded me using that term. In Poland, Christians felt the need to suppress the cult a thousand years ago. At the periphery, in Ireland, aspects of the cult survive to this day. If the reader is interested in more pyramids, they are to be found everywhere, in perhaps every European country and almost every nation on Earth. I would recommend looking also into Etruscan mounds in Italy, as well as some strange step pyramids in Sicily, and on the Azores, as well as in the Pacific.

In summary, it would seem that we are unable to truly reconcile mythology with ancient ritual. The peoples living with the current European pyramids, literally in their backyards in some cases, do not necessarily have descendants who are native to the area. This is more the case in centrally located nations like Poland and Germany, but less the case in Ireland, where ridiculously old folk traditions have been preserved in some form until present times.

The tree is also a gateway to the underworld, the region under the mountain. The sacred tree upon which wishes are attached is in part feeding off the life below. This was perhaps a worldwide religion at an early stage, though obviously there were still huge differences between each culture who worshipped at pyramids, perhaps similar to different churches or other temples existing in different countries today. As pointed out in Schoch's book, there are so many similarities. The snake guards the entrance to the 2nd level of the underworld in both Mayan and Egyptian traditions, for instance.

One of the most striking results to come out of the investigation of mounds in Europe is the that the larger mounds are generally for fertility. The smaller ones are for human burial. It may be little different in Egypt, where the Giza pyramids have presented a curious enigma for investigators for quite some time. Most, or all true pyramids seem to be fertility mounds, or harvest hills to use another term, even if they may also have been used as tombs for certain kings. They are tombs for fertility gods wherever it seems, they are to be found. It seems that certain pyramids have also been used as places of ritual and sacrifice to the fertility gods, with altars set up nearby. The Great Pyramid is possibly built for Osiris, and possibly even for Khnum (both fertility deities), perhaps as much as it is a monument for Khufu. It represents the world mountain, Earth, the *Axis Mundi* of Egypt itself, and a home for the gods.

Back in the old days there is usually just one afterlife. Either one's soul is instantly destroyed by the crocodile, or one continues to endure. We are on the cusp of uncovering details of an incredibly old religion, but the details are complex and uncertain. The crocodile may be related to the river Green Man, or even the snake of Eden or Midgard serpent. He is a kind of judge of souls. This makes sense since the snake of the mound religion guards the Yggdrasil which is placed on top of various mounds. It is the tree at the top of the pyramid which is the gateway to the afterlife. The river itself or nearby water seems indelibly linked to the pyramid and to the cycle of rebirth. The 'moat' around Silbury Hill might remind one of the waters of Charon. One must cross them to reach the afterlife, or Avalon.

We come to the name of the pyramid itself. For the Greeks it was, seemingly, 'fire in the middle'. In Europe one of the names is 'Hel'. In *The Cerne Giant*, Rodney Castleden points out the similarity of Heoloth (hell) and Helig (holy). This means basically that the tree on the pyramid is like an entrance to hell, or the 'holy' afterlife. When the Christian religion arrived, notions of damnation may have become associated with the hel ('holy' afterlife) of the old religion. In Germany I was taken down a ceremonial road called the 'hellweg', or Holy way. The hellweg was really part of a huge northern trade route stretching up to Moscow. Going through Dortmund it passes in between two Charlemagne churches. It is a kind of symbolic gateway. But where is the hill? Where is Hel itself that it leads to? Perhaps it is at nearby Hohensyburg. Perhaps it is another strange structure, waiting to be uncovered.

Certain central mounds and cairns of Europe, surrounded by burials, but not containing a burial themselves, should perhaps be 'reclassified.' It has become apparent that these tumuli or large cairns are not for burials of humans, but burials of gods. As above, so below. They are a home for the fertility gods who gave life to mankind. By placing burials nearby, man can enjoy eternal life, and the country can enjoy eternal fertility. There are no burials at Stonehenge (another tomb for the gods), no burials on the Krakus Mound, none in Silbury hill, yet all are surrounded by very real burials. People simply wanted to be close to god in the afterlife, close to the triple goddess and her entourage, the wells and world tree from whence fertility and life eternal would spring. A pyramid is also a place which is the artificial centre of the universe, brought closer to man by sympathetic magic. I cannot help but feel that 'pyramid' is perhaps most appropriate a name to give these large structures, designed to bring man closer to the gods. That term would highlight a certain pedigree between traditions and cultures once affected by the bearers of the old religion, across Asia and perhaps into Africa, at some scattered time in their history.

On the one hand the pyramids aim towards memorialising the ancestors. On the other hand they are renewal machines, and as such, 'good-luck' devices, rather than simple tombs or memorials (small barrows or cairns). They are the meeting place of Mother Earth and Father Sky, and they are associated with being a gateway to the afterlife. Their associated sacred festival-times later became church or neo-pagan holidays. There was 'May Day', and also the 'Halloween'. During such magical times, particularly associated with the changing of a season, the barrier to the other world broke down and people could ascend the hill towards the sacred mound. This was the place where they could bring their animals for sacrifice, and drink *soma* while perhaps being lectured and chanted at by a shaman wearing a horse's head or maybe even the very heavy golden 'wizard hats' such as that found in Germany, and dating to around 900 BC.

The pyramids themselves memorialise not any particular god, but the Stone-Age stories themselves, upon which gods could be superimposed. The story of the clash of the gods, geological and weather forces, perhaps became an early basis for the pantheon. The gods cannot be separated from each other due to the story of creation, involving many gods. The pyramid gives power and position to all the gods, who are locked together in a mythological association. These are the gods of the underworld, as well as the gods who drove them there.

Research can go on and on, but somewhere it has to end, and I think this book is big enough. It is time to define what it was all about. A pyramid may or may not have been a burial. The death of the Pharaoh was but an opportunity to build a pyramid. In the case of the Old Kingdom, he was a dead Horus, about to become Osiris, the resurrection god. Every time a resurrection god dies, there needs to be a new mountain to build a tomb upon, for his resurrection to take place, at least in the case of Ancient Ireland. In Egypt, pyramids were required to replace mountains. The fact so many pyramids and mounds built elsewhere were empty shows that pyramids could be built even without dead kings and Pharaohs. The resurrection god is always active.

Above all, a pyramid, or central large mound, was a place built for the resurrection of the gods who leave every winter, leaving the Earth a cold shell of its former glory. The reason, they could not fathom. The Sun, associated partly with dead Baldr in the mound, needed to return. By building him a home, his return was assured. The gods were honoured. There was now a tangible substance to the mythology. The old mythology was now enshrined into society. With more sympathetic magic, the king, perhaps buried nearby in a large mound, could take advantage of this cosmic resurrection, arising from the primary mound. This ensured his own afterlife and resurrection into a good version of the afterlife.

As well as being a representation of the underworld, perhaps for what lay underneath, with all its evil aspects like the Norns, Loki, Hel, the serpent, the wolf, the mound also, with its lofty height, was a pregnancy of mother Earth. The union of Father Sky and Earth gave birth to a son, Thor, the weather god. He could deliver fertility to the Earth. In an Egyptian version, Osiris the Earth god fertilised an Earth Mother, Isis. The child was Horus, sky god. Isis, a kind of Earth Mother, gave birth to Horus, the sky god. This creation occurred at Giza, next to the Great Pyramid, where the temple of Isis was later situated, to venerate the idea. Khufu, as pointed out by Herodotus, was buried nearby, along with many other people.

Here, upon the Giza plateau, was possibly the temple of the Triple Goddess, of life, death and rebirth, the premier life force of the Stone Age, together with her faithful hound, which would become known as the Sphinx. These possibly became known as Joseph's Granaries, from some vague memory of fertility as well as the huge food production, once required for the workers.

Rain, symbol of fertility also noticeably forms over mountains. They are holy places. The pyramid as mountain representation was a home for a collection of gods associated with creation stories. These gods were always actively re-creating initial creation, thus unavoidably re-fertilising the land and soil around the pyramid, and of which it was composed, in an infinite cycle.

Pyramids were quite huge. They needed to be, if they were a home for gods, who were certainly a lot bigger than the giants of old. The religion of the third millennium BC was interested in representing an underworld, on Earth. The pyramid represented mythology, and part of this other world. It was a gateway sticking up above Midgard, rising up to Asgard, but being built out of fragments of the fiery underworld below, a skewer between the worlds. With its lofty slopes, the pyramid was a nice place to visit. It was the great Babel, a place where people could ascend to heaven, without leaving Earth. Here they could exist at the horizon and at the periphery, as they conceived it, of space and time.

Appendix A

Pharaoh of *Exodus*

An interesting idea pops up from a reading of Manetho, an Egyptian historian who wrote in Greek during the Ptolemaic era. He mentioned that Khufu was also called 'Peroptes.' This may well be a Greco-Egyptian corruption of something similar to 'pharaoh,' which is also a Greco-Egyptian corruption of an Egyptian word or name. With his supposedly long reign and with other later ideas of oppression it is interesting that Khufu should not show up in the book of *Genesis*.

In the context of this book, I have mentioned that we have a king, Khufu, (with himself or his father Sneferu as a founder of the fourth dynasty) who came along, seemingly overturning existing ideas, being remembered as 'wicked' and engaging in all sorts of blasphemy against existing Egyptian gods, according to Herodotus. (Zahi Hawass also discusses Khufu's monotheism, in a 1990 work, claiming Khufu saw himself as a solar deity, a very reasonable and traditional argument. I believe however, that Khufu may simply have been of a different religion, as he represented a new dynasty and culture, rather than simply an exponent of influence and power of the priesthood of Heliopolis, city of the Sun, versus the cult of Ptah at Memphis.)

This may represent a migration into Egypt of a new culture of pyramid building, that of smooth sided pyramids, possibly, I would speculate, based upon the turf mounds of Eurasia. Notably, the previous form of pyramid, of the third dynasty, was a very Middle-Eastern style indeed, and may have been inspired by people that I can describe as proto-Jews, later perhaps remembered or conflated with a migration of Abraham, even if they themselves did not identify as such, in their own time. These were men who built with mud-brick shaped small stones.

Fourth dynasty architecture however, is certainly more 'Cyclopean.' They used much larger stones and Cyclopean architecture, wherever it occurred in the ancient world, continues to baffle and inspire.

With the coming of Khufu's dynasty, the 3rd dynasty builders may have had their knowledge utilised and enhanced, combining with another type. Furthermore, some may have been enslaved under a new regime, who totally overhauled the religion of the Giza plateau, possibly incorporating, for the first time, solstice and equinox properties into their final construction. (which were sacred to the builders of the megalithic civilisation of Western Europe) In later times stories about this era, in Egypt, may have become conflated with later legends originating from the actions of someone around the time of Ramses the Great, about fifteen hundred years later, who is said to have enslaved the Jews.

Exodus itself may have been formed out of various earlier ideas with the story assembled in later times based upon what was remembered or what survived, from any previous era. Oral legends and myths, upon which Exodus is based, are not historical and should never be treated as such. They are conflated myths based upon whatever was popular and whatever was demanded to be retold, conveniently sorted into a story which was easy to retell, as it dealt with an idea that held with the public imagination.

As a fascinating postscript to this idea, just prior to publication, one may note that the *Koran* places the time of the building of something resembling the tower of Babel, in the age of Moses. Furthermore, it claims that someone who was close to Pharaoh was called 'Haman.' God sent Moses to try and invite Pharaoh and Haman into monotheism but they rejected this call. (Here we have a possible memory of an idea the Egyptians told Herodotus, with Khufu as some kind of a heretic) They furthermore refused to let the Children of Israel go free. Interestingly, the historical name of Khufu's vizier and architect, was Hemon, or Hemiunu. Hamon was commissioned, in the story, to build a tall tower of burnt bricks, for Pharaoh to climb up, to talk to the God of Moses.

In other words, the legends about (possibly) Khufu, or his vizier (now no longer extant) were sufficiently interesting and similar to other stories, to possibly involve themselves into early versions of what would influence Biblical idea.

If we then consider that the collapse of the fourth or fifth dynasty resulted in such works as the *Admonitions of Ipuwer*, supposedly stories about the First Intermediate period, which people agree seem to strongly resemble the story of the Plagues of Egypt, in which time the 'oppressed' may have been released and Giza was certainly ransacked, (Temple speculates the Anubis face of the Sphinx was damaged in this time, resulting in a later re-carving in the Middle Kingdom, when prosperity returned) then we have the basis for an idea that earlier versions of the story of Exodus were perhaps based around an earlier historically-inclined template which was formulated as early as the Egyptian Middle Kingdom. This would have been based upon Old Kingdom and later events, which involved tales of oppression by an alternate form of pyramid-building heretics.

This template would then have been contaminated by later historical events, and subsequent written stories which incorporated the finer aspects of both events, as if they had occurred at the one time and place, resulting in *Exodus*, as we now know it.

Appendix B

Differences between 3rd- and 4th-dynasty pyramids

Further to the previous statements, we can consider the analysis of Kurt Mendelssohn, 1974, who somewhat counters the usual idea that there is a clear evolution in pyramid design, within Egypt, which explains all apparent paradoxes. (That is, there is a desire to increase the size of the pyramid, and then reduce it, across the dynasties, without resorting to arguments regarding foreign invasion) He wrote that 'the drastic change of the monument's shape and the equally novel conception underlying the layout and character of the whole pyramid complex indicate some profound alteration in the beliefs concerning the pharaoh's afterlife.'

He seems correct in this. The 4th-dynasty pyramid, though it followed directly after 3rd-dynasty attempts, was no longer stepped, possibly not made up out of buttresses, but built of huge blocks, and now smoothly faced, in the era of Sneferu. There was also a huge change in funerary practice. The wall around the pyramid became more token, rather than an imitation of a huge palace, as with Djoser's complex. Furthermore, instead of burying the king in a shaft in front of the pyramid, as in the case of Djoser, there was now a passage of about twenty eight degrees, an entrance to the underneath of the pyramid, which pointed up towards the north pole. This was a way of centring the pyramid to the north pole. It is a change in funerary custom. Instead of having many recesses filled with old pottery, there is none of this. Furthermore, an alignment of a sacred monument to the north pole is central to the incredibly widespread proto Indo-Germanic tradition of *Axis Mundi*. Djoser's pyramid complex is somewhat like a huge mastaba with central mound. The fourth dynasty pyramids seem like something very different indeed, a new religious practice partly derived from within but also from without.

Dr Leon Stover, writes in *Stonehenge City*, 2003, that archaeologists are not always aware of just how conservative funerary customs can be. A shift in customs generally indicates a different culture has arrived on the scene. In this case archaeologists are cautious due to the lack of evidence of invasion. Where are the weapons? Everyone seems to have been at peace. I would conjecture that what one might like to call a 'fourth-dynasty pyramid shift' is based upon the gradual and peaceful influx (during the third dynasty?) of a neighbouring pyramid-building culture, possibly from Europe (*cf.* Silbury Hill, Newgrange), or Libya, who desired the building of smooth-sided mounds, as found there, but employing existing stone technologies found in Egypt, combining them with some 'Cyclopean' ones of their own. (They may have been a re-invasion of the so-called 'dynastic race' which earlier helped found Egypt, by contributing various ideas or technologies, as well as population)

The subsequent (hypothetical) takeover by a new culture, in the 4th dynasty, while having, and continuing to coexist and mix with the natives, forged a new pyramid culture unique to Egypt. (These rulers eventually were remembered as having oppressed the natives and their gods) On the other hand, the contemporary nature of Silbury Hill with the Old Kingdom might indicate a recent common ancestry with Asian nomads, having swept across Europe, and also into Egypt, though more peacefully, in that location.

This hypothesis of various pyramid cultures infiltrating Egypt provides a sort of resolution to the eternal question many seem to ask: 'why did Egyptian civilisation appear from nowhere?' It appeared in part, because it was brought there, having spent part of its long evolution elsewhere. It then combined with existing Egyptian pyramid traditions. There is merit here as it is known that people were building variants on the huge-pyramid design outside of Egypt at the same time as the Egyptian pyramids were going up. Egypt was a place where a large population of quality workers was assured and where strong invading pyramid cultures could combine and develop their ideas, in a unique way, creating a unique civilisation, with peaceful formerly-nomadic invaders rapidly adopting Egyptian ways, having recognised themselves to be in the presence of a more exciting and older intellectual and civic culture, to that which they had been accustomed.

Appendix C

The Narmer palette and two pyramid cultures in Egypt

Further to the idea that the fourth dynasty seems to have represented a different culture to the third is that Egypt shows a mixing, sometimes violent, of various (pyramid) cultures in very early times, despite assertions that Egypt was not particularly warlike at this time. Egypt seems not to have had a warrior-type society. Grave goods are always civic rather than warlike. This may however reflect the Egyptian religion of wanting a pleasant civic afterlife, rather than a strife-filled one.

The famous Narmer cosmetic palette of about 3000 BC seems to show what may be Semites or Easterners, probably in Egypt itself, being 'smited' by a large figure, probably Narmer, or Mernar, as he may also have been called. Narmer himself has similar facial characteristics to the sandal bearer following close behind. Both the Semites as well as the other Egyptians, either of whom may have been variants upon the 'dynastic race' lived in Egypt since early times. In light of this, what does 'Egyptian' actually mean? Both may have been mound builders, forming a unique fusion of their own pyramid style, as the cultures mixed. The Narmer tablet shows that the mixing was not always pleasant.

It would be wrong to say categorically that the easterners would have been step pyramid builders, with westerners as smooth pyramid builders. Looking at Silbury Hill in England, we have a stepped mound, smoothed over with turf, just as the Great Pyramid and other edifices were stepped, with possible internal buttresses, which would have given the appearance of the Djoser step pyramid. Such structures were then smoothed over with casing stones. In the North East we may have had Kurgan burials, smooth mounds, but also to the east we had the stepped Ziggurats of Sumer. What occurred in Egypt is a result of a complex set of mixings of various ideas, which took on a direction of their own.

The Narmer palette relief, from the beginning of Egyptian history, seems to indicate the presence of two cultures, Egyptians and Semites, both of whom, we know built mounds and pyramids, from the earliest of times, in different geographical locations.

Appendix D

The Meidum Pyramid and the Tower of Babel

One of Kurt Mendelssohn's theories in *The Riddle of the Pyramids*, 1974 was that as a pyramid neared completion, the required numbers of workers would drop off. Instead of laying them off, it would have been more viable to have put them to work on another pyramid, explaining why Sneferu, first king of the Fourth Dynasty seems to have built three pyramids. (and was buried in not one of them!)

Mendelssohn introduces the supporting idea that Sneferu's first pyramid, at Meidum collapsed during construction, resulting in its abandonment. This is why, he explains, the Bent Pyramid of Dashur, the next to have been built, changes in angle from $pi/4$ to $pi/3$. It was thought safer to change the angle, as the outer casings of the previous pyramid had allegedly collapsed.

The subsequent Dashur pyramid possesses a curious bend in it, and so is also known as the 'Bent Pyramid.' Prior to the publication of Mendelssohn's book, a prevailing idea was that the builders had simply changed their mind, switching to a more shallow angle, to save time, in completing the top of the monument.

A more recent idea is that the pyramid itself may have collapsed much later on. It has occurred to me that this could be a reason why the Tower of Babel story was transformed in Biblical text.

For instance, the Tower of Babel story of Genesis (memories of Bronze-Age days, but written in the Iron Age) does not tell us that the tower collapsed. Instead, its building resulted in the mixing up of languages and the scattering of peoples. The 'later' *Book of Jubilees*, (10:18-27) says it was overturned with a great wind.

Later Egyptian dynasties reflecting upon past glory were rather sure of themselves in their cost-cutting efforts, and built rather poor-quality now-collapsed pyramids, such as the partially-ruined fifth dynasty pyramids, and the even worse Middle Kingdom mud brick pyramids, which are in even worse condition, and almost look like natural sand dunes on a rocky outcrop.

The *Midrash* seems closest in its description of Babel, to the Meidum pyramid. We are entering the realm of speculation here, but it is the buttressed core of the Meidum pyramid which remains standing. The casing stones have largely all fallen off. The Midrash claims that the top of the tower was burned, the bottom swallowed, and the middle left to slowly erode. That could refer, however, to any ruin. In the Meidum pyramid, the top was never finished, and the bottom was at least 'swallowed' by surrounding debris and what is possibly the original rubble ramp.

Recalling that the Jews in part came out of Egypt, it is perhaps in response to such ruins, as well as in response to the much larger collapsed Meidum pyramid, that the writers of the story of Babel found some inspiration, even if that story may be mixed in with ideas of another location in Mesopotamia, or another derived from elsewhere.

Appendix E

'The Great Smoothing'

The Meidum pyramid smoothing, seems to mark a cultural transition. The first of Sneferu's pyramids, it marked the first pyramid of the Fourth dynasty. It was larger than anything which had preceded it.

There is some evidence that the casing stones on this collapsed pyramid, employed for the first time, on such a huge scale, were not part of the original design. Kurt Mendelssohn pointed out that the pyramid was made up of two internal layers of buttressing. These already took up all the available bedrock foundation.

The external casing stones were to a large extent placed upon unsteady sand. In other words, this would seem to be a circumvention of architectural advice and building knowledge, possibly a tyrannical order from above. The pyramid had already been designed to maximum size, based upon the Djoser step format, when it was decided to tamper with the initial design, during building.

It is clear that a stepped structure is a platform. A smooth structure is far more like a natural hill or mountain and may have been more sacred to adherents of the mountain religion. There may have been a strong desire, therefore to create a smooth structure, where hitherto a stepped structure had been seen as adequate. This smooth structure, even if it was an abstracted type of hill with four sides, was seen as a better one.

The pyramid may not be entirely Sneferu's. For a long time, it was thought that the pyramid had belonged to Huni. In addition, Robert Schoch suggests interior components of various Old Kingdom pyramids may be older.

To be critical, the smoothing may not necessarily have been a result of cultural change but the desire to make a gnomon, easier to use for possible astronomical purposes.

Appendix F

Axis Mundi and the Olmecs

In an excellent book, *The Olmecs*, it is the opinion of author Jacques Soustelle, that the famous Olmec heads represent the features of native Americans who still reside in the vicinity of the old Olmec heartland, a swampy region of Mexico, to the west of the Maya areas.

The Olmecs were the first great civilisation of Mesoamerica. Like the Old-Kingdom Egyptians who influenced thousands of years of subsequent Egyptian culture, the bizarre (creepy) artistic style, number system and other ideas of the later-forgotten Olmec culture would continue to inspire all subsequent civilisations. The Teotihuacan pyramids seem to be representative of a very late Olmec culture, also known as Totonac, which may be a more appropriate name for the Olmecs. Aztecs remembered the builders as the 'Toltecs,' (perhaps having confused them, over the generations with the Totonacs?) and recalled with great admiration that they could built anything they wished.

Although archaeology does not really bear out the Aztec praise of the Toltecs as supreme artificers, their praise would certainly apply to the Olmec civilisation.

An early structure built by the Olmecs was nothing less than an artificial plateau, fifty metres in height, at San Lorenzo, and built in about the second millennium BC. It is 1.2 km in length. This monumental undertaking astonishes any archaeologist who writes about it. There are rectangular courts and pyramid-like structures on top. There is a huge system of underground tunnels (naturally, these always

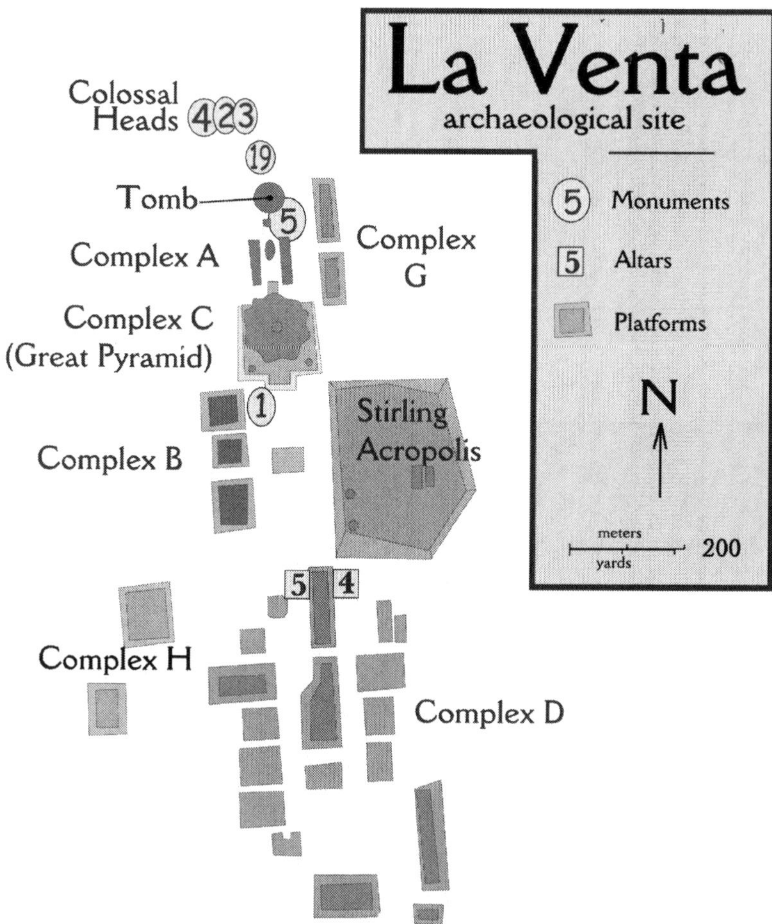

Figure F.1: This is a diagram of the complex at La Venta. The artificial volcano is marked out as Complex C.

show up in Axis Mundi sites!) built of basalt, underneath the plateau which have an unknown purpose. Soustelle suggests these could be for drainage.

Another of the Olmecs' earlier religious structures was nothing less than what appears to be a conical pyramid, designed to look like an artificial volcano, at the plateau of La Venta. La Venta has *Axis Mundi* properties. It is a raised pyramid complex on a plateau with a north-south alignment. In addition the complex is aligned to north. It is off true north by seven to eight degrees.

I would suggest the artificial volcano is something to do with a veneration for a fire god. Soustelle suggests there may be an agricultural purpose as well. One of the most fascinating Olmec offerings is called 'Offering No. 4.' This is a set of statuette figures facing a red statue. They seem to be all facing some standing stones, perhaps what in Germanic parlance would be called a *thinge* assembly. The lead statue, who may be the fire god, is made up of red granite. The addressees are jade and blue serpentine. It may be sympathetic magic, to show that humans listen and obey, or it may mean nothing. All the figures exhibit cranial deformation.

Although the Olmecs were certainly Native American, the definition of what this actually constitutes is certainly up in the air. The fact the Olmecs seem to have had their own version of the Axis Mundi pyramid religion makes it seem that they are based upon a recent cultural import from the Old World. That is why the Olmecs, perhaps like the Old Kingdom Egyptians 'appeared from nowhere.' On the one hand the large Olmec heads appear Chinese, or Khmer, or Filipino. (I have a Thai friend whose features greatly resemble one of these heads).

There is another type of Olmec figure that Soustelle describes as 'Uncle Sam.' This character certainly resembles a Caucasian and may be based upon stories of the Viracocha, or such people alive in America at that time. We may well be dealing with aspects of the possible Clovis migration from Spain, or a later people. The Uncle Sam images however are in the minority. (It is also pointed out by Schoch that the Teotihuacan pyramids are rather Chinese in their appearance, emphasising horizontal attributes) It is certainly the Mongolian type which predominates in the Olmec culture.

One fascinating link to Ireland, in particular Navan Fort, is the wedding-cake style soil offerings that the Olmecs made, with what is known in the Olmec literature as their 'mass offerings.' These feature at La Venta. These were a landscaped underground. In addition layers of various types and colours of clay were added, sculpting the underground as it were. A trench was dug, eight metres deep and seventeen across, twenty metres long. This was filled with 1000 tons of serpentine, a semi-precious stone treasured by the Olmecs. Huge serpentine mosaics of bizarre masks were constructed, five by seven metres, and immediately buried. One thing in common with the Egyptian 3rd dynasty, was the fact there were mass offerings of bowls, as well as other objects, such as fine mirrors, though there is certainly no link with Egypt. There may of course however have been a very distant common ancestry between various elements of these two peoples. (This ancestry relates to whichever set of cultures brought the *Axis Mundi* religion to Mesoamerica, possibly from both east and west)

The recipient, I believe, of all this ostentation, would have been the fire god, or Earth Mother. The purpose, as in the purpose of pyramids elsewhere, would have probably been agricultural.

Appendix G

The decline of pyramid building and Old Europe

Naturally the points and conclusions raised in this work have implications for datings regarding what was going on nearby, in a religious sense, at about the same time.

With Giza possibly as a vast temple for the Great goddess, in her last and most glorious incarnation, it becomes rather clear that Giza was built in the very final days of the worship of the Great Goddess, in Old Europe (the Balkans area), a stone's throw away from the delta. The worship of the Old Europe goddesses, perhaps reflected by similar deities in Egypt, had been built up over a period of 20,000 years. The implication is that goddess worship on the Giza plateau was incredibly ancient, existing long before the pyramids were built, as a final, possibly desperate reflection of her cult. Giza's ultimate development was not the beginning of her cult. It was the end, to be replaced with Isis worship. The ideas behind the building of Giza, recorded in yellowing and fragmenting pages, were distorted from the religious and historical record, long before the writing of the book that we know of as the Bible.

The great time of pyramid building, at least in the Old World, and in some respects elsewhere, corresponds to the third millennium BC. After this we have a new religion. The correspondence between the decline of pyramid building and the decline of the matriarchal culture of Gimbutas' Old European Civilisation, ending, she states, in 2500 BC, is an eerie parallel with Giza.

The book *Goddesses and Gods of Old Europe*, replaced the older edition, *Gods and Goddesses of Old Europe*, to emphasise the primacy of the goddess. (Various idols are masked, like Egyptian gods) Gimbutas' dates for the main period of the idols she discusses are 6500-3500 BC, a little early for Giza. The preface to the revised edition of Gimbutas' book, reveals the rationale for this. That former date is not a terminus, but a compromise between the start and end of the decline: 4500-2500 BC, brought about by waves of invaders. Gimbutas talks of a patriarchal society gradually overwhelming a sophisticated matriarchal society (Old Europe), of equivalent sophistication to cultures of the Near East, in this time.

I have no idea of whether the Indo-Europeans, a difficult and controversial enough topic, which Gimbutas refer to as a patriarchal people, may be equated in general terms with the Indo-Europeans, proto-Indo-Europeans or Indo-Germanics, I discuss in this book. I am merely taking about old inhabitants of Eurasia with a similar religion, over a very wide geographical area. Gimbutas suggests a conflation between the patriarchy of the invading Indo-Europeans after 2500 BC, and the previous culture, which clouds the issue of who worshipped what. I do not really make much distinction in this particular work, throwing the whole mass under the loose categories of Indo-Germanic or proto-Indo-European. I suspect, as many do, that the ancients were rather more flexible than many moderns will allow, with neither culture exclusively patriarchal or matriarchal. Reality is unavoidably complex.

The matriarchal society, Gimbutas argues, becoming extinct in Europe, resisted on the periphery, Greece, and in the Minoan empire, during the third millennium BC. The civilised survivors were the exponents, in their society, of a much earlier Stone-Age cultural pattern, becoming extinct elsewhere. I would add that it also survived a stone's throw away, in Egypt, declining rapidly in the later fourth, and even fifth dynasty, and perhaps largely nullified during the first intermediate period. Khufu may have been its greatest final champion. Elsewhere, in Greece, the Acropolis area, with its Caryatid females, was possibly Athens' version of the Giza plateau, updated with new temples in the Iron Age, towards the classical era.

The need for sharp corners at Giza may have been due to astronomical considerations and the drying of the Sahara, when the Sun possibly took over from the thunder god, as premier sky deity.

The pyramids which follow on after the decline of goddess worship, in the Middle Kingdom, are vague and slipshod imitations of what preceded them, by a people with slightly different religious views, attitudes and goals. Their re-carving of the Sphinx in a possible female form (as discussed, its later name was something similar to Hermes Trismegistus) was an expression of their understanding of earlier times. They were aware of their inheritance of a great legacy, and not too keen to disturb its enduring pattern, possibly re-interpreting pyramids within their own ideology, and for their own use.

Picture Credits

Cover (photograph used in composite): *Sun Over Pyramid* (http://commons.wikimedia.org/wiki/File:Sun_Over _Pyramid.jpg), A. Parrot, 2009. Licensed under Creative Commons Attribution–Share Alike 3.0 Unported licence.

Fig. 1.50: *The Cerne Abbas Giant* (http://commons .wikimedia.org/wiki/File:The_Cerne_Abbas_Giant_-_012.jpg), Peteharlow, 2001. Licensed under Creative Commons Attribution– Share Alike 3.0 Unported licence.

Fig. 5.13: *Mod. Bronzo nuraghe quadrilobato* (http://commons.wikimedia.org/wiki/File:Mod. _Bronzo_nuraghe_quadrilobato.gif), Shardan, 2008. Licensed under Creative Commons Attribution–Share Alike 3.0 Unported licence.

Fig. 4.22: *The Mount (Calvary)* (http://commons.wikimedia.org/ wiki/File:The_Mount_%28Calvary%29_-_geograph.org.uk_- _254994.jpg), Simon Carey, 2006. Licensed under Creative Commons Attribution–Share Alike 2.0 licence.

Fig. 5.4: *Pyramide von Hellinikon* (http://commons.wikimedia .org/wiki/File:Pyramide_von_Hellinikon.jpg), Schuppi, 2006. Licensed under Creative Commons Attribution–Share Alike 2.5 Generic licence.

Fig. 5.2: *Treasure of Atreus* (http://commons.wikimedia.org/ wiki/File:Treasure_of_Atreus.jpg), Atelier Joly, 2004. Licensed under Creative Commons Attribution-Share Alike 3.0 Unported licence.

Fig. 5.3: *The Treasury of Atreus* (http://commons.wikimedia .org/wiki/File:Treasury_Atreus.jpg), Carlos M Prieto, 2006.

Licensed under Creative Commons Attribution 2.0 Generic licence.

Fig. 5.14: *Altare prenuragico di Monte D' Accoddi (Sassari, Sardegna)* (http://commons.wikimedia.org/wiki/ File:Monted%27accoddisardegna.png), Gianf84, 2008. Licensed under Creative Commons Attribution 2.5 Generic licence.

Fig. 5.16: *The Circular Mound* (http://commons.wikimedia.org/ wiki/File:CircularMound.jpg), Ian and Wendy Sewell, 2007. Licensed under Creative Commons Attribution-Share Alike 2.5 Generic licence.

Fig. 6.5: *Göbekli Tepe, Siedlungshügel bei Şanlıurfa, Südost-türkei, Hauptgrabungsfeld von Norden* (http://commons .wikimedia.org/wiki/File:Göbekli2012-17.jpg), Klaus-Peter Simon, 2012. Licensed under Creative Commons Attribution-Share Alike 3.0 Unported licence.

Fig. 6.9: *Vue générale du mastaba de Ptahchepsès—Abousir* (http://commons.wikimedia.org/wiki/File:Ptahchepses12.JPG), Kurohito, 2010. Licensed under Creative Commons Attribution–Share Alike 3.0 Unported licence.

Fig. 5.8: *De Grote Galerij in de Piramide van Cheops* (http://commons.wikimedia.org/wiki/File:Cheops_grote_ gallerij.jpg), Peter Prevos, 2005. Licensed under Creative Commons Attribution–Share Alike 3.0 Unported licence.

Fig. 6.22: *Gott Chnum modelliert Ihy, Göttin Heket, Mamisi (Geburtstempel), Hathortempel, Dendara, Ägypten* (http://commons.wikimedia.org/wiki/File:DendaraMamisi Khnum-10.jpg), Roland Unger, 2000. Licensed under Creative Commons Attribution–Share Alike 3.0 Unported licence.

Fig. F.1: *La Venta site plan* (http://commons.wikimedia.org/ wiki/File:La_Venta_site_plan.png), MapMaster and Yavi-daxiu, 2006. Licensed under Creative Commons Attribution–Share Alike 3.0 Unported licence.

Creative Commons license deeds for the above works are available in full at http://creativecommons.org/licenses/

Bibliography

This bibliography contains a broad sway of books, as well as a few papers, which have inspired, entertained, and shaped various ideas. All of them have helped in some way. Some have helped far more than others. Some are directly related to the topics of the book—others only tangentially. They deal with topics from ancient Indo-European peoples, survivals in the modern world, to pyramids and ancient monuments themselves. They are either very conservative, or in other cases they are prepared to take a less orthodox view, pushing hard at the boundaries, sometimes breaking them.

Alessandro Achilli *et al*, 'Saami and Berbers—An Unexpected Mitochondrial DNA Link,' *American Journal of Human Genetics*, 76: 883–6, 2005.

Cyril Aldred, *Egypt to the end of the Old Kingdom*, McGraw-Hill, 1965.

Mark Baillie, *Exodus to Arthur*, Batsford, 1999.

Claudio Barocas, *Monuments of civilisation: Egypt*, The Reader's Digest, 1979.

A. L. Basham, *The Wonder that was India*, Fontana, 1971.

Robert Bauval & Adrian Gilbert, *The Orion Mystery*, Broadway Books, 1995.

Oric Bates, *The Eastern Libyans*, Macmillan, 1914.

Stefan Bergh, 'Knocknarea: the ultimate monument', in *Monuments and Landscape in Atlantic Europe: Perception and Society During the Neolithic and Early Bronze Age*, Christopher Scarre (ed.), Routledge, 2005.

Geoffrey Bibby, *Looking for Dilmun*, Alfred A. Knopf, 1969.

Aleister Blackwell (ed.), *Ancient Egyptian Spells not to try at home*, Plus Ultra Books, 2015.

Janet & Colin Bord, *Mysterious Britain*, The Garnstone Press, 1972.

Janet & Colin Bord, *More Mysterious Britain*, Paul Elek Ltd, 1976.

Janet & Colin Bord, *The Enchanted Land*, Thorsons, 1995.

Brian Branston, *The Lost Gods of England*, Thames and Hudson, 1957.

James Henry Breasted, *Ancient Records of Egypt: The First Through the Seventeenth Dynasties*, University of Illinois Press, 2001.

Martin Brennan, *The Stones of Time: Calendars, Sundials and Stone Chambers of Ancient Ireland*, Inner traditions, 1994.

William J. Broad, *The Oracle*, The Penguin Press, 2006.

Peter Lancaster Brown, *Megaliths and Masterminds*, Charles Scribner's Sons, 1979.

Marie-Louise Buhl, 'The Goddesses of the Egyptian Tree Cult', *Journal of Near Eastern Studies*, 6:2, 80-97, Apr., 1947.

Andrzej Buku, *The Archaeology of Early Medieval Poland*, Brill, 2008.

Wallis Budge, *Egyptian Magic*, Arkana, 1988.

Wallis Budge, *Egyptian Religion*, Bell Publishers, 1959.

Wallis Budge, *An Egyptian Hieroglyphic Dictionary*, 2 vols, Dover, 1978.

Wallis Budge, *The Gods of the Egyptians*, 2 vols, Dover, 1969.

Aubrey Burl, *Prehistoric Avebury*, Yale University Press, 1979.

Hubert Butler, *Ten Thousand Saints: A Study in Irish and European Origins*, Lilliput Pr, 2011.

Rodney Castleden, *The Wilmington Giant*, Turnstone Press, 1983.

Rodney Castleden, *The Stonehenge People*, Routledge, 1987.

Rodney Castleden, *The Cerne Giant*, Dorset Publishing Company, 1996.

Rodney Castleden, *King Arthur: The Truth Behind the Legend*, Routledge, 2000.

Rosemary Clinch & Michael Williams, *King Arthur in Somerset*, Bossiney Books, 1987.

Andrew Collins, *Beneath the Pyramids*, A.R.E. Press, 2009.

Andrew Collins, *Gods of Eden*, Headline, 1998.

Andrew Collins, *The Cygnus Mystery*, Watkins, 1999.

Philip Coppens, *The New Pyramid Age*, O-books, 2007.

H. S. Cowper, *The Hill of Graces: A record of Investigation among the Trilithons and Megalithic Sites of Tripoli*, 1897.

Patrick Crampton, *Stonehenge of the Kings: a people appear*, Barnes and Noble, 1992.

Kevin Crossley-Holland, *The Penguin Book of Norse Myths*, Penguin, 1980.

W. A. Cummins, *King Arthur's Place in Prehistory*, Bramley Books, 1992.

Michael Dames, *Silbury: resolving the enigma*, The History Press, 2010.

Michael Dames, *The Avebury Cycle*, Thames and Hudson, 1977.

Michael Dames, *The Silbury Treasure: The Great Goddess rediscovered*, Thames and Hudson, 1976.

John Darrah, *The Real Camelot: Paganism and the Arthurian Romances*, Thames and Hudson, 1981.

Fionn Davenport, *Ireland*, Lonely Planet, 2006.

Joseph Davidovits & Margie Morris, *The Pyramids: An Enigma Solved*, Hippocrene Books, 1988.

H. R. Ellis Davidson, *Scandinavian Mythology*, Paul Hamlyn, 1969.

Paul Devereux, *Places of Power*, Blandford, 1990.

Mircea Eliade, Philip Mairet (trans.), *Images and Symbols*, Princeton University Press, 1991.

Ralph Ellis, *Thoth: Architect of the Universe*, Adventures Unlimited Press, 2002.

David Else, et. al., *England*, Lonely Planet, 2009.

Walter Emery, *Archaic Egypt*, Pelican, 1961.

R. O. Faulkner, *Concise Dictionary of Middle Egyptian*, Griffith Institute, 1962.

Vergilius Ferm (ed.), *Ancient Religions*, The Citadel Press, 1965.

William R. Fix, *Lake of Memory Rising*, Council Oak Books, 2000.

William R. Fix, *Pyramid Odyssey*, Mercury Media, 1978.

A. T. Fomenko & G. V. Nosowsky, *How it was in Reality*, AST, 2012.

Lucia Gahlin, *Myths and Mythology of Ancient Egypt*, Anness, 2003.

Adrian Gilbert, *The Holy Kingdom*, Corgi Books, 1999.

Marija Gimbutas, *The Goddesses and Gods of Old Europe*, Thames and Hudson, 1982.

Zakaria Goneim, *The Buried Pyramid*, Longmans, 1956.

Robert Graves, *The White Goddess*, Faber, 1961.

Jacob Grimm, *Teutonic Mythology*, Dover, 2004.

L. V, Grinsell, *The Ancient Burial-mounds of England*, Methuen & Co, 1936.

Graham Hancock, Santha Faiia, *Heaven's Mirror: Quest for the Lost Civilization*, Three Rivers Press, 1999.

Selim Hassan, *Excavations at Giza*, Vols 1-7, 1932-53.

Zahi Hawass, *The Pyramids of Ancient Egypt*, Carnegie Museum of Natural History, 1990.

Zahi Hawass, *Pyramids: Treasures, Mysteries, and New Discoveries in Egypt*, White Star Publishers, 2011.

Jacquetta Hawkes, *Dawn of the Gods*, Book Club Associates, 1968.

Gerald S. Hawkins, *Beyond Stonehenge*, Harper and Row, 1973.

Thor Heyerdahl, *Aku Aku*, Pocket Books, 1960.

Thor Heyerdahl, *The Tigris Expedition*, Doubleday, 1984.

Ronald Hutton, *The Pagan Religions of the Ancient British Isles*, Blackwell, 1991.

Veronica Ions, *Egyptian Mythology*, Peter Bedrick Books, 1982.

T. G. H. James, *Myths and Legends of Ancient Egypt*, Grosset & Dunlap, 1971.

Nancy Jenkins, *The Boat Beneath the Pyramid*, Thames and Hudson, 1980.

Prudence Jone & Nigel Pennick, *A History of Pagan Europe*, 1995.

Gwyn Jones and Thomas Jones (eds.), *The Mabinogion*, Everyman, 1993.

Hugh Kearns, *The Mysterious Chequered Lights of Newgrange*, Elo Publications, 1993.

John King, *Kingdoms of the Celts*, Blandford, 1998.

E. C. Krupp, *Echoes of the Ancient Skies*, Harper and Row, 1983.

Ian Lawton & Chris Ogilvie-Herald, *Giza: The Truth*,

Jim Leary & David Field, *The Story of Silbury Hill*, 2010.

Mark Lehner, *The Complete Pyramids*, Thames and Hudson, 1997.

Thomas C. Lethbridge, *Witches*, The Citadel Press, 1962.

Norman Lockyer, *The Dawn of Astronomy*, Cassell, 1894.

A. Lucas & J. R. Harris, *Ancient Egyptian Materials and Industries*, Dover, 1999.

Chris Lynn, *Navan Fort: Archaeology and Myth*, Wordwell, 2003.

Nicholas R. Mann, *The Isle of Avalon*, Llewellyn, 1996.

Peter Der Manuelian, *Slab Stelae of the Giza Necropolis*, The Peabody Museum *et al.*, 2003.

W.H. Matthews, Mazes and Labyrinths, Longmans, Green, 1922.

Carmel McCaffrey & Leo Eaton, *In Search of Ancient Ireland*, Ivan R. Dee, 2012.

Terence Meaden, *The Secrets of the Avebury Stones*, Souvenir Press, 1999.

George Terence Meaden, *The Stonehenge Solution*, Souvenir Press, 1992.

Stephen S. Mehler, *The Land of Osiris*, Adventures Unlimited Press, 2001.

Kurt Mendelssohn, *Riddle of the Pyramids*, W. W. Norton & Co, 1986.

John Michell, *At the center of the world: Polar symbolism discovered in Celtic, Norse and other ritualised landscapes*, Thames and Hudson, 1994.

R Brzezinski & M Mielczarek, *The Sarmatians 600 BC - AD 450*, Osprey Publishing, 2002.

Siegfried Morenz, *Egyptian Religion*, Cornell University Press, 1973.

Anthony Murphy, *Newgrange: Monument to Immortality*, Liffey Press, 2012.

Jeremy Naydler, *Shamanic Wisdom in the Pyramid Texts*, Inner Traditions, 2004.

Henry O'Brien, *The Round Towers of Ireland*, 1834.

Harold Osborne, *South American Mythology*, Hamlyn, 1968.

R. I. Page, *Norse Myths*, British Museum Press, 1990.

Dick Parry, *Engineering the Pyramids*, Sutton Publishing, 2004.

Nigel Pennick, *The Ancient Science of Geomancy*, Thames and Hudson, 1979.

Nigel Pennick & Paul Devereux, *Lines on the Landscape: Leys and Other Linear Enigmas*, Robert Hale, 1989.

A. Pochan, *The Mysteries of the Great Pyramids*, Avon Books, 1978.

Richard Poe, *Black Spark, White Fire*, Prima Publishing, 1997.

T. G. E. Powell, *The Celts*, Thames and Hudson, 1980.

Francis Pryor, *Britain BC: Life in Britain and Ireland before the Romans*, Harper Perennial, 2003.

Berry Radice (ed.), *Early Irish Myths and Sagas*, Penguin, 1981.

Colin Renfrew, *Archaeology and Language: The puzzle of Indo-European origins*, Cambridge University Press, 1987.

Michael Rice, *Egypt's Making*, Routledge, 2003.

Christopher Robbins, *Apples Are from Kazakhstan: The Land that Disappeared*, 2010.

Anne Ross and Don Robins, *The Life and Death of a Druid Prince*, Summit Books, 1989.

John Romer, *A History of Ancient Egypt: From the First Farmers to the Great Pyramid*, Penguin, 2013.

John Romer, *The Great Pyramid*, Cambridge University Press, 2007.

Richard Rudgley, *Lost Civilisations of the Stone Age*, Trafalgar Square, 1998.

William Ryan & Walter Pitman, *Noah's Flood: The New Scientific Evidence about the event that changed history*, Simon & Schuster, 2000.

Byron E. Shafer, Arnold Dieter, *Temples of Ancient Egypt*, I.B. Tauris, 2005.

Robert M. Schoch & Robert Aquinas McNally, *Pyramid Quest*, Penguin, 2005.

Robert M. Schoch & Robert Aquinas McNally, *Voices of the Rocks*, Harmony, 2000.

Robert M. Schoch & Robert Aquinas McNally, *Voyages of the Pyramid Builders*, Tarcher, 2004.

M. V. Seton-Williams, 'Cairn', *Encyclopaedia Britannica*, Chicago University Press, 1971.

Alastair Service & Jean Bradbery, *Megaliths and their Mysteries*, Macmillan, 1979.

Colin Simpson, *The Country Upstairs*, Angus and Robertson, 1962.

Craig B. Smith, *How the Great Pyramid was Built*, Smithsonian Books, 2004.

Jacques Soustelle, *The Olmecs: The Oldest Civilization in Mexico*, Doubleday & Company, 1984.

Leon Stover, Bruce Kraig, *Stonehenge: The Indo-European Heritage*, Nelson-Hall, 1978.

Leon Stover, *Stonehenge City: A Reconstruction*, McFarland & Company, 2003.

Lord William Taylour, *The Mycenaeans*, Thames and Hudson, 1983.

Olivia Temple, with Robert Temple, *The Sphinx Mystery*, Inner Traditions, 2009.

Robert Temple, *Egyptian Dawn*, Arrow Books, 2010.

Robert Temple, *Netherworld*, Random House, 2002.

Robert Temple, *The Crystal Sun*, Century, 2000.

Nikolai Tolstoy, *The Quest for Merlin*, Little, Brown and Company, 1985.

Peter Tompkins, *Secrets of the Great Pyramid*, Harper and Row, 1971.

Joyce Tyldesley, *Pyramids: The Real Story Behind Egypt's Most Ancient Monuments*, Penguin, 2004.

Miroslav Verner, *Forgotten Pharaohs, Lost Pyramids: Abusir*, Academia Skodaexport, 1994.

Miroslav Verner, *The Pyramids*, Grove Press, 1997.

Colonel Howard Vyse, *Operations Carried on at the Pyramids of Gizeh in 1837*, James Fraser, 1840.

G. A. Wainwright *The Sky Religion in Egypt*, Cambridge University Press, 1938.

R. B. Warner, 'The Prehistoric Irish Annals: Fable or History', *Archaeology Ireland 4*, 1, 30-3, 1990.

R. B. Warner, 'Tree-Rings, Catastrophies and Culture in Early Ireland: Some Comments', *Emania 11*, 13-19, 1993.

Alfred Watkins, *The Old Straight Track*, Abacus, 1970.

James Wellard, *The Search for the Etruscans*, Bookthrift, 1976.

David Lewis-Williams & David Pearce, *Inside the Neolithic Mind*, Thames and Hudson, 2005.

John K. Young, *Sacred Sites of the Knights Templar*, Fair Winds, 2005.

Li Yuanlong, He Fei, Han Rongliang (trans.), *Temple of Heaven*, Morning Glory Publishers, 1999.

Index

28269297R00271

Made in the USA
Lexington, KY
12 January 2019